GALINA VISHNEVSKAYA

The author is an internationally renowned soprano. Formerly she was with the Bolshoi Opera. She and her husband, cellist-conductor Mstislav Rostropovich, have two daughters, Olga and Elena. They live in Paris, Lausanne, New York and Washington D.C. Their biennial Rostropovich Festival is now a regular feature of the Aldeburgh calendar as a tribute to their friendship with Benjamin Britten and Peter Pears.

'This book forces us to ask again how high a price the artist should be expected to pay for the inconvenience of his genius'

Listener

'This book is epic in its scale . . . Imperative reading for anyone interested in the lives of Russian artists'

The Literary Review

'A scorching read . . . Moscow's loss was the free world's gain, as this heartening book bears witness'

The Economist

'A ringingly forceful and uninhibited personal outpouring into which is also concentrated a social, musical and theatrical history of her country . . . written with sweeping vividness and a keen eye for detail . . . this book has an epic quality'

Financial Times

'One of the most remarkable autobiographies ever written by a singer'

The Field

'A devastatingly readable autobiography'

Standard

'A passionate, engrossing, personal as well as historical study'

Homes and Gardens

'A damning indictment of those who seek to impose state control on the arts'

The Stage and Television Today

'Vishnevskaya's life story proves just as absorbing as her artistic achievements'

Daily Telegraph

'A deadly account of the way musicians and composers are treated in the Soviet Union today'

Sunday Times

Galina Vishnevskaya

GALINA
A Russian Story

Translated from the Russian by Guy Daniels

First published in Great Britain in 1984 by Hodder and Stoughton Ltd

Sceptre edition 1986

Sceptre is an imprint of Hodder and Stoughton Paperbacks, a division of Hodder and Stoughton Ltd

British Library C.I.P.

Vishnevskaya, Galina
  Galina: a Russian story.
  1. Vishnevskaya, Galina
  2. Singers – Soviet Union –
  Biography
  I. Title
  782.1'092'4   ML420.V3975

ISBN 0-340-39453-6

Printed and bound in Great Britain for Hodder and Stoughton Paperbacks, a division of Hodder and Stoughton Ltd., Mill Road, Dunton Green, Sevenoaks, Kent (Editorial Office: 47 Bedford Square, London, WC1 3DP) by Richard Clay (The Chaucer Press) Ltd., Bungay, Suffolk. Photoset by Rowland Phototypesetting Ltd., Bury St Edmunds, Suffolk.

I take this opportunity to express my heartfelt gratitude to the American publisher of this book, William Jovanovich, for his complete understanding and support. I also want to convey my thanks to Guy Daniels for his fine translation and to my editors at Harcourt Brace Jovanovich, Inc. Jacqueline Decter and Marie Arana-Ward for their highly professional work on this edition.

To Slava, Olga, and Elena

A woman's voice glides like the wind
Of black, of damp, of night
And all it touches in its flight
Suddenly is other.
It courses, floods with a diamond's blaze,
Somewhere something for a second silvers
And with an enigmatic cloak
Of unearthly silks it rustles.
And what a mighty force
Draws that enchanted voice there
As if ahead were not the grave
But the ascent of a mysterious stair.

> — Anna Akhmatova
> December 19, 1961
> Lenin Hospital, on hearing
> Galina Vishnevskaya's voice over
> the radio singing Villa-Lobos's
> *Bachianas Brasileiras.*

CHARACTERS
in A Russian Story

With titles and positions held at the time they figured in Galina
Vishnevskaya's life. Nicknames are given where applicable.

Akhmatova, Anna Andreyevna: (1889–1966) Poet.
Brezhnev, Leonid Ilich: (1906–82) General Secretary of the
 USSR from 1964; President of the USSR from 1977.
Britten, Benjamin: (1913–1976) English composer, conductor,
 pianist.
Bulganin, Nikolai Aleksandrovich (Kolya): (1895–1975) Prime
 Minister of the USSR, 1955–1958.
Chaliapin, Fyodor Ivanovich: (1873–1938) Bass, most
 renowned singer of his day.
Demichev, Pyotr Nilovich: (1918–   ) A secretary of the
 Central Committee of the Communist Party, 1961–1974;
 Minister of Culture from 1974.
Evtushenko, Evgeny Aleksandrovich (Zhenya): (1933–   )
 Poet; author of 'Babi Yar.'
Furtseva, Ekaterina Alekseyevna (Katya): (1910–1974)
 Minister of Culture, 1960–1974.
Garina, Vera Nikolayevna: (1871–1956) Galina's voice teacher.
Hurok, Solomon Izrailevich: (1888–1974) American impresario.
Karajan, Herbert von: (1908–   ) Austrian conductor;
 director of Salzburg Festival since 1964; artistic director of
 Berlin Philharmonic Orchestra.
Khaikin, Boris: (1904–1978) Conductor of the Bolshoi Opera,
 1954–1978.
Khanayev, Nikandr Sergeyevich: (1890–1974) Tenor, soloist
 with the Bolshoi.

Khrennikov, Tikhon (Tishka): (1913–   ) Composer; head of the Soviet Composers' Union.

Khrushchev, Nikita Sergeyevich: (1894–1971) Prime Minister of the USSR, 1958–64.

Kondrashin, Kirill Petrovich: (1914–1981) Conductor of the Bolshoi Opera, 1943–1956; artistic director of the Moscow Philharmonic, 1960–1975.

Lemeshev, Sergei Yakovlevich: (1902–1977) Tenor, soloist with the Bolshoi.

Melik-Pashayev, Alexander Shamilyevich: (1905–1964) Conductor of the Bolshoi Opera, 1931–1964.

Mikoyan, Anastas Ivanovich: (1895–1978) Chairman of the Presidium of the Supreme Soviet, 1964–1965.

Nesterenko, Evgeny: (1938–   ) Bass, soloist with the Bolshoi.

Obraztsova, Elena Vasilyevna: (1937–   ) Mezzo-soprano, soloist with the Bolshoi.

Ognivtsev, Alexander Pavlovich (Sasha): (1920–1980) Bass, soloist with the Bolshoi.

Oistrakh, David Fyodorovich: (1908–1974) Violinist.

Pasternak, Boris Leonidovich: (1890–1960) Writer, poet, translator; author of *Doctor Zhivago*.

Pears, Sir Peter (Petya): (1910–1986) English tenor.

Pokrovsky, Boris Aleksandrovich: (1912–   ) Stage director at the Bolshoi Opera from 1952; chief stage director, 1952–1963 and 1968–1982.

Prokofiev, Sergei Sergeyevich: (1891–1953) Composer, pianist.

——Lina Ivanovna: first wife.

——Mirra Mendelson: second wife.

Richter, Svyatoslav Teofilovich: (1915–   ) Pianist.

Rostropovich, Mstislav Leopoldovich (Slava, Slavochka, Stiva): (1927–   ) Cellist, conductor, pianist; Galina's husband.

Rubin, Mark Ilich: Director of Leningrad District Operetta Theater.

Sakharov, Andrei Dmitriyevich: (1921–   ) Nuclear physicist, dissident.

——Elena Bonner: wife.

Samosud, Samuil Abramovich: (1884–1964) Conductor with the
    Bolshoi, 1936–1964.
Serov, Ivan Aleksandrovich (Vanka): (1905–   ) Head of the
    KGB, 1954–1958.
Shostakovich, Dmitri Dmitriyevich: (1906–1975) Composer.
——Nina Vasilyevna: first wife.
——Margarita: second wife.
——Irina: third wife.
Solzhenitsyn, Alexander Isayevich (Sanya): (1918–   ) Writer
    now living in exile in the US. Author of *One Day in the Life
    of Ivan Denisovich, Cancer Ward, The Gulag Archipelago.*
——Natalya Reshetovskaya (Natasha): first wife.
——Natalya (Alya): second wife.
Tito, Josip Broz (Iosya): (1892–1980) President of Yugoslavia,
    1953–1980.
Tsvetaeva, Marina: (1892–1941) Poet.
Vysotsky, Vladimir: (1938–1980) Actor; popular songwriter
    whose works are widely, though unofficially, available.
Zhdanov, Andrei: (1896–1948) Politburo member, from 1938
    entrusted with direction of Party propaganda.

PART ONE

ONE

Bright sunshine and emerald meadow. I am running. Like a shot, I dive after the boys off a bank and into the river – the water surrounds me, murky green. I stand on the bottom and thrust my hands toward the surface, clenching and unclenching my fists.

The grown-ups saw my hands and pulled me out. I don't remember being frightened – there wasn't time enough. All I remember is the good spanking my mother gave me. I howled, unable to comprehend why diving was all right for the boys but not for me. Just because I couldn't swim? If they could, so could I. I was defending my rights – asserting my independence – for the first time.

That was the summer of 1930; I was not yet four years old.

I don't remember that I ever had any particular attachment to my parents: they were always alien to me. But then, they had cast me out when I was very young, only six weeks old, and my father's mother had taken me in. After that I would often hear myself referred to by that pathetic word 'orphan.'

My mother was half-gypsy, half-Polish. She was seventeen when my father first met her – he was twenty. She had just broken with a former lover by whom she was pregnant, and was going through one of many crises in her life. My father fell in love and they were married. She had a son soon after, and two years later I was born.

My mother was very beautiful – a black-eyed blonde with long, shapely legs and strikingly pretty hands. I admired her, but from afar – she was never 'mine.' It was probably through her gypsy blood that I inherited a passion for singing. She would play the guitar and sing gypsy ballads – 'Dark Eyes,' for instance – and I would mimic her. Guests at our house would call out, 'Sing, Galya!' and I would respond by crawling under the table. Not that

I was afraid of an audience. On the contrary, I craved one. It wasn't enough to sing for myself, I needed people to live and feel along with me. But I needed that realm of mystery, that refuge from reality, where I could create my own world. And so, from under the table, would issue my own version of 'Dark Eyes': '*Ochi chor-nye, ochi strast-nye, ochi zhguchiye i prekra-a-a-snye . . .*'

I was only three but had the voice of an adult. I had been born with it. It must have struck our guests as strange to hear such rich chest tones from the throat of a little girl. But they would heartily applaud me. Inspired by my success, I would crawl from under the table, take a bow, and do my next act:

> '*A stern captain fell madly in love with*
> *An innkeeper's daughter, a sprite*
> *Of a girl who had eyes like a doe,*
> *And a smile like a mist late at night.*'

I sang that 'masterpiece' standing on a chair. The scene seemed effective enough: when the unfortunate girl's fatal hour came, I could throw myself from lighthouse to sea (that is, from chair to floor) and drown. My audience would be ecstatic. I would then launch into a dance, shimmy my shoulders, and shout the gypsy '*Chavella!*'

My mother had a small and pleasing voice, but my father was an impressive dramatic tenor. He had even dreamed of becoming a singer once, but had succumbed to the most Russian of 'weaknesses' – drink. Whenever he'd had one too many, he would bellow Hermann's aria from *The Queen of Spades*: 'What is our life? A game!'

That year, 1930, was the only one I ever spent with my parents. I had been brought to visit with them at their 'dacha' outside Leningrad. The brief time left me with few but vivid memories:

I was sitting by the window. Our dacha was a hut no different from the rest of them in the village, but it was clean, with chintz curtains and city furniture. It was a rainy day in autumn and the mud seemed impassable, but the street I looked out on was full of people running, shouting, weeping. Through the wide-open door of the hut across from ours I could see some men lugging out bundles, pots, blankets, and pillows. They hurled them into a cart tied to an emaciated horse. The woman of the house stood by. Her children, my playmates, clung to the hem of her skirt and bawled. Their grandmother darted to and fro, her weathered hands clutching a copper samovar. She was not about to turn it over to those burly men at any price, and screeched again and again, 'Herods! Herods! Herods!'

The memory of that gloomy autumn day remains: the muddy road, the crowd of peasants, and, against the gray of that scene, the copper samovar bobbing and gleaming in the old woman's hands. I had never heard that strange word 'Herods' before. Many years later, I understood that this was the beginning of collectivisation; that before my eyes the so-called kulaks were being stripped of their possessions – stripped of all rights. My child's mind had recorded a picture of the ruin of the Russian peasantry.

I remember, too, my mother and I walking on a road in the woods. A man driving in the opposite direction tossed us two loaves of bread. My mother stashed those treasures in her bag and ordered me not to tell anybody. Little did I know then the role that stranger was to play.

What I did know very well was that my mother did not love my father. When he wasn't home, other men would come around, and my mother would be transformed – she would become even more beautiful. It seemed to me she didn't love me either, and, to get back, I would spy on her. I sensed that she was afraid of me – afraid that I would tell my father. When my father was home, not a day passed without his making a scene. The neighbors had probably told him of the comings and goings while he was away.

One night I was awakened by shouting. My mother was running about the room in her nightgown, and after her, with an axe in his hand, came my father – drunk and raving. I screamed, and that must have brought him to his senses, because he ended up venting his rage not on my mother but on the mirrored armoire. The axe came crashing down against the glass, shattering it into a thousand pieces.

My father grabbed me and thundered, 'Who was with your mother? Who was it?'

I saw my mother's huge eyes trained on me. She wasn't begging for my silence – she simply looked at me and I knew that I could not betray her. As a female, I automatically sided with her.

'Who was here?'

'Nobody,' I said.

'You're lying! Tell the truth or I'll kill you! Who?'

'Nobody.' I had in fact come to know the sight of that stranger very well.

Toward morning the battle died down and they decided to separate – the marriage had lasted a short five years. My father asked me, 'Who do you want to live with – your mother or me?'

'With you.' That meant with his mother, in whose place I had been living before. I parted from my own mother as from a stranger.

I had been born prematurely. I was told that my mother took one look at me and turned away: 'Take her out of my sight! She's so ugly!' In fact I was a little monkey at birth. I was covered with hair, even on my face. And I roared, demanding to be fed constantly, but my mother denied me the breast. Having never loved my father, she transferred that indifference to me. It was her son she adored.

So when I was six weeks old my grandmother, Darya Aleksandrovna Ivanova, came and took me off to Kronstadt where she lived with my grandfather, a married daughter, Katya, and an unmarried son, Andrei. Grandma knew how to care for a baby. Quickly she found a woman who, by some miracle in those years of near-famine, still had a goat and could supply us with milk. In the evening, when the stove in the kitchen had cooled, she would tuck me in the oven to keep me warm. She would chew white bread into a paste and stuff it in my mouth – anything to shut me up. I survived.

My grandparents on my father's side were from Vologda Province. My grandfather, Andrei Andreyevich Ivanov, a stovemaker, was a master in his trade. (To this day, many an old home in Kronstadt has the handsome tile stoves and fireplaces he built.) They had settled in Kronstadt long before the Revolution.

Of their eight children, four died, leaving two sons and two daughters. My grandfather managed to provide them all with a good education and so enabled them to better their lot in life. Only the younger son, Andrei, followed in his father's footsteps and became a stove-maker.

I remember Grandpa vaguely. He was a kindhearted man who called me his 'little black cherry,' and always had a sweet for me. I loved him and knew that he loved me.

The 'weakness' claimed him, too: he went on binges, in the Russian tradition, although he was never a rowdy drunk. Every day I would wait for him to come home from work. I would sit on the floor in the hallway listening for him – the sound of his footsteps telling me whether he was drunk or sober. If he was drunk, he would fling the door wide open, strike a pose in the door frame, slowly survey the rest of us, and intone with majesty and dignity (he always said the same thing), 'So it is I . . . (pause), Andrei Andreyevich Ivanov!'

I would immediately bring him his *oporki* (the felt boots we wore as slippers), and he would slip me a candy, repeating, 'my little black cherry!' Grandma would scold him, but he would only smile, philosophise a while with the neighbors, and go to bed.

His was a horrible death. Drinking had given him an ulcer, and during one of his binges he was overcome by pain. To ease it, he poured boiling water into a glass bottle, stopped it up with a rubber plug, and lay down in bed with it on his stomach. The plug erupted from the bottle, and the boiling water spurted right into his eyes. He developed an infection and was soon gone. We were given a photograph of him in his coffin; his face was unrecognisable for the bandages.

The winter of that eventful year, 1930, found me crossing the frozen Gulf of Finland on foot. Aunt Katya and her son Boris, who was two years younger than I, had come to Leningrad to pick me up from my parents and take me back to Kronstadt. I was feeling resentful toward my mother and father, who had handed me over to these people. Like a wild little animal, I crossed my grandmother's threshold with a scowl. I ignored the old woman, and greeted no one.

Grandma was offended. 'So! What's eating you?'

I said nothing and didn't budge.

'Eh, you spawn of a gypsy! You've got your mother's blood all right!'

I was an unaffectionate child. It would be many years before I learned what it was to give and receive love, but at that stage I was unapproachable. With time and with the warmth of my grandmother's love, I began to thaw out. She was of peasant stock – thin, short, energetic – and spent whole days on her feet. First thing in the morning she was off scavenging the market for the cheapest food she could find. She did laundry and sewing for other people. After Grandfather died, she received a pension of forty rubles a month – at a time when meat cost eight rubles a pound. How we managed I don't know.

She was fond of her vodka. On the eleventh of each month, when she received her pension money, she would stop on the way home and spend three rubles and fifteen kopecks for 'a short one,' a half-pint. She would keep the little bottle in the cupboard, do her housecleaning, cooking, and laundry, then take a shot. By evening she would finish it off. And she smoked. She would send me to the shop for the cheapest cigarettes, Raketa, at thirty-five kopecks a pack.

A few women friends of hers would gather at our place on the day she got her pension. They would drink, sing, and eventually get around to the main thing – gossip. But I'd be sitting there, in their way.

'Galenka, go on out and have some fun.'

'But I don't feel like it. I want to sit here with you.'

'Look! All your girlfriends are out there. You're the only one inside.'

'No, I'm not going. I like it better here.'

And I would stall, knowing that the old biddies would eventually take up a collection for me – twenty kopecks apiece – for ice cream. Taking the bribe, I would go outside until sundown.

In general, Grandma spoiled me well beyond her means and I grew up pampered: I never washed a dish. From time to time, my aunts and uncles would let her have it: 'You're crippling her, raising her like a princess. She's not going to be living in a palace! She doesn't know how to do anything. She'll wear you out and you won't get so much as a thank you.'

'All right, now,' Grandma would reply. 'Why don't you just look after your own kids. You all think you're so smart – picking on a little orphan!'

I was terribly stubborn. Whatever I wanted, I got. Of course I never demanded money or anything out of the question, but I had to have my own way. If I wanted to wear a new dress that was meant for holidays only, I could carry on day and night. I would lock myself in the bathroom if I had to, and sit there on the floor, howling in the dark. Grandma would feel sorry for me, and I would hear her pacing back and forth outside the door. Uncle Kolya, who was a teacher at my school, sometimes got into the act, telling Grandma, 'Don't you dare go in to her!'

'I suppose it makes you feel good, tormenting an orphan!'

'Let her scream all she wants, but don't go in!'

'Who asked you anyway? Teachers!'

The scene was enacted regularly. 'So you've had your way, you pigheaded girl! Like mother, like daughter.'

The communal apartment we lived in had once belonged to an admiral in the tsar's navy. During the Revolution he fled abroad with his family, leaving all his furniture behind, including a Becker upright piano. The apartment consisted of five large rooms and a huge kitchen where all the tenants prepared their meals. Gas heating was unheard of; we fueled the kitchen stove with wood. One room was occupied by Grandma, Uncle Andrei, and me; another by Aunt Katya, Uncle Kolya, and their three sons; the third by a woman doctor who lived alone. The Davydov family – husband, wife, and two daughters – had the other two rooms. The one toilet and one bathroom were shared by all. There were fourteen of us, a small number compared to other communal apartments.

Aunt Katya worked as a bookkeeper, and Uncle Kolya taught physical education at my school. Uncle Andrei was a laborer.

Everyone thought him feebleminded and strange, but he was merely kind. My father, with his good salary, never sent me a kopeck, but Andrei, half-starved himself, fed me. For him it was only natural, but he was seen as a fool.

My father was a confirmed communist. He was born in 1904, graduated from *Realschule*, and in 1921, at the age of seventeen, took part in the suppression of the Kronstadt rebellion, killing sailors. The son of a worker, he found himself shooting his own people. This left its mark on him for the rest of his life. It maimed his soul.

And what does a Russian man faced with that burden do? He drinks. My father was a mean drunk, and even at age five or six I hated him. Eyes bloodshot, he would strike a pose before me and make speeches as if he were on a platform. 'Parasites! . . . Spongers! . . . I'll shoo-oot ev-err-y one of you! We're Leninists! What did we fight for? The Revolution, that's what!'

I would stand there with my mouth agape. For me, the entire Revolution and all its ideas were embodied in that drunken Leninist.

The tragedy was that he was not an ordinary, dull muzhik morally disfigured by the Soviet regime. If he had been, he simply would have given his life over to drink and died in some gutter. But no. He was an intelligent and educated man, and the bloody scenes of his youth – his hands spattered with the blood of his brothers – gave him no peace. Not even vodka could quiet the voice of his conscience.

All that became clear to me many years later. But as I stood before him then, my child's soul was aflame with fury and loathing for the man and his words. I was consumed by an overwhelming urge to sneak up on him from behind and wallop that odious head.

It was from such childhood impressions that my character was formed. Within my own family I was witness to disintegration of personality, distortion of morals, breakdowns. Uncle Kolya, too, was prone to drinking bouts. He died sprawled beneath the wheels of a bus. And Grandma's older daughter, Masha, was married to an alcoholic. A well-educated man, he degenerated to the point where he sold everything in the house, ruined the family, and died of drunkenness. They were all like that. It was a family damned to a horrible fate.

My great uncle had a daughter whose husband got drunk one evening and either out of jealousy or anger grabbed an axe, butchered her and her sister, and stabbed himself. What more is there to say? In the face of that unbridled Russian drunkenness, violence is bound to erupt over the slightest trifle. My childhood was filled with the fumes of drink, and I've had a horror of drunks ever since. Vodka and bombast – that's the Russia of today.

Kronstadt is a fortress town on the little island of Kotlin. In those days, it was two hours by boat from Leningrad. In winter you took the electric train to Oranienbaum, then a bus across the frozen Gulf of Finland. The town had few streets, verdant boulevards and parks, and pretty houses of two and three stories. The waterfront was handsome with its Officers Club building and Petrovsky Park with its monument to 'Peter the First, Founder of Kronstadt.' On a clear day the town's huge Morskoi Cathedral could be seen from Leningrad. Later, it was converted into a movie house. On the town square was a monument to Admiral Makarov, beyond that a deep ravine where we would go sledding in the winter.

The children would crowd the movie house for the morning show, each one of us wanting to sit in the first row. We made a dash for it – I along with the rest. We saw the films over and over, and knew them by heart, but we lived them anew each time: *The Red Sons of Devils, Chapayev, The Merry Boys*.

Those were the years when churches were being closed or destroyed. A beautiful chapel across the street from our apartment building was razed. I could never understand why – it had been so beautiful. It was rumored that the Morskoi Cathedral would be blown up, too. The Cathedral Ioann of Kronstadt was converted into a potato warehouse. Even it was scheduled to be blown up, but the war interfered.

Kronstadt was a sailor's town. There were few soldiers, and the sailors despised them. I often witnessed wild fights in the streets, especially when the sailors were on leave and 'on a spree.' They would get drunk and brawl with the soldiers – not one on one, but in groups. I saw them take off their belts and beat a man to death with the buckles.

In our building, an anthill of communal apartments, everybody knew the intimate details of everyone else's life. We went in and out of one another's rooms as if we were one big family. No one had secrets. A husband beat his wife, and everybody knew. A scream was heard, and everyone would be on the scene, getting into the act. We lived in plain sight, unbuttoned, unembarrassed. As a rule, it was one family, one room: there the parents slept, the son would bring his bride to a bed behind the wardrobe, and there children were born.

In our room stood Grandma's bed with a huge feather mattress; next to it was Andrei's bed and next to that the carpet-covered red ottoman I slept on. But often my grandmother's rheumatism would keep her awake and I would crawl in with her to rub her with ointment. Although it was warm in the feather bed – as warm as an oven – she would find it hard to sleep. 'Sing something, Galya.'

Quietly, I would sing a lament or two:

> *'I was born in this town, on the outskirts,*
> *My family was poor as could be.*
> *At seventeen, hopeless and wretched,*
> *I found work at the brick factory.'*

Grandma would shed a few tears, and I would try even harder:

> *'Marusya, oh Marusya,*
> *Open your eyes wide!*
> *But the doctor answered,*
> *"Marusya? She has died."'*

With that repertory, we would finally fall asleep.

We had an enormous samovar that could hold a whole bucket of water. Grandma used it three times a day – she wouldn't take tea from a teapot. Soup, bread, and tea were our staples. If there was no money for tea, Grandma would put chunks of dried carrot in the pot and pour boiling water over it. At least it had color and after a while you got used to the taste.

Butter we bought only on paydays. Sunflower oil was what we usually ate, and I still like it. And I will never forget the taste of the rye bread baked in Kronstadt before the war. It was made at the navy bakery in huge round black loaves weighing several kilograms, the bottom crust thick, the top one shiny as if lacquered. Recently, in a Russian shop in Paris, I spotted a similar loaf. The minute I got it home, I cut off a warm slice and smeared it with butter. A cup of sweet tea, and it was bliss.

We had a big, mirrored wardrobe, which, one fine day, told me I was pretty. In my eyes, it seemed a reservoir of countless treasures. There, Grandma would store old dresses and hats – no doubt they had belonged to the admiral's wife. There, too, wrapped in a sheet, were six silver spoons, a silver sugar bowl, and sugar tongs. Grandma always said she would sell anything before she would part with our piano or with that silverware – Galya's trousseau. But as time wore on, those things found their way to Leningrad, to the Torgsin, where they were pawned for food coupons.

The day came when Grandma withdrew from that magical wardrobe an ikon of the Holy Mother. I remember the silver mounting encrusted with turquoise and pearls and its light blue halo verging on white. It was very hard to break the mounting, but we did it, and converted it into a formless mass. The silver would not have been accepted at the Torgsin otherwise. Grandma ripped each pearl and piece of turquoise from the silver, weeping and whispering all the while. The image itself she stowed away somewhere.

We all would look forward to the summer, to Grandma's annual quest for berries and mushrooms in Kaporye, beyond Oranienbaum. Several times in the course of the summer she would go off into the woods for a day or two with a group of old women. We children would await their return on the dock and lug the big, overflowing baskets through town. We were like squirrels, absorbed with the carting of that free forest booty – to us it was not labor. In winter we would have barrels of pickled mushrooms, dried mushrooms, and bags of frozen cranberries. My favorite soup is still one made of dried mushrooms with pearl barley and potatoes.

Grandma would buy salted cod. At fourteen kopecks a pound, it is still the cheapest fish in Russia. First she would soak it for two days, then boil it. What a stench! The building would reek of it. Mixed with boiled potatoes, onions, and sunflower oil it was heaven. Even now I can eat that concoction after the most sumptuous French meal. This, herring-head soup, buckwheat kasha, and cabbage pies on holidays formed the gist of our menu.

The Davydovs, who shared our communal apartment, were a solid, well-off peasant family. The father was a truck driver, which was lucky for them all. If he was hauling food, he'd snitch a hunk of meat and smuggle it home. His wife, Marusya, would cook it furtively, blocking our view of it with her back. But the aroma! How I loved to come into their room and watch Filya, the father, as he ate. He would sit there gorging himself, forking up meat. He might notice the little girl with hunger in her eyes, but wouldn't concede so much as a crust of bread. The Davydovs never offered anyone anything and kept everything under lock and key. During the war Marusya died of a strangled intestine. Poor thing.

Ivan Glot was my grandfather's friend. He too was a laborer and a hard drinker. I never knew where he lived – in a dormitory, no doubt – but he would sleep in the streets on the nights he was drunk. He often came to see Grandma even after Grandpa died. And he would always offer us children fruit drops from his pockets – a few sticky pieces with shag tobacco clinging to them. His hands were always black and he never washed, but we didn't care – we loved him. He only had to come in and Grandma would feed him; and though he might lie down right there on the kitchen floor and go to sleep, she would never chase him out. She shared what little she had. Not like our prosperous neighbor Davydov.

Uncle Ivan drank himself to death. He got the shakes one night after a binge, passed out, and choked on the crosspiece of a bed. He had lived in utter poverty, and had no one other than my grandmother and Andrei to bury him. When his trunk was opened, it was empty save for a single piece of paper, an insurance policy for 1,000 rubles made out in my name. The great Russian soul! Grandma put the money in a bank, and little by little we withdrew it over a period of many years. For us, living on forty rubles a month from the pension, that was big money!

Once in a while something would come over my father and he would want to see me. Grandma and I would go to him. We visited him once in the town of Stalinsk in the Urals. A vast industrial complex was being built there and the town was full of foreigners; prisoners were doing the construction work. That was the winter of 1932–1933, the beginning of Stalin's purges, and a year before I started school.

My school years . . . I studied, like all the other students, but took no particular interest in the subjects. I never did my home-work and got by on my memory, easily recalling what the teacher had said in class. For chemistry, physics, and mathematics I had no patience. And, as in every other Soviet school, little time was given to history, literature, or foreign languages – the things that really interested me. Once I graduated, I quickly emptied my brain of everything that my teachers had so zealously stuffed into it. No force in the world can compel me to remember what I was taught there.

As a child, I had few toys – I didn't find them interesting – but I learned to read very young, on my own. Even in the lowest grades, I was a regular participant in all the school recitals, and I soon acquired the nickname of 'Galka the Artistka.' The other kids used to tease me with that name, chanting it over and over: 'Galka the Artistka, Galka the Artistka.'

In the first grade I won my first prize for singing: three meters of dotted chintz, from which Grandma made me a dress. Singing became my passion. I sang everywhere: on the street, in school, with my friends, at home. My voice could boom across a whole courtyard.

'Well, there goes Galka the Artistka,' the kids would say.

I was really no different from anyone else, except for my artistic gift, which had manifested itself so early. A few days after my grandmother had enrolled me in school, my teacher told her, 'Darya Aleksandrovna, I think there's a special fate in store for your Galya.'

I went to school because I had to, but after school I would waste no time getting out into the street to run and play with the other children until nightfall. Among the girls, I had no real friends. I preferred the boys, and they liked me – probably because I never put on airs or complained. A buddy on equal terms, I ran across roofs and threw stones with them. My elbows and knees were always bruised or scratched, and my nose was often bloodied.

In the third grade, I was transferred from one school to another. The teacher brought me into the classroom and introduced me: 'Meet our new student, Galya Ivanova.' I was wearing my only smock – a black-and-white checkered one that my grandmother had sewn for me. Although it was three years old and somewhat threadbare, I wore it proudly. More so, because my hair was crowned with a red silk ribbon I had been given at my former school for New Year's Day. For several years and for every major occasion, it had served as my main adornment.

I sat at my desk, and all the boys began to stare. I must have made a profound impression on one of them, because I saw him put an iron button in his slingshot and shoot it at me. It hit me right between the eyes and immediately produced an enormous welt. Panic broke out. Tears were streaming down my face; it was a miracle that I hadn't lost an eye. Some girls carried me to the teachers' room. The boy was terrified.

'Who did that?' the principal asked.

'I don't know. I didn't see him.' My reply stirred up a wave of admiration among the other kids: 'She's a girl, but she's not a tattletale!' I was put on a pedestal, and the culprit became my best friend, my bodyguard.

It was in that school that I encountered my first singing teacher, Ivan Ignatyevich. He was possessed by his love for music – a teacher by vocation, not out of necessity. Most music teachers in such schools are failed singers or pianists who drudge their way through their jobs, pounding out the crudest of melodies, or teaching 'mass' songs like:

> *Stalin is our military glory,*
> *Stalin is our youth as it takes flight.*
> *Our people, singing, battling, and winning,*
> *Follow Stalin to the end of night.*

Ivan Ignatyevich, too, had to fulfill his plan and the program of the Department of Public Education, which consisted of nothing but such masterpieces. But the school recitals gave him a chance to unleash his soul.

At the very first choir lesson he noticed me. 'You, the new girl. Stay in the classroom after the lesson.'

I stayed.

'What school did you transfer from?'

'Number eight.'

'Have you performed in amateur concerts?'

'Yes.'

'And what did you sing?'

'Songs.'

'Which ones?'

I sang for him:

> *'Crossing hills and valleys,*
> *The division kept marching on –*
> *On to capture the sea country,*
> *The White Army's bastion.'*

'And what else?'

'What else?' I issued even more loudly:

> *'Budenny, big brother, the people are with you!*
> *The order: look forward and never feel blue.*
> *With us is Voroshilov, the first Red officer.*
> *And we march ever onward – for the USSR.'*

'Fine. Now, sing a scale.'

'What?' I'd never heard the word before.

'I'll play it on the piano, and you repeat it. Can you?'

'Sure.' I sang after him, trying my best and enjoying every bit of it.

'Do you want to sing in our next school concert on May Day?' he asked.

'Of course. What shall I sing?'

'Well, what do you sing at home?'

'"Dark Eyes," "What's Our Life? – a Game!" Shall I sing them?'

He chuckled. 'No. For now we'll learn "A Spring Song."'

I learned it right off and have never forgotten it:

> *Come more quickly, spring;*
> *Bright May, come to us,*
> *Bringing back more quickly*
> *The flowers and the grass.*

> *Bring back the violets*
> *In the quiet dale,*
> *And the birds of springtime –*
> *The cuckoo and the nightingale.*

What did violets and nightingales have to do with anything? Reality for me was Old Vasya in the courtyard singing bawdy folk songs. The words of the songs were strange to me, yet sweet – unsophisticated and serene.

At the next concert I sang a duet with another girl – a barcarolle:

> *'I stand against the mast,*
> *And count the waves aloud . . .'*

For the first time I felt the beauty of voices singing in unison, and I wished it would never end. Ivan Ignatyevich accompanied us, a look of rapture on his face. We sang that duet at the Children's Olympiad, and for a prize I was given a piano transcription of Rimsky-Korsakov's opera *The Snow Maiden*.

That year I went to Leningrad to visit my mother. She knew that I was growing more and more fond of singing and for my tenth birthday gave me a record album of Tchaikovsky's opera *Eugene Onegin*, and a Gramophone. Tatyana was sung by Kruglikova, Onegin by Nortsov, Lensky by Kozlovsky. Strangely, my first roles in the Russian repertory at the Bolshoi were Tatyana in *Eugene Onegin* and Kupava in *The Snow Maiden*.

So it was that I heard opera for the first time. The sounds of the orchestra, the beauty of the voices, the poetry stirred up emotions completely new to me. I was in a fever for days. I noticed nothing around me, I forgot to eat, I no longer ran out in the street to play with the boys. I just sat and turned the crank of that marvelous machine, making it repeat for me, over and over, Tatyana's and Lensky's declarations of love, and Onegin's cold moralising.

Soon the whole apartment was moaning over *Onegin*. My grandmother would shriek from the kitchen, 'Stop! Turn off that blasted machine! I'm sick of it!'

But by now I was transported:

> *'Are you an angel watching by me?*
> *Are you a tempter sent to try me?*
> *I beg you, drive these doubts away!'*

The mystery of those words and the grace of the melody moved me to tears. I wanted not only to sing but to act – to interpret. I would put my hand on my heart, look at myself in the mirror, and sing with Lensky:

> *'I love you, Olga, I love you,*
> *As only the mad soul of a poet*
> *Is doomed to love . . .'*

Eventually the mirror interfered and distracted me from the most important thing – my inner feelings. I would turn away and see Olga in the garden. The yellow house with its columns, Tatyana on the balcony on a moonlit night:

> *'I drink the magic poison of desires,*
> *Dreams haunt me . . .'*

How sweetly does the heart beat! I so wanted to be on that balcony . . . to put on a white dress . . . Never had I known the meaning of the words 'the magic poison of desires.' Before, poison had meant only one thing:

> *Marusya has drunk poison,*
> *They've taken her away . . .*

Now there was a 'magic poison' that caused one's heart to melt, one's head to spin, that made one want to soar from happiness.

I learned the whole opera by heart. I knew all the parts and choruses. Like a madwoman, I would sing from morning to night. I would sit at the table, take my school notebook, and write as I sang:

> *'Let me perish, then, but first*
> *In a hope that blindeth me,*
> *I'll summon up an obscure bliss,*
> *I'll taste of life's felicity.'*

Such a state was perhaps bound to lead to a tragic denouement: I fell in love.

He, my Onegin, was the grade ahead of me, the fourth. He was not like the other boys, who were mop-headed and messy. His hair was always neatly combed with a part in the middle, and he wore long, well-ironed gray trousers, a matching jacket, and clean shirts. In short, it was clear to me that:

> *'The moment you came in, I knew you;*
> *I felt all faint, I felt aflame,*
> *And told myself: it's He!' . . .'*

But he paid no attention to me. Not the slightest. And because I couldn't very well go up to him and profess my love, I decided to write him a letter. Naturally I cribbed the whole thing from Pushkin:

> *'I write you. What more can one do?*
> *What else is there I can say?*
> *I know it's now within your power*
> *To punish me with scorn. But nay, . . .'*

It was a long letter of several pages. I asked a girl in class to pass it to him. Lord, how I waited for the next recess, for his verdict! And what came of it all? Calamity. My Onegin with his gray trousers and perfectly neat part didn't understand a thing. He said nothing – gave me not so much as a look. I ran home and wept bitterly. It was my first unrequited love, right out of Pushkin. How Russian!

That encounter with the great poet and with Tchaikovsky decided my fate once and for all. From my real life – filled with drunken scenes, with unvarnished lies, with bombastic propagandistic marches – I was transported to an exotic world of unimagined beauty, magical sound, and unearthly purity. I never came back. Everything I had known up to then simply ceased to exist, and I pictured my future in the most glowing of colors. It was decided: I would be an artist; I would sing.

Fifteen years later I would stand on the stage of the Bolshoi and sing Tatyana. My partner would be Pantaleimon Nortsov, the Onegin I had listened to as a child. He was ending his career; I was just beginning mine.

It's curious. When, at eighteen, I first heard *Eugene Onegin* at the Leningrad Opera I was terribly disenchanted. Everything on that stage seemed artificial after the power I had felt in the poetry and music alone. As a child, knowing nothing about professional theater and never having seen it, I had created my own theater, one born of an active imagination. But the ecstasies of my childhood only pointed up for me the lie of what I was seeing on the stage. It was false, it was deception itself, and for a long time it alienated me from operatic theater.

I developed an enormous appetite for reading after that: Pushkin, Lermontov, Tolstoy's *Anna Karenina*, Balzac's *Splendeurs et Misères des Courtisanes*. And then there were new distractions: a drama group and the ballet school, where I studied for two years. I didn't particularly like to dance, but I enjoyed standing at the barre making beautiful, flowing movements with my arms, straightening my spine, my neck, and gracefully turning my head. Or gliding, floating across the room. I felt myself an empress. But movement was not enough. I needed to express all that I felt – I needed *words*.

But aside from the new life opened up for me by the miracle of art, I was living the real, inescapable, everyday life of the people around me. Those were the years of Stalin's purges – the years of Yezhov's Great Terror. The teacher at school would read us the newspapers; we were obliged to know that the great Stalin had unmasked the Trotskyite enemies. The spies for foreign countries, Yakir and Tukhachevsky, the great Stalin had unmasked, too. And the list went on: Pyatakov, Bukharin, Kamenev, Zinovyev. With the murder of Kirov, the great Stalin again exposed, unmasked, unraveled . . . Stalin, Stalin, Stalin, Stalin, Stalin, Stalin, . . . until we finally realised that in fact no life was possible without Stalin. Loving Stalin came first, everything else was secondary. The Stalin Constitution and the *History of the All-Union Communist Party* (*Bolshevik*) were already being taught in the schools. And when parades were held in honor of the November 7 and May 1 holidays, we didn't simply go – we *had* to go. Not to go would have been to be against Stalin.

It didn't take long for volunteer informers to make their appearance. Those scum were the first to detect which way the wind was blowing, and the first to get to the trough. At Pioneer and Komsomol* meetings we were told that we were encircled by enemies, that it was our duty to report all suspicious events to the school or the police. Every kind of denunciation was encouraged, and informers were held up as models of behavior. Finally, we were offered up the model worthiest of emulation, a hero: twelve-year-old Pavlik Morozov, whom millions of Soviet children would glorify in song, poetry, paintings, monuments – all because he had informed on his own father and grandfather.

As in Hitler's Germany, Russia began deliberately to cultivate a generation of snitches, and the indoctrination would start with grade school. Or even earlier, in nursery school. Children who had barely learned to walk were lisping verses and songs – about whom? About Pavlik Morozov. The nursery school itself might bear his name. The message was plain: 'Children, if you're good little boys and girls, if you inform on Mama and Papa, songs may

---

* Communist youth organisations.

even be sung about you. So keep your eyes peeled, keep a close watch, and listen hard.'

It would be interesting to know who was first in that infernal work of corrupting children's souls – the Nazis or the Communists. It would seem the Soviet Union was a bit ahead.

'Thank you, Comrade Stalin, for our happy childhood!' For many years afterward, children at meetings would shout that slogan as a conclusion to their speeches. And for a long time we would continue to hear it from the screen in movie houses, from the stages in our theaters, and from every one of our vast country's loudspeakers. We believed in Stalin not as in a god – we knew nothing about God – but as the most ideal embodiment of Man on earth. And we were so brainwashed that we believed that with no Stalin we would all simply drop dead. 'Stalin is Lenin today!'

My first real triumph had something to do with Lenin. I was nine, and was singing in a school concert in celebration of his birthday. To this day I can hear the rigid, marching tune and the words:

> *'Ring out, O song of ours!*
> *Like a wave against the world.*
> *Lenin lives, Lenin lives,*
> *Lenin gives us life.*
>
> *In the cities, in the country,*
> *The great billow seethes.*
> *Sing it louder – this our banner!*
> *Hear it, Lenin? The earth is trembling!'*

When I finished, the auditorium erupted. Everyone was shouting – children and parents alike. I had to repeat the song two more times. And I sang like one possessed; like a tribune, like a member of the *Hitlerjugend*: 'Hear it, Lenin? The earth is trembling!' I must have believed those words. I doubt that my performance would have had such an impact otherwise. And yet I was still a child, only nine. Oh, how vividly I remember those first feelings on the stage – the ecstasy, the frenzy.

We became inured enough to think that the years were passing by uneventfully, although we often witnessed the 'resettlement' of some of our acquaintances – now and then of whole families. An Estonian family by the name of Gerts lived in the apartment across from us. But what kind of Estonians could they have been if they had moved to Kronstadt before the Revolution, and might even have forgotten their language? Nevertheless, they were hauled off with all their belongings, not to the capital of our great motherland, but to Mother Siberia or Solovki.* I clearly remember old Fenya, her feet swollen, barely able to move, leaning on her grown children as she inched along. She was wailing at the top of her voice, as over the dead.

All of the neighbors gathered on the stairway to watch. Russians enjoy seeing other people's suffering. For some reason, they feel sorry for themselves at such moments . . . No, I don't recall that anyone was outraged; such scenes had become commonplace. On the contrary, many even tried to find a justification for this monstrous lawlessness. 'Kronstadt,' they'd say, 'is a military stronghold, and the enemy never sleeps. Of course we've known Fenya all our lives – and you have to feel sorry for the old woman. At her age how will she ever get used to things in a new place? She may even die before she gets there. But what can you do in times like these?'

They would talk a bit more, have a smoke – to pacify themselves – and then go their separate ways.

My father served in Estonia in 1941, after its 'voluntary' annexation to the USSR. He invited me to spend the summer vacation with him, so I joined him in the city of Tartu. What a striking difference between the life I had known and the life I saw there! I had come to another planet. The people were so well dressed, so well fed, the streets so clean. Families lived in their own apartments; there were no communal ones here. And why did they say 'Thank you' to me in the store? Because I had been fortunate enough to afford that wonderful pair of shoes? No, that couldn't be. Something was wrong. But of course, all this was a

* A prison camp, formerly a monastery on Solovetsky Island in the White Sea.

capitalist plot! They wanted to entice 'Soviet man,' stupefy him, and then . . . But you can't fool us! Every day on the radio we're warned of this, even children know better. Besides, my daddy's job is to indoctrinate you Estonians: 'We'll soon put an end to these bastards! Parasitic gluttons!'

One light summer night, as I was coming home from a girlfriend's house, I noticed a truck in a deserted street. It was jammed full of people, standing there silently, ghostlike. Suddenly a girl jumped out of the truck and began to run. Some soldiers took off after her. First the clacking of her high heels resounded on the cobblestones, then the pounding of jackboots, and then . . . silence. They had caught her, of course, but she hadn't cried out. That was the way our 'Soviet brothers' rounded up 'voluntary joiners' and took them into exile, or to be shot. It went on before our eyes, without affecting us very deeply. We knew that we were surrounded by spies and enemies who wanted to annihilate us. But we also knew that the great leader and teacher was on the alert. Our benefactor would take care of us. He did not sleep nights, thinking about us. Hitler's invasion caught him sleeping, however, and it hit us like a snowstorm on a hot summer's day.

I was alone in Tartu when the Germans advanced – my father was out of town. I ran to the headquarters of an air force unit, where vehicles were being loaded in haste. Amid the noise and shouting, I managed to get out on a bus filled with pilots. A special detachment followed us, blowing up bridges in its wake. We traveled day and night. It wasn't a retreat at all; it was a flight in panic. We had reached Torzhok before we stopped to catch our breath. That's how the war began for me – that's how my childhood ended. I was fourteen.

TWO

On September 1, 1941, the schools in Kronstadt opened as usual. But no one had any interest in schoolwork. The Germans were marching across Russia. We were taught how to bandage the wounded, extinguish incendiary bombs, and handle weapons. During the first months of the war, the huge battleship *Marat*, at anchor in Petrovsky Harbor, was split almost in half by a direct hit. When we reached the spot, our eyes were met by a horrifying sight. Hundreds of sailors in nothing but their skivvies, many of them wounded, were swimming to shore and collapsing on the ground. The water in the harbor had turned red with that first blood . . . So that's what war was all about!

The Germans were already near Leningrad, bombing it and shelling it every day. The air was filled with the smell of pulverised brick and melting iron.

Once, the air-raid alert found me on the street; I sought cover in the nearest doorway. The shells crashed and whistled. One hit the far side of the building I was standing in. For a time, we couldn't see through the red dust. After the shelling, we rushed to that part of the building. The entire entrance was a heap of bricks; the dead and wounded lay among them. With our hands, we dragged the bricks out of the way, and pulled out the first woman. She was dead. My heart froze. Her eyes were huge – bulging out of their sockets – and she was covered with that terrible dust – her face, her hair. Only in her glazed eyes did the blue sky find its reflection. Nearby, a little girl of about five ran aimlessly about, crying, 'Mama! Mama!'

We put the woman on a stretcher and carried her to my school, close by. I had no idea the dead were so heavy . . . It was my first encounter with death. The little girl ran after us, weeping.

Not long thereafter, the famed Badayevsky food warehouses

in Leningrad went up in flames. They burned for several days, and melted butter and sugar flowed through the streets. The Germans had used their excellent knowledge of the plan of the city and obliterated almost the entire food supply.

A harsh winter set in. Not even the old-timers could remember such cold: the water mains froze, pipes ruptured, and the sewage system went out of order.

The blockade had begun. Nine hundred days of constant suffering. Even I, who went through all the circles of that Inferno from beginning to end, cannot watch old newsreels and believe that it actually happened.

Only a few months had passed since the outbreak of the war, but Kronstadt was already starving. The amount of food one could obtain with a ration book dwindled and dwindled. Soon the bread ration was down to four ounces for a dependent and eight ounces for a worker. The groats ration was ten ounces per month, the butter ration about three ounces. Eventually, nothing was issued but bread, if you could call it that. Those four ounces on which life depended were a wet, sticky, black mash of flour waste products that fell apart in your hands. But everyone made his hunk last as long as possible.

For a while, the schools continued to function. Those who had the strength attended. Bundled in our overcoats and caps, and gnawed by hunger, we would sit in the icy, unheated classroom. All of us had sooty faces: there was no longer any electricity, so people used wick lamps. They gave off precious little light and smoked mercilessly. Even our teacher had soot embedded in the wrinkles of her face. People gradually let themselves slide; they stopped washing, and were covered with lice.

There were cafeterias where for a coupon worth half an ounce of groats you could get a bowl of soup. Actually, it was soup in name only but it was better than nothing. One day I went to a cafeteria with a girl from my class. I tore off a coupon, put my ration book on the table, and went to the window to get my soup. When I came back, the girl with sitting there, but my ration book was gone. She had stolen it. When the bread ration is four ounces a day and the groats ration is ten ounces a month, stealing a ration book is tantamount to murder. I remember that girl well. She was one of those people in whom animal hunger had overcome reason. They were the first to die. The girl survived, however – she ate human flesh. She had a strange look in her eyes and an awful sideways gait. The only thing she ever talked about was food. Later, when the two of us happened to be living in the same room in a barracks, she stole from me again. But I couldn't bring myself to hide anything. It was debasing to me. I recall her now without judging or accusing. In that terrible time, the only ones to survive morally were the ones whose spirit had not been conquered.

People were dying in the streets; for days the bodies would lie where they had fallen. One often saw corpses with the buttocks carved out. When someone in a family died, the survivors would try to hold off burying him and reporting his death as long as possible, so that they could make use of his ration book. Mothers lay in bed with dead children for a few extra crumbs of bread. Frozen corpses were left in apartments until spring.

We all went hungry together, but the men succumbed sooner than the women. Uncle Kolya's whole body swelled up, and Andrei's legs were covered with sores from scurvy. He lost almost all his teeth and could hardly walk, though he was only thirty-two. Grandma was so weak from hunger that she could no longer stand up and would sit by the stove all day. One of her arms was paralysed.

Where were my parents in those days? Long before the war, my mother had gone off with a new husband to the Far East of Russia. Now and then I would get a letter from her. And my father, that eternal 'fighter for Leninist ideas,' had a civilian job in the provisions department of a military unit in Kronstadt. But he never even paid us a visit. He was living with his mistress, Tatyana, whose husband, a navy officer, had been killed in battle, leaving her with two small children, her mother, and a grandmother of eighty. My father stole food from the military warehouse and brought it to her. And for his beloved he arranged a party to greet the terrible New Year of 1942. Tatyana invited me to the celebration. I was so thin, so transparent, it was a wonder I could keep body and soul together. She looked at me and was amazed. 'Pavel, why is that daughter of yours so scrawny?'

Yes, there were people who took it into their heads to ask questions like that when corpses were lying in the street.

I looked at the table and couldn't believe my eyes: roast goose! I wasn't even upset by the monstrous luxury of it. The sight sent me into raptures. And the taste! I asked Tatyana for a piece to take home to Grandma. When I brought it to her, she stared at it for a long time in silence, then gave half of it to me and ate the rest.

There was a small iron heating stove in our room, a *burzhuika*.* No firewood was to be had, so we chopped up the admiral's wardrobes and tables and kept warm that way.

One night Grandma and I were alone in the room. I was sleeping on the sofa under a pile of blankets, and Grandma was warming herself by the burzhuika. She dozed off. The clothes she was wearing were dried out from the heat, and the hem of her dress was sucked into the open door of the stove. It began to smolder, but by the time she felt it her dress had burst into flames. She cried out, and I rushed to her and threw blankets over her to put out the fire. She was covered with third-degree burns from the knees to the neck. For two days she lay in bed, while I tried to take care of her by applying manganese lotion. But what good could lotion do when her entire body was one big blister?

She kept begging, 'Lord, let death come quickly! Galenka, don't touch me, for the sake of Christ!' The pain she endured cannot be imagined. On the third day we wrapped her in sheets and blankets and took her by sledge to the hospital. The poor thing moaned all the way there. The next day, toward evening, I went to the hospital.

'I'd like to see Darya Aleksandrovna Ivanova.'

'And who are you?'

'I'm her granddaughter.'

'You're Galya?'

'Yes.'

'She died during the night.'

Dear God! But it can't be!

* A corruption of 'bourgeois,' dating from the days of the Revolution.

'Yes, she's gone. She kept calling for you. She wanted to see you, and kept saying, "I have a granddaughter, Galya." Why didn't you get here in time?'

'Can I see her?'

'Oh no, they took her away this morning.'

'Dear God! Where can I find her?'

'There's no point looking for her now. If they've taken her away already, she's probably in a common grave by now.'

That was in February 1942. God rest your soul, Darya Aleksandrovna Ivanova, your good, kind Russian soul. Why did you have to die like that? Tormented by hunger and cold, covered with scabs and lice, with none of your children or grandchildren at your side. Strangers' hands closed your eyes . . . May the earth nestle you like down. And forgive me everything for which, intentionally or not, I am guilty before you.

An order was issued for the evacuation of women and children. It was the last chance to get out. The only route was across frozen Lake Ladoga, and spring was fast approaching. Aunt Katya prepared to leave with her three children. Andrei decided to go, too. They would have taken me with them, but I refused. Not that I had any good reason to stay, but utter indifference to my fate had crept over me – that state of mind which, when all was said and done, helped me to survive . . .

They traveled in overcrowded trucks by night to lessen the chances of being hit by artillery shells. The Germans knew full well that there were half-dead women and children on that road. Yet they swept it with fire, meter by meter.

The ice had already begun to melt, and the wheels of the trucks were deep in water. All around were craters from bombs and shells. Many trucks vanished under the ice. In those last days and hours of the evacuation, the trucks somehow managed to take tens of thousands of people across. Ladoga was the 'road to life.'

On the other shore food awaited those who made it. It was a great test. People driven mad by hunger threw themselves on the bread, disregarding the doctors' warnings that they should eat slowly. Many who had survived the famine did not survive the long-desired piece of bread. Aunt Katya's two younger children could not hold back and gorged themselves. Within a day both of them died of dysentery. She buried them in that very place, then traveled on with her remaining son. As for Andrei, after the evacuation we never heard anything about him again. Whether he died on the Ladoga 'road to life' or further down the line, God only knows.

And so I remained alone.

My father decided to save Tatyana and her family. But there was the problem of her old, crippled grandmother. They certainly couldn't take her with them. What could he do with her?

Then it occurred to him: 'Galka doesn't want to leave,' he told Tatyana, 'so your grandmother can move in with her. It will be jollier for both of them.'

Yes, of course. It will be jollier for two to starve together.

They brought her to me with her little bundle, sat her down on the sofa, and left.

I don't blame Tatyana. She had her own children and her mother to save. But as for my father . . . he was abandoning me to almost certain death.

The unfortunate old woman just sat on the sofa, sat there and said nothing. She died shortly thereafter. The neighbors across the hall sewed her up in a blanket, but there was no one to bury her. For two days she lay on the floor beside my bed. I was terrified, and couldn't sleep: there was not another soul in the apartment . . . She seemed to be stirring in the blanket . . . At last some men arrived. They didn't have enough strength to carry her, so they took her by the feet and dragged her across the floor and down the stairs. Then they threw her on a cart and hauled her off.

I slipped into a kind of half-sleep. Alone in the empty apartment, wrapped in blankets, I dreamed – not about food. Castles, knights, and kings drifted before my eyes. I was walking through a park in a beautiful dress with a crinoline, like Miliza Korjus in the American film *The Great Waltz*. A handsome duke appeared. He fell in love with me and married me. And of course I sang, like she had. I had seen that film at least twenty times before the war.

I didn't even suffer from hunger. I didn't suffer at all but simply grew steadily weaker. I spent all my time sleeping or daydreaming of beautiful, unattainable things . . . Only the cold tormented me.

One night I was awakened by strange sounds coming from the street. I went to the window; below was an open truck piled high with corpses. Spring brought with it fear of an epidemic, and a special detachment of women was organised to collect corpses from people's apartments. They received extra rations for this grisly job. Working at night, they would drag a frozen cadaver from an apartment to the street, pick it up by the hands and feet, swing it – one, two, three! – and throw it into a truck. It would make a ringing sound like a log covered with ice. This was the sound that had awakened me.

As I watched, they brought out a woman and tossed her on top of the heap. She had very long hair, and it billowed like a living wave. Lord, how beautiful! The day would surely come when I too would fail to wake up, and they would throw me into a truck – one, two, three! And I would make a ringing sound . . .

But the spring of 1942 arrived, and they began a door-to-door search – for those who were still alive. A team of three women came to my apartment.

'Hey, anyone alive here?' I heard them shout from the hallway. But I was dozing and was reluctant to answer.

'Look, there's a girl in here! Are you alive?'

I opened my eyes and saw three women standing beside my sofa.

'I'm alive . . .'

'Anyone else here?'

'I'm alone.'

'Alone? What are you doing here?'

'Living.'

If they hadn't come then, it would have been the end of me.

They returned the next day to take me to the headquarters of the MPVO (local anti-aircraft defense), a detachment of about four hundred women. They were quartered in a barracks and received a military ration. Their commanders were old men unfit to be sent to the front. The uniform was a light-blue coverall, and

the sailors jokingly nicknamed them 'the blue division.' I joined
that 'division,' and came back to life in their midst.

Our duty was to keep round-the-clock watch from the towers;
we had to report to headquarters the location of any flares or fires
we spotted; or, in case of a bombing or artillery fire, where the
explosions were, and what part of the town was being attacked.
Immediately after an air-raid alert sounded, we had to be ready to
help the civilian population: to dig people out of the rubble of
buildings destroyed by explosion, to minister first aid, and so on.
During the day we were involved in cleaning up the town. We
tore down wooden buildings for fuel and issued firewood to the
population. (The same thing was done in Leningrad, where not a
single wooden building was left standing.)

We had no equipment to speak of except our hands, crowbars,
and shovels. During the severe winter, sewage pipes had ruptured everywhere; and as soon as the ground thawed out, the
sewage system had to be repaired. The women of the 'blue
division' took care of it. We did it in a very simple way. Suppose
there was a street 1,000 meters long. First we would use
crowbars to pry up the cobblestones and would remove them
with our hands. Then we would dig the earth out of a trench some
two meters deep with shovels. In the trench there would be
wooden planking covering the pipe. We would pry up the planks
with crowbars and repair the part of the pipe that had ruptured.
The recipe was as simple and clear as in a cookbook. In the
process, I even learned how a sewage system is built. Of course
I had to stand in filth up to my knees, but that didn't matter – I was
being fed!

The bread – ten ounces of it – was issued in the morning, along
with a lump of sugar and half an ounce of fat. For lunch we had
soup and kasha, and for dinner more kasha. The portions were
minuscule, but it was royal fare – and every day. That was living!

A navy unit was quartered in the barracks next to ours,
and they had their own jazz orchestra. As soon as I felt my
strength returning, I began to sing with them. After a full day
of heavy, unwomanly labor, I could barely drag myself back
home. But youth is all-powerful. After a few hours, I would
dash off to rehearse with the jazz combo. In the evening we

gave concerts on ships, in the forts around Kronstadt, and in dugouts.

The room I lived in had twenty beds. In the centre was a table and a huge iron stove where we dried our clothes. Beside each bed was a little night table, and a trunk under the bed held all our belongings.

The women varied in age and background. I was the youngest, though in a few months' time I grew rapidly, put on weight, and began to look much older than my years. Though I did the same work as all the others, carrying planks on my back and moving cobblestones, I wore three pairs of canvas mittens. I didn't care whether my stomach muscles tore, but I spared my hands, because I knew I would perform one day.

Sailors would cluster around our building lying in wait. Our outfit was by no means an 'institute for high-born young ladies'; the 'blue division' had a bad reputation. During those terrible years, when the burden women shouldered taxed them beyond their limit, many led debauched lives. They drank like men, and smoked shag tobacco. I along with them. What sort of feast could I expect after a concert? A bowl of soup, a hunk of bread, a glass of vodka. And I thank the sailors who served it: they shared their last morsel.

The loss of husbands and fiancés led to the moral dissolution of many women. And yet there was much that was pure, much that was genuine. After years of looking death in the face, people sought more than momentary pleasure; they wanted lasting love, spiritual closeness. But that, too, often ended in tragedy. In his 'field wife' a man often found the spiritual strength that would lead him to break with his family. Many such tragedies took place before my eyes. But it was among just such people that I learned the real price of human relations. I came to know life as it really is – life as I never would have known it under other conditions.

Left to my own devices in that vortex of human passions, I realised that I would either sink to the very bottom or emerge from the mire unscathed. And I sensed – I knew – that only art could help me. So I longed to sing, to appear on stage. There, if for only a few brief minutes, I could escape from real life and find within me the power to bring others into my own special, beautiful world.

Then came love.

In winter, when the gulf was frozen over and the ships remained in port, the town swarmed with sailors. They flocked to the officers' clubs in their handsome new uniforms, complete with epaulets. Navy men took on a special charm. I spent many evenings at the officers' club. I would come there in my thread-bare dresses, my only accessory the sparkle in my eyes. It was there I met a young lieutenant from a submarine the sailors dubbed the 'Pike.'

The submariners were unique among navy men. In a catas-trophe at sea, not one would survive – the prospect of such a fate heightened their sense of duty and deepened their regard for friendship. Pyotr Dolgolenko, my lieutenant, was good-looking and a lot of fun. He was big and kind, and had the most infectious laugh I had ever heard. With such a man, one fears nothing. When he kissed me for the first time, I actually fainted. We were on the street, and when I came to, I was sitting on a bench. Above me was his face, and around it the stars, spinning.

We planned to marry after the war, and in order to be together in the meantime, we would go dancing night after night. There was no place we could be alone. All of the women in the MPVO had to comply with barracks rules and could get to town only on a pass. Anyone who went AWOL would be sent to the *guba* – the guardhouse in the basement – or be put on toilet-cleaning detail. But the women got out anyway, through the windows.

Once, coming back late from a dance, I thought I would be able to slip past the guard. But I was wrong. The platoon commander was up and waiting for me. 'To the guba!'

I knew the guba well. I shrugged my shoulders, changed into my uniform, and went down to the basement. The water came up to my knees, bits of ice were floating in it. My rubber boots were worn through and my feet were soon soaked. I complained to the guard.

'Tough luck. You'll just have to sit it out on that plank over there. You're no princess.'

'Oh, so that's the way it is.' I took off my boots and threw them in his face. 'I'll just stand here barefoot. My feet are wet anyway.'

'What are you, an idiot? You'll croak.'

'Fine. And you'll have to answer for it.'

He went away, and for more than an hour I stood in the icy water, not once getting up on the plank. Then I heard his footsteps again: he had a new pair of boots in his hands.

'Here, artistka!'

The usual punishment for going AWOL was three to five days in the guba. But for throwing my boots in the guard's face, I got ten days on bread and water. My third day there happened to be February 23 – Red Army Day. Above, a concert was scheduled. The jazz combo was waiting, the concert hall was full of officials, and the star of the program was in a flooded basement like some Princess Cockroach.

Footsteps again: 'Come on out, artistka. They're waiting for you.'

'I'm not going.'

'What do you mean, you're not going? I'm under orders to bring you.'

'Just try it! I'm not going anywhere!'

He tried to persuade me, first with kind words, then with threats. I sat there adamantly on the plank bed, my legs tucked under me, water all around. Then came the top officer in charge of women, the commander of the MPVO – a rather young, imposing man. He said cheerfully, almost gaily, 'All right, Ivanova. Come on out!'

Ah, I thought. So it's an important occasion, plenty of guests, but no dessert. Why else would he have come? 'Why should I? I'm fine right here.'

'Okay, enough. They're waiting. Go and sing!'

'No.'

I was stalling, knowing by now that they really did need me.

'Come on! Stop playing hard to get. Don't make us have to take you there by force – at bayonet point!' But he was looking at me as a cat looks at suet – smiling. Obviously, I pleased him. Such repartee in such a setting was provocative indeed.

I told him frostily, 'Sure, you can take me on stage at bayonet point, but you can't make me sing.'

He was practically purring now. 'So we can't force you?'

'You can't force me.' Every man for himself!

'Okay. How many days did they give you?'

'Ten.'

'And how many have you served?'

'Three.'

'I'm releasing you from the guba. Get on up there!'

I took off without a backward glance.

January 1943. I was sitting alone in the room one evening; everyone else had gone off to see a film in the barracks. Music was coming from the radio, and I sat by the stove, dozing. Suddenly the music stopped, and through my half-sleep I heard the voice of the announcer, Levitan: '. . . a report from the government . . . our valorous troops have broken the blockade of Leningrad.'

God in heaven! And only I had heard it! I had to let the others know, but then it occurred to me: What if I had dreamed it?

I ran to the hall where the movie was being shown, opened the door a crack, and peered in. Our platoon leader was right there. I whispered, 'Come! Quick!'

He stepped into the hallway. 'Well?'

My heart was in my throat: 'The blockade is broken!'

'What, are you crazy? Close the door and tell me calmly.'

'Come with me then, and listen to the radio!'

We ran to my room. Levitan was repeating the same news. We tore back to the hall, flung open the door, and turned on the lights: 'Comrades, the blockade is broken!'

The news was received with an uproar. We knew full well that much grief was still in store, but at least we would be cut off from our own people no longer. It was an opening, a chink, and help would get through. The situation didn't improve the very next day, of course, but soon another four ounces of bread was added to the ration, and on ships they began handing out American canned goods.

That summer, Pyotr went to sea on the *Pike*. For us, the women in the 'blue division,' the good weather brought a different kind of work – in truck gardens. We plowed the land and planted potatoes until we had such back pain that we couldn't straighten up. The work was hard, but we were grateful for the warmth of the sun.

I was weeding a garden and singing one day when one of our women pulled herself up to full height and shouted, 'Hey, Galka! Did you hear about the *Pike*, your Petka's ship? It was sunk the other day.' Her teeth were bared in a jeer. I was already kneeling in the weeds. I pressed my face into the earth. . . .

Alone again.

How miserable and hopeless everything became after his death. It was as if that woman's bestial grin had opened my eyes – I suddenly saw everything around me differently. Who were these people? Why was I here? Clearly, I couldn't stay any longer, but where could I go? Leningrad maybe? To study?

I asked for a discharge, but they refused to give it to me. 'Wait until the war's over,' they said. 'There's still work to be done.'

I went to the commanding officer who had released me from the guba and asked him to let me go.

'Why are you in such a hurry? You're still young – you have time. Right now you're needed here.'

'And when the war ends will I still be here in your vegetable gardens? I can't stay any longer. I want to study. Let me go.' He was a good man. He saw it my way and approved my release.

I had spent a year and a half in the 'blue division.' It had saved me physically, but a spiritual death was at hand, and I had to save my soul.

Leningrad. Little by little, the city was coming back to life. With a worker's ration book, you could get almost a pound of bread a day. My first priority became finding a job that would afford me that opportunity. But where? I had no qualifications.

A bit of luck came my way: I was hired at the Vyborg Palace of Culture as an assistant lighting technician. In those days, lighting booths were located just off-stage. I merely had to know how to switch the upper bank of lights on and off, and the spotlights right and left. The work wasn't hard. During the day I was free and could study, in the evening I sat in my booth enjoying plays and concerts. Most importantly, I had a worker's ration book and could eat.

More often than not, the actors who performed in our theater were from the Gorky Bolshoi Dramatic Theater. Many of them were fine artists. It was the first time I was exposed to acting of that caliber, and I became obsessed with the theater. After two or three performances, I would know a play by heart and was able to prompt the actors if they forgot their lines.

The opera theaters and the conservatory had virtually ceased to exist during the war, but a group of singers had remained in the city, and those who had managed to survive the worst days of the blockade organised an opera company. People literally rose from the dead to reach out for art.

So it was that, for the first time, I found myself sitting in the Mikhailovsky Theater listening to Tchaikovsky's *Queen of Spades*. Although by then I knew the arias and duets of many operas by heart, having heard them in movies or on recordings, this was my first 'live' opera. It turned out to be an historic performance. The blockade had not been fully lifted, but the Leningraders, still suffering under a frightful famine and a bitter winter, turned out for the opera. They sat there in fur coats and caps to listen to Tchaikovsky's great work. And the singers were no less heroic than the audience. Hermann was sung by Sorochinsky, Liza by Kuznetsova, the Countess by Preobrazhenskaya, Polina by Merzhanova, and Prilepa by Skopa-Rodionova. I can still see the emaciated Hermann; Liza – thin, blue, skeletal, her bared shoulders thick with a veneer of white powder; and the great Sofia Preobrazhenskaya, in the full flower of her career.

As they sang, their breath steamed in the cold air. The thrill I felt was not simply the pleasure of a great performance: it was pride in my resurrected people, in the great art which compelled those human shadows – the musicians, the singers, the audience – to come together in that opera house, beyond whose walls air-raid sirens wailed and shells exploded. Truly, man does not live by bread alone.

The Rimsky-Korsakov School of Music eventually reopened its doors in Leningrad; I was determined to find the best teacher in that school and was told it was Ivan Sergeyevich Did-Zurabov, an Armenian who had once studied in Italy. He had a sweet tenor voice that he commanded well, and he used it to demonstrate musical phrases. This he did very prettily, in the Italian manner.

I resolved that I would study with him. He was the most popular teacher, and he ruined voices with the greatest of ease. No one could figure out how he managed to do it, and only now do I understand.

There would always be at least twenty students in the classroom huddled around Ivan Sergeyevich. He was short and pot-bellied – the perfect caricature of an aging tenor heart-throb. Brandishing choice phrases, he dazzled them all. The setting was more a concert than a classroom.

I handed him some sheet music and said I wanted to be in his class.

'What will you sing, my beauty?' All women were either 'my beauty' or 'darling.'

'Liza's aria from *The Queen of Spades*, "Midnight Draws Near."'

'Aha! Let's hear it.'

I sang. I knew the aria well. It had been sung, after all, in the movie *The Flying Cabman*.

'So. How old are you?'

'Sixteen.'

'And where have you studied?'

'Nowhere.'

'Don't fib. Anyone can hear that you've studied. Your voice is trained.'

'But I've always sung like this.'

He called in several other teachers. 'Now. Sing it again.'

I could tell that he and the others were pleased with me, so I gave them my best. I flowed with the music – the higher the tessitura, the better.

I began to study with him and within three months I lost my top notes. The fact was that I had been endowed with natural voice placement – I knew intuitively how to project the voice, how to use the chest, and how to breathe. Singers spend years learning how to breathe correctly, yet often they don't master that most basic of techniques. What I was born with, my first teacher destroyed. He should have guided me cautiously, developed my musicality, given me easy arias at first. In class Ivan Sergeyevich always talked about firm support and a strong diaphragm, but he never explained what that meant. As a result, he had me tightening my diaphragm. My breathing was hampered, my larynx tightened, my voice became thinner, and good-bye, high notes! I realised that something was going wrong, but what could I do? I had lost the mastery of my voice and could not recapture it – I had never been fully aware what it was. For me, living, breathing, and singing had been equally simple, equally natural.

After six months, I left him. I wandered from one friend's place to another – I had no home of my own. The feeling of being alone and abandoned never left me, although men were attentive and young people sought my friendship. I built a wall around myself. Life had taught me self-reliance, and with the years I came to need that independence.

Leningrad, our 'Palmira of the North!' A miracle erected by edict of Peter the Great on drained swampland, a 'city built on bones.' The majestic beauty and mysterious charm of that city with its white nights, the cold, classical severity of its architecture, the lead gray of the Neva River, inclines one toward meditation, and . . . melancholy. I would wander through my favorite spots, content to be alone.

Ultimately, my loneliness led to marriage. In the summer of 1944 I married Georgi Vishnevsky, a young sailor. Within a week it was clear that the marriage was a mistake. He didn't want me to sing, study, or perform. Even my old singing teacher became an object of jealousy. He would spy on me to see who my companions were. It's a story as old as the world. And when, on September 1, 1944, I joined the Operetta Theater, a quarrel broke out that put an end to our marriage. We parted for good after two months; only the name Vishnevskaya remains to remind me that the marriage ever took place.

I was brought into the Leningrad District Operetta Theater by a girl I knew: 'Let's give it a try! We'll travel; it'll be fun.'

We went to see the director, Mark Ilich Rubin, and auditioned for him. He took us. At seventeen we were the youngest, and the prettiest. The positions paid seventy rubles a month for twenty performances, plus one ruble and fifty kopecks a day when we were on the road. Considering that our prima donna only got 120 rubles a month, I thought the salaries were generous.

'Come to rehearsal tomorrow,' Rubin told us. 'You can take part in the crowd scenes and chorus – we'll find something for you.'

That was how my singing career began.

There were forty in our troupe: soloists, chorus, extras, and a six-man instrumental ensemble. Within days I was singing the role of a lady at a ball in Zeller's *The Man Who Sold Birds*. They dressed me up in a powdered wig, a gown with a crinoline, and corseted my waist. When I saw myself in the mirror, it took my breath away. This was what I had dreamed of even as I was dying of hunger and cold! The gown looked as if it had always been part of me. From my first step onto the stage, I felt comfortable in my costumes and instinctively knew how to flourish a fan, how to handle a train, how to pose and move my hands. I probably inherited it from my mother – that natural gypsy affinity for the theatrical.

It was a road company and we were always on the move, playing at the military units of the Leningrad District. The Germans were retreating, leaving behind the remains of Novgorod, Pskov, and Volkhov. The only buildings left standing were the churches, which neither shells nor bombs had been able to destroy. And so, on the heels of the army, our troupe moved through the cinders of Russia. We would sleep huddled together, in whatever shelter we could find. There were no washrooms, no toilets – only the street, where the temperature hovered at thirty degrees below zero. We had only the most rudimentary sets and could perform on any stage. We played in bitterly cold club-houses, with snow lining the walls and soldiers and sailors hunched in their overcoats and caps. Shoulders bare, we danced and sang *The Czardas Princess* or *The Merry Widow* – twenty to

twenty-five performances a month. I would either sing in the
chorus or sit backstage and listen. I knew our entire repertory by
heart – every one of the roles.

Almost three months after I joined it, the troupe was in a panic:
the soubrette had broken her leg. And we were on tour with only
the basic cast – there were no understudies. The evening of the
calamity we were to perform Strelnikov's *The Bondwoman*, and
the next day, Zeller's *The Man Who Sold Birds*. The director
turned to the chorus. 'Girls, which one of you can save us? Who
can sing Polenka in *The Bondwoman*?'

This was the moment I'd been waiting for. 'I can.'

'You know the role?'

'Yes.'

'Well then, let's rehearse!'

They called for the pianist and the dancers. I sailed through
without a hitch. But then I knew the show so well that I could
have taken any role, a man's as well as a woman's. I could have
played a comic if I'd had to.

The show went on. The next morning, another rehearsal:
Christina in *The Man Who Sold Birds*. That evening, another
show.

I had become a soloist, the company's soubrette. And the part
of the music-hall flirt suited my voice – I lacked the top notes for
the romantic leads; I couldn't even reach G in the second octave.

That troupe became for me a genuine school – my only one. It
was from those performers that I learned to serve art selflessly:
to respect the stage – the performing artist's sanctuary. Working
under the most intolerable conditions, the members of the troupe
nurtured and protected their art, making no concessions to
fatigue or illness. Whatever sooty underground shelter or
wretched remains of a clubhouse we were playing, an hour and a
half before the show the singers would put on their makeup and
step into their costumes as carefully as if it were the most
splendid of stages. Our troupe included a number of aging actors
who lived and performed according to the great stage traditions,
and we young people learned from them. I saw with what spirit
those old actors entered the stage, never allowing themselves a
half-hearted performance, no matter how undemanding the audi-

ence was. I wanted to be like them – to love the theater as they did. From them I understood that art was not crinolines or make-believe, but hard, exhausting work. Becoming a good actress would take many, many sacrifices.

We had to go on every day. It was the discipline I learned at the very outset of my career that helped me to preserve my voice and carriage for so long. Conditions were so severe, in fact, and our training so demanding, that one of our young actresses, Shura Domogatskaya, unable to make the superhuman effort, died on the stage from a brain hemorrhage. She was thirty-five, and we buried her in her makeup.

Her entire repertory fell on my shoulders. I had to sing regardless of my health: with tonsillitis, with abscesses in the throat, with fever. Our troupe was self-supporting – there could be no question of canceling a performance – and we all depended on one another. When you have to perform so often with a hoarse voice, with a cold, you can't rely on your youth or the vigor or your voice alone. You have to master your body. Then you will be able to shift the accent subtly – at the critical moment – and compensate for a lack of vocal resonance by acting, by involving the audience in your personality. My experience with that troupe didn't make me a singer, but it did make me an actress. In the course of four years I performed in hundreds of shows. I learned to be comfortable on stage. I learned to dance, I learned to *move*.

Life with our troupe did have its lighter moments. Performing in Gatchina, we lived for two weeks at the headquarters of a military unit. The regimental commander's son – a boy of sixteen, droll, with rosy red cheeks – got a crush on me. He was too shy to declare his love, but he came to every show. At Gatchina, I shared a room with our prima donna, Tamara Triyus. She was forty – an experienced actress with a good, strong soprano voice. Although Tamara dressed smartly, she was an extraordinarily homely woman. The rosy-cheeked boy finally screwed up his courage the morning we were to leave town, and, as Tamara and I still slept, rushed into our room, cried my name out wildly, and began kissing the first head he came to. He had failed to notice, in his passion and in the semi-darkness, that there were two of us in that room. Tamara's screech awoke me, and the unfortunate teen-ager, eyes bulging, recoiled with a yelp. I leapt from my bed bewildered, only to see the poor boy flee.

I married Mark Ilich Rubin, a former violinist and the founder and director of our troupe. He was forty, I was eighteen. I moved into his communal apartment, and felt I had finally found what I had been lacking: a home, a family, and a man who loved me and would care for me. He was a mature man, experienced in life. For the first time I felt at ease and secure, and I was grateful to him for that. We had our work and our creative interests in common, and not for a day were we apart.

I was soon pregnant. Young, and frightened by my lack of experience and our life of semi-starvation, I didn't want a child. But the thought of an abortion was worse: I feared it would leave me unable to bear children. I had to have the child, and I had to work – twenty shows a month, with a move every other day. I squeezed myself into a corset and sang and danced until my eighth month. It never even occurred to me that I should be pampered because I was pregnant. People were living in dug-outs, in half-wrecked buildings – half of Russia was in ruins, and everybody was going hungry. We would all survive!

Our tour brought us to Murmansk, where we got a room at the municipal hotel. The first night there I was awakened by what I thought was someone walking in the room barefoot. I switched on the light and saw gigantic rats milling about in our room. I was terrified and kept the light on all night, but even so they kept crawling under the door into the room from the hallway. In the morning I went to the communal washroom and as I opened the door, rats leapt from the basins onto the floor. Murmansk was crawling with them. In the full light of day, rats ran along the streets. They scurried among restaurant tables like cats, huge and red. But they didn't bite. Our oldest actor, Isai Shulgin, would take a crust of bread, crumble it, and offer it to them as if they were chickens, calling out, 'Chickie! Here, chickie!' They would run up to him and be fed. When we asked a restaurant manager why Murmansk didn't destroy its rats, he said there were simply so many that if the city tried to poison them, the poison would get into the people's food. After a while we scarcely noticed them.

Later, we went on a tour in Eastern Prussia, which is now annexed to the Soviet Union. The war had just ended, and riding the train with us were German POWs, among the first to be released and on their way home. They were young, but many lacked teeth and had scurvy. They looked pitiful. The sight of them reminded me how, in Leningrad immediately after the blockade lifted, I had seen a column of German prisoners being led along Nevsky Prospekt. The Russian guards literally had to create a living wall to protect them from the enraged Russian women.

The war had been over for only a month, and yet they, our former enemies, were there in the train beside us, and we shared with them our scant supply of bread. They were human beings, could we have done any less? They took their share and thanked us, smiling in an ingratiating way, and all that we felt was compassion.

We arrived in Königsberg. In the last days of the war, the Allies had leveled that great city to the earth. One night a cloud of steel passed over disgorging its cargo, and for miles around the earth was flat except for a half-ruined building here and there. The clean, swept streets pointed up the horror: the German survivors had been forced to clear them of rocks and plaster. It was a dead city. The smell of death was everywhere. Corpses lay rotting in the rubble, and there was no one to pull them out.

In front of the house where we were staying, an old German woman sat on a rock. I saw her there every day. She was singed black, like a dried-out mummy – only her burning eyes were proof that she was alive. Had they gone hungry, too?

On the way to the officers' mess where we ate, I ran into a little girl of about five – blonde, pretty, a little angel. I noticed she was wearing men's boots with rags wrapped around them so her tiny feet wouldn't slip out. 'What's your name?' I asked her.

'Helga. Do you have any *brot*?'

I took her with me to the mess, and there we fed her, sharing our can of soup, our meat and bread. Thereafter, whenever we went to the mess, we would find her in the same spot. *'Guten Morgen*, Helga.'

'Guten Morgen. Do you have any *Brot?'*

The time for me to have my baby was drawing near. All the women I knew advised me, 'Don't go to the big hospital. There are hundreds of women lying there, screaming. You could yell "Help!" all day long and nobody would hear you.' But where to go?

I learned of a small maternity clinic with about sixty beds. But it was virtually impossible to get in. I was advised to go there as soon as my labor pains began, shout that this was my first baby and refuse to leave. They'll find a place for you, I was assured. They always keep a bed or two free for VIPs.

That's precisely what I did. As soon as my labor pains started, Mark took me to that clinic. There we were told, 'We have no free beds. You'll have to go to the hospital.'

I broke into tears. 'But this is my first baby! I'm afraid! What if I give birth in the street?'

They summoned a doctor.

At that point my labor pains stopped entirely. The doctor looked me over and pronounced, 'It's too soon. You'll deliver tomorrow. But don't come back here. I'm warning you – we won't be able to take you in.' I wasn't about to go anywhere. I was going to sit right there in the corridor until the baby came.

And so from six in the morning until midnight I sat there in my overcoat on a wooden bench in the corridor. The doctors went to and fro all day long, and remarked at my persistence: 'You're still here?'

I stuck to my guns. 'Yes, and I'm going to stay here. It's my first baby, and I'm afraid.'

The nurses kept telling me, 'Afraid of what? You're not the first, and you won't be the last. Go on home! It's already night.'

'No! And if anything happens to me, you'll be responsible.'

Seeing that there was nothing they could do, they took me directly to the delivery room. Being a nobody I didn't get one of the reserved beds. They put me on a table covered only with a sheet, and there I lay for two days. The labor pains would start and stop. I lacked strength; I was thin, exhausted. All around me I heard screams and moans. No one there had ever heard of anesthetics. Beside me a woman was giving birth: the baby was coming. I was scared, and covered my head with the sheet so I wouldn't see. Another woman couldn't push her baby out – she didn't have the strength. I peeked, and saw that they were bringing long forceps to pull it out. Lord help me!

My labor pains became more frequent and stronger. I bit my lips.

One kind nurse kept coming to comfort me. 'Oh, you poor dear thing! You're a child yourself! How can you have a baby? Why should you have to suffer for so long? Here, let me pat you.'

'Help me, Aunt Tanya. I can't stand it any more!'

'Go ahead and yell. That'll make it easier. Yell!'

I didn't scream once.

I gave birth to a son. I managed to make the sign of the cross on my forehead – instinctively, and for the first time in my life. After that I don't remember anything. I had an attack of eclampsia. And little wonder. I had sat for eighteen hours in the corridor, and spent two days on a wooden table watching women give birth! Eclampsia during a delivery can kill both the mother and the baby. The body is so racked with convulsions that you can bite off your tongue, or be left cross-eyed or with twisted features for the rest of your life. I've seen women like that. Perhaps the sign of the cross protected me from such a fate. It was then I first thought about God.

The baby was named Ilya in memory of Mark's father.

They brought my son in for a feeding. He was healthy and strong, and as soon as he took the breast, my nipples cracked. I developed large abscesses on both breasts, and ran a high temperature. But they discharged me after nine days. At home there was no one to help me. Who would look after me and the child? Mark was a man – what could one ask of him? The diapers had to be washed and hung to dry right there in the room. I had to eat. The baby had to be fed.

I lay there for a month with a temperature of 104; I couldn't get up. The baby kept crying to be fed. What could I afford to give him except the breast? I would bring him to the breast, and then shriek at the top of my lungs. That trial would be repeated every three hours. The sores on my nipples had no time to heal before the baby would open them up again.

My father chose that time to show up. He had heard that I had had a baby, and he came by – drunk, of course – with his latest wife in tow. He sat there for a few hours, seeing very well what a desperate situation I was in, and then left. His wife, who was a stranger to me, wanted to stay and help, but he didn't let her. It might have saved my son if she had stayed.

I was indifferent to my father's disregard. I had but one desire – to close my eyes and die so that I wouldn't have to hear the crying of my unhappy baby. So that there would be no more of this accursed life.

The baby contracted an infection. There were no antibiotics then, and he couldn't be saved. He died at two and a half months. Mark and I knocked together a little coffin out of planks, lined it with white cloth, and laid our son in it. We hired a car and went to the cemetery. Spring was late that year; it was snowing, and the ground hadn't thawed. The grave was hard to dig.

Two weeks later our troupe went on the road. I was only half-alive, but Mark took me along. Things would have been worse for me at home with no one to take care of me, and he had to go. Scarcely recovered, I too began working – and I slaved like a cart horse. I was nineteen.

I returned from that tour to our home in Leningrad – to the room where my son no longer cried. Scattered all about were his swaddling-clothes, his little bonnets, his diapers. My heart was so wrung at the sight, I could hardly breathe. Forty days had passed since his death; according to Russian Orthodox custom a memorial service should have been held exactly on that day. No one had ever told me about that, but my heart ached, and I was fretful. Perhaps his little soul was calling out to me. 'Let's go to the cemetery,' I blurted to Mark.

Seeing that I was overwrought, he tried to keep me from going. We quarreled, and I set out alone. It was early summer, and warm. The cemetery was swarming with people celebrating Whitsunday. I entered, tears streaming down my face – I was feeling sorry for my little one, and sorry for myself, as I made my way to the grave without my husband, without his father. I stumbled along, sobbing, oblivious to the people cavorting about me. Some danced, some sang, others drank and ate.

I couldn't find the grave, I couldn't orient myself – everything seemed changed. When we had buried him, the ground had been hard and bare, but now flowers were everywhere. The more I strayed, the more I despaired, and I wept out loud. I weaved in and out, a solitary figure among the gravestones, wailing.

Some boys saw me and called out, 'Why are you crying, girl? Come on and have a drink with us. You'll feel better.'

I tore myself from their clutches and finally found the grave. I had suddenly remembered the name of the person buried next to him, having glanced at the gravestone briefly forty days before. When I saw the little mound, still bare with no gravestone or cross, I fell to the ground and lay there for a long time, weeping.

I don't know how much time passed before I heard someone call my name: 'Is that you, Galya?' I raised my head. Aunt Tanya – the nurse who had commiserated with me at the clinic – stood before me. Whether she was one of the revelers or whether one of her family was buried there, I never knew.

'Oh, you poor thing! Your baby must have died. Did he?'

'He died, Aunt Tanya. He died . . .'

'But just look at you! What a sight you are! So skinny! You aren't sick, are you?'

'No, Aunt Tanya. I'm only sick of living.'

She sat down beside me, stroking my hair. 'Hush, dear. Don't wear yourself out with grief. Everything is in God's hands now. He giveth, and He taketh away.'

THREE

A strange woman came to see me, saying that she was my father's wife and had had a daughter by him. It was she who told me he had been arrested and convicted under Article 58 – the 'political article' – of the Criminal Code and sentenced to ten years. When I asked why, she said that once while drunk he had told a joke about Stalin. Someone had informed on him, the authorities prosecuted him, and he would now pay for that joke with ten years of his life. So the confirmed Marxist-Leninist had fallen into the same meat grinder he had been so eager to push others into. I didn't feel sorry for him. It was cruel of me, perhaps, but after he had abandoned me during the blockade, after he had failed to lift a finger when he saw me dying with a newborn baby on my hands, I erased him from my life once and for all.

Those days brought a new wave of arrests. Anyone, everyone, was being thrown behind bars. The country was in ruins and in need of unpaid slave labor – of an entire army of slaves. Under the new system that had been established in our country, the state could not pay labor what it was worth. But the 'wise Party' had a great deal of experience in that area. Even before the war, imprisoned slaves had built the White Sea Canal, gigantic electric power stations, plants, industrial complexes, and so on – the glorious industrial achievements of socialism and communism. And after the war, under the leadership of the wise Father and Teacher, zealous officials packed the Gulag with their fellow Russians, making up political excuses as they went. A person could work himself to a frazzle for a minimum of ten years, and the government would not have to pay him a kopeck. No expenditures, no unemployment. It was a stroke of genius!

Then came the campaign against the Formalists and the

Cosmopolites. The first to take the blows were our Leningraders, Anna Akhmatova and Mikhail Zoshchenko. Andrei
Zhdanov's newspaper article in which he called Akhmatova a
'rabid society matron going back and forth between the boudoir
and the prayer house' provoked the first domestic protests. What
was going on? Anna Akhmatova was the pride of Russia. How
could Zhdanov, with such impunity, brazenly and publicly smear a
great poet and insult her as a woman?

The Party decree on Formalism in music in which the 'Formalist' composers – Prokofiev, Shostakovich, and others – were
vilified, was insane gibberish. The great Communist Party of the
Soviet Union was instructing the musical geniuses of our era in
musical literacy.

Under the slogan 'Down with the Cosmopolites!' a black plague
spread throughout the Russian theater, and many of its best
works were buried for years. One after another came the
directives ordering theaters to stage contemporary Soviet plays
glorifying the Party. And the talentless writers, the playwrights,
poets, and composers who for years had sharpened their quills
waiting for their hour, rushed pell-mell to the trough, to pay
hysterical tribute to the Soviet regime and its Great Leader, 'the
genius of all time and all people.'

What did it matter that, because of him, millions of virtually
unarmed Soviet soldiers became cannon fodder during the first
months of the war; that the Germans marched triumphantly
through the Ukraine and Belorussia, coming up to the very walls
of Moscow and Leningrad; that in Leningrad alone more than a
million and a half of the civilian population – old people, women,
and children – died of starvation? That was all forgotten. The
important thing was that the Great Leader had spoken, and
opportunity was at hand. Forward, leaders of art and culture!
Curry favor, music critics! Get the traitors! Sic 'em! Sic 'em!

'Ah, so you're a genius? Well, we the people take our collective
peasant shoe and mash it in your face. Hurrah! Long live the
Father and Teacher!'

1947, 1948, 1949 – actors were performing in theaters that
were almost empty. The public had simply stopped going. It was
too painful to hear the great actors of the Aleksandrinsky Theater

strain with false pathos and shout those bombastic, propagandistic phrases. They were visibly ashamed of themselves, and one could only feel sympathy for them, for their public humiliation. There was one consolation, however: hardly anyone was listening. In the splendid Aleksandrinsky Theater, with its velvet and gilt and seats for twelve hundred, only a few dozen people sat. I was among them.

When the new Soviet repertory achieved dominance and we were forced to perform the rubbish that the zealous pen-pushers were dragging into our theaters, I left our troupe for concert work. That was in 1948. I preferred to leave, rather than be obliged to join in the choruses of 'Hurrah!' when what I really wanted to shout was 'Help!' It was not a political protest. I could no longer bear that universal, pathological lie – I wanted to get away, crawl into a hole, hide. I prepared a program of music-hall songs, and began to give solo concerts. Soon, Mark, too, left the theater. He became my manager, organising my concerts and handling all my business affairs.

We bought a car, a Pobeda, for a thousand rubles and always drove to our concerts. There were four of us: the accompanist, either a violinist or a reciter for the beginning of the program, Mark, and me. For the most part, we played in little provincial towns or villages. We would go on the road for a month or two, following a planned itinerary and giving a concert a day. We moved from one town to the next, staying in filthy hotels and putting up with the bedbugs. Even the names of those places were appropriate: New Mouse, Old Mouse.

It was a hard way to earn a living. But since I was paid thirty rubles a concert, two months on the road would earn me a decent amount and, once back in Leningrad, I could live another two months without working. I would use this time to go to the theater or to Philharmonic Hall where I could hear famous singers on tour in Leningrad. When the money ran out, we'd get back in the car and set out to earn more.

I had no desire to try out with the Leningrad Operetta Theater or the Leningrad Variety Show Theater. I had already tasted freedom: nobody stood over me with a stick, forcing me to do what I didn't want to do. I wanted to become a well-known

personality first so that later I could join the big concert organisations with the right to set my own conditions.

I was not fond of opera then, and went only rarely to the
Mariinsky Theater. I preferred to hear singers in concert, where
I could follow closely the vocal line, the phrasing, and the
technique. Whatever I liked I would imitate at home. In listening
to the singing, I could create the character in my imagination, but
seeing someone else's interpretation of that character on stage
would destroy my own conceptualisation. Even good singing
could not make me believe that some 216-pound Aïda was 'a
celestial creature, the marvelous flower of the Nile Valley.'
All those heavy, aging matrons – rolling their eyes in *Faust* as
they plucked the petals of a daisy: 'He loves me, he loves me
not'; or lowering themselves onto a creaking bed in *Onegin*, to
write a naïve and girlish letter – only provoked annoyance and
embarrassment.

I began to look for a teacher who could help me recover
my voice, now so thoroughly wrecked by the 'darling' Ivan
Sergeyevich – that oh-so-sweet adherent of bel canto. I worked
with one teacher after another, but nothing came of it – my voice
could manage the low notes, but my upper register was blocked.
The loss didn't especially vex me, however, since the repertoire
I used in recitals required a beautiful middle register and low
chest tones.

I had decided to become a music-hall singer. My ideal was
Klavdiya Shulzhenko. I liked everything about her. I would go to
her concerts as one would to the finest conservatory. And I
learned a great deal. From the moment she came on stage, I was
under the spell of her voice, her presence, her movements. Each
song would have a definite personality. Each was a finished work
of art, with its own prelude, development, and finale. The
music-hall genre is a dangerous one – there is always the
temptation to use cheap effects and to overdramatise, with only
one object in mind: to dazzle the audience. Klavdiya Shulzhenko
never lost her sense of what was fitting. She was an artist.
Beautiful, expressive hands, a richness of facial expression –
these things reflected inner, spiritual stirrings. All was sincerely
felt, clearly projected, intelligently planned. She never used a

microphone although her voice was small. And hers was a pleasing timbre – it was as if she weren't singing but crooning, never forcing the sounds. It was the ease of her performances and their atmosphere of intimacy that captured her audiences.

She created her own style, and she reigned on the music-hall stage for decades. Her excellence can only be compared with that of Edith Piaf, although in their actual gifts they were very different. In Piaf there is sadheartedness, tragedy, anguish. In Shulzhenko there is a soft lyricism and radiant femininity. Hearing her sing, one wants to live.

Of course I wanted to sing her repertoire in my own concerts. But the sheet music couldn't be bought – her songs had never been published. So I would go to her concerts three times. At one concert I would learn the words; after a third hearing I would have them committed to memory. I would go to my accompanist and sing the songs for him. He would pick out the accompaniment on the piano, write it down, and we were set.

Once I came home from one of my tours exhausted, and found a note from my mother's sister, who was living in Leningrad: 'Come and see us when you get back. Your mother is here.' Mama! I had long ago forgotten that word, not having seen her for thirteen years. And I could conjure no love for her – I had known her too little. But neither did I feel any hostility; she wasn't repulsive to me, as my father was. I had only rarely thought about her, but when I had, it was with warmth and a feeling of pity for her failures. From time to time I would hear rumors: she had married again, divorced again . . . But in recent years she had not written me at all.

I rushed to my aunt's. She lived in a communal apartment in the Vyborg quarter and even though we lived in the same city, we scarcely knew one another. I opened the door of a little room. My aunt and uncle and their son were sitting there, and next to them a woman with a little girl of about four. I recognised my mother right off. I went in, my heart racing, and somehow produced the word 'Hello.'

She looked at me, no glimmer of recognition on her face.

'Hello.' As if she were speaking to a stranger.

At that, Aunt Vera shot out, 'Zina! What's with you? Don't you see who it is?'

She looked at me mutely, and those seconds of silence pounded in my head like a hammer: What's wrong? What's wrong? It's me! It's me!

'No. I don't recognise her.'

'Look closer!'

'I don't know . . .' More silence. '. . . Galya, is that you?'

Lord, how I wept that day! There they'd sat, expecting me, and even so she hadn't recognised me. No maternal bond – no call of the blood – had prompted her to. And I, I couldn't even pronounce the word 'Mama.'

How rapidly the Soviet regime had managed to corrupt its people, to destroy the blood ties linking children to parents and sister to brother. Forcibly torn from the concept of 'my' or 'one's own,' people would easily come together and just as easily split apart. And, away from one another they dispensed with the relationship entirely, having unlearned to accord importance to the meaning of the words 'my family,' 'my children,' 'my parents.' When you are indoctrinated with the notion that everything belongs to the Party and the State – your soul as much as the chair you're sitting on – you finally begin to understand the 'science of indifference': the simple fact that you belong to no one and no one belongs to you.

My mother was like a cuckoo without a nest. All her belongings consisted of a few suitcases full of dresses, and that little girl. She had neither home nor family. At the age of forty-three she was still a beautiful woman. She had a charm, a feminine softness, a quiet voice, and a certain sweetness – it was these that attracted men to her. I knew what a stormy life she had led – how she had thrown herself headlong into love affairs. It was strange for me to see her now, helpless and defenseless. It was hard to imagine her so resolute in her relations with men, but I knew that was the case. Or was it perhaps her femininity and defenselessness that so attracted men? It was as if she were always pursuing some impossible dream: she would fall in love quickly, and just as quickly grow disenchanted. And then no force could stop her. Remorselessly abandoning everything that, only a short time before, had been her essence and a source of happiness, heeding only the call of her heart, she would go off . . .

Her golden hair, her black, languorous eyes . . . I looked at her, aware that a tardy feeling of love – a daughter's love for her mother – was filling my heart.

She had come to Leningrad for medical treatment. Some time before, she had developed cancer of the uterus, and by then it had gone badly neglected. I was racked with pity for her.

We put her in the hospital, and I went off on tour. Our itinerary took us away from Leningrad for several months. When I returned, I found a letter waiting for me: 'Come! Your mother is dying.'

I rushed to the hospital. There they told me what ward she was in, and said it was on the fourth floor. I flew up the stairs. The corridor seemed never-ending, and I could find no numbers, no nurses, nothing. I began to run, my legs weak beneath me. Suddenly something within me made me stop before one of the rooms. The door was open, and I looked in. On the bed, on her knees and all bent over, was an old, shriveled woman, her two huge black eyes looking directly at me. It was my mother – now it was I who didn't recognise her. I realised it was she only because her sister and stepmother were standing by the bed. But what was this? Why was her hair black and streaked with gray? My mother was a blonde. This woman couldn't be she. And yet the ends of her hair were yellow. She'd been dying her hair, and I hadn't known it! I'd never known it. Lord! That little dried-up thing was all that was left of my young, beautiful mother? At first I froze with fear. Then with a cry of 'Mama!' I threw myself at her.

They took me into another room, where I sobbed uncontrollably for a long time. But I had to pull myself together. I had to go back in there calmly, so that she wouldn't realise how frightened I was. I must not destroy her hope.

They gave me a sedative of some kind, and I went in.

She was dying and in terrible agony. The pain was so bad that she couldn't lie down: she stayed on her knees all the time. She slept that way. She was only skin and bones, but her healthy young heart wouldn't let her die. During those brief periods when the morphine injections would ease her pain, she would look at me dreamily. I stroked her leathery hands. 'It's all right. Be patient. You'll get better soon, and you and I will go to the Crimea.'

She looked at me hopefully. 'Yes, to the seashore. It'll be warm, we'll have a piano, and you'll sing . . . you'll sing . . .'

'Yes, yes. By all means.'

'I know I've wronged you, but you must forgive me. Don't judge me.'

'Of course not. Never! What are you saying? Hush.'

She couldn't eat; she couldn't swallow. I wanted to give her something, anything, even if only now before death.

'What can I bring you? Tell me what you want. I'll bring it tomorrow.'

'I don't want anything.'

'Please. It's so important to me. I want to give you pleasure.'

'Well, all right, bring me some *petits fours*. Nothing more.'

I brought them the next day. Of course she couldn't eat them. But she was happy just to look at those elegant, pretty delicacies amid those wretched hospital surroundings.

On the last day of her life – somehow she knew she would die that day – she was in a hurry to tell me all the most important things that she had not, or could not, tell me earlier. She spoke with great difficulty. 'Don't be afraid. Cancer isn't contagious and it isn't hereditary. That much I know.' She paused, then looked closely at me, 'When I was young I had tuberculosis. Take care of yourself.'

And later, 'Don't trust men. None of them is worth anything.'

Toward evening she died, still on her knees, her face buried in the pillow.

Her stepmother sighed, 'Well, Zinaida, because of your prayers, your sins will be forgiven you.'

It was hard to straighten her out so she could be laid in her coffin. In it, she looked small as a child.

It was I who buried her. I took her in the car; as we crossed the city my mind reeled with the images of my miserable childhood and her accursed life. Beside me sat her four-year-old daughter, orphaned now, and faced with the prospect that had once faced me.

My meeting with Vera Nikolayevna Garina – a voice teacher – changed my life. I don't know what direction my professional career would have taken without her, but I'm certain I never would have become an opera singer.

A friend Tamara stopped by one day and as we were chatting over tea, she suddenly said, 'You know, I've been meaning to tell you about a very interesting old woman, a singing teacher, who lives nearby. Why don't we go and see her?'

'I don't really want to. I've had it with singing teachers. They're all charlatans.'

'Look, the weather is glorious. Let's go for a walk, and on the way we can stop by her place. What have you got to lose? If you don't like her, you won't go back.'

'All right, let's go.'

The door was opened by a gray-haired woman, who led us into a little room, narrow as a pencil-case. After we had been introduced, I asked her if she would listen to me sing.

'What kind of voice do you have?'

I thought: Why should I bother explaining the whole story to her? I'm sick and tired of it. Besides, even when I do, no one understands why I lost my high notes. 'Mezzo-soprano,' I said.

'Good. Let's sing some scales.'

We began with the lower octave, and I sang the low notes like a bass to prove that I was a true mezzo-soprano, perhaps even a contralto. I had always had very strong low notes anyway.

'I see, I see. Interesting, very interesting.'

I kept on descending.

'All right. Now higher, higher.'

But how could I go any higher when my voice didn't reach beyond G in the upper octave? 'I can't go any higher.'

'All right, then, that's enough. My dear, you're not a mezzo. You're a real soprano.'

I was dumbfounded. 'Really? I remember the high notes I used to have, but I lost them, and nobody believes I ever had them. All the teachers I've studied with have told me I was a mezzo. How did you know? I've been singing professionally for six years now, and you're the first person to recognise it.'

'I could tell from the transitional tones of the upper octave. For a soprano, those notes are D, E flat, and E. You don't know how to use head tones for them, and – remember this for the rest of your life – *that* is the key to the high notes. You have to be cognisant of the process. You must consciously find and pass through your chest, middle, and head registers, and learn to control your breathing. Having a naturally placed voice may suffice for the foolish and lazy. The reason many splendid voices are lost early in singers' careers is that, without having had professional training, they perform, and rely only on their natural gifts. So, it's decided. I'm going to teach you, and we start today. First: How do you breathe? Show me!'

'I don't know.'

'All right. Take a breath and sing this phrase.'

She put a hand on my diaphragm, and I began to sing.

'Do you feel how tense your diaphragm is? When it's cramped like that, it's impossible to talk, no less sing. Here. Breathe the way you do when you sing, and try to say a few words.'

I did as she told me, and my speaking voice became tense and muffled, as if coming from under a pillow.

'Do you feel how the sound is trapped in your throat? With that kind of breathing it may still be possible to sing in the middle register, but high notes are out of the question. So. Go on home now, but don't you dare sing a note this evening. Don't try to understand everything all at once. It's impossible, and you'd only damage your voice. We'll work together every day – that's my chief condition. I usually charge ten rubles a month, but since you work, I'll charge you fifteen. Can you afford to pay that much?'

'Of course. But that's so little. Why don't you ask more?'

'Because I have ten students, and with my pension that comes to one hundred and fifty rubles a month, which is quite enough to feed me and my cat. I have no need for more than that.'

When I met Vera Nikolayevna, she was eighty years old. Before the turn of the century, she had studied voice with the famous singer Pauline Lucca in Vienna and for most of her professional career, she sang abroad. After her marriage to a musical-instrument manufacturer in Petersburg, she gradually gave up her singing career. Her husband – a bourgeois – was shot during the Revolution.

She lived on Mayakovsky Street in a huge communal apartment building that had once been a private home. Her narrow little room was on the sixth floor. The elevator hadn't worked since the beginning of the war, and in her later years she stopped going out because she couldn't climb the stairs. Every day, one of her students would buy food for her and fetch wood for the stove. The room was furnished with a wardrobe, a bed, a table, four chairs, and a piano made at her husband's factory. Atop the tile stove, which was almost ceiling height, sat her huge black cat, Gypsy. Often, while students were singing, he would leap off the stove and fly through the room like a black panther. Old, yellowed posters advertising Vera Nikolayevna's concerts, and a few rotting ribbons from wreaths and bouquets adorned the walls.

And so I began to study with her. As the sun rises in the east and sets in the west, I was at her place for my lesson every morning. It was a law.

After about two weeks, when she was putting me through a warm-up, she suddenly stopped and looked at me intently.

'Vera Nikolayevna, why are you staring at me like that? Did I do something wrong?'

'You have a star on your forehead,' she said.

I didn't attach any importance to those words. If anything, they made me uncomfortable. I thought: the old woman is praising me so I won't leave her. All teachers do that. But with or without her compliments, I'll go on studying with her.

More than anything else, we worked on breathing, to loosen up my diaphragm. Through special exercises, I learned to relax my tongue, lower jaw, and larynx. Within six months I had reached my full range, two and a half octaves. I worked like one possessed. I fell asleep thinking of Vera Nikolayevna, and I woke up thinking about her. I had no other life beyond touring to earn money and returning to Leningrad to work with Vera Nikolayevna.

We had remarkable rapport. Sometimes I would stand behind her; she couldn't see me, but as she listened to me sing, she would make comments: 'Keep your chest up. Relax your larynx. Keep your tongue down. Raise your upper lip.'

It was astounding, but even at eighty she could demonstrate

these techniques with her own voice. Of course, a soprano at that age couldn't possibly have made it sound the way it should, but I would understand her immediately. First I would mimic her, then I would try to analyse why one phrase or another sounded the way it did.

I made such rapid progress that by the end of a year I was singing arias by Verdi, Puccini, and Tchaikovsky. I adopted her method one hundred percent, which none of her other students was able to do.

A few months went by, and quite suddenly, I began to feel run down. It had happened to me before. At my lessons I tired quickly and was short of breath. I would lie down as soon as I got home, and I completely lost my appetite. I didn't know what was the matter with me, but I thought it was the usual spring lethargy and that once summer came I'd regain my strength.

The time for our regular summer tour arrived. We set out in the car, giving concerts in the Leningrad, Moscow, and Kharkov regions as we gradually made our way toward our final destination, the Crimea. My condition steadily worsened. Never before had I experienced such a loss of strength. I could not get myself out of bed in the morning and would lie there until time for the concert. Nevertheless, we continued on our way south. The heat in the car was unbearable, and I was so weak I was more dead than alive. As we neared Kharkov I began to cough up blood. In Kharkov, Mark took me to a hospital. We had to wait in line for hours. Finally a doctor listened to my cough, took my temperature (it was 100.4), and told me I had the flu.

I explained to him that I had coughed up blood, that I sweated heavily at night. 'I might have pneumonia. At least take some tests.'

'Your lungs are fine, and the blood only means your coughing broke a blood vessel. Next!'

'No! I demand that you take tests and X-rays.'

'Listen! You saw the line out there, and you're holding everybody up . . . Well, all right. Take this slip and go for a test and X-rays. Next!'

The test revealed tubercle bacillus and the X-rays showed lesions in half of one lung and a cavity under the clavicle. The diagnosis: an acute form of tuberculosis. There it was – my dying mother's prophecy.

For my husband, it came like a bolt out of the blue. He was so used to my endurance – I never complained, and never stopped working – that now he was at his wits' end. It occurred to him that I would be better off getting treatment in a warm southern city than in Leningrad, with its damp climate, and he took me to a tuberculosis clinic in Kharkov.

After examining me, the doctor there said that the situation was especially dangerous because I was so young, and galloping consumption could set in. The case called for artificial pneumo-thorax, that is, forcing the collapse of the lung. There was no alternative.

Mark blamed himself for failing to recognise the seriousness of my illness early on. Of course there was a grain of truth in that. He knew that a collapsed lung would mean the end of my singing career. But I myself did not understand the full gravity of the disease, perhaps because it had hit me so suddenly. I was certain that in a month or so I would be completely well.

A bed was brought in to the doctor's office for me, and I fell asleep full of optimism. The next morning two sullen orderlies came in and draped me in a horrid gray flannel smock. When I looked at myself in the mirror it seemed to me that I was wearing a shroud. I was not frightened, only taken aback: before me stood a complete stranger. And I felt the cold breath of death.

I didn't want to be alone, so I quickly left the room. In the corridor were tables covered with oilcloth. Seated at them, in a deathly quiet, were people in the same gray smocks, which seemed purposely designed to create an atmosphere of hopelessness. Slowly they were making their way through their miserable breakfasts.

I sat down at a table. Good lord, what unhappy, ashen faces! These were men and women, all much older than I, who must have been afflicted with tuberculosis for many years. In their eyes I could read my own sentence. Only now did I fully understand the tragedy of my situation, and terror froze my heart.

An elderly woman sitting across from me looked at me for a

long while, then suddenly began to weep loudly. Feeling that I
was about to choke with tears myself, I jumped up from the table
and fled to my room. I threw off the smock – it was as if a bony
hand had been lifted from my shoulders. No, and again, no! I must
go home at once! And if I'm fated to die, please, God, don't let it
be here – not here!

That very evening I returned to Leningrad by train. When I got
home, I fell into bed, nearly unconscious.

In a Leningrad hospital, a group of doctors examined me and
decided unanimously that my lung should be collapsed immediately, because galloping consumption had already set in.
They were, in effect, handing me my death sentence.

'Doctor, isn't there a way of doing without it? I'm a singer.'

'My dear, what should concern you now is not your singing but
your life. I can see that you don't fully understand the danger of
your situation, so I am obliged to tell you outright – you'll be lucky
if the pneumothorax helps. To put it bluntly, you have galloping
consumption, and I cannot guarantee that you'll live.'

I found myself on the operating table. Thoughts flashed
through my mind like lightning: If they collapse my lung, I will sing
no more. If I can't sing, there's no point in living.

The preparations were underway. One doctor was wielding an
enormous needle. My left side was rubbed with alcohol. I asked
myself why my life should be saved only to prolong a miserable
existence, only to become one of those gray smocks? . . . Not for
anything in the world! I'd rather die!

'Don't touch me! Don't you dare! Don't you dare!' I leapt from
the operating table, pushed the doctors aside, and ran off. They
made me sign a paper stating that I had refused the prescribed
treatment and would take full responsibility for the consequences
of my decision. I went home.

Apathy overcame me, and I didn't resist the disease. All I
wanted was quiet, to doze and think of nothing. I couldn't eat. My
revulsion toward food was so strong that even if I took a bite, I
couldn't swallow it. To be sure, my health had taken quite a
beating – the blockade, famine, the birth and death of my child,
and work, work, work. I lay there, and it was as if I were resting
for the first time in my life. I didn't have to go anywhere or

perform for anyone. All I wanted was to be left alone; I wanted to talk with no one. I had peace of mind, and wasn't suffering physically or emotionally. I was so tired . . .

It was the summer of 1951 and I rapidly approached death. The white nights of Petersburg made everything seem unreal: the majestic imperial boulevards and squares, the still gardens and parks . . . and in all its blinding beauty the whole phantom city, rising into a fathomless white sky, mysterious and spellbinding . . . To die there would not be terrible at all: to close one's eyes and stop breathing . . . it would be easy, so easy . . .

'Can I get you something?'

'No.'

'Are you in any pain?'

'No.'

I had the urge to reread Turgenev – 'Asya,' 'Spring Freshets,' 'First Love' – the poetic descriptions of our magnificent Russian landscape, lofty human feelings. Was such love really possible?

The blood rushed to my cheeks. With a pounding heart I accompanied the heroines of my favorite books – faster, faster – through the splendid, lush park of *A Nest of Gentlefolk*, my cape flapping in the wind . . . A storm was raging, but I ran on. I feared nothing – in the summerhouse *he* was waiting for me . . . Tears fell from my eyes onto my favorite pages. I couldn't tear myself away. I was breathless with excitement.

And suddenly I wanted to get up. It couldn't be that I was going to die – I was as young as the heroines of those books! I wanted to live! It was as if I had seen a blazing light ahead, and was drawn toward it. As of that moment, I began to fight for life.

Forcing myself to overcome my revulsion, I began to eat. I drank warm melted lard, honey with butter, and up to ten raw eggs a day. Streptomycin had just appeared in Russia, but it was not available in drugstores. You could only get it on the black market at outrageous prices. My doctors said we could try injections of it, though they doubted it would help. We decided to take the chance. Once a week, Mark went to the airport, where a black marketeer would come from Moscow, bringing little vials of the antibiotic at 30 rubles a gram – my fee for a single concert. And I needed 120 grams; that is, 3,600 rubles. Where would we get the money? Even if I had been working, I would have had to give 120 concerts! We began to sell our belongings.

With great difficulty, Mark managed to get me into a tuberculosis sanatorium near Leningrad for two months of treatment. It was located in a pine forest and had little resemblance to a hospital, although from time to time corpses were removed from it at night.

I was given two injections of streptomycin a day. In those days, the drug was very impure, and the injections were terribly painful. When they gave me the last of my 120 shots, there wasn't an unmarked place on my body. I was covered with bruises and swellings, because the medication hadn't resolved well. I was just lucky that I wasn't allergic to it. It saved my life.

Those fortunate persons who had the drug kept it under lock and key, and others would look at them with envy. Because of its cost, the drug was inaccessible to most patients (that's our free medical care for you!).

I showed marked improvement, but the doctors categorically forbade me to sing. But that didn't stop me – I went off into the woods and sang. With each passing day, I could feel the life surging back into me, and I wanted to shout it from the rooftops. I wanted to sing, to love – I was only twenty-three. I would light a bonfire and, standing over it, sing Marfa's aria from Mussorgsky's *Khovanshchina*: 'Secret forces! Great forces! Souls who have departed for the unknown world! I call upon you!' At those moments I felt I was queen of the world.

The doctors considered my recovery a miracle. The tuberculosis had disappeared, and the cavity had filled up. Over the two months I gained thirty-five pounds, and people didn't recognise me. A month later I was concertising – we had no money and were badly in debt.

At first I tried not to overwork or catch colds. But soon we were back to the old routine: into the car, and off we'd go! We'd have plenty of time to rest in the next world.

FOUR

When I came back to Vera Nikolayevna's I was strong and had gained weight. My voice was simply bursting to be heard, and I was full of energy. Vera Nikolayevna counseled me, 'Don't listen to the doctors. Start your studies again. If you breathe correctly and sing on the breath, it can only help to cure you for good.'

It did.

With fresh strength and enthusiasm, I plunged into my favorite exercises. Vera Nikolayevna had helped me to master the fundamental techniques quickly and I developed a big, open, operatic sound. But apart from her, several of her students, and my pianist, no one had ever heard – no one knew – my real voice. Not even my husband, for I had continued to concertise with my old repertory, and that required only light crooning. To most of those who had heard me I was a talented, charming, but 'voice-less' singer.

I myself felt that I would soon take another path. I had never thought about a career as an opera singer. As far as I was concerned, I was preparing for a concert career; and, since I was by nature an individualist, I had dreams of establishing my *own* theater.

My husband was skeptical about my lessons. 'Why do you need them? You're on your way to a fine career. Work on your music-hall repertoire, and in a couple of years you'll be famous. Who knows what will come of your 'pure art'? Maybe you'll get there, maybe you won't. But here you have a sure thing. And you can look forward to a lot of money in the future, and to running your own show.'

Mark never came to my lessons; he was convinced that it would only be a matter of time before my enthusiasm turned to boredom. He treated me well – as I did him – and fussed over me like a nanny. He did the food shopping, and would hold my hand as we walked down the street. With him I felt secure, even happy, until I realised that he was more a loving father than a husband – than my man. With that realisation, our marital relations began to seem wrong. Mark felt this change in me and we grew distant. He had hoped to hold on to me through our work, knowing that in my life, as in the life of any performer, work was paramount. But his lack of interest in my lessons stung me. I withdrew into myself and stopped sharing my thoughts and dreams with him. And extricating myself from him as quickly as I could, I would run off to Vera Nikolayevna.

I had been on the professional stage for almost eight years by then, and had gained much experience. I knew vocal literature well, and had come to love symphonic and instrumental music. Whenever I had a free evening, I would slip away to concerts in the Great Hall of the Leningrad Philharmonic.

I was coming to the end of my second year of lessons with Vera Nikolayevna. Technical difficulties no longer existed for me. I had learned how to fill a room with my voice, and how to sing *piano*. I now had strong high notes that never failed me.

Life was beautiful! One day in the spring of 1952, I sauntered along Nevsky Prospekt feeling young and happy. The sun was out, the weather wonderful. I turned right, toward the Field of Mars and my beloved Summer Garden, and came to a screeching halt. A poster on the Actors' House proclaimed boldly: 'The Bolshoi Theater of the USSR announces a competition for the *stazher* group. Register in advance.'

Others were reading the announcement too. I turned to them immediately, 'What does *stazher* mean? Do you know?'

'The younger group. They're holding the third day of the competition today.'

Representatives of the Bolshoi Theater were auditioning singers in nearly all the big cities that summer: Leningrad, Kiev, Kharkov, Saratov, Odessa, Minsk, Sverdlovsk, Novosibirsk, and many others. The first round of auditions was held locally, and the second and third in Moscow at the Bolshoi Theater.

Should I go in and listen? I had never taken part in a competition. I hadn't wanted to before and I didn't particularly want to then. But I was curious.

I went in. The auditorium was small, dark. At a table near the stage sat the jury: Solomon Khromchenko, a tenor from the Bolshoi; the pianist Solomon Brikker; and Nikolai Dugin, the secretary. I looked around and saw my pianist, Lyuda Patrusheva; she had come to hear her friend audition. We sat together. A few young singers came on and sang. They were conservatory students, all of them inexperienced on the stage, although their voices were good.

'Lyuda,' I finally hissed, 'what is this? The whole thing is such a bore.'

One contestant had only to sing a bit better than the others and the jury would come to life: 'Sing this aria, sing that one.' I was appalled. It was so amateurish! I simply couldn't listen to any more. Clearly, nothing interesting was going to happen here, but I stayed anyway.

We sat there for an hour, and then another, and suddenly Lyuda leaned over: 'You should try out.'

She had read my mind. 'You really think I could?'

'Of course. You're more experienced than all of them put together.'

'And what shall I sing?' My heart was already pounding.

'Why not *Aïda*?'

Well, why not? When the break came, I found the jurors' room and went in. 'I'd like to sing for you.'

Of the three, the first to react was the tenor Khromchenko. 'Well, so you want to sing?' He was already giving me the once-over. A true tenor, he was reacting to a woman as a war horse reacts to the call of the trumpet.

Dugin chimed in: 'Did you register?'

'No.'

'Why not? The procedure –'

'I didn't know there was to be a competition. I just saw the announcement today.'

'So you haven't prepared for it. Tomorrow is the last day, you know.'

Khromchenko couldn't restrain himself. 'Listen, why are you

giving her such a hard time? Whether she's prepared or not is none of your business.' Then to me, 'Come and sing.'

'When?'

'Today.'

'Today?'

'Yes, at four. It has to be today. The competition was supposed to run through tomorrow, but if we can get everyone auditioned by four, we'll leave tonight.'

'All right.' But I was worried. What if I wasn't in good voice?

'What will you sing?'

'*Aïda.*'

'*Aïda*? What aria?'

'"*O patria mia.*"'

He must have thought I was out of my mind – as young and attractive as I was, it was by no means imperative that I sing a difficult aria.

'Do you study or are you working?'

'I'm a concert singer. I work with the Leningrad District Philharmonic Society.' That would impress no one from the Bolshoi. 'So,' I went on, laying down my conditions, 'first I'll sing a Rachmaninov song, "O, Do Not Grieve."'

They responded in unison, 'We don't need the song. There's no time for it. The aria is enough.'

'No, I'll sing the song. First, because I can warm up on it. Second, because if you don't like my voice, why should I continue to try and sing the aria? I won't do it any other way.'

'All right, then.'

I had piqued their interest – I was an intriguing case. Not every young singer sings *Aïda*, not to mention '*O patria mia.*'

My pianist and I agreed to meet at four at the Actors' House, and I ran off to see Vera Nikolayevna.

'Vera Nikolayevna, warm up my voice. I'm in a competition!'

'Just look at you – you're all flushed. What competition?'

'The Bolshoi, the young group. I've already talked to the jury. I have to sing at four, and it's already almost two. Quickly, quickly!'

She didn't say a word.

'Why are you so quiet? What are you thinking about?'

'About you. I would have liked another year to work with you, but I can see your time is now. Don't worry, you'll get on very well by yourself. As for the competition, don't be nervous. They'll take you, you're ready. Come, let's start.'

She warmed me up and gave last-minute instructions: Don't waste breath in the longer passages, keep on top of the transitional notes, sing *piano* passages on the breath, don't force the breath when making a complicated approach to a high C, keep a cool head.

I dashed along Nevsky Prospekt chanting her rules again and again to myself. Don't forget a word of it. When you're on stage, think of nothing but Vera Nikolayevna.

Lyuda and I entered the jurors' room. 'We're ready.'

'You have a pianist? But you don't need one. We have the Bolshoi's finest rehearsal pianist here. He knows our tempos. You'll have to sing with him.'

Getting nervous, I snapped at him, 'I have the greatest respect for your pianist, but I'm used to working with my own accompanist. She knows me, and she knows *my* tempos. I'm an artist.'

'Okay, go ahead.'

Lord, help me! I went on stage and gathered my wits. My mind still raced with the things Vera Nikolayevna had insisted I remember: You must create the atmosphere with the first sounds; bring the audience into your own world; keep yourself in control; always a cool head . . .

'I will sing Rachmaninov's "O, Do Not Grieve."'

I began to sing in a hushed, disembodied voice:

> '*O, do not grieve for me.*
> *For there where ends all sadness,*
> *My past with all its pain,*
> *Shall be as vanished dreams . . .*'

The voice of a dead woman addressing the man she loved . . . An ethereal sound, with almost no vibrato . . . I sensed that the audience was holding its breath. Later in my career, Khromchenko would recall that he had literally felt a chill.

Further on, the voice must grow stronger – as if the departed soul were gradually filling with the sap of life, 'O, do not pine for me!' And then, with repressed passion and in a quivering, muffled whisper, as if fearing to be heard, she confides:

> *'This parting cannot sever*
> *My soul from yours;*
> *It may return and hover near.*
> *Just as in days gone by,*
> *My love and care shall ever*
> *Protect your life from grief and fear.'*

And then, no longer able to hide how well she remembers the flesh she has left behind, she sings passionately:

> *'It is your part!*
> *And should some force be given,*
> *Renewing strength and comfort,*
> *Joy and peace . . .'*

And, like a final 'Forgive me!' on a climactic high B flat that signifies the majesty of death, the endlessness of life in it:

> *'Then know, 'tis I am sent,*
> *A messenger from heaven . . .'*

She shifts suddenly in thought and tone, as if coming to her senses, ending broadly and serenely:

> *'To dry your tears, and bid them cease.'*

I finished, and silence reigned in the auditorium. No one asked me to sing more. I whispered to Lyuda, 'I guess that's it.'

Her voice was confused. 'I don't know. Ask them.'

I turned to the audience and the jury. 'You don't need to hear anything more?'

'What do you mean? Sing! We're waiting!'

'O patria mia' from *Aïda* is another thing altogether. One has to be able to draw out the high notes, to sing with a big, rich sound in order to compensate for the full orchestra, and to have a

resonant lower register – all on a large scale. I had worked on that aria with Vera Nikolayevna, polishing each phrase. When I finished singing it – after the last high C, the following A dying away into a *pianissimo* – the audience buzzed: 'Who is that? Where did she come from?'

No one in the audience knew me. I had not performed in the city of Leningrad, only in the district.

In the jurors' room they asked, 'Did you graduate from the conservatory?'

'No. I've taken private lessons, and I sing in concerts. For four years I sang in an operetta company.'

'In *operettas*? . . . We're leaving for Moscow tonight. The next round is held at the Bolshoi. Can you come?'

'Of course.'

'Wait for our call.'

Even strangers were congratulating me as I emerged from that room. But I had only one thing on my mind: to get to a telephone. 'Vera Nikolayevna, sweet, dear one, I made it to the second round in Moscow! I'm going to run home right now and change my clothes' – I was drenched with perspiration – 'and then I'll come over and tell you everything, everything!'

I charged down Nevsky Prospekt like a locomotive. Sparks must have flown from my feet, because people on the sidewalk saw me coming and shied off to one side. If a wall had suddenly appeared before me, I surely would have broken it to smithereens.

I burst into our room. 'Mark, I sang in a competition for the Bolshoi!'

'*What?* What competition? What Bolshoi?'

'They're auditioning for the youth group, and I made it into the second round. I'll soon be called to Moscow – understand? Now I'm off to see Vera Nikolayevna.'

He was stunned, he couldn't believe it. My husband! How could I expect others to react? The news spread like wildfire; no one believed it – I scarcely did myself. I was plagued with the thought: They're back in Moscow now, and they'll forget all about me. One week went by, an eternity. And then the telegram asking me to come.

I took my last class with Vera Nikolayevna, and soaked up her last bit of advice: 'On the day of the competition, get up earlier than usual. Eat well. Go to the theater two hours before the audition. Walk around the stage so you can get a feel for it. Vocalise for an hour, and don't talk to anybody. Concentrate only on what you're going to sing.'

'Vera Nikolayevna, now what if they ask me to sing something else? Maybe something easy as a warm up?'

'If you sing *Aïda* they won't ask you to do anything else. A singer warms up backstage, not on stage. You're not a student, you're an artist. By doing *"O patria mia"* you'll show everything at once: range, mastery, endurance. That will impress the conductors. If you sing it the way you've sung it for me, there will be no questions. Go with God!'

I passed a long, sleepless night on the train. By morning, I was in Moscow and at the Bolshoi Theater – the dream of every singer in the Soviet Union. I stood before it struggling to sort out my thoughts, so fantastical had it all been. But that colossus didn't frighten me. On the contrary, it filled me with resolve: I was ready to fight for my place in it. From provincial clubs, from poverty, having no musical education to speak of – my weapons were my voice, my talent, my youth, and I was entering a struggle for the highest, most honored placed in the country. With life as my teacher, I had to emerge victorious.

The second round was held in the Beethoven Hall of the Bolshoi Theater. The company's soloists had turned out to hear the contestants – more than a hundred of them – who had come from every corner of the country to compete. The jury included famous singers: Maria Maksakova, Vera Davydova, Alyona Kruglikova, Natalya Shpiller, Nikandr Khanayev, Sergei Lemeshev, Ivan Kozlovsky, Mark Reizen, Alexander Pirogov; the theater's chief conductor, Nikolai Golovanov, the conductors Vasili Nebolsin and Kirill Kondrashin, and the theater's chief stage director, Boris Pokrovsky.

My day came. I sat in the round auditorium waiting my turn, trying not to hear the other contestants so that I could concentrate. But I could not help noticing the many good voices, female and male.

'Vishnevskaya. Verdi, *Aïda*, *"O patria mia."*'

I walked down the aisle past the singers, past the jury's table. I walked as if in a dream, skin flushed, eyes burning – even my eyelids felt feverish. Lord keep me from getting carried away, from looking directly at the people out there. I mounted the platform bursting to sing.

Into that one aria I put enough emotion and inspiration for a whole opera. I felt a kind of inner triumph – as if I were walking through the music and before me walls were dividing, falling. I wanted to go on singing . . . on and on but the last note sounded, trailed off, and fell into a void of silence. And then from that great distance, drawing me, pulling me back to earth: applause.

I stepped down from the platform and made my way again past the jury. Someone stopped me to ask a question, but I heard nothing. Within me, everything trembled. Slowly, surely, words became audible: 'Are you from Leningrad?'

'Yes.'

'Do you have relatives in Moscow? Is there a place – an apartment – where you can live?'

'An apartment? No, I have no apartment.'

'All right. Thank you.'

As I left the auditorium, my fellow contestants congratulated me. For good reason – artists were simply never applauded at Bolshoi competitions. It was an event.

I felt myself staggering and sat down on a chair in the lobby. I took off my shoes – the only high-heel dress shoes I had – and stretched my legs. Suddenly, Nikandr Sergeyevich Khanayev peeked out from the auditorium.

'Where is the girl who sang *Aïda* just now?'

He came up to me. 'Well done! Well done!' And he looked at me with a twinkle. I knew what a famous singer he was, and felt honored that he had come to encourage me.

'Thank you – and please forgive me for not standing. My legs are all wobbly.'

He laughed. 'Don't worry. You've already made it to the third round. But I must tell you one thing to keep in mind the rest of your life: think of a stop signal when you sing – think of little red lights. Otherwise, with your temperament, there'll be nothing left of you.' I listened, absorbing every word from the mouth of that old, splendid singer; and my heart overflowed with gratitude.

Three days later the third round was held at a branch of the Bolshoi. We would be singing with an orchestra and a conductor. It was all so unfamiliar to me, and there would be no rehearsal.

Word was out that a certain young woman offered great promise, and the female singers in the company were looking me over with great interest.

The third round. About fifteen of us had made it. As Vera Nikolayevna had counseled me, I came to the theater two hours early to get a feel for the hall. A young, good-looking man came up to me.

'I'm the conductor, Kirill Petrovich Kondrashin. You'll be singing with me. Why don't we go and rehearse with a pianist, so you can learn the tempos and get a bit used to me.'

'Let's go.'

We began to rehearse.

'Have you ever sung with an orchestra?'

'No, never.'

'It doesn't matter. Don't worry. I'll cue you on every entrance. All you have to do is watch me. Good luck.'

I went backstage. Someone was already auditioning, and I didn't want to hear it. I paced around like a lion in a cage. Then I looked up and saw the old singer Nikandr Sergeyevich Khanayev heading for me.

'So here you are! How do you feel?'

'Oh! I'm nervous!'

'That's all right, everyone gets nervous. But I'll tell you a little secret: the decision has already been made. You'll be accepted. So sing, and don't be afraid.'

He left. How could a decision have been made? What if I sing badly? I don't have the right, and that's all there is to it. If you have crossed the threshold of this theater, I told myself, you will be good enough to sing as you have never sung before. And if you die after that, who cares!

I was on stage and the sounds of the orchestra were welling up around me. All those musicians here to play for me, for Galka the

Artistka. And here am I in this splendid hall, with these famous singers come to listen. I was full with the grandness of the moment. The orchestra died down, and I began:

'I wait here for Radames . . .'

It was a large hall, and my performance had to fill it. Don't hurry – each word is worth its weight in gold. Project each sound to the most distant point. I watched the conductor. With his eyes and arms, he was showing me what to do so that I wouldn't lose the tempo. To hell with that! If I look at you and think of nothing but entrances and rhythms, what then? I closed my eyes and kept them closed until the very end. When I was done, I opened my eyes – the orchestra was giving me an ovation. Victory!

The jurors went off to confer. An hour later they announced that Nechipailo, a young bass, also from Leningrad, and I were the only ones accepted into the youth group of the Bolshoi Theater.

'Go to the personnel department – they'll give you a form to fill out. The theater assumes no obligations until you have been cleared by them.'

I was surrounded by singers from the Bolshoi. Some congratulated me, others warned me, telling me in effect not to rejoice yet. Winning the competition and having the orchestra applaud you is only half the game, they said. The main thing is filling out that form.

'Is there anything in your background . . .'

'No, nothing.'

And then the realisation like a knife slashing: my father. He had been convicted under Article 58 – proclaimed an enemy of the people! There wasn't a person in the country who didn't know what Article 58 meant. Tens of millions of people were rotting in prisons and camps under that article. If they dug up the facts about my father, the Bolshoi would drop me with no discussion whatsoever.

If you stand on Sverdlovsk Square facing the Bolshoi Theater, to your left is a small building, in no way remarkable. It houses the personnel department of the Bolshoi – a purgatory through which anyone who dreams of linking his fate to the mighty government theater must pass. In that little edifice, KGB agents work in the sweat of their brows. The chief of the department has a high rank, but always wears civilian clothes. He sits in his office behind a thick door covered with quilting and black oilcloth. Nothing said there will ever leak out. He lives as if in a vault with the rarest valuables – the 'personal files' of the Bolshoi's artists. Though you may be the greatest singer in the world, you will never stand on the stage of the Bolshoi if that harmless-looking little building doesn't want you to.

The Bolshoi Theater does not serve art alone; first and foremost, it serves the state. Government officials are frequent guests, and artists 'deemed worthy of the honor' perform at government receptions and banquets. Accordingly, the chief task of the Bolshoi's personnel department is to ensure the complete safety of the precious lives of government members. How many talented artists have been caught in the security nets spread by zealous KGB men in civilian clothes!

Life had taught me not to fear, not to cower, not to tolerate the slightest injustice. Those people with their grim, unsmiling faces could not unnerve me; they only caused me to muster my forces and steel myself. How well I knew those attentive, 'vigilant' looks that bored into you as if they knew things about you that you yourself didn't even suspect. Like hell you knew, damn you! Only an hour ago, I had triumphed in the most difficult competition of one of the world's best theaters. I was still brimming over with happiness greater than I had ever known before. And now I was supposed to tremble before the significant glances of those scum? Don't hold your breath! You're after the wrong woman, overlords of art!

I took the form – good Lord, it was at least twenty pages long – and started to write. Then I heard a honeyed voice: 'There's no hurry. Give yourself time to remember and think things over.'

And what was I supposed to remember? My hungry childhood? Working since the age of fifteen for a hunk of bread? What other memories did I have? Yet something else was gnawing at me: I would have to lie about my father. He had shown me nothing but scorn, and now, because of him, I might be denied everything – everything I had slaved for, lived for.

There was no end to the questions: Who were your grandfathers and grandmothers? What did they do before the Revolution? Did they own any property? If they are deceased, where did they die? Your parents: Where were they born? Where did they receive their education? What did they do before the Revolution? What are they doing now? Where do they live? If they are deceased, where are they buried? Do you have any brothers/sisters? If so, what do they do? Where do they live? Where do they work? Do you have any relatives abroad? Was anyone in your family held prisoner by the Germans? Did any of them live under the occupation? And so on, and so on.

I wrote that my father was declared missing in action during the war – taking the chance they wouldn't dig up the facts, the bastards.

'Here, I'm done.'

'That was quick. Yes, a bit *too* quick. Are you sure you didn't forget anything?'

'I'm sure.'

'Well, all right.'

'When will I know the results?'

'You're always in a hurry, heh, heh. When you've been cleared, you'll hear from us.'

(Nechipailo mentioned on his questionnaire that as a fourteen-year-old boy he had lived in the German-occupied Ukraine. As a result, he was not cleared for almost two years, and joined the Bolshoi only after Stalin's death.)

Like a bullet, I flew out to the street. The Bolshoi Theater! So that's what you're like, you 'mighty colossus!' You have feet of clay; and a worthless dwarf hiding behind a padded door can wring your neck at his whim.

I returned to Leningrad, robbed of my feeling of triumph. In my mind's eye, I could see the pages of the form, and one thought obsessed me: Would they discover the truth, or not? It was somewhat comforting that no one knew anything about it but Mark and me – at least there was no one to inform on me. But what if they found out anyway? Any day could bring a summons to the KGB office, and those people knew how to 'chat.' They were specialists . . .

The days dragged on like years . . .

After all the excitement of the competition, I fell to pieces. My voice had no resonance, my energy was sapped.

A month went by – not a word. Our money ran out; so, after the splendid stage of the Bolshoi Theater, I found myself back on the road, into the car and making the rounds of villages and collective farms once again. Two, three months crept by. Then suddenly, a telegram: 'Come. You have been accepted to the youth group of the Bolshoi Theater. Anisimov, Director of the Theater.'

It had come true! I would sing in one of the finest theaters in the world! I was twenty-five.

PART TWO

FIVE

The Bolshoi Theater! Grand, monumental, unequivocal. I joined the company at the end of an epoch, at the borderline between two generations. There were still a good number of first-class singers who had begun their careers in the early thirties and essentially carried on the traditions of the prerevolutionary Russian theater. *Bon ton* obtained in their relations with one another; and although there was competition and intrigue, as is only to be expected in our profession, none of it overstepped the bounds of decency.

Though many of these singers were in their fifties, and a few were over sixty, on the whole they were still fine vocalists, and among the men there were some whose artistry was unique. The next, or middle, generation of singers was much weaker in its creative potential, although there were some good voices.

When I burst into that 'high society,' I brought with me the unvarnished real life – full of deprivation and suffering – that went on outside the walls of that sumptuous, mighty theater. I belonged to another era than the female singers whose careers had begun before the war. Not only were they older than I, their perception of life was different. They had their own style, those famous matrons with their grand manners, covered with decorations and furs. All of them lived in beautiful apartments, surrounded by hosts of sniveling toadies.

As I looked around me with amazement, it seemed that I had settled in with a huge family: more than a hundred soloists, the chorus, orchestra, ballet dancers, conductors, and stage directors.

A Soviet collective is not merely a group of people working together, but a commune with rigid regulations and rights over each individual member. In Soviet theatrical companies there are no contracts. The artists of the Bolshoi are assigned to their place of work like workers to a factory. They get a monthly salary, and are obliged to fulfill a quota of performances. The season lasts for ten months.

A singer must be prepared every day to be summoned to replace a soloist who has fallen ill. No one has the right to go on tour anywhere in the country without special permission from the management. Yet, to meet a performance quota, one may be sent to another city to give a concert without extra pay. In a word, the artist is at the disposal of the management. A singer must work twenty-five years before receiving a pension, and all those years, if not longer, every detail of his life is open to view before that huge family, the commune.

There is nowhere to go from there. There is only one Bolshoi Theater. All the other theater companies are much worse: the pay is half as much, and the routine is the same. Once accepted, therefore, artists cling with all their might to their positions in the Bolshoi and to their apartments in the capital, afraid even to think about the drabness of provincial life.

The Bolshoi was run with iron discipline. To get into the building, you had to show a special pass with your photograph, even if you had been working there for decades. This procedure was enforced in the event that the personnel department issued an order to bar a certain employee from the theater. The year I joined the troupe, the chief conductor was the great Nikolai Semyonovich Golovanov, who had worked at the Bolshoi for decades. For quite a long while, persistent rumors had been circulating that Golovanov was to be removed from his position because the Kremlin was dissatisfied with him. One day, as he was entering the theater without showing his pass to the guard – he was the chief conductor, after all – he was stopped. 'Your pass!'

'What pass? What are you talking about? Don't you recognise me?'

'Your pass, please.'

Golovanov took out his pass and showed it. Right then and there, at the entrance, it was taken away from him, and he wasn't allowed to enter the building. So it was that that highly placed, seemingly all-powerful man learned that he was no longer chief conductor of the Bolshoi Theater and that he no longer worked there.* Such was the Bolshoi in 1952.

My work schedule in the Bolshoi youth group included two major roles: Tatyana in *Eugene Onegin* and Leonore in Beethoven's *Fidelio*. After a one-year probationary period, the theater had the option of dismissing me entirely or transferring me from the youth group to the main company as a soloist. I later learned that I had been taken into the Bolshoi in view of the forthcoming production of *Fidelio*. Boris Pokrovsky, a brilliant stage director and reformer of Soviet opera theater, would be staging the production, and for the role of Leonore, who wears a man's costume throughout the opera, he wanted a young singer with a slender physique.

The Bolshoi attached great importance to that production of *Fidelio*. Indeed, it was a major event for all of musical Russia: Beethoven's only opera, never before staged in Soviet times! The famous soloists were to sing, and the conductor was to be Alexander Shamilyevich Melik-Pashayev, who had just been named to replace Golovanov as chief conductor. From the very first I found myself handed opportunities no beginner could even imagine.

The fact that Boris Pokrovsky had taken a liking to me was all well and good, but there was more to it than that. Melik-Pashayev had to be satisfied with me; if not, I wouldn't get the role. He hadn't heard me sing at the competition – he had been out of town.

Melik-Pashayev, a great master of his art, was most discriminating in selecting his performers. He did not trust inexperienced young singers; it was harder to get into his productions than anyone else's. He had his own favored soloists, with whom he had worked for many years. Now, suddenly, into the conductor's sanctum sanctorum – *Fidelio* – Pokrovsky wanted to bring an

---

* A few months later Golovanov died, not having been able to survive the humiliation. He was only sixty years old.

unknown young singer, and one trained in operetta at that! Melik-Pashayev agreed to listen to me – for Pokrovsky's sake – but he was hardly pinning his hopes on me.

An audition was arranged. It would be my first meeting with him. At the time I lived with some of Mark's relatives, far from the theater. The trip by trolley bus took an hour, and I arrived a full ten minutes late. I dashed into the classroom short of breath from the cold, my cheeks glowing and my eyes like saucers. There they were, *waiting*! The chief conductor, the chief stage director, the chief rehearsal pianist. When I saw them, I thought: It's all over for me!

'Sorry I'm late.'

Melik-Pashayev inclined his head and said nothing. I should note that he always showed everyone the greatest courtesy; he never shouted. But at that moment even screams would have been preferable to his silence.

'Well, what are you going to sing?'

I was puffing like a steam engine, and little wonder. I had raced up six flights of stairs – there had been no time to wait for the elevator.

'You know,' I said, 'I haven't had a chance to vocalise, and I really must. Please wait in the hallway for a few minutes – then I'll sing.'

How could I have been such a fool!

The rehearsal pianist, Vsevolod Vasilyev, who had worked for many years with Melik-Pashayev and worshiped him, looked at me with despair, as if to say, 'What impertinence!' But something – my directness, perhaps – had won Melik-Pashayev over, and though he should have booted *me* out of the classroom, he and the others filed out.

I warmed up as quickly as I could, then opened the door: 'You may come in.'

'Thank you, thank you . . . Now, what will you sing, my child?'

'I can do Aïda, or Liza.'

'Aïda would be fine.'

When I was done, I could see that Pokrovsky was satisfied. Melik-Pashayev was more reserved, 'Well, not bad. Of course it's still too soon for you to do Aïda, but do look the part over, do look it over.'

I knew he was stingy with compliments, but *Aïda* was his favorite opera, so the words 'look the part over' augured well for the future.

'What else can you sing?'

Okay, I thought, now I'll flatten him. 'Well, I can sing you a song.'

'A song? What kind of a song?'

'A Spanish one, from my music-hall days. I've brought my castanets with me.'

He opened his eyes wide and even leaned back in his chair. What an odd bird had landed in the Bolshoi Theater!

Pokrovsky said, 'Go ahead, sing!'

I gave the music to the pianist, who almost fainted with terror. Poor dear. He must have thought the walls would cave in. Everyone knew how strict and academic Melik-Pashayev was when it came to music, and now, of all things, a song from the repertory of Klavdiya Shulzhenko!

I grabbed my castanets and began to sing and dance. Pokrovsky, barely stifling his laughter, watched as Melik-Pashayev squirmed in his seat, looking now at the floor and now at the ceiling. It was all so unexpected that he didn't know how to react. Castanets clacking, heels stomping, at an audition for Beethoven's Leonore! Nothing like it had ever happened in the Bolshoi before.

'All right, all right, child. Study the part, and then we'll see. Good-bye.' And he quickly left the room.

I don't know what kind of talk he had with Pokrovsky, but I was officially cast as Leonore in *Fidelio*, and began to study the part in earnest.

From that time forward, my life evolved within the walls of the Bolshoi Theater. I went home only to sleep.

At the Bolshoi there is no limitation on individual rehearsal time: you can work with a rehearsal pianist as much as you wish. In the mornings, after my lessons with the pianist, I would hurry to rehearsals with the ensemble and the orchestra. There I would listen to the singers and try to learn from them. I knew those magnificent voices well, having often heard them on the radio or at concerts. And so it was with eager anticipation that I would go to hear them in actual performances. But to my disappointment, most lost their best qualities on stage. As actors they were unable to fill that great hall – to project the essence of their roles to the audience. Many lacked the technique, and, worse, the opera stage pitilessly exposed their physical shortcomings. Only a few of them – a very few, like Lemeshev and Pirogov, who were brilliant actors – seemed to blossom on stage.

Every evening I would stand for hours in one of the boxes, listening, looking for a role model, an ideal as an actress. I didn't find her. Among the women there was not one outstanding artistic personality I wanted to emulate; the interpretations on stage struck me as artificial and wrong. By then, apparently, I had developed a personal sense of the beautiful, and I would have to give this vision flesh myself. But I had yet to appear on stage.

Waiting for that moment to come, I went from one concert hall to another, gradually becoming part of the life of the theater and getting to know its art. That season, the Bolshoi was staging a new opera, *The Decembrists*, by Yuri Shaporin, and I often attended the rehearsals. It occurred to me that I was constantly encountering strange, unfamiliar people at those rehearsals. Who were they, those grim-looking men, silent intruders in the hall's dark corners? And why did the directors always treat them with such servility? I soon learned that they were officials from the Central Committee's Department of Agitation and Propaganda (Agitprop), that they were overseeing work on that 'thesis opera,' and that they were torturing both composer and performers half to death with their endless demands for changes. Those officials had no concept of art whatsoever. Their only concern was with words. They wanted the opera to convey that the aristocrats who, in December of 1825, demonstrated and were massacred on Senate Square were actually revolutionaries – working-class. Innumerable 'commissions' from the Central Committee saw *The Decembrists* before it was allowed to be presented to the public. The staging was done over a period of several years, and in the process history was reshaped in every way. Lies oozed from every chink in the production. There is 'sacred art' for you!

As I was to learn, this rewriting of history affected more than the Soviet operas: even in classical operas, the directors would come up with some outlandish characterisation or bit of stage business to correspond to the Soviet ideological line. In Puccini's *Madama Butterfly*, as produced during the Cold War, for example, the American consul – a fine, kindhearted man – was transformed into a hard, cynical 'Uncle Sam.' In the second act, instead of tenderly stroking the little boy's head as he exclaims in admiration, 'What a head of hair! What's your name, little one?' he touches him squeamishly with two fingers, as if the child were a source of contagion. And this is conveyed although the words and music remained unchanged.

Invariably, the Bolshoi's best artists performed in *The Decembrists*. For any Soviet work that addressed contemporary or revolutionary subjects, the company always put forward its most famous singers, hoping that with talent they could mask falsehoods and musical drivel. In such cases the management did not stint on promising artists decorations, honorary titles, apartments, and extra pay. I would sit there in the hall, witnessing the agonies of a Soviet opera's birth, and it seemed criminal that singers should so stupidly squander their art. It was clear that such a production would at best be mounted three or four times a season, that the public wouldn't come for love or money, and that – as a result – the opera would soon be plucked from the repertory. And how much money was thrown down the drain! But nobody cared – it was state money after all. Perhaps they got what they paid for: the plan for a Soviet repertory would be fulfilled and the fortunate director could have the honor of reporting that fact to the government. For me, such hack work was humiliating. From my first days at the Bolshoi I tried, by hook or by crook, to avoid performing in those short-lived operas.

The next premiere after *The Decembrists* was to be Kabalevsky's *Nikita Vershinin*, and I was given the leading part. Even though Melik-Pashayev was scheduled to conduct, I didn't

want to sing in that production at any price, not only because the
music was uninspired but because I can't bear to see primitive,
crude everyday life depicted on the opera stage. But you can't
just say that you don't want to sing in a Soviet opera, and one on a
revolutionary subject on top of it! That alone is criminal, and an
open invitation for a political charge. I finally thought of a solution:
I began to learn the part, but after some ten days I stormed into
the repertory department in tears and said I couldn't continue,
the part was too high, and a young, inexperienced singer like me
could ruin her voice.

When Kabalevsky was told, he protested, 'What does she
mean, she can't! She sang Aïda at the competition, and is
preparing *Fidelio*. Nonsense!'

He came to one of my lessons, and I started to sing him an aria,
but I deliberately cracked on two B flats. I grabbed my throat and
bawled, 'I'm scared of ruining my voice. It's too hard for me. I'm
an inexperienced singer.'

He tried to calm me down. 'It's too bad you can't sing the part.
But if you're afraid of it, I can't persuade you otherwise; I won't
take that responsibility.'

I'd managed to wriggle out!

In the same way, I wormed out of the next 'masterpiece,'
Khrennikov's *Mother*.

The other singers wondered why I refused to sing in Soviet
operas. After all, they were considered great opportunities for a
young singer: the production could win a Stalin Prize, and every
leading performer could get a badge as laureate, which is a boon
to anyone's career. They didn't understand that from the very
beginning I had set myself a goal far above badges or titles. I
wanted to become a great artist like Chaliapin; his kind didn't
exist at the Bolshoi anymore. All the glitter of a medal couldn't
divert me from my goal.

Stalin personally watched over the Bolshoi. For the most part,
he went to Russian operas, and so the best singers were assigned
to those: *Prince Igor, Sadko, Khovanshchina, Boris Godunov,
The Queen of Spades*. They were the Bolshoi's gold mine. Each
opera is still mounted identically from year to year, and to this
day not one has ever been removed from the company's

repertory. The same stagings have weathered thirty-five or forty years.

The Bolshoi has never known any financial difficulties. The state spares no money to advertise itself. Sets and costumes alone cost millions of rubles, since all the work is done by hand. Materials are constantly in short supply and machine-made goods virtually nonexistent. And although the nation has always been proud of its theater, people do not realise that it is they who pay to maintain it. You can be sure Stalin did not pay one kopeck from his own pocket for all those life-size cathedrals and huts that cluttered the stage.

During the Stalin era every singer, regardless of his health, would try to perform in a production if his name appeared on the roster. The imperial theater! One had to appear not only for the sake of art, but for the sake of one's own status in the country, in the eyes of the nation. Everyone aspired to perform for Stalin, to please him; and Stalin went to great lengths for the artists of the Bolshoi. He himself set their high salaries, generously conferred their decorations, and personally presented their Stalin Prizes.

During my first season, 1952–1953, Stalin came to see several operas, and I remember the fear and panic of those evenings. His visit would be announced beforehand. All night long, guards would scurry about examining every corner of the theater inch by inch; singers who were not performing in the production were banished from the theater that day and would even be denied entry the day before. The performers were issued special passes and had to carry their passports with them. At the last minute, the management might remove even the most famous singer from the program and substitute another for him, depending on the whims of the Great Leader. No one ever openly voiced any grievances, but took such treatment as his due. And each tried to pander to the tastes of the Soviet monarch to become his favorite, even if being elevated turned out to be at the expense of someone else's public humiliation. This serf-theater mentality continued long after the death of Stalin.

Stalin always sat in Box A, hidden from the audience by a curtain. If you face the stage, Box A is the first one on your left, directly above the orchestra. And only by the clump of bodyguards in civilian clothes and the frenzy in the eyes of the performers would you know that sitting there was none other than 'he himself.' Even today, when heads of state attend a Bolshoi production, the public is prevented from driving up to the theater in cars. Hundreds of KGB men surround the theater, and the artists are checked several times for their papers. The first checkpoint is at the entrance, and is overseen not by Bolshoi guards but by the KGB: the performer must produce his special pass and his passport. The thugs in civilian clothes man the backstage, too. In my day, if VIPs were in the hall, I would have to show my pass one more time – when my makeup was done and I was ready to go on stage. There were purely technical difficulties in all of this. For instance, where could you put your pass, especially if you were one of the dancers? They were practically naked, after all! Their only option would be to tie it to one of their legs like a tag in a communal bathhouse.

Did Stalin like music? No. What he liked was the Bolshoi, its splendor and pomposity. There he felt himself an emperor. He enjoyed his role as patron of the theater, and of its artists. They were his serfs. He liked being generous to them, rewarding the outstanding ones as a tsar would have. The only difference was that Stalin didn't sit in the tsar's box – the central one. The tsar had not been afraid to sit before his people. Stalin's place was behind a curtain. In his *avant-loge* – the singers called it the bathhouse locker room – there was always a big bowl of hard-boiled eggs on a table; he ate them during intermissions. When Stalin came to a performance, as when chiefs of government do today, KGB men sat in the pit beside the musicians – in civilian clothes, of course.

Stalin had his favorites among the singers, and especially liked Maxim Mikhailov's interpretation of Ivan Susanin in Glinka's opera *A Life for the Tsar* (*Ivan Susanin* in Soviet times). He attended that opera often, probably thinking himself the tsar, and taking pleasure in seeing the Russian muzhik die for him. Surely, more than once, sitting in his Box A and listening to *Boris Godunov*, did he mentally swap his modest gray field jacket for sumptuous tsar's vestments, did he seize the scepter and grasp the orb. He adored monumental productions. And they were mounted to suit his taste, with exaggerated majesty and unnecessary pomp – in short, with every symptom of gigantomania. From stage, from rigid sets, the huge, booming voices would not only sing but prophesy. The message became more 'significant' than the art. The Bolshoi was oriented solidly toward Stalin's personal taste, and it mattered not whether that taste was good or bad. When Stalin died, the Bolshoi lost all its bearings, and began to be buffeted from side to side – from the tastes of one incumbent to another.

Stalin's female favorites were the soprano Shpiller and the mezzo Davydova. Both were beautiful and stately, and always sang at his banquets. Stalin enjoyed playing the patron to those haughty, elegant Russian women. He liked to be in their company, to offer them toasts, to instruct them or rebuke them in a fatherly – in an imperial – manner. But for all his favors, no one was spared his petty tyranny. Once, at a banquet in the Kremlin where both the competing beauties had sung, Stalin pointed to Shpiller and trumpeted to Davydova within earshot of everyone, 'There's the one you should learn singing from.' With that remark the 'little father' probably took several years off Davydova's life.

The distinguished conductor Samuil Samosud, who had worked many years at the Bolshoi, told me of one occasion when he was conducting a performance attended by the entire upper echelon of the government. During the intermission he was summoned by Stalin. Samosud had only just stepped into the *avant-loge* when Stalin declared to him without mincing words, 'Comrade Samosud, your production tonight is . . . somehow . . . lacking flats.'

Samosud went numb and was totally confused. Could it be a joke? But the members of the Politburo and all the others were nodding seriously and adding, 'Yes, do pay attention to the flats,' although among them were the likes of Molotov who surely understood that they were making idiots of themselves.

Samosud collected himself and replied soberly, 'Good, Comrade Stalin. Thank you for your comment. We will not fail to pay attention to that.'

Another interesting incident involved the opera *Eugene*

Onegin. The last scene takes place early in the morning, and
Tatyana, according to Pushkin, must be in her peignoir:

> *The princess sits there all alone*
> *Before him, pale and unadorned,*
> *Reading a letter of some kind,*
> *And with her hand holding her cheek,*
> *Softly sheds tears she cannot check.*

And that's the way the scene was played, until Stalin saw a
performance. When he saw Tatyana in her sheer gown before
Onegin, he complained, 'How can a woman appear in front of a
man dressed like that?' Since then, Tatyana has worn a cherry-
colored velvet dress in that scene and her hair is up as if she were
ready to receive visitors. There is no doubt that Stalin knew what
Pushkin had in mind. He couldn't have cared less. Dress her,
period.

But on the whole he was a 'good tsar' for the Bolshoi. He liked
to invite the singers to the Kremlin for drinking bouts, and have
Maxim Mikhailov, a former archdeacon, sing *Mnogaya leta** in his
thundering bass. The repressions and purges of 1937, when
millions of Soviet citizens were thrown into prison, hardly
touched the Bolshoi – its leading singers at any rate. It was
Stalin's theater. He even allowed ordinary mortals from the
street to hear performances; and he was no doubt proud of his
magnanimity, considering himself a patron of the arts.

From time to time, Stalin would summon a singer to Box A and
grant him the honor of looking on the Great Leader, or of hearing
a few of his words. The singers got so nervous before him that
they would be speechless. And Stalin would take great pleasure
in seeing what an impression he had made on those celebrated
singers who, only minutes earlier, had strode the stage imper-
sonating tsars and heroes. Here, then, were the mighty –
powerless before him. They awaited his word, his glance,
whatever pittance he might toss them – ready to snap up any

---

* *Mnogaya leta* (Church Slavonic for 'many years') is one of the most
beautiful songs in the Russian Orthodox liturgy.

bone from his table. Although he had long since become used to the fawning, it was especially sweet from those whom God had endowed with art. Their humiliation, their obsequiousness, reinforced his conviction that he was no ordinary mortal.

He spoke slowly, quietly, and very little. As a result, each of his words, glances, and gestures took on a significance it did not in fact have. But long after those encounters, the singers would go around parroting those words and trying to guess at their meaning – to decipher their ambiguity. The truth was that Stalin had a poor command of Russian. No doubt he, like an actor, had long since assembled a whole arsenal of expressions which never failed to affect those around him, and trotted them out according to the circumstance.

In all his portraits, in all the sculptures, he looks like a great hero; and people who saw him close up, who even stood next to him, actually believed that the short man was much taller and bigger than he was. Stalin's habits and style were bound to make their way to the stage of the Bolshoi. Men padded their clothes to expand their chests and shoulders, and walked slowly, as though weighted down by that 'hero's' ponderousness. (Films made during Stalin's era are full of this walk.) The staging of those days also demanded certain qualities in the performers: loud voices and exaggerated enunciation. The performers had to conform to the inflated majesty, the monstrous grandiosity of those spectacles. Today those colossuses, without the performers they were intended for, make a ludicrous impression. They are the dinosaurs of an era, like those megalithic buildings Stalin left us to remember him by.

I never heard anyone express doubts about the rightness of his actions. And when the 'doctors' plot'* was exposed, all were amazed (or so they said) that they themselves had not recognised them as enemies of the people. Those very doctors, after all, treated the Bolshoi singers.

The final weeks of the evil genius's rule were passing by. The

* In November 1952, leading physicians, primarily Jews, were accused of plotting to murder members of the political and military elite. The campaign against them threatened to become a general purge of Jews, had it not been for Stalin's death.

last opera he attended at the Bolshoi was Tchaikovsky's *Queen of Spades*. Pyotr Selivanov was singing the part of Eletsky. When he came on stage in the second act to sing the famous aria and saw Stalin sitting in his box close by, he became so agitated that he simply lost his voice. The orchestra played the opening bars, and Selivanov began to *speak* the words: 'I love you, I love you beyond measure, without you I couldn't think of living through the day . . .' And he kept right on for the whole of the aria – a recitation accompanied by the orchestra. One cannot imagine what was going through his mind. It's a wonder he didn't die right there on stage. Backstage, and in the hall, everybody froze.

During the intermission, Stalin sent for Anisimov, the theater's director, who came running, quaking – more dead than alive. Stalin drilled him, 'Who's singing Prince Eletsky tonight?'

'Selivanov, Comrade Stalin.'

'And what title does Selivanov have?'

'People's Artist of the Russian Socialist Republic . . ."

Stalin paused, then said, 'The *good* Russian people!' He laughed. He had made light of it! A joke!

A happy Anisimov skipped out of Stalin's box. And the next day all of Moscow was repeating the great witticism of the Leader and Teacher. We singers were full of love and gratitude for the great charity of our Master. Our Benefactor could have expelled the transgressor from the Bolshoi – he had every right to – but he had been merciful and only laughed.

Yes, great was the belief in The Chosen One. When he died, the genuine mourners rushed to Moscow to be together, nearer him and nearer one another. The railroads had to shut down, the trains had to be stopped, so that Moscow would not be inundated by a sea of people. And I wept along with the rest of them. Life had come to an end. The nation was seized with a panic, full of confusion and a fear of the unknown. For thirty years we had heard only Stalin, Stalin, Stalin . . .

If, encountering difficulties, you should doubt your own strength, think about him, about Stalin, and you'll find the necessary confidence. If you feel tired at a time when you should not, think about him, about Stalin, and your fatigue will leave you . . . If you have planned something big, think about him, about Stalin, and the work will be a success . . . If you are seeking a solution, think about him, about Stalin, and you will find it. During the war, people died 'for the motherland, for Stalin.' (*Pravda*, February 17, 1950)

Now, suddenly, he was dead – he who would live forever, who would think for us, decide for us.

Stalin had annihilated millions. He had destroyed the peasantry, science, literature, art . . . But he was dead, and the slaves were simpering, moaning, crowding the streets with their tear-swollen faces. As in *Boris Godunov*, it was the starving who were lamenting:

> *For whom are you leaving us, our Father?*
> *For whom are you abandoning us, dear one?*

All day and all night the loudspeakers on the streets of Moscow blared the strains of heartrending funeral music.

The sopranos of the Bolshoi were urgently summoned to rehearse Schumann's 'Daydreams' to be performed in the Hall of Columns of the House of Unions, where Stalin's body was lying in state. We sang without words, with closed mouths, mooing. After the rehearsal, everyone was taken off to the Hall of Columns but me. I had been screened out by the personnel department because I was a newcomer with only six months at the Bolshoi. Plainly, I wasn't trusted. Only the tried-and-true herd were allowed to moo.

In those days, when life itself seemed locked in expectation of further horrors, someone striding through a corridor in the theater flung out the words, 'Sergei Prokofiev is dead.' The news swept through the theater, and hung in the air like an impossibility. Who had died? Another person besides Stalin could not have dared to die. Stalin alone had died, and all of the people's feelings, all the grief of loss, should belong to him alone.

Prokofiev died on the same day as Stalin: March 5, 1953. Fate had not afforded him the pleasure of learning that his tormentor was dead. The streets of Moscow were blocked off, and traffic had come to a standstill. It was impossible to find a car; and it cost a tremendous effort to move Prokofiev's coffin from his apartment across from the Moscow Art Theater to a tiny room in the basement of the Composers' House on Myausskaya Street for a civil funeral.

All of the hothouses and florists' shops had been emptied for the Leader and Teacher of All Times and All Peoples. Nowhere could one buy even a few flowers to place on the coffin of the great Russian composer. In the newspapers, there was no room for an obituary. Everything was Stalin's – even the ashes of Prokofiev, whom he had persecuted. And while hundreds of thousands of people trampled one another in the frenzy to get to the Hall of Columns so as to bow one last time to the superman-murderer, the dark, dank basement on Myausskaya Street was almost empty – the only people present being Prokofiev's family and friends who happened to live nearby and could break through the police barriers.

Mother Russia, how much longer will you grieve for your hangmen? Fight back! Avenge your ravaged, tortured children! Clearly your time has not yet come.

The death of the great patron marked the end of an epoch in the history of the Bolshoi Theater. The genius, the divinity, was gone; after him came mere mortals.

SIX

To my delight, Mark finally managed to exchange our room in Leningrad for a room in Moscow. It was hard to call that space a room, however. I had lived in communal apartments all my life, but I had never seen anything quite like our new dwelling on the corner of Stoleshnikova Lane and the Petrovka. At one time, before the Revolution, it had been a comfortable seven-room apartment, but now it was swarming with people and bedbugs. Each room was occupied by one entire family if not by two. A total of thirty-five people called that apartment home, and naturally we all used the single toilet and only washroom. The washroom was not used for bathing – people would go to a public bathhouse for that; rather, it was used for laundry, which was hung up to dry in the kitchen. Laundry tubs and washbasins lined the walls. In the morning, one had to stand in line to use the toilet, and then in another line to wash and brush one's teeth. Lines, lines . . . In the kitchen there were four gas stoves, seven kitchen tables, and in the corner a *polaty** where an old woman slept. Under the *polaty* was a closet that accommodated two. Did this not fill the bill for the 'Crows' Village' in Ilf's and Petrov's book *The Little Golden Calf*? At one time the apartment had had two entrances, front and rear. But they had closed off the rear entrance, broken up the stairway, and built a ceiling and a floor. The result was a very narrow room with a cement floor and a huge window that looked out upon a courtyard.

Mark and I settled in. To get to our room we had to pass through the kitchen, where from six in the morning until midnight a dozen women clattered pots on the gas stove and created the fumes that permeated our little room. But I didn't see all this as

* Planking fixed between the ceiling and the stove, used as a place to sleep.

distressing. Having holed up in corners of other people's rooms for so long, I was even happy: We had been given a Moscow resident's permit, we had a roof over our heads, and it was a three-minute walk to the theater. Into our room we squeezed a sofa, a wardrobe, a table, four chairs, and a rented upright piano. And it was here that I worked on my first roles at the Bolshoi: Leonore in *Fidelio*, Tatyana in *Eugene Onegin*, Kupava in *The Snow Maiden*, and Cio-Cio-San in *Madama Butterfly*. It was my home for almost four years, well into the time when I had become a leading soloist with the Bolshoi.

I worked on *Fidelio* like one possessed. From the very beginning I tried to give my voice an instrumental sound, and I would imagine the instruments of the orchestra and work on blending with them. I tried for longer breaths, variety of coloration, and clarity in the *piano* passages. Every day I sang through the whole opera in full voice, as if I were actually performing. I knew well what a demanding conductor I would be working with. Melik-Pashayev was eager to begin rehearsals as soon as possible, but the male soloists weren't ready yet. He was told to hear me first, because 'Vishnevskaya is the only one who has learned her part.'

He couldn't have forgotten the scene I had made dancing before him with castanets. He probably recalled it all too well, and had no great faith in me. Perhaps he only intended to use me as an understudy for the part, in case something happened to the lead, but he was in a hurry to begin rehearsals, and so summoned me to a lesson. I was not going to be late that time! During the six months I had already been with the Bolshoi, I had attended every production Melik-Pashayev conducted. I had great admiration for his work and dreamed of singing with him.

Two hours before the lesson, I was in the theater warming up. In came Melik-Pashayev – smartly dressed and elegant as always – carrying the score. I never saw him come to a rehearsal or a lesson without the score in hand, even if he had conducted the opera all his life and knew it by heart.

'Hello there, young lady. So. What can you sing from your part?'

'Everything. Whatever you want.'

'You know the whole part?'

'Yes.'

'Well, then, let's begin with the first quartet.'

I took my piano transcription, which was lying open on the grand piano, and with an obvious, sweeping gesture closed it and set it aside. He acknowledged my move, 'You're going to sing it from memory?'

'Of course.' I said it as if it went without saying – as if I had done nothing all my life but sing Leonore in *Fidelio*.

I sang him the whole part from the first note to the last, without stopping and without any interruption from him. For a whole hour, I literally did not close my mouth. In that most difficult of heroic soprano parts, Melik-Pashayev was testing me for endurance, seeing whether I had enough stamina for the whole performance. I was ready, like a soldier prepared for battle – as if the slightest mistake could have been fatal. I didn't make one. I felt that my fate was being decided right then and there: either I would sing in the production he conducted, or I would lose him now and never have this opportunity again.

I sang through to the final bars of the glorious ensemble.

He looked at me attentively, as though seeing me for the first time. 'Wonderful, my girl! I wasn't expecting that. I just wasn't expecting it.' I saw that he was moved. The great Melik-Pashayev would be my first conductor – I knew I had become a singer. He patted me on the head, went out, stopped at the repertory department, and gave the unequivocal order, 'For all my future rehearsals of *Fidelio*, call Vishnevskaya.' The troupe hummed with the news that a new favorite had surfaced. But never mind, they all agreed; in a part like Leonore, she'll break her neck.

A novice's career depends on her first roles – Leonore was an infinitely difficult part even for an experienced singer. As it turned out, *Fidelio* would serve as basic training for my whole career. Working on it, I learned not to force my voice and, where necessary, how to cut through the orchestra not with volume but by concentrating and focusing the sound. And when, after several months, the stage rehearsals with the orchestra began, it was

Fidelio that taught me how to extend my breathing, how to regulate it, and how to conserve my strength. My long familiarity with the stage enabled me to monitor myself during rehearsals and performances – to control my voice, diversify its coloration, and change its timbre. Within seconds after difficult scenes I was able to calm my breathing, dispel my tension, and begin in again melodiously and with a clear, serene sound.

It was important for me that Russia had known no previous productions of the opera. Since I had never seen it performed or even heard a recording, I was able to create the role of Leonore for myself – relying only on my own resources and interpretations of the role. The role was all the more mine since Melik-Pashayev never allowed his singers to force their voices: my natural voice, then, became the one associated with *Fidelio*. And the director Pokrovsky, too, built the character around my traits. In his conception, Leonore had to be young and agile. Pokrovsky had me darting about the stage while singing; fortunately I knew my part well – I didn't need to watch the conductor even during the most complicated ensembles. I could have sung standing on my head.

The Bolshoi worked on *Fidelio* for almost a year and a half. We had daily lessons, staging rehearsals, chorus rehearsals, and orchestra rehearsals. As the production progressed, Melik-Pashayev came to love my voice, its 'pure, virginal sound,' as he said. Later he admitted that tears had come to his eyes when he first heard me sing. In the future, the touch of silver in the timbre of my voice would help me create the characters of young heroines, especially Tatyana (*Eugene Onegin*), Natasha (*War and Peace*), Marfa (*The Tsar's Bride*), Cio-Cio-San (*Madama Butterfly*), Marguerite (*Faust*), and even Aïda, a role traditionally performed by a dramatic soprano.

I was caught up in *Fidelio* because I was creating something new; in contrast, it was because *Eugene Onegin* had been done for so long that I did not want sing Tatyana. The clumsy and passive character presented by all the Tatyanas I had seen ran counter to my notion of Pushkin's and Tchaikovsky's heroine. Every time I attended a performance I could not help but think that the singer, whom I knew and for whom I had great respect, looked as if she had been fitted out in Tatyana's dress and wig as for a masquerade and had forgotten to take them off. I had a strong urge to tell her that, so that she would assume a more natural air, and I would be spared embarrassment for her, so much did that masquerade fail to correspond to Tatyana's inner and outer character.

In a letter to Baroness von Meck dated December 16, 1877, Tchaikovsky wrote:

Where will I find that Tatyana whom Pushkin imagined and whom I have tried to illustrate musically? Where is the singer who will even somewhat approach the ideal of Onegin, that cold dandy to the marrow of his bones, imbued with worldly *bon ton*? Where will I find a Lensky, a youth of eighteen with thick curls and the impulsive and original traits of a young poet à la Schiller?

How Pushkin's charming picture is vulgarised when it is transferred to the stage, with its routine, its senseless traditions, and its male and female veterans, who shamelessly play the roles of sixteen-year-old girls and beardless youths!

Tatyana! In my childhood she had captivated me. To me, she embodied everything that was most beautiful and valuable in Russian women: a deeply passionate nature, tenderness, boldness, and a willingness to sacrifice herself . . . For Russian women there is a special sweetness in the willingness to sacrifice oneself. It is as strong in them as love.

It was that kind of Tatyana I would have liked to be; but age-old traditions and famous singers had created a Tatyana that disillusioned me. The voices were good enough, but it was Tatyana's 'vocal image' that I longed to see embodied on the stage. And it was not just that all those singers were older than I. Galina Ulanova danced Juliet until she was fifty-three, but I never saw a younger Juliet. In order to be young on stage, one must have an inner airiness, a tremulousness. These lend lightness to one's movements, elegance to one's gait, chastity to one's look, and, most important, a girlish ring to one's voice. But it is not enough to understand and feel those qualities; one must embody them and project them to the audience. Precisely for that reason is it essential to have special training in movement – in gestures and expression. My operetta and music-hall experience had stood me in good stead. In the course of eight years I had become accustomed to appearing on stage before any kind of audience: to sing and dance for it, to feel it, to 'penetrate' it, and reach it emotionally. The music-hall stage demanded that I refine my gestures and movements, that I create a definite picture or provoke a specific emotion merely by shifting my posture or moving my arms. As I switched from song to song, I would glide from one life to another. The music-hall stage is the theater of a single actor; no conservatory can teach that. Young singers in an opera company spend many years feeling their way to vocal mastery. And one must also take into account the fact that in their early careers they perform rarely, so they are agitated at each performance. Acting is not an issue; it suffices that they sing well, don't get off tempo, and don't fluff notes. But when vocal mastery and maturity come, one's career is already near its end. *Si jeunesse savait, si vieillesse pouvait!*

When I joined the Bolshoi, however, I was already a creature of the stage, ready not only to sing the opera parts but to act the roles – to create stage images in the full sense of the words. Having been on stage since childhood, I was not at all afraid of the audience. On the contrary, I was eager to get on stage and open myself up completely – to tear myself away from the earth, to rise above it, and to project the pictures of my imagination. And with my vocal technique in hand, my stage images began to resound accordingly.

A production of *Eugene Onegin* was in preparation under the direction of Boris Pokrovsky, and since the on-stage rehearsals of *Fidelio* had not yet begun, I was allowed to rehearse with him. It was the first time I had worked with this man, who was to change all my notions of operatic theater. (Later, I created all my roles with him.) From the very first, he became for me an absolute authority, a repository from which I could draw all the secrets of the art of opera. If I had not met him, I surely would have left the Bolshoi.

I underwent such inner conflict over the role of Tatyana that I almost came to hate it. I came to the rehearsal not only without any desire to work but with a firm resolve to refuse the part. But I couldn't imagine arguing with Pokrovsky, since I hadn't yet demonstrated my artistic worth.

'Sit at the desk, take a sheet of paper, a quill pen, and sing.'

I began: 'Let me perish . . .'

How many Tatyanas had already been heard in the theater! The Bolshoi had seven at that time.

I sang, and with every facial expression I could muster I tried to show him how boring and uninteresting it was: This scene is insufferably long – let it be over soon!

I sang the whole scene through. He said nothing, and I didn't care. Here it comes – I thought, he'll say that it was bad, that I'm not suited for the role. Fine. Maybe I'll get Aïda.

Finally he began, 'I watch you, and I'm amazed. Such a young girl, and she whines like a little old woman suffering from rheumatism. How can you sing Tatyana like that?'

'Of course one shouldn't sing Tatyana like that, but I don't like the part. I find it boring.'

He shouted, 'You don't like the part? You find it bor-r-ring? Why do you sit there like an old woman on a feather bed? You have to understand that Tatyana is seventeen. You have to understand what kind of novels she has devoured, and the state that she – a well-bred young lady – must have been in to make a declaration of love out of the blue and write it in a letter to a young man. And you're bored! All you sopranos want to play African and Ethiopian princesses, anything the audience doesn't understand. Just try to play Pushkin's Tatyana and see how far you get! Did you read what Tchaikovsky wrote? "Rapturously! Passionately!" But you singers are all fools. You don't even know how to read. Did you read this? Did you understand it?'

I jumped to my feet and shouted back, 'What do you mean, "understand"? I look at the stage and see nothing of what you describe. But you staged this production, and so it must suit you, it must be what you want!'

'Don't look at the stage. Learn to use your own brains. "Rapturously! Passionately!" She shouldn't get out of bed as if she were being hoisted by a crane. She should fly! Have you ever been sledding?'

'Of course.' I saw that his eyes were shining, that he was shouting and on fire.

'Well, if you've been sledding, that's what Tayana's letter is all about. Without thinking, she got on a sled and, from a high, steep hill, flew down! It took her breath away. It wasn't until she reached bottom, until the sled stopped, that she came to her senses. In the same way, Tatyana wrote the letter and sent it to Onegin. Only later did she realise what she had done.'

I was listening, mouth agape, unaware that tears had long been streaming from my eyes. Suddenly, as if by magic, I saw myself as I was in Kronstadt – Galka the Artistka, writing her first love letter to the boy with the part in his hair. My heart began to ache sweetly, to flutter in my breast, and the radiant, sweet image of Tatyana, the Tatyana of my childhood in all her unique charm, appeared before me.

From the very first, that remarkable director and psychologist took into account my individuality, and my young, resonant voice. With his keen insight into personalities, he had sensed my impulsiveness, my temper. That day, without my even suspecting it, he gave me the key to 'my theater' – a key I had long carried within me. And from then on, I threw myself headlong into work – into shattering those traditional conventions that had seemed as indestructible as the world.

Without looking back, and as one emancipated, I entered the struggle, defending my own art. Had I been an inexperienced novice, the Bolshoi would have soon broken me, relegating me to the ranks of ordinary, good singers. I would not have become an individual personality and certainly never could have created a new operatic style at the Bolshoi.

With my appearance on the scene, the conductors' and directors' requirements rapidly changed. Those playing the young roles were expected to bring to them the entire scope of their creative talents. Being overweight became a liability to one's career. When I joined the company there were fifteen sopranos with my repertory. I was seen by them as the saboteur of an established sanctuary. They were annoyed by my boldness and obstinacy in art as well as in life. And they were beginning to say that I had a difficult character, that I was short-tempered and hard to work with.

One day I went to see a rehearsal of *Carmen*, with Maria Maksakova in the title role. She had once been a brilliant Carmen, but now it was her last season: she was retiring. I had never talked with her, and had seldom seen her, but I felt somehow that she took a dim view of me. She was a good actress, nevertheless, and I wanted to see how she worked in a rehearsal. I took a seat in a corner of the hall. During a break, she came up to me, looked at me silently for a while, then said, 'You're stubborn, you know?'

I was dazed by the suddenness of the assault. 'Why do you think so, Maria Petrovna?'

'I've been watching you now for some time, and I've concluded that you're stubborn. In any case, I wouldn't want to be with you in the same collective . . . or in the same dormitory.'

I was infuriated by her incivility, and those words I couldn't tolerate: 'collective,' 'dormitory.' I barked back, 'But I needn't worry you at all, Maria Petrovna, since you're on the point of retiring.'

Of course, that was the sort of thing one wasn't supposed to say, and later I was ashamed of it. But to this day I don't understand why she went at me like that. I was sitting there quietly in a corner, like a mouse under a broom, watching and learning. Plainly, however, for her as for many others, I was a foreign body in that well-adjusted organism.

The Moscow concert organisations soon heard about me, and I began to get many invitations to perform at concerts. Just what were those 'concerts'? People in the West seldom have had exposure to them, so it is best to explain. Many famous performers would take part. They would include such varied features as circus numbers, famous violinists, the Moiseyev Dance Company, magicians, prima ballerinas from the Bolshoi, balalaika players and *chansonniers*, actors from the Moscow Art Theater, trained dogs, and, of course, soloists from the Bolshoi Opera Theater. An especially great number of such concerts – literally hundreds of them – are scheduled for holidays: New Year's Day, Soviet Armed Forces Day, International Women's Day (March

8), May Day, November 7, Lenin's birthday, and so on. Each time, the concert hysteria lasts about a week. The concerts are given at ministries, institutes, academies, schools, and in concert halls. Often the public goes to them directly after work, and usually admission is free. (That is to say, one doesn't pay to get in.) In truth, a Soviet citizen does not see the money, because it is deducted from his salary; the same applies to 'free' education, 'free' medical care, 'cheap' apartments, and the rest. So that, whether you wanted to go to the concert or not, the money was taken from you long ago. You don't see it, you don't miss it, and no one has bothered to ask you what you would have preferred.

Soloists from the Bolshoi get about fifteen or twenty rubles for such a concert; and during the 'holiday harvest,' some of them manage to perform six or more times in one evening. They hop like fleas from one club to the next. It often happens that after such feverish work they lose their voices and can't sing at the theater for months, collecting their salaries and licking their wounds like disabled veterans after fierce battles for the glory of the Fatherland. Many young and inexperienced singers of the Bolshoi have lost splendid voices to that hack work. Even though you need only sing two songs and one aria at a concert, each must be a crowdpleaser. You may not feel tired, but each performance in a new auditorium is bound to shake up your system. Not to mention six performances in one evening!

Why do they do it? Because the young singers want the same things people in civilised countries want: a car, a private apartment – even if it's only a studio – a decent standard of living for one's family. But today, in the Soviet Union, a car costs from 10,000 to 18,000 rubles. So that if you worked only at the Bolshoi, you wouldn't earn enough for a car in a lifetime: your wages would only suffice for food, a pair of shoes, and one suit per year. In order to buy a car at 15,000 rubles, at the rate of 20 rubles per concert you'd have to sing 750 concerts. It would be interesting to know what such astronomical prices are based on, since the average wage of a Soviet citizen is no more than 150 rubles a month.

But I am describing the holiday concerts in Moscow. For the celebrations, a Leninist theme is a sure thing. The composers, poets, writers, and singers know that very well, and they exploit the fact outrageously. If a composer writes an oratorio about Lenin, he can be sure it will be bought: one hundred percent sure. He takes it to the Ministry of Culture, where they must listen to it and buy it. A group of officials is assembled for an audition. One swears under his breath, another sleeps with his eyes open (they've become skillful at that), and yet another snores unabashedly, but all of them obediently and significantly nod their heads in approval. Then the composer is congratulated on his new creative triumph, the goods are purchased, and usually after two concerts (the first and last) in one evening, it is put on the shelf and forgotten for all eternity. And who pays for that prostitution? That same Russian citizen who half-starves on his miserable wage.

During holidays, all the big names in Moscow hurried from one concert hall to another, reaping the harvest. At first I was not tempted to earn a bit more; I preferred to spare my voice. But I was getting only 180 rubles a month, and it simply wasn't enough for food, clothes, and the life of an adult woman, however minimal her requirements might be. I, too, joined the marathon.

Once I was rushing off to a concert in the Hall of Columns, and in the lobby I ran smack into Lenin! Lord!

'Where are you going in such a hurry, young lady?'

Everything was so unexpected that I confess I thought 'the eternally living one' was standing next to me on two legs just as sure as if he'd been pulled out of his coffin. But it was Gribov, and behind him, Massalsky, another actor from the Moscow Art Theater. They were hurrying in to play a scene from *The Kremlin Chimes*:* the conversation between Lenin and H. G. Wells about electrification.

I went on stage and did my number. The audience applauded, and demanded an encore, but backstage, Gribov and Massalsky, who were waiting their turn, kept looking at their watches. They were late for their next concert, and pawed the ground like horses in a stable.

Gribov said to me (he was already 'in character' and was

* A play from the early forties by Nikolai Pogodin (Nikolai Stukalov).

practicing his guttural *r*'s, getting tuned up for the whole evening): 'Get it ovegh with in a hugghy, deagh young lady! We'ghe algheady late.'

It was laughable – Lenin's mummy from the mausoleum come to life and talking to me. The woman who was managing me helped me into my fur coat. And Lenin, one hand tucked in his vest and the other stretched out in front, strode out on stage, followed by the monocled H. G. Wells. I jumped into another taxi and went on to the next concert hall.

'Hurry up! You're on!'

I looked, and couldn't believe my eyes: Lenin was standing there on stage. But I had just left him at the other place! How could he have made it here before me? Or was I so worn out that I was seeing things? Looking more closely, I noticed that he seemed thinner . . . It was another pair from a different theater!

So, during the holidays, different Lenins scurried about Moscow far into the night, trying to turn up an extra kopeck. Each of them would make himself up in his own theater, and then put on his cap with the bill lowered so that anyone who saw him on the street or in an elevator wouldn't get frightened. After all, someone could have dropped dead in a minute, if he thought he were seeing 'the eternally living one' next to him. Ilich has risen!

It was in October 1953 that I first sang the role of Tatyana in *Eugene Onegin*. Tatyana! Dear Tatyana! In my childhood, it was under her tutelage that I came to know what tears of happiness were. She brought me my first success in opera. And thirty years later, in October 1982, together with her I bade farewell to the opera stage in a series of eight performances of *Eugene Onegin* at the Paris Opéra.

Like a loyal and devoted friend, she accompanied me throughout my career, giving me joy and inspiration. I have sung that opera hundreds of times, and yet my heart always stops in the last scene, with the words 'I love you.' It is there, in her confrontation with Onegin, that we see the wholeness and directness of her nature. Already married and a woman of the world, she acknowledges to him with chaste simplicity, 'I love you . . .' For her, loving him all her life is as real and as natural as the fact that her life had ended on that day in the distant past – on the path in the garden – when she had listened to his cold moralising and could only whisper, 'My God! How humiliating, how painful!'

> *'I love you. Why should I lie?*
> *But I belong to someone else*
> *To whom I'll be true all my life.'*

When the Bolshoi Opera was on tour in Paris in 1969, Marc Chagall came to see *Onegin*. After the performance, he came backstage and told me, 'What majesty, what simplicity you have!' For me, it was the highest praise. Majesty and simplicity were exactly what I had been striving for in art throughout my life.

The premiere of *Fidelio* did not take place until after I had played Tatyana, until spring of 1954, and it became a musical event of great importance. What good fortune to have had the opportunity to sing that work of genius at the outset of my career. The purity and manliness of Beethoven's soul left an imprint on my fate – not only on a creative level but on a human one as well.

There is a point in Leonore's famous aria when, after the prayerlike slow section, the French horns come in as if sounding an invocation. At that moment I wanted to seize a banner and lead regiments, to break through iron bars, to liberate prisoners in the name of freedom and the human spirit.

The performances of *Fidelio* were attended by the creative intelligentsia, singers, and musicians. At the premiere I met Dmitri Shostakovich. A star had begun to shine on me.

Then I was given my third role, that of Kupava in Rimsky-Korsakov's *The Snow Maiden* (conducted by Kirill Kondrashin and staged by Pokrovsky). Those roles – Tatyana, Leonore, Kupava – were perfectly suited to my temperament, my youth, candor, sense of principle, and determination. In earlier productions of *The Snow Maiden*, Kupava had been sung by a hefty woman, a dramatic soprano, and it was comical to see her alongside the Snow Maiden, that little block of ice.

For a long time I couldn't make sense of the role – couldn't arrive at its essence – until one day at rehearsal it occurred to me that it would be interesting to know how old Kupava is. I had thought she was about thirty; the vocal part is dramatically very intense. But those village girls were only sixteen when they married, and by the age of thirty they had a bunch of kids! And she was a friend of the Snow Maiden, who was fifteen.

I heard the voice of Pokrovsky: 'Galya, why are you clumping around the Snow Maiden as if you were an old matron? Jump! Run! You should be bursting with joy!'

'Yes, I know that I'm not doing the right thing, but I'm confused.'

'Why?'

'The vocal part is very high-pitched and assertive, and not for a young girl.'

'How old do you think Kupava is?'

'I'm not sure. Maybe sixteen?'

'Right. You're a girl, the same age as the Snow Maiden. But the Snow Maiden has water in her veins. What does Kupava have?'

'Blood!' I shouted triumphantly.

We had found the key to the role. Like blood and water, the image of the young, passionate Kupava had to be in sharp contrast to that of the cold, crystalline, and infantile Snow Maiden. Kupava was the life of the village. She was full of the simmering juices of life. The high tessitura and assertiveness of the vocal part was merely an expression of her abundance of strength and youth. She is as pure and guileless as nature itself, and throws herself into Mizgir's arms without thinking twice. For her there are no shades of feeling, no conditions. And when Mizgir reproaches her:

> 'For a lover, modesty is the dearest thing of all . . .
> But you loved me quite heedlessly,
> You put both arms around me . . .'

the sky falls in on her. How was such betrayal possible? As if loving and talking love were shameful! Like a madwoman, she appeals to the birds, the trees, the stream for help. Human beings, in their hypocrisy and sanctimony, do not understand her. She runs to Tsar Berendey, not to complain but to demand justice. During the performance, I flew to Berendey's palace and only in the last fraction of a second jammed on the brakes and threw myself at the tsar's feet so violently that he always skittered aside in advance – away from the proscenium, afraid that I would send him flying into the orchestra pit. I implored the tsar, demanding that the offender be punished.

Kupava had become a young girl once more.

That production brought me a special kind of success. I completely altered the traditional character. There was a definite shift of focus, resulting – people said – in an opera about Kupava. At the discussion after the dress rehearsal, the famous baritone Alexei Ivanov said that Pokrovsky had ruined the production by giving the role of Kupava to Vishnevskaya because Mizgir could not have jilted such a Kupava for the sake of the Snow Maiden. To do that, he would have been a complete fool, and the audience would never believe it. It was flattering for me to hear that, but I knew that without Pokrovsky I would not have played the role that way.

As soon as I appeared as a young singer on the Moscow horizon, I was snapped up by officials from the Ministry of Culture who began to parade me around at concerts and government receptions. These were usually held at embassies or at the Metropol Restaurant, but the most important ones were held in the Kremlin, in St George's Hall. To be taken there was considered a great honor for the artists. They would drive us to the Kremlin and have bodyguards escort us to a room near St George's Hall. Sometimes you had to wait several hours before going on stage. Your nerves would be stretched taut, and you'd be afraid that your voice would collapse under the stress of waiting . . . And waiting with you were such luminaries as Ivan Kozlovsky, Mark Reizen, Maxim Mikhailov, Maya Plisetskaya, Emil Gilels, David Oistrakh . . .

Most loathsome was to be expected to sing toward the end of a reception. The huge hall would be swarming with hundreds of

people; a long table in front of the stage would hold the members
of the government, already duly 'under the influence' and with
faces like boiled lobsters. One shouts something to the man
beside him, another looks at you with glassy eyes . . . You stand
there on the stage feeling so ashamed and humiliated you'd like to
melt into the floor. People drink and chew, their backs turned to
you. They clatter their knives and forks, clink glasses, smoke.
And in that huge pigsty you sing for their pleasure like a serf girl.
You may be given the great honor of being called to their table, of
sitting with them and gulping down glasses of cognac.

Once, after such a performance, the crudeness and vulgarity of
the scene sent me into hysterics backstage. A magician who had
gone on before me paled with fright and took me off into a corner
where he could shield me so the bodyguards would not see my
reaction. 'Calm down! What's the matter with you?'

I couldn't stop. How dare they? How dare they?

I was fortunate in that I was soon able to refuse that 'honor'
once and for all – something I shall recount later. But in that I was
a unique phenomenon at the Bolshoi; all the other soloists
elbowed one another and lunged for the government feeding
trough. It made them feel important; and there was always the
remote possibility that they would get something out of it for
themselves.

Years later when I was living in Paris, I read in a copy of the
Bolshoi's weekly newspaper that in answer to the question 'What
was the strongest emotional experience you had this year?' the
leading soloists Evgeny Nesterenko and Elena Obraztsova replied, 'The great good fortune of singing at a banquet in honor of
Leonid Brezhnev's 70th birthday.' Well, one can only feel sorry
for them if they could dredge up no greater emotions.

Today, the artists continue to compete with one another as to
who has more acquaintances in the government, and who drinks
vodka with whom. These ways are passed on from one generation to another like a baton in a relay race. The young people see
that the mediocre can garner titles and positions not through
talent but through acquaintances and by singing at drinking bouts,
wherever it is necessary and to whomever it is necessary.
They see that singers may have long since lost their voices,

but cannot be dismissed because they have protectors in the Kremlin.

Closer relationships with the Soviet government elite are formed at receptions in honor of foreign delegations. Such functions generally take place in private dwellings that have been specially designated for that purpose. During my first years at the Bolshoi, I often performed at them. The most positive impression I got from all our *grands de ce monde* was made by Mikoyan, who was simple in his dealing with others and was humanised by his individuality, by the lively temperament of a Southerner. I remember our other leaders as a collection of gloomy, squat idols – silent and motionless figures at the center of a whirling carnival of sniveling toadies.

You could be summoned to those receptions by telephone at any time – often late at night, just as you were getting ready to go to bed. This meant that after a drinking bout, some leader had decided, quite capriciously, that he had to hear the voice of a favorite artist. You would never dream of refusing: you got dressed, and five minutes later you were in a black ZIL limousine. Singers were never invited with their wives or husbands; and the members of the government never brought their wives – they kept them well hidden in their 'women's rooms.' It happened, too, that favorites of the Soviet elite would often be exempted from an evening performance in order to sing at a banquet (I was called in this way).

It was while circulating in that unfamiliar 'high society' that I first saw the Party courtiers in action. If an important government official pays attention to you, a herd of hangers-on from his retinue immediately stampedes in your direction. They fawn on you, hoping to render their boss some service through you. How repulsive and sickening it all is! All of them, like overgrown eunuchs, like pimps, are eager to curry favor with the big shot and put a pretty woman in his bed. Having given themselves over to toadying, and having stuffed themselves with *bliny* and caviar at too many banquets, these courtiers return to their little bureaucratic offices to play the tyrant like feudal lords; and in compensation for their abasement, for having been compelled to subservience, they in turn humiliate their own subordinates.

Having lived in Leningrad, I of course knew there was a privileged class of society among us – that not everyone huddled in a communal apartment like me. But before joining the Bolshoi, I could not imagine the size of the ruling class in the Soviet Union. Essentially, they live in another state built by themselves for themselves, a horde of many thousands exploiting Russia's impoverished, bitter people for their own ends. They have their own restricted stores for food, manufactured goods, clothes, and shoes, which are guarded by husky bouncers, where everything is of top quality and the prices are far below the official prices for the people. They live in excellent, rent-free apartments and dachas with a whole staff of servants, and they all have chauffeur-driven limousines, not only for themselves but for members of their families. They have at their disposal former tsarist palaces in the Crimea and the Caucasus, converted especially for them into sanatoriums, hospitals, and vacation villas. Their 'state within a state' contains everything. Sincerely believing in their divine exclusiveness, they remain haughtily aloof from the life of the Soviet plebs, securely protected against them by the high, impassable fences of government dachas. In the theaters they have their own individual boxes with special exits to the street; and even during intermissions they don't go out into the lobby so they won't have to lower themselves by mingling with the slaves.

Often, standing before a banquet table in St George's Hall in the Kremlin – a table laden with yard-long sturgeons, gleaming hams, and caviar – and raising, along with everyone else, a crystal goblet to the happy life of the Soviet people, I would study the swollen, flabby faces of our self-appointed leaders of state, as they chewed their way through many a splendid still life. I would remember my wanderings through the huge country, with its wretched daily life, impassable mud roads, and beggarly standard of living. And I would ask myself: Do these people – drunk on power, self-important, stupefied by food and drink – know how we live? Plainly, they knew it, but knowing is not enough. One must feel it with one's skin, with one's belly. To understand it, one must live, if only for a month, the vile life of a Soviet slave. Let them shout their toasts to the victory of communism throughout the world, not at this Lucullan feast, and not stuffed with caviar and salmon, but in the stinking kitchens of communal apartments. Install each Politburo member there and see what happens. Let him live, say, in my tiny room with the cement floor – the room of a soloist with the celebrated State Order of Lenin Academic Bolshoi Theater of the USSR. Let him – after emerging from this hovel in the morning, exchanging abusive remarks with his neighbor, and thirsty for his morning hair of the dog – let him stand thirty-fifth in line for the bathroom. Only if, of course, he wants to risk washing in that filth. Let him go to work not in an armored limousine but in a tightly jammed subway car or hanging off the steps of a bus. And let his wife, in the meantime, stand in line for three or four hours to get food for the family. Well, all right, let our leader not go to a worker's cafeteria during the lunch break to stand in line and rattle his tin plate with a blue, frozen potato on it, or the grateful citizens of the Soviet Union may never again see their favorite leader robust and well at the nation's helm. Let him come, instead, to the Bolshoi Theater, to the snack bar for the artists, the favorites of Melpomene, where he may be lucky enough to get a piece of boiled sausage called the *doktorskaya* – that meatless, mysterious, fantastic concoction consisting half of starch.

We have a joke on that subject. Two friends meet on the street, and one says to the other, 'Listen, Van, you look kind of blue to me. Did you get frostbite?' 'No,' replies the other, 'the thing is, I ate a *doktorskaya* and couldn't breathe afterwards, but at least my collar got a good starching!'

But let us continue. At the end of the day the 'servant of the people' comes home from work – again in the subway and not in a limousine. Blue from his sausage-starched collar, and with people pushing against him from all sides, he hears the toilers of the Land of the Soviets colorfully cursing out the entire Soviet regime and Comrade X personally.

At home he is met by his wife – disheveled and infuriated from standing in lines. If she has been lucky, she may have gotten her hands on a half-rotten fish or the stump of a shinbone with bits of meat on it for his dinner. Store managers sell the meat itself 'under the counter' to their favored customers, and pocket the money.

When his vacation time approaches, he will race around for weeks in advance, trying to secure accommodations in a holiday home. If he doesn't succeed in that, the best lesson in communism is to go south and rough it. Upon his return from such a vacation, he can write whole novellas describing how, after arriving at a seaside resort and searching all day in the infernal heat, he finally rented a cot in a tiny room where several other lucky people like himself had already found lodging; how, early in the morning, he made a dash for the beach in order to claim a miserable meter and a half of our boundless Motherland; how, under the broiling sun, he stood for hours in a line at a restaurant for his one meal of the day; and how, holding his nose, he hopped about the entrance to the beach toilet, trying to slip in, skipping delicately around the little piles left on the ground at night by others who were roughing it.

Many were the times I 'vacationed' in the south in just that fashion, and I could provide much useful advice on how to survive under such primitive conditions without losing one's dignity. Let our leaders live the way the average Soviet citizen does for a time, without global problems and fulsome rhetoric, and they might realise that Soviet people live like cattle. Humans, though, look after cattle. But who looks after the Soviet citizen?

Despite the fact that I was singing lead roles and was being 'served up' like a dessert at government banquets, I still lived in that tiny room on the Petrovka, the only difference being that now there was one more bed to set up at night: I had hired a housemaid. Her name was Rimma, she was seventeen, and for a long time she had been doing cleaning and laundry for a number of the tenants in our communal apartment. She would work from morning till night, singing all the while. Often she slept on a trunk in the corridor like Cinderella. Homeless and lonely, she reminded me of myself in my youth. I felt sorry for her, and decided to take her on. In our converted staircase landing of a room there was no place to install a permanent bed for her, but there was a small, built-in closet which had at one time been a servant's dressing room. At night we would open a folding bed into it lengthwise, and there our Rimma slept half in and half out of the closet. Though she was strong and of great endurance as only

Russian women can be, she had one drawback – she did not know how to cook at all. But she tried as best she could, testing her skills on our stomachs. In the evenings she accompanied me to concerts or attended my performances at the Bolshoi. She loved to sing and had a good ear.

Soon there was a fourth full-fledged member of the family. One winter day, Mark and I went to visit some friends out of town. Knowing my love for animals, they gave me a tiny, three-month-old puppy, a white griffon named Jerry. On the way home, we decided to stop the car and take a walk. I held the puppy to my breast as we strolled past some generals' dachas surrounded by impenetrable fences. Since there was no one in sight, I put Jerry down and let him run. Suddenly, up ahead, a gate opened and a good-sized German shepherd came bounding out.

I shouted, 'Jerry! Jerry! Come here! Come here!'

But Jerry, having seen the monster, sat down in the snow and wouldn't move.

The other dog charged like a wolf, perhaps taking Jerry for a cat. I ran right at him, hoping to snatch up my puppy before he did.

Behind me, Mark was shouting, 'Come back, Galya! Come back!' But I wasn't thinking clearly. The beast snapped Jerry up in his mouth, so that only the puppy's tail and head were visible, and began shaking his head furiously. Beside myself, I jumped on his back and, pressing my legs into his flanks with all my might, dug my nails into the corners of his eyes and lips, trying to tear them apart. He howled from pain, and my poor little dog dropped out of his mouth onto the snow where he lay in a motionless heap.

But what could I do now? If I let the big dog loose, he would rip me to shreds.

Some men in uniform rushed out of the gate, along with the woman who owned the animal. I shouted, 'Come and get your damned dog!'

'I'm afraid to,' she said.

Then Mark came running up. 'Don't let the dog loose! Don't let him loose!'

He tore off his belt and tied it around the dog's throat. My hands were cramped, and I couldn't unclench them. And I had spasms in my legs. The frightened military men came running with a muzzle and a chain.

'Well, young lady, you'd better thank God. It's a miracle he didn't bite you.'

I myself didn't understand why the dog hadn't torn me asunder. Most likely he was shocked at finding me so brazenly astride his back.

Only when I looked him over afterwards did I realise just what a huge, fearsome beast he was. So that was the steed I had straddled!

Grabbing Jerry, we hurried back to Moscow and took him to an animal hospital. When we got home, I collapsed into bed. For several days I couldn't move my hands.

That's how we came to be, as in the story by Jerome Jerome, 'Three in a boat, not counting the dog.'

A separate apartment! To live alone, to escape the accursed commune, is the ultimate dream of any Soviet person. Since I was appearing at one government banquet after another, I could easily have asked one of the leaders to find me an apartment as we clinked our glasses of vodka. But I would rather have bitten my tongue off than demean myself by begging from our arrogant idols. And I fully expected that the Bolshoi would allocate housing to me because the management knew what my living conditions were. But the country's eternal housing crisis had even affected the Bolshoi. When new artists were hired, they were warned that the theater could not provide them with housing. And if the Bolshoi couldn't, then who the hell could? After all, there were no private proprietors: everything belonged to the state. So you did what you could: you formed the necessary acquaintances, offered bribes, or paid in kind – quite simply, you slept with the right person. There had been a time when the theater management addressed its requests directly to Stalin, the Boss. But with a collective leadership looming into sight, just try to figure out whom you should ask about housing for newly hired soloists. For that matter, the new government had no time for the theater: a power struggle was in progress. As a consequence, until the end of the sixties the Bolshoi had a dormitory where young soloists of the opera and ballet would live for years, several persons to a room. If a young married couple was hired, the husband lived in a room for men and the wife in a room for women. Not surprisingly, the marriage often ended in divorce. The housing problem can be blamed for crippling the lives of many people at the Bolshoi. Without a place of her own, a young woman could not get married and have a family. And if luck descended upon her in the form of a one-room apartment, measuring a mere 25–30 square yards including kitchen and bath, the long-desired peace of mind she had finally acquired was dearer to her than a future family. Besides, she never knew what kind of husband she might get, and she would think twenty times before getting married and allowing a husband into her precious abode. After all, in the event of a divorce he would have the right to claim one-half of the room she had acquired through so much suffering; that might be the reason he wanted to get married in the first place, something that happened quite often. One young soloist at the Bolshoi, T. T., not only had a beautiful voice, she even had her own room in a communal apartment – she was a most desirable catch! After picking and choosing for a long time, she finally married a ballet dancer with the theater. The marriage didn't work out and they got divorced. But for more than a year her ex-husband didn't leave: there was no place for him to go. So they lived together in one room, divorced and hating each other. She slept on the bed, he on the floor.

Once she told me, sobbing, 'I'm simply going mad, do you understand? It's not just that I can't sing, I can't even live! I don't know what to do – how to kick him out. Just the other night I came home after a performance, opened the door, and there he was lying on my bed with some woman. I gave him hell for daring to bring a prostitute into my room. But he answered right back, "What business is it of yours? I'm not your husband, and you're not my wife. I have no place to go, and if you don't like it, get out." And last night – imagine! – he woke me up and said, "What's the point of sleeping separately? Why don't I crawl in with you? We used to sleep together, so what difference does it make?" It's enough to make a person hang herself, and I have to sing in *Aïda* tomorrow!'

Situations like this are by no means rare at the Bolshoi. You would think one could check into a hotel. But no – out of the question. In the first place, a hotel room costs no less than ten rubles a day – that is, 300 rubles a month – and young singers earn only 200 rubles a month. The decisive factor, however, is that Muscovites do not have the right to stay in Moscow hotels; only out-of-towners do. And even if the theater can wangle special permission for one of its artists, it is only for a very short period of time.

One gets the impression that the Soviet government deliberately creates difficult living conditions in order to distract a person from more important problems and stifle his intellectual and spiritual life, to insure that, after a day's work and jostling in lines, he has only enough strength to drag himself home, drink a bottle of vodka, and go to bed. Soviet people spend their whole lives in 'getting,' whether it be groceries, which are always in short supply, or an apartment, which one must not only 'get' but 'merit.' In the Soviet Union there is a shortage of everything, from toilet paper to automobiles. But just think of the opportunities to rejoice! When a Soviet citizen finally gets something he needs, he is filled with the joy of victory. If there is a good dinner on his table, he eats it with a sense of pride because he has overcome the obstacles blocking his path in the form of long, slow lines. He has given a store manager a bribe and emerged a victor from the field of battle – something that his neighbor has perhaps not managed to do. And his neighbor envies him and respects him. If he has succeeded in getting a separate apartment, he is great and powerful not only in his own eyes but in those of his fellow workers. As he obtains all these trifles, he begins to think that life in the Soviet Union is improving; that the government is looking after him. Granted, for many years there wasn't any toilet paper or washing detergent in the stores, but now there is, thanks to the Party and the government and Comrade X personally. Hurrah! Forward to communism!

And before you know it, life has gone by in a daily, exhausting war with tragic defeats and brilliant victories – the endless struggle against mighty Shortage. For shortage is like a Hydra: if you cut off one of its heads, two more will instantly take its place. If today the stores have teakettles, which have not been available for several years, tomorrow will necessarily witness the disappearance of, say, enameled saucepans, or irons, or absorbent cotton in the drugstores, or children's socks, or brassieres, or sheets and towels, or . . . or . . . or . . .

And the struggle continues, creating the illusion of a dynamic, active life. The poor individual so deceived does not even have time to notice that his best years and strength have been spent on that petty activity. If the man in the street were to be spared that daily struggle, he might have time to think about his position as a slave drudging for the convenience of the Party elite. And he would finally take up a cudgel and oh, how he would swing it! No, Shortage is vitally necessary to the Soviet regime!

After Stalin's death, as soon as the adored idol had vanished from the famous box, there was a change in the government's attitude toward the Bolshoi, and the new generation of singers found themselves in a very different position. First and foremost, as if by magic the high salaries that Stalin had personally set for leading soloists (700 rubles a month for four performances) vanished. One fine day, when they went to the cashier's window to get their pay, the singers learned that from then on the top salary would be 550 rubles for six performances a month. Under Stalin, the period of employment before getting a pension was twenty years; after him, it was twenty-five. Earlier, pensions for People's Artists had amounted to 400 rubles a month. After the Soviet monarch's death, pensions dropped to 200 rubles for People's Artists and 120 rubles for all others.

Needless to say, there was no strike. In a communist country there cannot be any strikes, because there cannot be any malcontents. And it must be assumed that the singers of the Bolshoi were very content, and even happy, with that drop (of more than half) in their standard of living. Those salaries are still in effect, although in the meantime the cost of living has increased severalfold.

At the Bolshoi, a leading soloist earns only about twice as much as a singer doing small parts. The same goes for the number of performances required: an artist singing the role of Otello must sing six times a month for 550 rubles, while one singing the part of the servant Emilia in the same opera – a part which consists of a few phrases – sings in ten performances for 250 rubles. Every-one realises that this is unfair. But the only recourse the leading soloists have to equalise the situation is to perform less often for the same amount of money – to sing in two or three performances per month instead of six. I did it too. It wasn't difficult: all I had to do was claim I wasn't up to it and get a slip signed by one of the doctors at the Bolshoi's polyclinic. No doctor would refuse.

Artists in secondary roles, as soon as they join the Bolshoi, begin occupying key posts in the 'social organisations': the trade-union committee, the local committee, the shop commit-tee. They willingly collaborate with the KGB, and become Party members so that they can all be together. If the leading singers begin to complain about the existing pay scale, the others simply consolidate and crush them with their sheer numbers.

So to provide incentives for the soloists – to distinguish them from the masses without using money – there exists a system of honorary titles. The first rung is the title of Honored Artist of the RSFSR (Russian Republic), the second is People's Artist of the RSFSR, and the third and highest is People's Artist of the USSR. And there are the prizes (the Lenin Prize and the State Prize, formerly the Stalin Prize), the orders, and medals. Artists vie for these badges as early in their careers as possible, hoping to distinguish themselves from the common herd. The title of People's Artist of the USSR brings many privileges with it: a good apartment rent-free, for example, or permission to make trips abroad, or vacations in government sanatoriums. And if you become sick, you can get the best medical care free, a private room in the Kremlin hospital, the most scarce and expensive medication, and delicious food offered on a menu. Everything there is as it is in the best clinics abroad. These advantages are rare – in Russia you cannot buy them for any amount of money. They are granted to you only if the government itself, by awarding you its prizes and titles, singles you out from the endless gray Soviet masses. They, too, get free medical care. But they lie on broken-down mattresses with dirty linen, nine or more people to a room, or in the corridors of overcrowded hospitals. They are given nauseating food and second-rate medication – the best is always in shortage. Across the street from the Kremlin hospital, however, there is a pharmacy (it sports no sign, of course, and has restricted access) where you can find any kind of Western medication. Behind the door lurks a muscle man who, with one hand, can grab and eject whatever Soviet scum dares trespass those green pastures.

The right to be treated at the Kremlin hospital is awarded automatically along with a title, and the recipient rises to a different, higher stratum of society. As soon as I became a People's Artist of the USSR – literally within a few days – I got a telephone call from the Kremlin hospital, and a woman with an unfamiliar but gentle and tender voice inquired about my health. I couldn't understand the reason for her concern, or just what it was she wanted, until she explained that she was the doctor assigned to me.

'Dear Galina Pavlovna, we await you at your leisure. Please come. We'll arrange all the examinations. Perhaps you want to spend a few days here, darling, and rest? We've prepared a good room for you in our hospital outside the city. You can stroll in the woods. Your children will be taken care of, too.'

I was unaccustomed to such unctuous words, and I didn't know how to reply. 'Thank you, but nothing seems to be wrong with my health at the moment. Of course if something happens . . .'

'Oh no, Galina Pavlovna! You must take care of yourself. Don't hurt our feelings – come! We're responsible for you. Our duty to the people . . .' Et cetera.

What to do? Soviet people are as used to badges of excellence as meat is used to stamps of quality; without them, a person is simply a workhorse. Artists bustle about, frequenting government receptions and banquets in the hopes of making influential contacts. They strain their voices and blister their feet; an artist with no title simply has no credibility.

And there is one last advantage that a People's Artist of the USSR has over other Soviets: after he dies, a civil funeral is held for him in the main foyer of the Bolshoi. The Bolshoi's orchestra plays and the chorus sings. In short, a first-class affair. For those who cannot crowd in, there is space below in the lobby; a tape recording suffices there.

The title of People's Artist of the USSR may even mean a

chance to be buried in the Novodevichy Cemetery. Right now, the Moscow City Council has a list of perfectly healthy people who will be honored by burial in that famous graveyard. If the deceased has a high title, it means his relatives will experience less torment in securing a tombstone for him. Special workshops for making marble tombstones simply do not exist. People toil for years, giving bribes to whomever necessary, to get a factory to make an ordinary marble gravestone on the side.

A certain pianist had been driven to desperation trying to get a marble tombstone for his deceased mother. On a tour in Vienna, he bought an antique marble gravestone with a name already engraved on it, and lugged it back to Moscow. There the engraving was sanded away and replaced by his mother's name. But not everyone gets to Vienna!

In Russia there are no stores that sell burial supplies. There are only white cloth slippers and coffins crudely assembled from painted boards. And there are no establishments which, for a certain sum of money, might spare the deceased's grieving relatives the nightmare of arranging for the funeral. But at all institutions – including the Bolshoi – there are public-spirited people, enthusiasts, who have spent years acquiring skill in these matters. As soon as a comrade departs for a better world, they know where to go and whom to talk to. There is not a minute to be lost: bodies are not kept in the morgue for more than three days, because there is no cold storage. During that time they must make the rounds of dozens of institutions to get the needed documents, secure a place in a cemetery, arrange for cars, organise a civil funeral, and see to it that there are speeches, wreaths, and an orchestra. They have to stand in lines to get food and vodka for the funeral feast. They work zealously, 'for conscience's sake.' All try to serve the deceased. Soviets may not do so well in other areas – they may not know how to let you go about living – but they certainly know how to bury you.

A funeral at the Bolshoi is the event of the year. The theater's doors are flung wide open. There is no admission charge, and the crowds stream to the upper foyer where the coffin is, knowing they will see a spectacle on a par with the best of productions. Naturally, the artist's friends, acquaintances, and fans all come.

But the crowd surges through just to have a look. (As they say, 'they were in the neighborhood and dropped in.') If the artist was very famous, the funeral lasts for several hours. Representatives of every kind of organisation – people who may never have known the deceased nor seen him on stage – read speeches, frequently getting the 'unforgettable comrade' and dear friend's name wrong. The theater's directors and artists, like fifteenth-century Meistersingers, vie with one another in eulogising the dead person. Had he heard it all when he was alive, he might have lived longer!

The Bolshoi orchestra plays the funeral music. The guard of honor beside the open coffin changes every three minutes. The Bolshoi chorus sings, and famous instrumentalists play. Opera stars sing sad ballads, tearing their own hearts out – not to mention the hearts of the deceased's family, and of the public. Only the famous ballerinas are not there to dance.

The opera soloist Daniel Petrosian was once asked to sing at such a funeral. He readily agreed. He placed the music in front of his accompanist and with great feeling began to sing Dargomyzhsky's song 'I'm sad because I love you . . .' But he had completely overlooked one little detail; namely, that the song ends with the words 'I'm sad because you're so cheerful.' *And* there was a reprise! When he had sung the fatal phrase for the first time and was still in a state of consternation at what he had heard from his own mouth, he bugged his eyes, turned toward the deceased, bowed low, and ended, looking at him with an anguished expression: '. . . because you're so cheerful.'

Russians harbor a rather hysterical fondness for funerals. Even total strangers can feel sorry for the deceased and weep over him. The gossip-mongers who hang around the theater are the first to show up. Lining the walls, they try not to miss a single sigh. And, through their tears, they manage to have a look at the famous artists, noting who is wearing what, how many wrinkles this one has, and how much that one over there is weeping. 'See that one? She's hardly crying at all, the callous bitch! But that other one is really suffering. Maybe there was something between them, eh?'

In different corners of the huge foyer people pursue their own interests.

'Citizens, whose funeral is this?'

'I don't know.'

'Must be an important person – so many flowers!'

'Yes, he was a remarkable singer and a wonderful actor! Remember how he sang Lensky?'

'And did you hear his Romeo?'

'Just look at her – covered with grief! How pretty she is in her sorrow. Mourning becomes that face. I've always adored her. Hand me the binoculars.'

'Who's that standing by the coffin, dear? Family, perhaps?'

'No, artists.'

'Well, what d'ya know? A-a-a-artists! And was he an artist, too?'

'Yes, Mama.'

'Well, well, so he was an artist. May the kingdom of heaven open up its gates!'

At a rehearsal once, a colleague took me aside and asked, 'Galina Pavlovna, why don't you apply for housing? You're living in frightful conditions.'

'I'm waiting for the theater to offer it to me.'

'They never offer anything of their own accord. The Bolshoi has just been given several apartments in a high-rise. You should go and see the director.'

'All right, I'll go. Thanks for telling me.'

What kind of a country is it that always makes you ask for things and go to great trouble trying to get them? It would seem that the simplest thing would be to pay a person what his work is actually worth, so that he himself can dispose of his own income as he sees fit. But then there wouldn't be any 'free' apartments or any 'free' medical care, and you wouldn't be obliged to the Soviet regime for anything. In fact, there wouldn't be any need for the regime at all, or its millions of Party parasites who determine your needs at their discretion. From the day you're born, they think for you, they decide for you; your whole life is subordinated to someone else's will. And the terrible thing is that gradually, with the waning of your needs, your desires, and your initiative, this subjugation even becomes convenient. You may have only a hovel in a filthy communal apartment, but it is there and it is cheap. Your food may be wretched, but it too is there. You're alive and thank God!

And so I went to see Anisimov, the director of the Bolshoi.

'Hello, Galina Pavlovna. You hardly ever come to see me. How are you? Is anything wrong?' He said all this with an air of concern.

'No,' I said. 'Nothing is wrong. I feel a bit awkward turning to you for a favor, but –'

He visibly stiffened and interrupted me. 'We can't raise salaries right now. But we'll soon be retiring a number of the old-timers, and that should free some funds.'

'But I'm not asking for a raise. I came about another matter.'

'What?'

'For three years I've been living in terrible conditions in a communal apartment, thirty-five tenants in all. There are three of us in a tiny room off the kitchen. I can't get a decent sleep before performances because the pots and pans are rattling by six in the morning. My repertory is very demanding – it's essential that I be in good shape. I understand that the Bolshoi has recently acquired several apartments. Can I count on two rooms? Even a communal apartment would be all right if it's not too crowded.'

Lord, how disgusting it is to ask favors! It was the first time in my difficult life that I found myself in that position.

For a while he was silent. Then he leaned toward me, looked me in the eye reproachfully, and shook his head. 'I'm surprised at you, Galina Pavlovna. Your career is just beginning, yet what pretensions you already have! It's impudent. At least you have a roof over your head. Do you know how our charwomen and elevator operators live?' And his eyes were filled with sorrow for all mankind!

A hot wave of blood rushed to my head. He was reproaching me for the immodesty of my needs, while he himself had a huge, rent-free apartment! He ought to give *it* to a charwoman then!

Not to speak of his state-owned dacha, his car and chauffeur, the perks from the Kremlin he was entitled to as director of the Bolshoi. Why was it that I, a leading soloist, should not live better than charwomen and elevator operators? Damn! You sit there in that office like the personification of the Soviet regime. That's the way all of you care for the people; but look a little closer and one sees that for one of the 'people' – the official's own son or daughter – a dacha or apartment is built at government expense.

Feeling the tears welling, I got up and left the office without a word.

Where could I go now? To the trade union? The Party committee? The theater's local committee? To grovel, weep, and badger, trying to prove my human right not to live under bestial conditions? But the *raison d'être* of those state organisations is to protect the Soviet regime from us, the bothersome slaves. That's what they get paid for and why they so fervently serve their masters. The minute you poke your nose in, they'll gang up on you and tag you with such labels that all you will want is for them to back off and leave you alone.

I hid in a dark corner of the corridor burning with humiliation, and remained there for a long while, trying to come to my senses. I wanted to give it all up – the all-powerful theater, those insufferable people – and disappear.

I got a call from the personnel department and was asked to come in the next day. Every time it happened I felt sick. What if they had found out that I had lied about my father on the questionnaire? What would become of me then? Stalin had died only a short time before, and as yet there had been no talk at all about exposing the 'cult of personality.' As in the song, 'Lenin is one falcon, and Stalin is another,' the two of them were lying in a virtual embrace under the same roof in the mausoleum.

I didn't sleep at all that night. The next morning, however, I arrived at the personnel department, giving no sign that I was overwrought, playing a perfectly carefree, lighthearted creature.

I opened the familiar padded door. 'Hello.'

Two other men were there besides the chief of the personnel department.

'Hello, Galina Pavlovna.'

One was middle-aged, gray-haired, and stocky; the other was young – about thirty. They both played up to my bold gaiety, plastering smiles on their faces. But their eyes bored right through me.

'Let me introduce myself. My name is Vasili Ivanovich, and this is my friend Nikolai Petrovich.'

I waited. They were in no hurry to begin the conversation, so I remained silent.

Vasili Ivanovich took his identification card out of his pocket. 'I am KGB Major So-and-so,' and gave his last name.

My heart sank. My fatal hour had struck: they had discovered the truth about my father. But I kept myself under control. Take it easy . . . take it easy . . . My mind raced with every possible connection I had in the government.

'Galina Pavlovna, you are such a talented singer – our great hope, one might say.'

Whew! What was he up to? So they hadn't discovered a thing – if they had, they would have begun the conversation in quite a different tone. Thank you, Lord!

I even leaned back casually in the chair and crossed my legs. Let's hear what they have to say.

'We'd like to get better acquainted with you, have a little chat.'

'My pleasure.'

'It's not convenient here. Come to the Metropol Hotel tomorrow, room such-and such, third floor, on the right. We can talk there.'

'About what? And why the hotel instead of here?'

'Don't worry. Nothing will happen to you. You've seen my identification, and your chief of personnel is here. We're asking you to come tomorrow. And don't tell your husband about it. Good-bye.'

'Good-bye.'

I had already figured that they would recruit me as an informer for the KGB – that highly moral communist society of the Land of the Soviets. Today, as before, all soloists of the Bolshoi are approached, and many are recruited. At the time, informing for the KGB was not a ticket to travel, since in those years no one went abroad. (The Bolshoi Opera's first foreign engagement, in Milan, was in 1964.) The objective then was to have everyone keep an eye on everyone else, and be at the beck and call of the KGB. Those people had to have something to do, didn't they? The KGB represented hundreds of thousands of mouths, and they all needed to be fed.

I knew that sooner or later I, too, would have to pass through 'purgatory.' The KGB recruits artists during their first years with the theater, before they are awarded any high titles or make important contacts and acquaintances, while it is still easy to blackmail and frighten them.

I went to the Metropol Hotel, located right across the street from the Bolshoi. They no doubt maintained rooms there to get information from their informers quickly. And it still may be the case today, since the Maly Theater, the Moscow Art Theater, and the Operetta are nearby as well. As I entered the room on the third floor, the same two men greeted me joyously, as if I were one of their own.

'Hello, dear Galina Pavlovna. How good to see you! Please sit down.'

And right off the bat, without wasting a minute, Vasili Ivanovich said to me, 'Galina Pavlovna, we're asking for your help.'

'How?'

'You move in government circles. You are often among foreigners at receptions and banquets . . . And the Bolshoi Theater – we don't have to tell you what a responsible place it is. Our country is surrounded by enemies, and it is the duty of every Soviet person to help our security organisations expose them.'

He spoke without trying to persuade me but simply to explain the honorable work of an informer. An inconsolable anguish, a sense of utter hopelessness enveloped me. How could I escape this death grip? Dear God, what could I do? If I said no, they'd squash me like a fly. So once again I had to be tricky, lie, and pretend I was a naïve featherbrain.

I opened my eyes wide, and asked, 'How and where am I

supposed to expose enemies? My work is nerve-racking, you know. I'm a singer – I often have hysterics, I talk in my sleep, and I'm very scatterbrained . . .'

I babbled whatever nonsense came into my head. But he stuck to his guns. 'There now, Galina Pavlovna, you're such a wonderful actress, so young. As for your poor little nerves, we'll see to it that you get treatment. We'll get you a pass to a sanatorium. We can arrange it in a minute, heh, heh.'

'Thank you, but it won't be necessary.'

'We're not asking you to do anything serious – just to observe certain individuals and give us your opinion of them. Is that really so hard? And you were so frightened! My, my! There's no reason to be afraid of us. Now, sign this paper.'

'What paper? Why?'

'It's only pro forma. That what we have talked about here is not to be divulged.'

I signed.

'I'll give you my telephone number at work. If you need anything, call me immediately.'

'And what is it that I might need of you?' Inwardly, I was shaking, and wanted to spit in his face.

'Well, if you have any trouble at the theater, if they give you a hard time, call us right away, and we'll quickly put things in order. We help our friends.' He was already talking to me like a protector, as if henceforth there would be a lifelong bond between us.

'No, thanks. I myself always –'

'That's all right, call us. We just may come in handy. Well, we won't take any more of your time right now. We'll call you when we need you. Till then.'

A month went by and Vasili Ivanovich didn't call. I was overjoyed, thinking that perhaps they had forgotten about me. But no, those people don't forget. He called – the very sound of his voice made me shiver – and again I had to go to the Metropol.

'Hello, Galina Pavlovna. My, but you're blooming! How are things at the theater?'

'Fine, thank you.'

'If the slightest thing comes up – we're on guard!' (They

wanted to be of service to me, so that I would feel obliged to them. That's how they snare the small fry.)

'But there's really no need. Everything's perfectly fine.' (Damn you, I don't need your help! Leave me alone!)

He got right down to business. 'You're on friendly terms with the ballet pianist Petunin. We have information that he often says things against the Soviet regime. Is that true?'

He said all this in a confidential tone, with a smile. About Petunin, they were correctly informed. He did talk against the regime; in fact, that was our only topic of conversation.

I assumed an expression of extreme astonishment. 'You don't say! Really? I never heard anything like that from him.'

'Does he tell you any jokes?'

'Yes.'

'What kind?'

'Oh, I can't repeat them to you. He's so vulgar, he tells only dirty jokes.'

'You mean to say that although you're friends, he's never told you any political jokes? We have reliable information . . .'

Clearly, someone from the theater had informed both on him and on me. 'But who told you such nonsense? Petunin is so stupid! Where would he get the brains to tell political jokes?'

'All right. Put that in writing.'

I wrote: 'I often see the pianist Petunin. He likes to tell frivolous jokes.' I signed with a hand that seemed to be made of cast iron. A deft movement by Vasili Ivanovich, and the little sheet of paper was gone.

'Thank you. Good-bye for now. We'll call you. In the meantime . . .' And he gave me an assignment: 'Petunin is a friend of the chess player Smyslov, who has just returned from abroad. Find out what Smyslov has told Petunin.'

In the days that followed, I tried not to run into Petunin. But as if on purpose, he kept bumping into me everywhere – in the snack bar at the Bolshoi, on the street – rattling on with his twaddle and jokes.

Two weeks later I had another call from Vasili Ivanovich. I said I had a performance and couldn't come. Two days after that he called again. I asked my husband to tell him I was sick. Another few days, another call . . . There was no way out – I had to go . . . The Metropol, third floor, on the right . . .

A broad grin. 'Hello, Galina Pavlovna. So you were a little under the weather. How do you feel? How are things at the theater? They haven't given you any trouble yet?'

'Everything's fine, thanks.'

'So Smyslov met with Petunin? What did he have to say?'

'He told Petunin how he played, and what a hard tournament it was.'

'And what did he say about things abroad?'

'He didn't say anything. You know, I've been working so much – I have a premiere in two days – that I can't remember what this or that person carries on about.'

'All right, all right. Don't get upset. Did he bring back any presents?'

'Yes, he gave Petunin a beautiful tie.'

'Nothing else?'

'Nothing.'

'Thanks. Write it down.'

How idiotic, I thought. What does he need it for? I wrote: 'Upon returning from his trip abroad, Smyslov brought Petunin a beautiful tie,' and I signed it.

In all likelihood, however, by giving me such 'petty' assignments to carry out, he wanted me to get used to the idea that I was *already* working for them, and that I had reached the point of no return. That was their system, no doubt. They could see, of course, that I was trying to wriggle out of the situation, and they had decided to drive me into the trap gradually. It was clear that this was only the beginning, and that I could not succeed in playing the fool for long.

And suddenly it occurred to me: What if Zhenya Petunin is a provocateur? What if he is working for the KGB and tells political jokes at the theater on their instructions, then reports who reacts to them and how? Vasili Ivanovich may have a denunciation of me in his pocket at this very moment. The thought bit me like a snake. But no, it couldn't be. I must have been losing my grip on reality.

After leaving that bandits' den, I walked the narrow side-streets of Moscow for a long time. God, how terrible that we all lived in eternal, degrading suspicion of one another! But how could we live otherwise? It was no secret that the majority of artists in the opera and ballet collaborated with the KGB, and still do. Some do it for fear of being deprived of a successful career. Others, the less talented ones, in the hope of gaining powerful support (and they get it). Still others cooperate in order to insure themselves for the future, in the event they lose their voices. No insurance policy in the world pays off as well. There have been many cases at the Bolshoi when singers who have lost their voices go for years without performing, yet continue to collect their salaries. The management makes no attempt to dismiss them, knowing that they are highly ranked informers and that, however hard one might try, it is impossible to get rid of them.

I didn't want to go home, yet the thought of going to the theater and seeing my colleagues was abhorrent. Lies, lies, lies everywhere; like a sticky spider web, they entangle one's consciousness, they twist the soul . . . they hang over you from the cradle to the grave.

And yet I succeeded in eluding the trap laid for me by those hunters of human beings. Never again did I go to the Metropol Hotel, 'third floor, on the right.' I succeeded because I soon made the acquaintance of Nikolai Bulganin, who was then chief of state. I complained to him, and he extricated me from that spider web once and for all.

There were occasions when artists were invited to receptions for foreign delegations as guests rather than as performers. In April 1955 I attended one such reception at the restaurant in the Metropol. My husband, of course, was not invited. A bunch of us were sitting together at a table when a young man strode up and greeted everyone.

'Let me introduce you,' someone volunteered. 'This is the cellist Mstislav Rostropovich, and this is the new star of the Bolshoi, Galina Vishnevskaya.'

He sat at our table. I was chatting away, and didn't pay any more attention to him. I had never heard his name before, and it was such a difficult one that it went in one ear and out the other. He was in the midst of telling the others some amusing stories when I suddenly saw that an apple was rolling across the table from him to me. He was playing Paris in *La Belle Hélène*: 'He gave her an apple . . .' As I was getting ready to go, he jumped up. 'May I see you home?'

'If you wish, I live nearby.'

We walked together past the Maly Theater and the Bolshoi. The weather was marvelous; it was already warm. When we arrived at my building, he said, 'I was supposed to go to a friend's birthday party, but after meeting you, I don't want to go anywhere.'

The flattery didn't affect me in the least. I heard that kind of thing every day.

'May I give you this candy?' From somewhere he produced a big box of chocolates.

'Oh . . . why don't *you* have them? I never eat them.'

'Please. It's very important to me.'

I took the box, said good night, and went up to our apartment. Mark asked where I had gotten the candy. From some musician, I answered.

I didn't read anything into that meeting. And it was Mark who ate the candy.

By then I had been married ten years. Having been on stage from the age of seventeen, I had always been surrounded by admirers, and was used to regarding men in general as a kind of obligatory and customary backdrop. They existed in order to give me flowers, to compliment me after performances, or to turn around and look at me on the street. But in recent years I had been so deeply involved in the theater and so full of my art that I was oblivious to anything else. Relations between Mark and me had become well defined. It was clear to both of us that a break was inevitable; but for the time being we lived under the same roof like old friends. Every day, at rehearsals and performances, I met my imaginary heroes. I endowed them with all the traits I longed for in a man, and continued to wait for someone I could love unto death – someone to love the way I could love my men on stage.

A short time later I was called to the Ministry of Culture and was instructed to fill out a questionnaire for foreign travel. The destination was to be Czechoslovakia, the 'Prague Spring' Festival, where I was to sing in *Eugene Onegin* and give several solo concerts. It was a great joy – my first trip abroad.

I learned later how I had been nominated. When my name came up at a session at the Ministry of Culture, someone interjected that, since I was young and had never been abroad, I might not be desirable for the 'Prague Spring.' One of the department chiefs, Veniamin Boni, stood up and declaimed, 'I don't know whether Vishnevskaya is desirable for the "spring," but in spring one desires Vishnevskaya!' With such a weighty argument, the decision was made to send me to Prague. Long after that, the witticism was still making the rounds of Moscow.

SEVEN

I flew to Prague with another singer from the Bolshoi, Alexander Ognivtsev. His bass voice was unique for its power and beauty, and he was handsome: young, tall, broad-shouldered – a regular Russian epic hero. He looked like Chaliapin. From the beginning our friendship was especially close and it always remained so.

We were driven to the Alkron Hotel, and taken to the restaurant for breakfast. All the other visiting Soviet artists were already there. I went in looking for a free table for Sasha [Alexander] and me when I spotted that cellist whose name I couldn't pronounce. He was heading right for me.

'Hello, how good to see you! There's an empty chair at our table – please sit down with us.' He had known that I would be flying in, and had kept that place especially for me. I had scarcely managed to look around when I found myself sitting next to him at his table.

'But I don't know. Where is Sasha going to sit?'

'He'll sit at another table.'

My bearlike friend appeared. 'Where have you been? I've been looking for you. Isn't there a place here for me?'

But Rostropovich told him matter-of-factly, 'You can sit at that table over there.'

As we sat and talked, his thoughts and ideas came pouring down on me like hail. It was only then that I got a good look at him. He was extremely thin, wore glasses, and had a typical intellectual's face. He was young, though already balding, and had an elegant look about him. I later found out that when he learned that I would be in Prague, he brought all his jackets and ties and changed them morning and night, hoping to make an impression.

He was all movement, impulsive, bubbling with jokes; but his eyes, in contrast to his mannerisms, were steady and attentive.

It was as if there were two persons within: one trying his best to please, the other observant and shy.

I turned to him. 'Mst . . . Mtl . . . Pardon me, but it's hard to pronounce your name.'

'Just call me Slava. And may I call you Galya?'

'Well, all right.' I wasn't used to being addressed that way; for many years people had been calling me only Galina Pavlovna. All my male acquaintances regarded me as, above all, a famous singer, and our relationships amounted to flowers and compliments; they all perceived me as the person they had seen on stage and whom they had applauded. And they were all middle-aged. Also, I had a reliable husband much older than myself, and that left a certain imprint on my behavior. This Slava was treating me like a girl!

And he saw me as such. He had never seen me on stage – for him I was not a spoiled, capricious prima donna but simply a young woman. With all his directness and impetuosity, he began to court me. Neither my past nor my rising fame interested him. It was a strange experience for me, but the impression it produced was special: his was a naturalness and sincerity that I was unaccustomed to.

When we went out to the street near the hotel, we saw a woman with a basket full of lilies of the valley. He took the whole armful and gave it to me.

Rehearsals, performances . . . and at my side would appear, then disappear, a man with a kind of frantic motor inside him. I didn't have time to analyse my own feelings and motives, but there I was looking forward to our meetings.

He came into my hotel room, sat down at the piano, and played. 'Too bad I have a concert and won't be able to hear you in *Onegin* tonight. You must be a marvelous Tatyana.'

Suddenly he leapt from the piano and sank to his knees. I was startled. Should I turn the whole thing into a joke?

'Forgive me, but in Moscow, the first time we met, I noticed that you had very beautiful legs – I wanted to kiss your feet then. You have to be at the theater soon, so I'll go. Till tomorrow!'

My head was in a muddle. At the theater there were flowers from him. Although I was often pampered, his attention was unlike any other I had ever known. Or perhaps I was now different?

Sasha sang the role of Gremin in our *Onegin*. After the performance he asked me, 'Why do I see you so seldom? Let's go for a walk tomorrow.'

'Fine, five o'clock.'

Slava later confessed that Sasha had asked to be awakened at five. And he had told Slava about our walk. At four-thirty, Slava showed up at my door. 'Let's go for a walk. The weather is marvelous. Have you been to the park on the hill?'

'But I promised Sasha I'd go with him. He'll be offended.'

'Your Sasha is sleeping like a bear in the dead of winter. If he isn't awakened, he'll sleep right through until morning.'

'Nonsense.'

'Here's how we'll settle it: We'll knock on his door three times. If he doesn't wake up, we'll call it fate, and you can come with me.'

We went to Sasha's door and Slava knocked three times. Of course he could have knocked more loudly, but I didn't insist. No answer. Slava took me by the hand, and we ran out to the street.

Never before had I felt so free and natural with someone. He talked about his mother and sister as if he and I had known each other for a long time. And how young he was! Although we were the same age, it seemed to me that he was a mere boy.

We left the path and walked into a deep thicket. Ahead of us was a high stone fence. 'Slava, we have to go back and look for the road.'

'Why go back? We'll climb over the fence.'

'What do you mean, "climb over the fence"? I can't . . .'

'Why not? I'll give you a boost so you can get up on top of the fence. Then I'll climb over it and catch you from the other side.'

That was the last straw. But what could I do? I climbed up, trying not to lose my composure. He was already on the other side, shouting at me, 'Jump!'

'Where to? Look, there are puddles and mud everywhere!'

'You're right, I hadn't noticed. But never mind. Here.' And he threw his coat over a puddle.

It was getting close to dinner time and we had to go back. We hurried along the street. 'Look, Slava, pickles! Too bad the store is closed.'

'Do you like pickles?'

'I adore them!'

In the hotel we sat down at the table as if we had just met up with each other in the lobby. God forbid that the others should notice anything! I was well-lodged in the first stages of a love affair, and on my first trip at that! It would have been considered a disgrace to the moral standing of the Soviet people. If anyone found out, I would never be allowed to go abroad again.

My 'bodyguard,' Sasha, came into the restaurant like a bear coming out of its den. He really did look sleepy. 'Where have you been? I've been looking for you everywhere. And you! Why didn't you wake me up?'

'But I knocked! We both knocked! We almost broke the door down. You sure can sleep!'

Then Slava began to tell stories. Jokes flowed from him as from a cornucopia. Never in my life did I laugh so much as I did that evening. Then, quite abruptly, he jumped up and ran off. What an odd sort of man! Within, he seemed to be all perpetual motion.

I came back to my room and threw open my closet to get my night clothes. The sight behind the door made me leap back in fear. In the closet, like a white specter, stood a huge crystal vase overflowing with lilies of the valley and pickles. Now, when had he found time to do that?

I called him in his room. 'Why did you do that?'

'Did you like it? I'm glad. Good night.'

We were hurtling toward one another, and no force on earth could stop us. As a woman of twenty-eight who had been taught much by experience, I wholeheartedly felt his young, unrestrained passion. And all my feelings, which for so long had been pent up within, went out to him in response.

We had only been in golden Prague for four days, but we were already in fact man and wife, although no one else knew about it. We decided that when we got back to Moscow we would get married.

Neither of us had ever heard the other perform. And to be honest, a cellist to me was some nameless individual in the orchestra pit. But my future husband had told me with some pride that he was also an assistant professor at the Moscow Conservatory.

At the end of those four days in Prague I got a telegram from the Ministry of Culture telling me to prepare for a trip to Yugoslavia right away. A government delegation – Bulganin, Khrushchev, Mikoyan, and others – was going to Belgrade, and would be accompanied by a group of artists. I wasn't asked whether I wanted to go – I was merely told to pack my things and get into a car.

Slava would be in Prague for another week. He flew from store to store, buying dishes, chandeliers, blankets . . . He saw himself as the future head of a happy family. With an intensity typical of him, he decided that when I got back to Moscow I should go directly from the airport to his place, without stopping at home.

'But how can I part in that way from a man I've lived with for ten years? He never did me any harm.'

'Then tell him everything, get it over with, and call me when you're through. I'll be waiting for you.'

'All right. But give me your word that you'll tell absolutely no one about our plans. I don't want Mark to hear about it from anyone but me.'

In those days, when Soviet government delegations went to Western countries to improve relations, they often took along a 'heavy artillery' of artists. The singers, violinists, pianists, and beautiful ballerinas helped the government officials, who were lacking in urbanity, to create a relaxed atmosphere at receptions.

This time the mission was especially ticklish: it was the first visit to Yugoslavia by a Soviet government delegation since the break between Stalin and Tito. We were going hat in hand to make peace with the man who for many years our leaders had called at best a mercenary traitor. I was present at that peace parley.

They all came to a reception at the Soviet Embassy in Belgrade after a whole day of conferences. There I made the acquaintance of Nikolai A. Bulganin, then chairman of the council of ministers – chief of state – and Nikita S. Khrushchev, general secretary of the Central Committee of the Communist Party. The others I had met earlier. After a concert in a small hall, Bulganin came up to me, said that he had heard me at the Bolshoi several times, and invited me to dine at the head table. So it was that I found myself next to him, Khrushchev, and Mikoyan, and across from Tito and his wife, a beautiful young woman. I was getting a close look at the famous Yugoslav 'traitor' whose name in Soviet newspapers had been mud for several years.

Tito struck me as completely different from his portraits, in which he was shown either in uniform, on a yacht, or on horseback. All Yugoslavia was hung with those portraits: the stores, the markets, any room you entered. Even Stalin in the Soviet Union had never enjoyed so much advertising. Staring from every Yugoslavian wall was a young, courageous, broad-shouldered man. But here at the table the great man looked diminutive. He was about sixty, of short stature, with fine features. His behavior reminded one of Stalin: the same slow, 'significant' movements and gestures, the same taciturnity. And in the same way, I thought, our artists had embellished Stalin, who was – in the flesh – a short, pockmarked, unhandsome man.

The atmosphere at the table was tense. It was plain to see that our 'solicitors' had not had an easy time at the talks. Tito was exaggeratedly calm and reserved. He had put up a wall between himself and his guests and was not about to take it down in one day.

It was obvious that for our people, all the roles had been sketched out in advance. Mikoyan proposed toasts like a toast-master; Bulganin tried to keep the conversation at a sophisticated level; and Khrushchev, for all the world like some kind of hail-fellow-well-met, kept trying to kiss everybody.

'Iosya, quit being angry! What a thin-skinned one you are! Drink up and let bygones be bygones.'

But everything in Tito's expression showed that he had a good memory, that he wasn't about to let bygones be bygones. In this country he was tsar and god. Serenely, very much the boss, he lorded while the emissaries of the great power abased themselves before him. One felt that he wanted to prolong the pleasure – that he had waited for this moment for a long time. Every now and then an ironical smile would glide across his face. Yes, I mused, he's a hard nut to crack – too hard even to put between the teeth of Old Man Stalin.

Ivan Serov, who had become head of the secret police after Beria, slithered up behind me and whispered, 'Propose a toast to Tito's wife!' What the devil! There were plenty of men at the table – the right thing would be for one of them to offer a toast to the lady. What did I have to do with it? It would be embarrassing, one woman to another. But there was nothing I could do. I stood up and issued wanly, 'I propose that we drink this glass to Madame Tito.'

My toast sounded completely out of place, and Tito responded with a laugh – his first that evening. 'Madame! What kind of "madame"? All during the war she was a partisan. She shot and killed people!'

'Really? I never would have imagined it. Such a beautiful woman.'

He chuckled. 'Now you know that there are beautiful partisans.' And he looked proudly at his wife.

The tension in the atmosphere was broken. The KGB man had been right.

Then Khrushchev joined in. 'Now, girls, let's dance!' And our leaders began to trip the light fantastic – with us. Forward, the 'heavy artillery'! Tito didn't dance.

Where did the Soviet rulers get their passion for dancing? They dance clumsily – as if they work at it. At receptions abroad, I've never seen presidents of great nations go into folk dances when they're tipsy. Bulganin eventually told me that Stalin made them dance at his nocturnal banquets. That, perhaps, was where they got their mania.

The next day I got a beautiful bouquet from Bulganin. That was all I needed! I knew that our new tsar and sovereign didn't present you with flowers just for singing well; those people aren't versed in the ways of gallantry. The next day it was the same thing. There could be no mistaking it – the chief of state was courting me, and that was no laughing matter. But I was not going to let it worry me. I'd get out of it somehow. Right now the most important thing for me was to get back to Moscow in a hurry. Slava was waiting.

As soon as I got home, I announced to Mark that I had met Slava, that we had fallen in love, and that I was going to move in with him that very day. Mark had always treated me well, and I had never heard an abusive word from him. He was a kind, good man, and it was painful for me to deal him that blow. He begged me to take some time to think it over and called the whole thing a passing infatuation. He even threatened to kill himself. 'I won't let you go!'

'Let me out. I have to call him.'

The telephone, a communal one, was in the hallway. I broke loose and ran through the apartment, with him after me.

'Don't you dare!'

'Go away!'

The neighbors were listening at all the doors. It wasn't every day they could enjoy a good fight.

'Slava, I'm home.'

'I'm coming. Wait for me outside.'

'I can't. My husband won't let me out.'

'*He's* not your husband, *I* am! I'll come to your apartment.'

'Don't!'

'All right. I'll come to your building and stand on the street until you come out. I'll stay there for days if I have to!' And he hung up.

I knew that once he'd promised something, he'd do it. The thought of a scandal terrified me.

In the meantime, Mark had locked the door. Then came a hit below the belt, 'You're forgetting where your father is. If people were somehow to find out that he's in prison, it would mean the end of Rostropovich's career and yours.'

'You mean they'll find out from you? Mark, nothing can help you now. Open the door, or I'll shout so everybody can hear. You know me. I'm capable of anything.'

'Go, then! But I'm going to stand right here at the head of the stairs. If you're not back within five minutes, I'll throw myself down!'

I bolted down the stairs, and Slava was already there. He grabbed me and pulled me out to the street.

ABOVE: In Krondstadt, aged one and a half.
BELOW: With my mother and my half-brother in 1930. I was not yet four.
RIGHT: My father, Pavel Andreyevich Ivanov.

ABOVE: With Grandma in 1932. She was
my father's mother and looked after me
when I was only six weeks old.
BELOW RIGHT: In 1943 with the 'Blue
Division', which was the sailors'
nickname (because of our light-blue
overall) for the MPVO, the local anti-
aircraft defence detachment in
Kronstadt.
BELOW LEFT: At seventeen, on tour with
the Leningrad District Operetta Theatre.

ABOVE: My debut at the Bolshoi as Tatyana, in *Eugene Onegin* in 1953. RIGHT: In the same role, my farewell performance at the Paris Opera in 1982 (Photograph: Daniel Cande).

ABOVE: As Leonore in the Bolshoi première of *Fidelio* in 1954. Beethoven's only opera had never been staged in Soviet times. BELOW: As Kupava, my third role, in Rimsky-Korsakov's *The Snow Maiden* in 1955. The lavish costumes and life-size sets were typical of the Stalinist period.

ABOVE: With the Bolshoi's
chief conductor, Alexander
Shamilyevich Melik-
Pashayev, who took me
under his wing. His favourite
opera was Aïda and he said
that in me he had finally
found a singer capable of
interpreting Verdi's music as
he wanted it.
RIGHT: Backstage at La Scala
as Sofia in Prokoviev's
Semyon Kotka (Photograph
Piccagliani/La Scala).

Aïda at the
Metropolitan Opera
during the Bolshoi's
tour in 1961
(Photograph:
Metropolitan Opera
archives).

During the recording of
Benjamin Britten's *War
Requiem* with Britten
himself in London in 1963
(Photograph: the Erich
Auerbach Collection).

ABOVE: With Elena Obraztsova after she received first prize in the Glinka
Competition in 1963 ... and in 1969, with Maria Callas (Photograph: AGIP).
BELOW: After receiving the title People's Artist of the USSR at the Kremlin on
October 5, 1966. Dmitri Shostakovich is seated third from the right, next to
me. Nikolai Podgorny (seated centre) conferred the awards.

'Come on! Let's get out of here!'

'How? I'm in my bathrobe!'

'It doesn't matter.'

'Wait! You see him up there? He says he'll throw himself down if I don't come back right away. I must talk with him – we must part decently. And . . . well, I'm afraid.'

'Of what?'

'When I tell you you'll understand that I can't be your wife.'

'Have you gone out of your mind?'

'Listen to me, Slava . . . my father is in prison.'

'If you were a direct descendant of monkeys, it would make no difference to me.'

'You don't understand. He was imprisoned under Article 58, the political article. I concealed that fact. But if I become your wife and that whole story comes out, your career will be finished. You can be sure they won't ever let you go abroad again.'

'To hell with *them*! I'm not interested in this nonsense. Tell me: Do you love me?'

'Yes.'

'Then you'll be at my place today.'

'Don't hurry things. I'll go back to my place now, and tomorrow at noon let's meet at the Moscow Hotel across from the Hall of Columns.'

'But he'll only refuse to let you out.'

'I'll tell him I'm going to the theater.'

Slava finally agreed, and we arranged to meet as I suggested. I went back home, and Mark and I quarreled and argued through the night. I felt terribly sorry for him. I was breaking his heart.

The next day, at noon, I got ready to go out.

'Where are you going?'

'To the theater.'

'I'll go with you.'

'Fine.'

He took me to the theater. I went in through the Petrovka entrance and ran clear across the stage to the exit on Sverdlov Square. Not feeling my feet beneath me, I ran past the Hall of Columns and across the street to the Moscow Hotel. No Slava! A taxi stood there with a swarm of people around it, all staring inside. I panicked, thinking something awful had happened to him. I dived into the crowd, elbowing people aside to look into the car. Rostropovich was sitting in the rear seat, surrounded by lilies of the valley. They completely filled the cab. He had been waiting for me on the corner, when several of his acquaintances passed by, and he leapt into the taxi to hide. Then he bought up all of an old woman's flowers to decorate the interior. You don't often see that kind of thing in Moscow – so a crowd gathered to find out what would happen next. He was sitting there like a bridegroom in a flowerbed; and the cab driver's eyes were glazed from the solemnity of the moment. In that short time he had been convinced that Slava's fate would be decided right then and there.

'You! Finally!' he said to me. 'Kolya, let's get out of town. Step on it!'

We stopped somewhere near Barvikha. There, we jumped out and ran into the woods, glad to be alone. We could talk undisturbed, and discuss everything.

I had a brilliant idea: 'You know, two months' vacation is coming up for us at the theater. Let's separate just for that long – you know me so little. That way we'll have a chance to think things over and examine our feelings. In two months we'll meet, and all will be clear.'

'Two months? I don't have to examine my feelings. All is clear to me as it is. If you need that, you must not love me.'

I was in tears. 'But I feel sorry for Mark.'

'And not for me?'

'I love you. Why should I feel sorry for you?'

'Here's what we'll do. We'll go back. If you don't show up by four o'clock, I'll know you don't love me and everything will be over between us.'

I slowly climbed the stairs to my apartment, thinking that my only solution was to write Mark a letter and leave. But for me to do that, he'd have to be out of the house. I'd ask him to go to the store for strawberries.

As soon as he was gone, I snatched up a sheet of paper and scratched out a letter asking him to forgive me. Then I threw a robe, a few dresses, and some toilet articles into a small suitcase . . . But where was I going? I didn't even know Slava's address!

I raced out to the telephone in the hall. I had the neighbors' attention once again. 'Slava, I'm coming. Give me the address!'

I hung up and ran down the stairs. My temples were throbbing. I was afraid of forgetting his address, and my legs were near paralysis. I barely made it to the cab stand. 'Nemirovich-Danchenko Street, number –'

The driver looked at me as if I were crazy. 'But that's right around the corner. You can walk there.'

'Go! Fast! I'll pay you well.'

It seemed to me that in those three little minutes we had inched through half of Moscow. We drove up to the entrance. A tall girl waiting there came over to the cab as I was getting out. 'Are you Galya?'

'Yes.'

'I'm Mstislav's sister. He asked me to meet you.'

'And where is he?'

'He went to get champagne.'

I could see she was frightened to death. This had probably hit like a bolt from the blue. He hadn't told his mother anything, because he was not sure I would come. He was a good son who had always heeded her advice – and she hadn't wanted him to get married. She had systematically interfered in his relations with women, and he had obeyed her – until I came along. When I phoned to say I was on my way, he announced, 'Mama, my wife is coming. Veronica, you meet her out in front. I'm going for champagne.' One can imagine the state he left them in.

We climbed up to the third floor and went in. Standing in the middle of the room was a petite old woman with a single braid hanging down almost to her knees, and wearing a man's under-shirt. She was trembling with excitement and struggling to get herself into a robe. And that is the way I remember her still: Sofia Nikolayevna in a man's undershirt (she always wore her late husband's shirts) with one arm in the sleeve of a robe, the long, white braid dangling, and a cigarette lodged in her mouth.

I couldn't say a word, and she too was speechless with fright. I sat down on my suitcase and began to cry at the top of my voice, and both of them joined in.

At that point, Slava came in carrying a string bag with bottles of champagne and a fish sticking out of it. 'Thank God you've already met!'

And that's how I became Rostropovich's wife.

The three of them lived in two rooms of a communal apartment which housed twenty people all together. Sofia Nikolayevna and Veronica occupied the space behind a screen in the main room off the hallway, and after my arrival Slava and I had the second room – a very tiny one. We lived there for six months.

Sofia Nikolayevna (née Fedotova) was born in Orenburg into a family of intellectuals who ran a little music school. Sofia Nikolayevna herself was a pianist and had graduated from Moscow Conservatory in Konstantin Igumnov's class. Slava's father, Leopold Vitoldovich, had been a splendid cellist. He died during the war, and Sofia Nikolayevna, left with two children – Veronica, who was sixteen at the time, and Slava, fourteen – had to work day and night to support them. Hers had always been a hard life, and even when her weak-willed husband was alive, it was she who assumed responsibility for the family. That petite, thin woman with the indomitable spirit ordered the family around like an admiral on a flagship. Since she always wore her husband's undershirt beneath her dress, Slava called her 'Vovka the Commander.'

Day by day, bit by bit, and not without pain she tore her adored son away from herself and yielded him to me. There were no conflicts between us. I knew we would soon be moving, and tried not to interfere in her well-ordered household. Before Stalin died, he had personally authorised construction of a cooperative building for the Composers' Union on Ogarev Street. Since Slava had just won a Stalin Prize, he signed up with the cooperative and invested all his prize money in an apartment. By the time we got married, construction of the building was being completed.

Despite the lightning-quick marriage, we never encountered any unpleasant surprises. Because we had never seen each other on the stage, we had no illusions about one another. On the contrary, a human relationship devoid of glittering theatrical tinsel brought out the most genuine and sincere aspects of both of our natures. The only surprise for me was that he turned out to be an outstanding musician, and for him, that I was a good singer. But the first impression always remained the most important. For me, he was the man whose wife I had become only four days after meeting; and for him, I was the woman before whom he had fallen to his knees.

For us, our art was a separate life, a domain apart. And if we chanced to meet there, things did not go nearly so easily and smoothly as in our private life: each of us was too intolerant and individualistic within our own professions. And it is probably a good thing that during the first years of our married life we seldom performed together. I went to concerts and enjoyed his music from the audience, and he went to hear me at the Bolshoi.

At the time, I was so shaken by the sudden change in my life that for a week I was afraid to go out of the house. Although we were very happy, my guilt about Mark tormented me for a long time.

In his new role as husband, Slava was frightfully amusing. The first morning he appeared for breakfast in an impeccable jacket and tie. I sat in an ordinary robe.

'Where are you going at such an ungodly hour?'

'Nowhere. I'm just having breakfast with you.'

'But why are you all dressed up?'

Sofia Nikolayevna and Veronica were all eyes.

'Sergei Sergeyevich Prokofiev never took the liberty of appearing at the dining table in a dressing gown, and I, too, intend to be dressed first thing in the morning.'

'So! Do you mean for us to squeeze ourselves into our corsets first thing in the morning?'

'No. You are ladies – you can make your appearance as you like.'

Toward the end of breakfast he asked permission to take off his jacket because it was hot. The next morning he asked if it was all right to come to the table without a tie. The morning after that we found him sitting at the table in his underwear, boundlessly happy.

For several years, when Slava was still young, he was on close terms with Prokofiev, who had a tremendous influence on him, not only as a great composer but as a man. He was often at Prokofiev's home, and spent summers with him at his dacha in Nikolina Gora; he saw in Prokofiev his ideal and tried to be like him in everything, even in trifles. Prokofiev liked perfumes – Slava developed that same fondness. His penchant for neckties also came from Sergei Sergeyevich. If someone told him that he outwardly resembled Prokofiev, Slava was richly complimented. It also pleased Sergei Sergeyevich, who would ask Slava the question (it had become a kind of game between them): 'Sir, may I tell you something abominable?'

Slava, in an equally dignified tone, would answer, 'Tell me, if you're so inclined.'

'You resemble me to a frightful degree.' And then both of them, happy as children, would giggle.

Slava simply worshiped Prokofiev's art. From the very first days of our marriage he told me about Sergei Sergeyevich with so much love and inspiration that I, who had never known him (Prokofiev died the same year that I joined the Bolshoi), began to feel toward his memory as I might have felt toward the memory of a man near and dear to me.

One of the first visits we paid was to Prokofiev's widow. I remember how agitated I was when I went up the stairs in the small building across from the Moscow Art Theater to meet her for the first time. We talked in whispers, as if in a church. Until his death, Prokofiev lived in a communal apartment in three small rooms with his wife and her stepfather. I was shocked by the modesty of those living quarters. Sergei Sergeyevich's widow, Mirra Prokofiev-Mendelson, honored his memory religiously, and kept everything just as it had been when he was alive. One got the impression that he had just gone out and would be back any minute. We often visited that apartment, and I almost always caught myself waiting – as if I expected the door to swing open and Prokofiev to sweep in.

Twice a year, on Prokofiev's birthday and on the anniversary of his death, his friends would gather there to pay him tribute.

There were not many of them, and one came to expect the same faces.

I soon felt well acquainted with Prokofiev; I could conjure up the facial expression he usually wore, his gait, his long hands. I could hear his voice and his manner of speaking. Although I had never worked on Prokofiev's music, I loved him as a man. And when I came to know his song cycle based on poems by Akhmatova – when I sang it – everything within me quivered from the radiant tenderness, the virginal purity, of his music. I wept when I learned his *Ugly Duckling*. Slava told me that Sergei Sergeyevich had written it about himself, about his own childhood. Prokofiev's music has run like a bright stripe through my life as an artist. In addition to singing his chamber music for voice in 1958, I sang Natasha Rostova in the opera *War and Peace*; in 1970, Sofia in *Semyon Kotko*; and in 1974, Polina in *The Gambler*. Polina was my last role at the Bolshoi – my farewell to Russia.

Prokofiev left Russia shortly after the Revolution, in 1918, and for a time he lived in France. He married abroad, and his two sons were born there. His first wife, Lina Ivanovna, was a Spanish singer. Several times, at the invitation of the Soviet authorities, they came to the Soviet Union to concertise. The authorities played up to Prokofiev in every way. They paid court to him, treated him with kid gloves, and tried to persuade him to return to Russia. They even paid his fees in foreign currency. Prokofiev had always felt that a composer should live in his native land, and in 1935 he came back to Russia with his two sons and his lovely young wife. She had only a vague idea what a mysterious, enigmatic country Russia was . . .

We don't need to go into the details of the relationship between Prokofiev and his wife. For the first few years in Russia they lived happily, but it was difficult for her to assimilate, and for all intents and purposes they separated in 1947. Sergei Sergeyevich moved into the apartment of his future wife, Mirra Mendelson; and Lina Prokofiev, a citizen of Spain, was arrested soon after.

One morning in February 1948 she got a telephone call from a stranger. 'I've just come from Leningrad, and I've brought you a package from your friend.' He gave the name of the person from whom Lina was in fact expecting a package, and continued, 'I'm now at the Leningrad Station. Come quickly. I'll wait for you on the street.'

'Why on the street?' she replied. 'Come to my place, it's close by.'

'No, I'm in a great hurry. I'll be standing on the corner. You'll recognise me by my naval uniform.'

How little she wanted to go! She had the flu, and it was bitter cold outside. But what could she do? She put on her fur hat and a warm fur coat, and went out. When she got to the appointed place, she saw a man in the uniform of a naval officer.

'Lina Ivanovna?'

'Yes.'

And the free citizen of Spain felt herself pushed toward the sidewalk where a car was parked. The door swung open . . . two more were in the car.

'Excuse me, I don't understand.'

But the naval officer then shoved her into the car and asked one of the men inside, 'Is this the one?'

'That's her.' It all happened within seconds.

Lina Prokofiev returned to Moscow eight years later. How well the fur coat must have served her in the Siberian labor camps!

Despite their great difference in age, Prokofiev was Slava's friend, and he valued that friendship. Of course, he recognised Slava's talent, his genius, but he also liked him because, even as a youth of twenty, Slava had come to him during those dark days of 1948 when the government had banned works by Formalist composers. While others were keeping their distance, Slava's utter devotion had never faltered; he had visited Prokofiev almost every day.

Sergei Sergeyevich shared his ideals with Slava, and played him his new compositions (which the state had not bought). He came to love him like a son, and frankly voiced his deepest anxieties. He worked together with Slava on his Symphony-Concerto for Cello and Orchestra, and dedicated it to him. Tikhon Khrennikov called that great work 'senile decay' – its final version was first heard not in Russia but in Copenhagen, where Slava performed it in 1954, after Prokofiev's death.

After 1948, Prokofiev's music was seldom, if ever, performed; he had no income. Slava went to pay him a visit once and found him helpless and bewildered; it was clear that he didn't have a single kopeck.

'What's happened, Sergei Sergeyevich?'

'Just imagine, Slava. Today there's nothing to pay the cook with.'

'Don't worry, Sergei Sergeyevich. I'll get it.'

'From where?'

'I know where!'

Slava ran to the headquarters of the Composers' Union. He burst into the office of the president, Khrennikov, almost grabbing him by the throat in his rage. 'Do you know what you've done to Prokofiev? Do you have any idea what is happening to that genius? Prokofiev has nothing to eat! Why don't you help him? He's there without a kopeck to his name!'

'Why doesn't he say that himself?'

'It's humiliating for him! Isn't it enough that you taunt him, you want him to beg bread from you besides? You know full well that Prokofiev's music is not being performed; that he isn't getting any official commissions for new works. Where is he supposed to get the money to live? I never would have come to you, but I have nothing to give him myself. You call yourselves "the Composers' Union" – it's your duty to save Prokofiev.'

Khrennikov called in his secretary and instructed him to give Prokofiev a grant of 5,000 rubles (500 in today's money). Slava snatched up the money and sped back to Prokofiev's place, buying a cake and champagne on the way.

'Hurray, Sergei Sergeyevich!'

'Where did you get all this splendor, Slava?'

'Off of Tishka,* Sergei Sergeyevich! I soaked him!'

The only time I saw Prokofiev was at the premier of his Sixth Symphony at the Leningrad Philharmonic in 1947. The people of Leningrad loved him. The symphony was a great success, and he

---

* Diminutive for Tikhon.

took many curtain calls. He was wearing a gray suit, his Stalin Prize badge, and, for some reason, light-colored felt boots that reached up to his knees. I was sitting far back and couldn't make out his face. But I have always remembered his music: sharp and ringing, like the dripping of snow in spring.

I also attended the premiere of his opera *War and Peace* at the Leningrad Maly Theater. I never dreamed that a few years later in 1958 I would sing the part of Natasha Rostova.

After Prokofiev's death, his widow, Mirra, spared no effort in putting his archive in order. She and Slava went to a lot of trouble trying to get one of the Moscow music schools named after Prokofiev. And they filed for permission to have the dacha in Nikolina Gora made into a museum; they were never granted it. When we left Russia in 1974, some twenty years after the death of the great composer, his house was abandoned, and only a tiny plaque on its door reminded people that Sergei Sergeyevich Prokofiev had ever lived there.

Mirra died in 1968. She had looked after the affairs and memory of Sergei Sergeyevich until the last minute of her life: she had been on the telephone with the director of the Prokofiev Music School about matters relating to the composer's archive, when suddenly her voice stopped. Thinking that the connection had been broken, the director hung up and called again, only to get a busy signal. He tried again a bit later, and the same thing happened. Since it was already late, he decided not to try again until morning. But in the morning the telephone was still busy. He went to her building and buzzed, but no one opened the door. Desperate, he called her neighbors, and together they broke the door to her room. They found her sitting in an armchair, dead – the telephone receiver in her hand.

Legally, I didn't have to get divorced, because my marriage with Mark had never been officially registered. We had been married during the war, when no one worried about paperwork, and after the war we never did anything about it.

And so Slava and I set out for the ZAGS (Registry of Acts of

Civil Status). It was the first time we had come out on the street together and I felt terribly awkward. It seemed to me that all the passersby were eyeing us, as if to say, 'Such a matron walking hand in hand with a boy!' To boot, he was walking very fast, so that I, who was used to strutting like a peahen, practically had to run to keep up with him.

The ZAGS was on Pushkin Street across from a second-hand store, in a courtyard, in the right corner near a rubbish heap. I don't know how things are today, but it remained unchanged until our departure in 1974. In a small, wretched room on the second floor, people got married, got divorced, and registered death certificates.

We entered the room. Behind the desk sat a portly dame right out of Babel's story: 'To the left a ficus, to the right a cactus, and in the middle, Rozochka.' Naturally, there were portraits of Lenin and Stalin on the wall. Because the ZAGS office was in the same district as the Bolshoi Theater, it was well tuned-in to artists.

'Ah, Galina Pavlovna! What a pleasure! I've heard you at the Bolshoi, and I simply adore you! Are you getting married?'

'Yes.'

'Sit down, please. Give me your passport, darling.'

And to Slava in a cold, official tone, with a little sigh, as if to say some people have such good luck: 'Let's have your passport, too.'

She began to write, repeating all the while, 'Ah, Galina Pavlovna, how marvelously you sing! Is there any way one can get into your next performance? Let's see, we'll write: The spouses Galina Pavlovna Vishnevskaya and Mstislav Leopoldovich Rotr . . . Rosr . . . Heavens! What a difficult name! Comrade, what is your last name?'

'Rostropovich.'

'What is it?'

'Rostropovich!'

'What kind of name is that, Comrade Rassupovich? Now you have a wonderful opportunity here. You can change that bothersome name, you can be' – she rolled her eyes and sang it out – 'Vishnevsky!'

Slava sat there as if he were perched on a hot skillet. 'Thank you, no. I'm used to my own name somehow.'

'Think about it! Later, you'll regret that you didn't take this chance . . . think how lovely it would sound!'

EIGHT

In the course of those happy days, it suddenly came to light that I was being sought throughout Moscow. My new admirer, Bulganin, whom I had completely forgotten about, had tried to call me at my old apartment and had learned from the neighbors that I had fled.

'Where to?'

'We don't know.'

The Bolshoi didn't know either, since I hadn't yet shown up there. Bulganin issued an order: Find her! But where to look? His lackeys made a hurried search throughout the city. Nothing, the bird had flown. Not until evening of the day Bulganin wanted to see me did they find Mark at home; he told them where I was. The minister of culture himself called me. 'Galina Pavlovna, we've been looking for you everywhere. Today is Bulganin's birthday. There'll be a reception out of town, at his dacha, and N. A. personally asks that you take part in a little concert. A car will be at your door in half an hour.'

I scarcely had time to dress and do my hair.

I hadn't even told Slava that in Yugoslavia the old man had sent me flowers. I was sure everything would blow over when I got back to Moscow. Far from it.

Bulganin's dacha was in Zhavoronki, on the way to Nikolina Gora, and the reception was in honor of his sixtieth birthday. But the word 'reception' is really not apropos here. One immediately thinks of a table beautifully laid out; of waiters, white napkins, goblets, and other things that inhibit the revelers. No, this was a good old Russian drinking bout, and I arrived when it was in full swing – things were really jumping. Plainly, they had been waiting for me: Serov himself, the KGB chairman, marked time impatiently on the porch. From the car I was taken in tow, hurried into the house, and presented to that honorable company. The birthday boy, beaming, escorted me to a place beside him, and, under the meaningful glances of everyone, I sat down between him and Khrushchev. I was overcome by a feeling of trepidation that hung on me heavily the whole evening.

A very intimate circle of guests had assembled there: members of the Politburo, their families, and a few marshals (including the famous Zhukov, who after the war had been sent into exile by Stalin). Since childhood I had known these leaders from their portraits, but I certainly had never seen them all together, 'at home,' with their whole households. How odd they looked to me in that domestic setting, elbow to elbow around a table laden with food and bottles. They were talking loudly and imperiously, and they were drinking hard. One sensed in them a kind of unnatural tension, as though they were leaders of wolf packs who had gathered there but did not want to risk showing one another their weaknesses. So these were 'the brains and heart of our Party!' The only ones lacking were Stalin, now 'asleep in the Lord,' and the recently shot Beria. All the other loyal brothers-in-arms were in their places, and I had a chance to look upon them.

They all had flabby, mongrel faces, coarse voices, and vulgar mannerisms. Above that hubbub rode the sharp, raucous voice of Kaganovich, with its strong Jewish accent. Even there, among their own kind, instead of toasts they recited slogans: 'Glory to the Communist Party!' 'Long live the Soviet Union!' With the usual awkwardness and transparency, they flattered Bulganin, calling him 'our intellectual' over and over because they knew he liked that.

The women were short, fat, quiet most of the time. They were tense. It was plain that each wanted to get out of there as soon as possible and be all-powerful in her own home. Not one wore an evening dress, and not one had a pretty hairdo. Chic or elegance were alien concepts here. The women were so faceless that if I had met one of them on the street the next day, I wouldn't have recognised her. Their husbands never appeared with them in society, and I never saw those ladies at any official receptions.

And from all sides came the waves of reminiscence.

'Nikita, do you remember . . . ?'

'Remember how in the thirties . . .'

The brashest of the women – homely and masculine – shrieked from one end of the table to another, 'Do you remember, Kolya,* how you showed up at our place in Turkestan as a very young officer? I said to Lazar: "Look how handsome he is!"'

Aha, that was Kaganovich's wife.

'. . . an intelligent young man. You have always been special to us, you know. You were our pride.'

And from the other side of the table, the deaf and toothless Voroshilov barking, 'Do you remember what a dashing cavalry officer you were?'

Then it suddenly occurred to me. Several of those women who sat there in silence – wives of leaders – had spent many years in Stalin's penal camps! And their husbands? They had roamed free in those years, having handed over their wives to be brought up on false charges. They hadn't defended them, but cast them out to save their own skins, the cowards! And now that Stalin had died, those women were back with their husbands and beside them at that table. It would have been interesting to know what they were thinking. I looked them over, trying to guess which of them had been in prison. The wives of Molotov, Kalinin, Budenny, Andreyev, and Poskrebyshev, as well as the wives of marshals, had been arrested as Zionists. Which of them had survived to return to this?

Oh, Lord! Why was I sitting there listening to those cynical lies? Why was I putting up with those meaningful glances? I hated them, and had no desire to be in their company. And that old man daring to look at me like that! But I knew full well that I was only a serf girl and he was the master. There was no point in playing naïve – that number wouldn't go over here. And this was just the beginning! The Soviet tsar beside me even had the same name as the last Russian sovereign – Nikolai Aleksandrovich.

I heard an insinuating voice in my ear: 'I called you at home, but I was told you don't live there any more – that you had run away.'

'I didn't run away. I got married.'

---

* Diminutive of Nikolai. She is addressing Bulganin.

'Really? Congratulations.' He played the fool, pretending surprise. But the form that Slava had filed probably had already been checked.

'Thank you.'

'And whom did you marry?'

'My husband is the cellist Mstislav Leopoldovich Rostropovich.' I enunciated the name proudly, and as agitated as I was, it came out correctly – something I would not manage to do for a long time thereafter.

I raised my head and encountered a fixed stare. It was Zhukov. He was sitting not far from me, and had apparently been observing me for some time. He was middle-aged, heavyset, and wore a general's uniform without decorations. The face was strong, with a stubborn, jutting chin. He was the only man who hadn't said a word all evening: I never did hear his voice. He just sat there studying the others silently, thinking . . . (He had much to remember!) Suddenly he jumped from his chair, grabbed me, and dragged me to the middle of the room to dance a *russkaya*. And did he dance! Fervently, furiously, never once smiling. I did my best, tried this and that, but he only looked straight ahead, as if intent on stamping something – someone – into the ground with his heavy boots. I realised then that Russians dance not only from happiness – they dance from rage.

The next morning someone rang the bell of our apartment, and Sofia Nikolayevna opened the door. A husky young colonel with a huge bouquet saluted her as if it were a review of troops. 'I'd like to see Galina Pavlovna.' His voice reverberated against the walls, and all the neighbors spilled into the hallway as if on command. Sofia Nikolayevna became flustered: 'She's still sleeping. Who are you?'

'Nikolai Aleksandrovich Bulganin has asked that these flowers be presented to Galina Pavlovna.' And he thrust the bouquet into her hands. It was so heavy that she began sinking to the floor. He barely managed to catch her.

'Well, thank him then.'

That was the beginning of my honeymoon with Slava.

Toward evening there was a call from the Kremlin. 'Hello, Galya. This is Nikolai Aleksandrovich.'

I fully understood the seriousness of the situation, but I opted for a light, noncommittal tone of voice.

'Hello, Nikolai Aleksandrovich! What wonderful flowers! Thank you.'

'I'm the one who should thank you. I was glad you could come to my place last night. Would you dine with me today? I'll be in town.'

He was talking to me as if my husband had never existed! I kept trying to shift the conversation to the level of social chat, but the voice at the other end of the line was serious and immutable. He had no intention of taking up my tone.

I began to hem and haw. 'I have a rehearsal at the theater tonight. It won't be over until late.'

'That's all right. I'll wait.'

Feigning utter naïvete, I agreed. 'How marvelous! Thank you. *We'll* come.'

There was a long pause at the other end of the line. Then: 'I'll send a car.'

Three black ZIL limousines glided into our narrow street that night. There were bodyguards in the first and third, and our new master himself was in the middle one. His appearance clearly indicated that he was arranging his chess pieces right off the bat; that he meant serious business, and was not one to fool around with. People were peering out of the windows of every building. What an honor for our street! The chief of state himself!

From that night on there were daily invitations, sometimes to his dacha, other times to his Moscow apartment. And, naturally, there were endless libations. N. A. drank a lot, and he made Slava drink. But Slava didn't need to be persuaded; he drank out of sheer wrath.

When they would both get tipsy, the old man would stare at me like a bull and start in on Slava, 'Yes, you beat me to it.'

'It looks that way.'

'And do you love her?'

'Very much, Nikolai Aleksandrovich.'

'No. Tell me, *how* can you love her? You're just a boy! Can you really understand what love is? *I* love her. She's my

swan song. But, all right, all right! Let's wait. I know how to wait
– I've had my training.'

I would sit there between them and listen. He didn't acknowledge that Slava had any right to me. Every drinking bout ended
with an explanation to my husband of how much he loved me and
that anything I asked for I could have.

'But we don't need anything.'

'What do you mean, you don't need anything? Aren't you
proud! My adjutant told me that you're living in a communal
apartment. Why?'

'We're living with my mother, Nikolai Aleksandrovich. But I'm
a member of a cooperative building on Ogarev Street that will
soon be ready.'

'Do you mean to say you *paid* for it? Where did you get the
money?'

'When I was awarded a Stalin Prize I put all the money into
it.'

'But why pay? I can get you a rent-free apartment in any
building – any kind you want.'

'Thank you, Nikolai Aleksandrovich, but I'm already used to
the idea that the apartment is my property.'

'How do you like that! A proprietor! Today property, tomorrow pass the hat!'

'But times have changed, Nikolai Aleksandrovich.'

'If only I'd gotten my hands on you sooner! No, no, I'm only
kidding.'

I think N. A. often regretted the good old days as he looked me
over with drunken eyes and told us about Beria's adventures.
How Beria had raped young girls; how, after they'd shot him,
they found a list of more than a hundred women who had been
delivered to him by secret police agents on his orders. The
agents had simply lain in wait for them on the street, pushed them
into a car, and brought them to their boss for his sexual pleasure.
What lingered in our memory was not the fact that he had met a
just reward in being shot, but that, although a villain, he had
been a member of the government for twenty years, and that
his brothers-in-arms were still in their places, serving the
regime. As far as we were concerned, Bulganin was an heir of

Stalin, whose terrifying, sinister shadow still hovered above us all.

Among the coarse and craggy faces of government, Bulganin stood out because of his intellectual look and his gentle, pleasant manners. He looked for all the world like a retired general under the old regime, and he very much wanted me to see him as an enlightened monarch, a Nikolai III. He always tried to emphasise that I need have no fears about being at his place. It may be that he actually loved me.

He used to tell Slava, 'You mustn't get angry because I call her so often. Let me be infatuated with her. You're young and have everything ahead of you, I'm just an old man.'

Although it sickened Slava to have to listen to all those effusions, there were times when he even felt sorry for the man. At home he would say to me, 'You know, he's really very nice. But why does he court you? If it weren't for that, I'd gladly be his friend.'

'As if he needed your friendship! He'd have wrung your neck with pleasure long ago if he'd had the chance.'

And it was true that Bulganin did not want, at any price, to face the fact that I had been snatched away from under his very nose. And snatched away by whom? By a 'mere boy,' as he would call Slava. Slava couldn't bear that, and would get even by calling our premier a 'cornball' behind his back. (Those were the days of Khrushchev's corn orgy, the idea being that if we planted corn from one end of the country to another, we would instantly achieve perfect communism.)

At first it was a game, and Slava enjoyed being the victor in such a high-level battle. But he soon came to realise the awkwardness of his position. On the street his acquaintances did everything but congratulate him. In a country where everything is bogged down in slavish toadyism and lies, even such a situation raises you to inaccessible heights. From an ordinary slave of the state, you are suddenly transformed into a personality. With complete sincerity, people begin discovering magnificent traits they hadn't seen in you before and which, quite possibly, you never had. No one judges, they only envy and admire. They seek your acquaintanceship, flatter you, fawn on you – why? So that through you they can put in a request: for a title, for an apartment, or simply for having a telephone installed without having to put up with the waiting list.

One night as we returned from the usual drinking bout at Bulganin's place, Slava started quarreling with me. 'I'm sick of it! I can't stand how that old man looks at you. I won't go there any more! You probably like it – being courted by our new tsar . . . Can't you see that it's humiliating for me?'

I was in tears. 'But what can I do if he refuses to understand? I can't tell him to go to hell! When the car shows up tomorrow – just try getting out of it!'

Slava – in nothing but his underwear – was climbing onto the windowsill. 'If that's the case, I'm going to throw myself out right now.' In his tipsiness he had forgotten that the drop to the ground was only about twelve feet.

Sofia Nikolayevna rushed into the room and grabbed him by one leg. Veronica grabbed him by the other, and I screeched hysterically, 'Stop, you madman! How can you think of jumping? I'm pregnant! What will happen to me?'

That was how I announced to my husband that we were going to have a baby.

It was as if a wind had swept him down from the windowsill and into the room. He was at my side, happy. 'Really? No, really? Why didn't you say anything?'

Tears were running down my face. 'Because – I wuh-wanted to-to sur-surprise you.'

The first thing Slava did was pick up a volume of Shakespeare's sonnets and begin reading them to me rapturously so that I, without losing a minute, would be imbued with lofty thoughts and would create something special and beautiful within. From thence forward, the book lay on our night table. And just as the male nightingale serenades his mate when she is hatching the little birds, so my husband would faithfully read me those beautiful sonnets at bedtime.

We decided to break off our strange relations with Bulganin gradually. The question was how to go about it. In that situation, we had to avoid making a deadly enemy. I began to decline invitations to his place, pleading fatigue and a full schedule at the theater. But he caught on to my strategy, and began to act through the Ministry of Culture, inviting me to sing at receptions in the Kremlin where it was the custom to appear without one's spouse.

First, a call usually came from an official at the ministry. 'Galina Pavlovna, there is a reception at the Kremlin this evening, and you have been asked to sing.'

'I have a rehearsal at the theater.'

'We'll have you exempted from it.'

'I'm not in good voice.'

The next call would come from the minister of culture himself. 'Galina Pavlovna, you have to sing at the Kremlin this evening.'

'I don't feel well, and I have a performance in three days.'

'I'll arrange to have you exempted from the performance.'

'But I can't sing. I'm tired.'

But they just couldn't comprehend my being tired. To their way of thinking, the honor was so great that even a corpse would have sung.

Finally, the premier himself would call. 'Galya, I'm asking you to come to the reception.'

'Nikolai Aleksandrovich, I don't like to sing at receptions.'

'Come. I want to see you.'

Finally, one day, I got sick and tired of the whole farce and couldn't restrain myself. I stood there in the stinking hallway of our communal apartment and, in a rage, yelled into the telephone: 'Why are you playing the fool? You call several times a day, as if you didn't understand that we can't come to your place. I'm tired of the gossip! I don't want to sing at your receptions! Why? Because it disgusts me! I don't want to see all of your chomping jaws while I'm singing. You have to get it through your head that it's humiliating for me. It may be a great honor for me to *your* way of thinking, but I ask you once and for all to spare me that honor. That's all. Good-bye!'

A few minutes later he called back. 'Galya, forgive me. Calm down. I'm asking you and Slava to have dinner with me at home tomorrow. I have to see you.'

What could we do? Again we went, and it started all over, with no end in sight. Truly it was said: 'Spare us from the worst of evils: a master's anger and a master's love.'* But from that time on I never sang at another government reception. My name vanished forever from the list of honored buffoons obliged to clown before our drunken leaders. It was Bulganin who rid me of that, just as he rid me of my 'chief' at the KGB, Vasili Ivanovich.

One morning I got a telephone call and heard a familiar voice. 'Hello, Galina Pavlovna! Vasili Ivanovich speaking. What a long time it's been since we had a chat.'

'I don't have the time, nor the desire to talk with you. I'm in a hurry to get to the theater.' And I hung up.

That evening we had dinner at Bulganin's place, and I decided to complain to him. 'Nikolai Aleksandrovich, I'm being hounded by the KGB.'

'What's going on? What do they need from you?' And he reddened.

'They're demanding that I write denunciations.'

'*What?* Have they gone out of their minds?' And he shouted to his adjutant, 'Fedka! Get Vanka Serov on the line. Oh, those bastards!'

He went into the next room to pick up the phone, and from snatches of the conversation we could hear the dressing down he was giving the KGB chief.

In a short while he was back. 'Don't worry. No one from *there* will ever call you again. You can take my word for it.'

And in fact that put an end to it. It was precisely then, in that period of my life, that help in such matters was crucial. Later on I had gathered enough strength to defend myself. And, knowing my high connections, everyone was cautious with me. Just let some Vasili Ivanovich try and touch me!

In December, just before the New Year of 1956, we moved into our new home. Although we were both well-known artists, it was the first time in our lives that Slava and I had our own apartment, and were able to close the door behind us. Four big rooms, a bathroom, and a kitchen – all to ourselves! Accustomed to being huddled together in one crowded room, we walked around as if in a forest, looking for each other. We had literally

---

* A famous line from Griboyedov's great play, *Gore ot uma* (*Woe from Wit*).

nothing: no furniture, no dishes. That very day I went to a store and bought some knives and forks, towels, sheets, and plates. We celebrated our housewarming sitting on the floor, because we had neither a table nor chairs. That's the way we began our independent family life.

In those years it was hard to buy furniture: the stores were empty – you had to put your name on a list and wait for several months. Slava gave someone a bribe so that we could buy a dining-room set, and we were thrilled that finally we could eat sitting at our own table. My former housemaid, Rimma, came to work for me again.

But our joy was premature. The fact that we had moved into our own apartment, for which we had paid good money, still didn't mean anything. We had to get a permit to reside there. In the Soviet Union each individual is officially allowed a maximum living space of nine square yards. But there were only two of us, since the housemaid didn't count. Well, if you took my belly into consideration, there were three of us. So at best we were entitled to twenty-seven square yards. And our apartment measured one hundred square yards.

Slava went to the regional Soviet, and to the Moscow Soviet, where apartment matters were handled; but they wouldn't issue a permit. Four rooms for only two people – impossible!

'But I paid good money for that apartment!'

'Why did you sign up for such a big apartment then?'

'Because at the time I was a bachelor and didn't yet know what my chances of having children might be. And as you can see, I did the right thing. My wife is pregnant – we're expecting a child in three months. Maybe she'll have twins, and the same thing could happen next year.'

But the brilliant prospects for the multiplying of the Rostropovich clan didn't convince anyone. They refused him a residence permit, and demanded that we vacate our apartment for one with only two rooms in the same building. I didn't want to appeal to Bulganin, and I don't know how the whole ruckus would have ended up, but the New Year of 1956 arrived. We had been invited to the Kremlin, but in view of my condition we decided to stay at home. At midnight we wished each other Happy New Year and went to bed. At two in the morning, the telephone rang. It was Bulganin.

'Happy New Year, Galya! May I stop by to convey my New Year's greetings?'

'Of course. We'd be delighted.'

Slava and I got dressed quickly and met our guest. He had come directly from the Kremlin, and caused a panic throughout our building. The elevator operator nearly fell ill from fright, and for a long time afterward she would recall how 'the boss' himself had appeared before her. Cars full of bodyguards were parked in the courtyard all night, and the general in command sat on the landing outside our apartment. It was his duty to guard the doors of the chief of state, so the poor thing had to sit on the floor for several hours. It didn't occur to me to bring out a chair for him.

The next day the whole building was abuzz with the news that Bulganin himself had spent New Year's Eve in the Rostropoviches' apartment. What important people we were! And how lucky it was that we were living in that building! The upshot of all this chatter was that the following day we had visitors from the Moscow Soviet and were handed, almost on a silver platter, a permit for our apartment. They congratulated us on our new home, and added: 'Don't worry about another thing. If there's anything you need, call the Moscow Soviet right away. Everything will be at your service.'

When I think back, I wonder what would have happened to me if I had not been sent to Prague but had gone directly to Belgrade with the government delegation. Slava's and my paths would probably not have crossed, and if not, there is no way of knowing what turn my fate would have taken. I might have reacted very differently to the courtship of the Soviet monarch. Like Marina Mniszek,* I might have sat as an impostor-tsarina 'on the throne of the Muscovite tsars.' Though the lot of impostors has long been known to all, the temptation has always been great!

---

* The Polish wife of the impostor Dmitri, who was tsar for a few months in 1605 after the death of Boris Godunov.

NINE

Nineteen fifty-six was a year of firsts. Though I was pregnant, I went on tour to East Germany, where I sang in *Fidelio* and *Eugene Onegin*. Upon my return to Moscow, I was awarded my first title – Honored Artist of the Russian Republic. And I made my first operatic recording, *Eugene Onegin*, with Boris Khaikin, a conductor from the Bolshoi, and the singers Evgeny Belov (Onegin) and Sergei Lemeshev (Lensky).

In the Soviet Union, a country of 270 million inhabitants, with forty-six permanent opera theaters and thousands of opera singers, there is only one recording company, Melodiya, and only once in twenty years does it produce a new recording of any given opera. The first and (at the time) only recording of *Onegin* made in Russia – the one that kindled my love for singing as a little girl – had been done in 1936, with Kruglikova singing Tatyana, Nortsov as Onegin, and Kozlovsky as Lensky. The next was my 1956 recording. How many Tatyanas, Lenskys, and Onegins vanished into thin air during the two preceding decades! And how many more will fade into oblivion until a new recording of the opera is finally made!

Singers in the provincial theaters never make recordings and have no illusions in that regard. Since an opera is recorded only once in twenty or twenty-five years, it stands to reason that it will be recorded at the Bolshoi, where the best voices in the Soviet Union are gathered. But even at the Bolshoi not every singer gets a chance, as there are several qualified soloists for each part. At one time, for instance, there were a number of basses in the theater, all noted for their interpretations of Boris Godunov, Khovansky, and Mephistopheles: Pirogov, Reizen, Ognivtsev, Ivan Petrov, and a few younger ones besides. Naturally, all soloists vie for what may be their one opportunity to record a part. The things that go on in the theater when a new record is planned or rumored! Anonymous letters, intrigues, denunciations, complaints to the Ministry of Culture and the Central Committee of the Party – anything to get on a record. For months the singers don't greet or talk to one another, and some become so overwrought that they develop heart conditions.

And it's not a question of money. For an entire opera a singer may earn 500 or 600 rubles at the most, and Soviet performing artists are not paid royalties on sales. The recording of an opera is done bit by bit, phrase by individual phrase, and often takes years. Before the agonising process is over, someone is liable to lose his voice, another may even die. In the free world, where there are many competing record companies, singers do not encounter these problems, and God forbid they ever will! Can one imagine that a recording of *Aïda* in America by a Renata Tebaldi would have prevented a Maria Callas from ever recording it? Or that a Mario Del Monaco would have to wait twenty-five years to record *Otello* simply because someone else had already done it?

When I began to record *Eugene Onegin*, all of the other women in the theater took up arms against me, and they had every right. I understood their predicament and their resentment, but I couldn't very well refuse the recording, because I might never have had another chance. (And I wouldn't have, if the Bolshoi had not gone to Paris in 1968, where EMI recorded *Onegin* in only four days. But that was a special case: the state was paid for our work in foreign currency.) So, although I was eight months pregnant, with my unborn daughter kicking me in the sides like a soccer player, and my huge belly resting on the music stand, I finished the recording and couldn't conceal my happiness. Sergei Lemeshev, by then fifty-four and for decades the most famous Russian tenor, rejoiced like a child that he had finally had the opportunity to record his favorite role. How fortunate for future generations of singers and the listening public that this outstanding singer has left his unsurpassed interpretation of Lensky to posterity.

It is tragic, in our age of highly developed technology, that so many fine voices from the Bolshoi and the operas of Kiev, Riga,

GALINA

187

Tallinn, Leningrad, Sverdlovsk, and Novosibirsk have disappeared without a trace, unheard of abroad and forgotten in their own country. The state organisations justify the limited production of records by claiming a lack of demand for them. A lack of demand? But what about the forty-six opera houses? Who goes to them? Very few people in fact. It must be admitted that even for an art form as popular as opera, we no longer have an audience. I'm not talking about individual devotees of singing, but about a general public which ought to be filling the nation's opera houses daily.

In the large provincial cities such as Petrozavodsk, Novosibirsk, Chelyabinsk, Donetsk, Voronezh, Kazan, and Saratov there are year-round opera and drama theaters with permanent companies, symphony orchestras, conservatories, and hundreds of music schools. All this costs a tremendous amount of money, and is maintained at government expense; that is, out of the pockets of the whole population. Does the sheer abundance of musical and theatrical institutions indicate that the material and cultural level of the people is high? Not at all. The concert halls in the provincial cities are usually empty, unless a celebrity from the capital is performing. And at the opera houses, there are almost always more people on stage than in the audience. Since there is no regular public on a sufficient cultural level, with the means and the spiritual need to attend concerts or operas, there is no necessity for such a great number of symphony orchestras, opera houses, and theaters in the country. But the government cares only about the statistics: the number of theaters there were before the Revolution, and the number there are now.

Who were those people who went to the opera before, who understood and loved it, for whom our great composers of the past created their works? They were the intelligentsia, the students – simply the educated people of society. You didn't have to be a distinguished noble to love music. What happened? Why has the public abandoned the opera houses? Our Soviet intelligentsia – the doctors, teachers, and engineers – are the lowest-paid people in the country. Their salary is less than that of the average worker. So the people who have a need for art do not have the means to satisfy it.

But that's not all. After an exhausting day's work caring for the sick or teaching school, a woman must hurry to the store where she shoves her way through the lines for several hours just to buy the barest necessities. On the way home with her heavy bag of rotten potatoes, cabbage, and groats, she is trampled in the bus or subway. After trying to concoct a meal she feeds the family, baths the children, washes the clothes, does the sewing, picks up around the house, and then, half-dead from fatigue, collapses into bed at one o'clock in the morning. At seven she's up again, and so on throughout her life.

Theater? She can barely drag herself home at night. That's what's become of the very public for which opera could fill a spiritual void. Nonetheless, the tickets to the Bolshoi are always sold out. The long lines at the box office are made up of people in Moscow on business, whose primary goal is to get to the Bolshoi and Lenin's Tomb, so that they can tell the folks back home that they've been there. Many have never been to the opera before and have no interest in it. They'll buy tickets for any opera on the principle 'take what you can get' – though even these inexperienced out-of-towners wouldn't be willing to pay for operas such as Khrennikov's *Mother*, Muradeli's *October*, or Kholminov's *An Optimistic Tragedy* if these 'masterpieces' were not palmed off on them in 'package deals' with tickets to crowdpleasers like *Aïda*, *The Queen of Spades*, *Tosca*, or ballet performances. People may have no alternative but to buy tickets for that rubbish; they don't have to attend them, however, and often throw the tickets away rather than sit through those insufferable Agitprop performances, watching the unfortunate singers strain to stuff them with that over-chewed cud. This system of piggybacking tickets is used at all theaters.

The swarms of out-of-towners besieging the box offices daily have gradually pushed the Muscovites out of the Bolshoi. Fed up with long ticket lines and with the impossibility of going to the theater when they please, the Muscovites have ceased regarding the theater as their own – as a place where they might run into friends and acquaintances – and they have gotten used to doing without it. The ones that do go usually attend premieres, or performances featuring the theater's one or two outstanding artists or perhaps a singer from abroad. But these are rare occurrences in the course of a season; even those diehards cannot be considered a regular opera public. And foreigners prefer the ballet to the opera.

'Collective trips' to the Bolshoi are frequently organised for office personnel, factory workers, and deputies to congresses of the Supreme Soviet. The cultural level of these chance visitors to the theater tends to be rather low. From their response, one cannot judge either the quality of the production or the merits of the singers, and the artists must rely on their own feelings and the reactions of friends in the audience. Once, back in the days of Stalin, a congress of distinguished kolkhoz women was held. In the morning, Stalin pinned decorations on their mighty bosoms, and in the evening they were all sitting in the first rows of the Bolshoi, listening to an opera. The most outstanding woman of all was seated directly behind Samosud, who was conducting that evening. For a few minutes she put up with it. Then she stood up abruptly, walked to the edge of the orchestra pit, slapped Samosud on the shoulder with her meaty hand, and lectured him loudly. 'Why are you waving your arms around like a windmill? Get out of the way! You're blocking my view!'

Hundreds of thousands of tourists from all over the country pass through Moscow every day. If each of them comes to the Bolshoi only once in his life, full houses would be guaranteed forever. The constant turnover in the public is a great misfortune for the theater – there's no need to be concerned with restaging old productions, nor with the quality of new Soviet operas. And for a public that knows nothing about theater, the individuality of a given artist has no meaning.

The typical visitor, harried from a whole day of business meetings and shopping for gifts, his briefcase bulging with oranges and sausages from some ministry's snack bar (in Moscow all men carry briefcases!), finally ends up at the Bolshoi in the evening. There he can settle comfortably in an armchair, take off his shoes, and gaze in wonder at the gilded loges, the gold curtain embroidered with hammers and sickles, the huge chandelier hanging from the ceiling, and the sumptuous costumes and sets. Soon, after taking stock of all the family errands he has run, he falls soundly asleep to the soothing strains of the music.

I would often observe the audience as I sat watching a performance in a box seat. What vacuous faces! They have no interest in what is happening on stage, don't applaud the singers, and can't distinguish one conductor from another. Something had to be done to rouse that impassive crowd and involve it in the performance. Unless everything was greatly overemphasised, the audience wouldn't understand. And to communicate the meaning of the operas, the words had to be given precedence over the music. Hence the excessive emotions, the exaggeration of words and gestures, the forced voices that have come to characterise Soviet opera. When Soviet singers perform abroad, they have often criticised for their overacting, the shrillness of their voices, and a lack of vocal blending and musical phrasing in their singing. But that is our style, the style of the Soviet theater. It is no accident that the music of Vivaldi, Handel, and Haydn is so rarely performed in Russia, and that Mozart's operas are not staged. In my twenty-three years at the Bolshoi, the only Mozart opera to be produced was *The Marriage of Figaro*. Such pure music simply cannot be enjoyed or appreciated in an atmosphere where nerves are strained to the breaking point and Party pronouncements are running through the mind.

For other reasons, sacred music is also rarely performed. It is beyond belief that Beethoven's *Missa Solemnis*, that extraordinary work, has never been played in Russia. After singing it at the Edinburgh Festival with Lorin Maazel in 1962, I wanted to sing it in Moscow, and I mentioned the idea to Alexander Sveshnikov, for many years the director of the USSR State Chorus. He told me that his chorus had never sung it. When the conductor Igor Markevitch came to Russia on tour, he wanted to conduct Haydn's *The Creation*, and asked me to take part in the concert. I advised him first to talk with Ekaterina Furtseva, the minister of culture.

'But why?' he asked with surprise.

'Just talk with her, and you'll see.'

He did, in fact, go to see her, and she gave her consent, but on condition that the text be revised so that there was no mention of God! *The Creation* according to Marx!

The untheatrical atmosphere in the hall carries over into intermissions. The people in the audience do not mingle or exchange impressions. One can see that they are chance visitors who feel awkward and ill-at-ease. Some head for the theater café to kill time. Others, alone or in pairs, silently wander about the lobby. The Bolshoi has about 2,000 seats; but even when every one of them is filled, the performers sing primarily for a few dozen people: for those in the director's box; for colleague rivals; for relatives; and for the fans that every famous artist has. In Russia, fans are called 'admirers,' so I shall refer to them as such. If during intermission you see a group of people engaged in lively talk and arguing about the production, you can be sure they are admirers.

Since an opera singer remains with one theater throughout his life, his admirers can accompany him from the beginning to the end of his career. They enter into his life, grow old with him, and walk behind his coffin. They are very dear to the artist, because they have come into his world through his art. He needs them. And often a singer finds in them even more feeling for, and understanding of, his artistry than he finds in his own family. I had many admirers who stood by me from the very outset of my career at the Bolshoi. And it was they, unafraid of being recognised by the KGB agents, who came to see me off at the airport when I was leaving Russia. It was they, and not a single one of the colleagues with whom I had sung on the same stage for a quarter century.

In addition to young people, my admirers included quite a few middle-aged men and women who had been coming to my performances for years. Some of them became my friends, and in time I learned much about their lives. For the most part, they were teachers, laboratory assistants, engineers, and technicians – in a word, our Soviet intelligentsia. Unmarried and childless, they lived in communal apartments on 90 to 120 rubles a month. Their love of opera was their one escape from an otherwise grim existence. It gave their lives meaning. At the theater, they could go off into another world for a few hours, and they looked forward to each performance as though it were a holiday.

Admirers deeply experience an artist's troubles and joys, and after a successful performance, they are the happiest people on earth. At work the next day, they might even forget the drabness and frightful monotony of their lives, for they have their memories and their dreams. But on a meager 90 rubles a month one has to eat, pay rent, and buy medicine. There are books one would like to have, and a woman enjoys going to the hairdresser from time to time. She needs to buy shoes and a dress at least once every two years. A pair of shoes, though, costs fifty to sixty rubles, a pound of coffee twenty. Yet admirers are willing to go without such things just to buy a ticket to the theater. And they prepare for a performance no less than the artist himself. They telephone one another to ask about the artist's health. If he isn't well, they suffer more than he. For him it simply means he won't be singing, but for them it's a tragedy.

I had admirers who came to my performances from other cities. There were times when I wasn't feeling well and didn't want to sing, but if I knew that one of my admirers had flown to Moscow that day, having spent her last kopeck on a plane ticket, and would skip dinner to buy flowers for me, I would crawl out of bed, force myself to get ready, and go and do the performance for her. Had it not been for such admirers, the Bolshoi would have been a dead place. They made up our genuine public. They knew the singers, they knew the repertory, and wouldn't miss a single performance of their favorite artist. They empathised completely with everything that happened on stage. They applauded their favorite singers with such enthusiasm that the people sitting next to them were caught up in it, and they tried to create the atmosphere that an artist needs – that inspires him to perform. If a few dozen admirers don't come to a performance, it will not be a success, not even for leading soloists. Opera singers and ballet dancers alike know this very well, and they make sure to reserve tickets at the box office for their admirers.

Tenors' admirers are a special breed. I remember Sergei Lemeshev singing in *Fra Diavolo* when he was about sixty. The part was very high, and he sometimes had trouble with the top notes – one could tell by looking not at the stage but at the tense faces of his admirers in the audience. They knew all the dangerous places in the arias, and if they sensed the least lack of confidence as Lemeshev approached the top notes they would begin to shout 'Bravo!' in advance, covering him just in case he fluffed. It was essential to them that he continue to perform. They idolised him and, as best they could, bolstered his waning faith in his own strength, trying to prolong his career.

In contrast to the Bolshoi, at concerts in the Great Hall of the Moscow Conservatory you always encounter the same crowd, Muscovites all. Half of them are well-educated older women who come directly from work, lugging their grocery bags. For the most part they are lonely souls without families, and music plays a very important role in their lives. The other half is made up of professionals: instrumentalists, singers, students, and teachers from the conservatory and music schools. This is the Moscow public remembered so warmly by all Western artists who have visited the Soviet capital on tour.

TEN

The Twentieth Party Congress opened in February 1956. No one was preparing for anything new; everyone expected the same empty blather. But suddenly the rumors shot through Moscow like a spasm: Stalin's cult of personality . . . the mass shooting of innocent people . . . the annihilation of the armed forces' top echelon . . . torture . . . denunciations. Khrushchev made his 'secret speech' to a congress of amazed delegates. They were amazed not by the information itself – they had known it all already – but by the fact that for the first time in Soviet history they were hearing truth from the Party rostrum.

The rumors began to spread, acquiring monstrous detail as they went. Stalin was a hangman . . . Stalin was a coward . . . Stalin was a criminal . . . Stalin was a maniac . . . Astounded by the opportunity of saying aloud things that they had earlier been afraid even to contemplate, people stopped in the bold light of day to talk – without noticing that they were not doing the most natural and most important thing: holding their own government to account. The cult of personality! But who had created it? The members of the Politburo, what had *they* done during the years of the cult? And Comrade Nikita Khrushchev? They had been the first to sing Stalin's praises, to flatter and glorify him – to dance for him at his nocturnal drinking bouts, this one the *lezghinka* and that one the *hopak*.

The report provoked a feeling of national humiliation. Would we finally awake from our spiritual somnolence? From the apathy that had brought us to accept the lies meekly?

Although Khruschchev had exposed the perversions of the communist regime, he concluded his report with the following peroration:

We cannot allow this matter to go beyond the limits of Party
circles – in particular, to get into the press. We must keep
within limits. We must not furnish weapons to our enemies.
We must not wash our dirty linen before their eyes.

Lord! What kind of a soul thinks in such terms? The destruction, the shooting, the savagery – all that is only 'dirty linen'! So
we'll wash it on the sly, among ourselves, and appear before the
public in white, bearing palm branches like peacemaking angels!

Of course nothing appeared in the press, but even though
Khrushchev had implored his cronies to keep quiet, all of
Moscow knew everything within a few days. It would seem that
the people were obliged to act – to express their indignation. But
no: the 'wrath of the people' was never openly manifested in any
way. Russians merely began talking aloud about things that many
of them had known for a long time, and others had surmised.
Typed copies of Khrushchev's speech were passed from hand to
hand, and the public was confused, perplexed. Before, there had
at least been a loophole – a person could hide behind his
ignorance. But now every Soviet citizen, in failing to call the
criminal government to account, had become an accomplice. It
seemed to me that it was with this very aim in mind that
Khrushchev – a clever, cunning Russian peasant – had made that
report: to throttle a whole nation with a single rope.

The revelations of those years made me feel worthless,
morally inferior. What kind of a people were we? Were we really
devoid of any sense of dignity or honor? Were we so crushed by
primal fears that we allowed such things to be done to us? No, the
Russian people are not cowards. During the war, unarmed
Russian soldiers attacked although death was a certainty – they
were prepared to die defending their country. But who wants to
die for nothing? Somewhere in a cellar, secretly humiliated, and
tortured by one's own hangmen-compatriots? In the name of
what? Though you scream, no one will hear. No, that isn't fear,
it is something far worse: it is utter hopelessness. With
Khrushchev's speech, I got my first clear glimpse of the pathological falsehoods of the entire past, present, and future in the
land of the Soviets.

Two months after the Twentieth Congress, the first – and so far as I know, the only – person who responded to it as the situation demanded was the aged general secretary of the Writers' Union, Alexander Fadeyev, whom Khrushchev called in his report 'a Stalinist agent who had personally denounced writers to me.' Many lives were on Fadeyev's conscience. He had acted, however, not out of self-interest but because he had regarded it as his duty. When his idol was cast from his pedestal, and when the shadows of former human beings filed out of the prison cells, Fadeyev put a bullet through his own head.

My father also came back from prison, and although he had served for almost ten years, he remained a confirmed communist. He traveled to Moscow to try to regain membership in the Party, but stopped first at the Bolshoi's personnel department and denounced me. He reported that I had withheld the fact that he had been arrested under Article 58, that I had known it all along. How could he reconcile such base behavior with the 'purity' of his ideas as a confirmed Leninist? Of course he hoped that I would be kicked out of the Bolshoi. But Papa had miscalculated: times had changed. He died of lung cancer two years later, one more moral monster spawned and destroyed by the Soviet regime.

The Bolshoi had a remarkable dramatic tenor, Georgi Mikhailovich Nelepp, an artist of impeccable taste, with a beautiful, youthfully resonant voice. I have yet to hear a better Hermann in *The Queen of Spades*. When I first joined the Bolshoi we worked on *Fidelio* together; that time ranks among the best memories of my career. Before coming to the Bolshoi, Nelepp had been with the Kirov Opera in Leningrad for many years. He was a Party member, a recipient of all the highest awards and titles, had won the Stalin Prize several times, and enjoyed great prestige, the respect of his colleagues, and the love of the public. His was a hobby unusual for a man: he did fine embroidery on towels and men's shirts – it calmed his nerves.

One morning I was waiting in the director's box for Nikandr Khanayev, who was director of the opera company at the time. On stage they were rehearsing Rimsky-Korsakov's *Sadko* with the orchestra, and Nelepp was singing the lead role. Khanayev was late, and I impatiently paced the landing near the box anxious to get my meeting over with so that I could watch the rehearsal. One floor below, by the cloakroom, a shabby, middle-aged woman sat quietly. Khanayev came in from the street and as he was being helped out of his coat, he was told, 'Nikandr Sergeyevich, the woman over there has asked that Georgi Mikhailovich (Nelepp] be called out of rehearsal. She's been sitting there a long time, and I don't know what to do.'

The woman addressed Khanayev directly: 'I have urgent business with Nelepp. I came to Moscow just today. I beg you. Please summon him.'

'And what might your relationship to him be?'

'He doesn't know me, but I have an important message for him from an acquaintance.'

I stood watching from above, and Khanayev called out to me, 'Galya, tell the secretary to call Nelepp off stage if he isn't busy.'

I did as he asked, returned to my perch on the landing, and watched as the scene below was played out: Georgi Mikhailovich Nelepp, People's Artist of the USSR, laureate of the Stalin Prize, the well-groomed, famous tenor of the Bolshoi, descended the red-carpeted stairs slowly and with dignity, like a lord. The woman rose to her feet as he approached.

'How do you do,' he said.

She only stared silently.

'You wanted to see me?'

Suddenly she opened her mouth and spat in his face. 'Take that, you reptile! You ruined my husband! You ruined my family! Only I survive to spit in your face! Damn you!' She spun around and staggered out the door.

Nelepp went white as chalk. Khanayev, embarrassed, walked past him and up the stairs. The usher didn't know which way to look, and I dodged quickly into the *avant-loge*.

Khanayev called me into his office. I was shaking like a leaf, and couldn't say a word. 'Take my word for it,' Khanayev told me, 'we haven't seen anything yet. In his day at the Leningrad Theater, Nelepp ruined a lot of people. It doesn't seem likely, does it? But that's just it. One look at him, and you'd trust him.'

Nelepp soon died of a heart attack. He must have been fifty-two, no more.

The mood of those years is best described by Solzhenitsyn in *Cancer Ward*. When a middle-level Party worker responsible for many denunciations learns that the authorities are beginning to release falsely convicted people from prison, he is sincerely astonished, even shaken. 'Why are they letting them out? They've been imprisoned for years, they're used to it . . . And what will happen to us? Why didn't they think of us? After all, we were carrying out the will of the Party! (Just as the Nazis carried out the will of their party.)

That was one part of the population, and not a small one. But a larger part was the one made up of those who had been rehabilitated. The era of the late Rehabilitance!* Into the capital from all parts of the country streamed the exhausted, the downtrodden – those who had survived the Soviet concentration camps. They were easily recognisable on every street corner – their miserable clothes, their vacant, emaciated faces. Come to Moscow in search of justice, they spent months haunting the thresholds of the Party Central Committee, the USSR Supreme Soviet, and the Office of the General Prosecutor, some of them seeking restoration to the Party and others documents certifying their rehabilitation. Those scraps of paper officially informed the half-dead with cynical simplicity that they had been falsely convicted. That now, after ten or twenty years in prison, and in the absence of a corpus delicti, they had been released and pardoned. By their irresponsibility – their indifference toward human life – those wretched scraps of paper were reminders that no amount of human sacrifice would change the bestial character of the Soviet regime. The atrocity of the imprisonment was only replaced by the travesty of the 'rehabilitation.'

As ever, Stalin's comrades-in-arms sat it out behind the walls of the Kremlin. None of them was put on trial, and their faces continued to adorn the nation's walls, brazenly looking out at the rehabilitated ones and the rest of the brainwashed population. Historians set about rewriting the history of the Communist

* A coinage by the author.

Party and the history of the Great Patriotic War as well. With the blessing of the loyal comrades-in-arms, the 'immortal' works of the former beloved leader were shredded, and his name deleted from all the pages of Soviet literature – a task at which poets and writers labored mightily and untiringly. Overnight, they took away from the dead usurper the cities he had taken as his own – cities that had borne his name for decades. In general, the history of the Soviet government was being recut and patched like an old, ragged pair of pants, and both the dead man and his memory were handed over to the people for reprisals. Bonfires blazed all over the country, burning any and all pictures of Stalin. Heads were hacked off sculptures of the Leader and Teacher of All Times and All Peoples – this took quite a bit of time, since there was not a single factory, school, theater, university, street, square, or park in the country that was not adorned by a likeness of the General Secretary of the Communist Party. And now, in a marvelous display of boldness and heroism, the whole nation could tie a rope to his feet, pull him down from his pedestal, and execute him, pounding the mute, dead mass to their heart's desire.

In early March of 1956, Slava went on his first tour to England and I stayed home, waiting from one day to the next for the birth of the baby. He called me from London every day; and from far off, through the noise of the line, his desperate shouts came to me. 'Don't you dare give birth without me! Wait! I'll be flying back in only a few days.'

'Do you know what you're saying? As if it depended on me!'

'It does! You can do anything if you put your mind to it. Give me your word that you'll wait for me.'

'What are you babbling? How can I give you my word?'

'Just lie there and don't move. My mother carried me for ten months – maybe that's why I'm so gifted and intelligent! Don't read scary books . . . Read Shakespeare's sonnets, hear? And look only at beautiful things.'

'But where will I see beautiful things? I never go out.'

'And so you shouldn't. Look in the mirror, and you'll see something beautiful.'

So he sat in London and commanded the parade.

And indeed, why should I give birth in his absence, going through the fear and agitation alone? He had gone abroad, garnered success and a great many new impressions, and would he now come home to a baby ready and waiting? No! Let my husband stand at my side, worry, even suffer a little along with me. Not only would I not move, I wouldn't even breathe. I would wait. On the evening of March 17 he returned, elated by his tour, happy and proud that the distaff side had carried out all his orders. His wife, hardly stirring, was sitting in an armchair waiting for her sovereign. And then, as marvelous things appear from an illusionist's magic box, so out of Slava's trunk came flying fantastic silks, shawls, perfumes, and other incredibly beautiful things. Finally, a gorgeous fur coat flew out and landed on my lap.

I could only gasp, unable to say a word. But Slava beamed, and kept pacing around and explaining: 'This will go with your eyes . . . You can have a dress for concerts made out of that . . . As soon as I saw *that*, it was clear that it was especially for you. See how good it is that you waited for me? I'm always right. Now you'll be in a good mood, and it'll be easier for you to give birth. As soon as the pain gets unbearable, just remember some beautiful dress, and it will all pass.'

He was simply bursting with pride and satisfaction that he was such a remarkable, wealthy husband who could offer me beautiful things the likes of which no other singer at the Bolshoi had. But I knew that my 'wealthy' husband – as they were already saying in the English newspapers, 'the great Rostropovich' – had probably not eaten much of anything during the two weeks of his tour so that he could buy me all those gifts. All he got from his concerts was eighty pounds per concert: the rest of his earnings had been turned over to the Soviet Embassy.

Long after midnight, when the travel-weary Slava was already sleeping soundly, I still couldn't close my eyes. First I would imagine the marvelous dresses that could be made out of those divine silks, then how I would put on my new fur coat to go to the theater . . . But all of a sudden my long-awaited child let me know, sharply and unequivocally, that it wanted to make its appearance into the world. My first thought was to awaken Slava right away and go to the hospital. But when I remembered that my first labor had lasted two long days on a table in the maternity ward, I decided to wait and stay at home as long as possible.

Again, a sharp labor pain. But no, that was only the beginning. It could last for many hours yet . . . No, it would still be a while . . . Tensely listening to, and taking part in, every movement of the life flailing about within me, I felt as if I were being filled gradually with a gigantic force that would propel me toward a great moment.

Finally, by five o'clock in the morning, it was clear that I had to awaken my husband right away. Trying not to moan, I shook him gently by the shoulder.

'Slava.'

'Mmmmm.'

'Slava.'

'Aaaa . . .' He was tired, and wouldn't wake up.

Then I whispered to him, 'Slava, I think I'm about to give birth.'

How quickly he leaped out of bed! He rushed about, waking everyone up. 'Mama! Rimma! Get up, all of you! Galya is having the baby!'

I was right on his heels. 'But I'm not having the baby yet! Don't shout so everybody in the building can hear you! It's just time to go to the hospital. O-oh-o-oh!'

He had forgotten all the telephone numbers for taxis, he had mislaid his trousers, and his fingers were all thumbs. In short, he was a man.

He ran from room to room, wailing at me, 'Don't walk fast! Don't jerk yourself around. Don't bend down – we'll dress you . . .'

'Now, Slava, don't get all worked up! There's still time. Oh!'

'Rimma, dress her right away – let's get her into the taxi immediately!'

'Never mind, the pain's gone. Don't rush me – I can't think straight myself.'

I saw my mother-in-law, with her loose, flowing white hair,

going silently around the apartment like a specter, opening all the doors and the drawers of the closets, buffet, and bureau.

'What are you doing, Sofia Nikolayevna?'

'Quiet, Galya, this is absolutely necessary. Everything must be wide open so it will be easier for you to give birth.'

Although I was in misery, I put on my new fur coat (to my husband's horror) and, still writhing in pain, went into our room to admire myself in the mirror.

'But you've gone out of your mind! How can you do that?'

'Well, I can! I've never had anything like it . . . Oh! . . .'

'Mama, this is too much! Tell her we're going right now!'

I gritted my teeth all the way and tried not to moan, seeing that my pale husband was faint with fear that I might give birth right there in the taxi.

At the Pirogov Hospital a bed was ready for me in advance; they were waiting for me. It was not like ten years before in Leningrad when the scrawny girl who had barely survived the blockade sat in a hospital corridor for almost twenty hours demanding to be admitted. Now they were admitting Galina Pavlovna Vishnevskaya, a soloist with the Bolshoi Theater, and everyone did his best to fuss over me.

On March 18, 1956, at one in the afternoon, my daughter was born.

The birth of a much-desired baby! My daughter struck me as the very epitome of beauty. And in fact she was amazingly beautiful, perfectly proportioned and with pure white skin. Within five minutes she was staring at me attentively, not with the cloudy eyes of the newborn, but with a clear, meaningful look. She seemed to want to tell me something terribly important. Plainly, Slava's nightly readings of Shakespeare had not been wasted. Even the midwife said to me, 'I must say, Galina Pavlovna, that of all the babies I have brought into this world, never before have I seen one like this.'

I wanted to call her Ekaterina, but Slava pleaded, 'I beg you not to call her that. There are serious technical reasons: you know I can't pronounce the letter *r* clearly. She's bound to tease me. Let's call her Olga.'

A week later I descended the steps of the hospital. A nurse-

maid carrying my treasure walked ahead of me, and Slava, Sofia
Nikolayevna, Veronica, and friends waited below.

Soviet hospitals do not allow mothers of newborns to have
visitors, and so Slava was seeing his daughter for the first time.
He grabbed her, clumsily shifted the little bundle in his long arms,
and dug his fingers in, afraid of dropping her. He was so excited
that he lost his hat and gloves somewhere along the way. The
sight of that tiny being threw him into paroxysms of ecstasy.
Laughing – almost crying – he repeated, 'It's a miracle! Simply a
miracle! Mama, look how beautiful she is! Look, all of you! Isn't
she the most beautiful thing you've ever seen?'

And Sofia Nikolayevna, looking over her first granddaughter,
nodded her head in satisfaction and pride. 'Oh yes, she takes after
our family. Now, don't be offended, Galya, but she doesn't look
like you one bit. Her lips are definitely from our side. We all have
that kind.'

And Veronica echoed her: 'Slavka, she has your nose and
eyes. Oh yes, she's pretty. She's a Rostropovich.'

'Well,' I sniffed, 'you've divided everything up among
yourselves. But, don't forget, it was I who had her. Have you
perhaps left a little something for me?'

And all of them smiled blissfully over 'our family' who, sweetly
smacking her tiny lips, rested happily in Slava's arms.

Two weeks later my husband left on his first tour of America.

I was even glad to see him go, hoping that during the two
months of his absence it would be easier to adapt to the new daily
routine that had descended upon us with the appearance of Olga.
Perhaps we might put our domestic life in some order once again.
Rimma worked like a factory from morning till night. In the
morning she stood in line for hours on end to get food; and when
she came back, she cleaned the apartment and made dinner at the
same time. She really had to rack her brains to come up with a
recipe for a meager piece of meat that had to be put through the
grinder three times before anyone could chew it; or for a stringy,
bony chicken that stubbornly resisted being transformed into
something edible.

But the inventiveness of Soviet woman knows no bounds. To
this day no one has arrived at a method for stewing a Soviet

chicken until it is tender without producing a miserable, charred corpse, but Rimma had her own method – ingenious in its simplicity. She would boil the chicken in a pot, throw in a glass stopper from a carafe, and declare that it helped. Although I secretly felt – with jaws numb from chewing – that there was no difference whatsoever, I refused to deprive her and myself of our illusion of victory over the stubborn stringy fowl. And when I myself boiled one of those unfortunate chickens that had obviously led a hard life, I too would toss a big glass stopper into the pot. If to that rich assembly you add potatoes, cabbage, and pickles, you have the full assortment of groceries from which a heroic Soviet woman must, every day of her life, prepare a meal for her family.

In the morning, Rimma would punctually appear in the door of my room and gloomily put forward the challenge, 'What are we going to have today?'

And every time, I trembled with the premonition of an impending, insoluble conflict worthy of Shakespearean tragedy. There was not another question in my life before which I remained so utterly silent, before which I so hopelessly lost heart. Realising that all human passions were as nothing when compared to Eternity, I would be reduced to dust, paralysed by agonising hesitation, like Hamlet. 'To eat, or not to eat?' And if yes, *what*?

A spasm of effort, and a few wretched ideas would spin like millstones, slowly, heavily, carrying me off to other spheres . . .

'Did you hear what I asked?'

A sick feeling in the pit of my stomach. I would descend to this earth and face implacable Fate standing there in the doorway. With superhuman will I would try to stir up my imagination. In vain.

'That's it, that's it! Come back to reality . . . this is no stage fantasy!'

Dully, I would begin with a few uninspired suggestions.

'*What?* Fish? Ha, ha! And where do you propose I find it? Spring chicken? Some sense of humor! Have you been on the moon, or something? When was it ever in the stores? Vegetables? Do you realise what you're saying? Have you forgotten that there's nothing but cabbage and potatoes? A person can't talk seriously with you. I'll ask you again: What are we going to have today?'

When she was finally sure that I was completely aware of my utter uselessness, she would savor my impotence a second longer, straighten her big shoulders like a commander on whom the outcome of the battle depends, and take upon herself full responsibility for the lives entrusted to her. Condescendingly, she would fling out: 'All right, then. It's impossible to get anything out of you! I'll think up something myself.' Full of noble valor and unsparing with her own sacrifices, she would throw herself into an attack on the stores.

If the campaign was successful, she would return home and triumphantly march into the kitchen. Upon hearing Delilah's aria 'My Heart at Thy Sweet Voice,' I would know that she had brought back trophies from the field of battle. But more often, she would return and go silently and gloomily into the kitchen, slamming the door behind her. In the ominous wordlessness that followed, only the rattling of saucepans and the breaking of plates would warn me that it would be better if no one entered that domain.

Now, in addition to all the household chores, she was burdened with the daily washing of the baby's diapers. In those days there were no washing machines available, and she hand-washed the baby's things, dozens of which would accumulate within twenty-four hours. Then she would boil them in a cauldron on the stove, dry them, and iron them. Laundry hung on cords in the kitchen, the hallway, the bathroom, and on all the radiators in the rooms. New buildings equipped with laundry drying facilities had not been built yet, and we had never heard of dryers. So far as I know, the Soviet Union still doesn't have them, and you can be sure disposable diapers will be a long time coming.

From morning till night Rimma tore through the apartment like a meteor, singing arias, doing first one thing, then another, and leaving broken articles in her wake. When it seemed she was about to collapse from fatigue at any moment and a welcome peace was at hand, she would present herself before me and ask, 'What else is there to do?'

'Leave me alone, and sit down for God's sake. Stop this commotion in front of me.'

'But I can't just sit there doing nothing. Give me Olga, *I'll* take care of her.'

When I wouldn't hand the baby over to her, her feelings would be hurt. But I had lost a baby son when I was just a girl, and I couldn't bring myself to leave my daughter with anyone, nor could I allow anyone to come near her. I breast-fed her for eight months. I would spend whole days diapering her, changing her clothes, feeding her, bathing her. And in between I would rush to the piano; I had to start vocalising after three months of silence. I was so exhausted that by evening I would not be able to straighten my back. All I wanted was to lie in bed and sleep straight through until nine in the morning. My daughter slept well during the day, and I sometimes even had to wake her to feed her. But as soon as midnight arrived she would announce that event with an imperious squawl – with the accuracy of the clock in the Kremlin tower – and demand that I pick her up. I would take her and pace the room with her for hours. Or I would sit on the bed, rocking her quietly, until she finally calmed down and dozed off. But no sooner had I myself fallen asleep than I would hear a wailing and puffing, which was her way of letting me know that her diapers had to be changed in a hurry. And so it went, on and on throughout the night. But when my adored daughter was four months old, I put her crib in the nursery. And now the one who slept next to her was Rimma, and it was Rimma who would be awakened punctually at midnight.

Had it not been for Rimma, with her superhuman physical endurance and her devotion, I would have been faced with a simple choice: the opera or a family. It is virtually impossible to combine a career as an opera singer with the endless problems of raising children and maintaining a home. It is the rare woman singer at the Bolshoi who has even so much as one child.

Rostropovich finally came back from America, stunned by the scope of that country's cultural life, its splendid symphony orchestras and concert halls. He was amazed by the number of daily newspapers and the fact that they ran to several dozen pages, whereas our central paper, *Pravda*, consisted of a meager four pages – six at the most. The Sunday edition of *The New York Times*, he marveled, weighed several pounds. He was astounded at the efficiency of the press, which could cover all the events in that society's teeming life, and he never ceased to wonder at the daily feats of the morning papers, which could print reviews of a concert given only the night before.

Listening to his stories, we found it hard to believe that every American family had its own automobile, sometimes two; that there was a television in every room of an American hotel, and that a viewer would have access to so many channels. (At the time, if I am not mistaken, we had only one.)

But what he talked about most of all was the wedding of Grace Kelly and Prince Rainier of Monaco, which had taken place during his tour. He showed us American newspapers full of photos, interviews, and accounts of the Cinderella turned princess. It was plain that this alliance had stirred up his imagination, and he couldn't understand why it was making no impression on me. But having spent my life playing princesses and queens, I found it quite normal for a prince to marry a beautiful actress, a Hollywood star. Some Cinderella! Whom else should he have married?

Along with such revelations, Slava had picked up some new, 'progressive' ideas in America and returned with a huge supply of powdered baby formula, plastic bottles, pacifiers, and some splendid little dresses à la princesse. He heatedly let us all know that we were behind the times. Only savages breast-fed their babies, he said. Civilised women use formula, which contains all the vitamins newborns need; in fact, it is precisely because of formula that children in American grow up healthy and strong. He was eager to demonstrate how easy it was to feed a baby that way; but we all kept a sharp eye on him, and didn't let him near Olga with his 'progressive' bottles. We took a skeptical view of this American novelty, it seemed too good to be true. The handsome boxes were put away in a closet, and I happily continued to unbutton my blouse every three hours and feed my daughter myself.

Shortly thereafter I got a call from the Leningrad film studio informing me that they planned to film the opera *Eugene Onegin*, and inviting me to take a screen test for the role of Tatyana. What could I do? I could hardly drag a three-month-old child to Leningrad on the train; she might catch a cold or be exposed to an infection.

In the morning, we called an urgent family council, and my mother-in-law took the floor. 'Listen, Galya, here's the plan. You can leave on the night train. But during the day drink as much tea as you can – by evening you'll have plenty of milk. Express it into bottles, and we'll put them in the refrigerator. Before you leave, feed Olga as usual, and go with God. Don't worry, I'll spend the night here. The baby will be fed, and you'll be back within twenty-four hours.'

They saw me off to the station, and I took the overnight train as planned. But it wasn't until the next morning at the studio as I was making up for the test that I felt the results of my mother-in-law's wise advice. The huge quantity of tea I had drunk the day before had taken this long to be converted into milk. Looking at my catastrophically swollen breasts, I wondered in horror how I would ever survive the day.

During the takes, I requested a break every hour and rushed headlong from the desk with young Tatyana's letter to a dark corner of the studio where I had discovered a sink. I would return with breasts somewhat more resembling those of a young girl. That carousel went on until late at night, when I finally boarded the overnight train to Moscow. But it had only started! I procured a few glasses from the conductor and spent the entire night filling them with milk, as if I were a prize cow. I was counting the minutes until I could walk through the door of my home where my daughter would release me from that nightmare. It seemed that I was constantly minutes away from an explosion; my skin was threatening to burst and fly into little pieces.

When I got home, I tore off my coat and sweater on my way up the stairs, and the buttons of my dress flew off in all directions. Rimma opened the apartment door, and in her arms was Olga, howling at the top of her voice.

'Hurry and give her to me! I'm dying, too!'

I put her to the breast. She took it, but spat it out immediately. I offered her the other; she scornfully refused it. Then she threw up all over me.

'Sofia Nikolayevna! Slava! What have you done to Olga?'

Little by little the story came out. The morning after my departure, Rostropovich had decided to feed our daughter himself. He demanded that she be brought to him along with a bottle of milk, and Rimma naturally did as he asked. Breast milk is thin and light blue, and during the night mine was covered with a thin film. Needless to say, it looked rather unappetising.

'What's this? Have you two gone out of your minds? You expect to feed my baby this rot?'

He grabbed both bottles and dumped everything into the sink before Sofia Nikolayevna and Rimma had time to gasp. Doomsday was approaching. Rostropovich, a can of American formula in one hand and a dictionary in the other, read the instructions on how to prepare the magic potion; how many spoonfuls of powder, how much water. Rimma screamed in a voice laced with agony that only over her dead body would he feed Olga that bourgeois poison. And Sofia Nikolayevna bellowed that she was disclaiming all responsibility if something awful were to happen to the child. Accompanying it all were the deafening yelps of hungry Olga.

But once Rostropovich had made up his mind to do something and had decided he was right, no force on earth could stop him. On measuring the amount of powder necessary to feed a three-month-old baby and dissolving it in water, he had decided that the mixture was too thin and had added just as much powder again, so that Olga would 'eat her fill and get fat,' as he said to the women clutching at the baby. One can imagine his shouts of rejoicing when, in one minute, Olga sucked up the mixture her father had prepared and, smiling blissfully, fell off to sleep.

'Well? What did I tell you, you uneducated, ignorant old women? There's how you raise children! No problems.'

And he fed her that way all day, victoriously awaiting my return from Leningrad. But during the night her stomach began to ache, and none of them could sleep a wink, she was yelling so.

And then I came home. Olga's stomach was rigid, and my head was pounding with my own predicament. We called our doctor.

When she arrived and discovered what had happened, she joined the other women in the general outcry.

Slava was so upset he didn't know where to turn. 'But she ate with such pleasure!'

'But you should have done it gradually, weaning her from the breast with only one bottle of formula a day at the beginning. You could have killed her! Since the day she was born, she has had nothing in her stomach but mother's milk. And here for a whole day you feed her something as thick as kasha.'

After a few sleepless nights, everything returned to normal, thank God!

In June we received the news from Leningrad that Vera Nikolayevna Garina had died. I couldn't go to her funeral – Olga was too small. All I could do was send a garland for her grave. Vera Nikolayevna had never heard me in an opera. But a year before her death I sang a solo concert at Leningrad's Philharmonic Hall. She sat in the first row surrounded by her pupils, and glowed with happiness and pride. Two years of studying with her had given me all the foundation I needed for the rest of my career. I never studied voice with anyone after her. That remarkable woman had made me the generous gift of a life in art – a long and beautiful life. Not once since then have I rehearsed or gone on stage without her in my thoughts.

PART THREE

ELEVEN

I have seen half this book go by without discussion of a man whose friendship cast a brilliant light over my whole life, and whose spiritual qualities captured my soul once and for all time. Dmitri Dmitriyevich Shostakovich – a titanic, deeply tragic figure in the world of art in the twentieth century. I am overwhelmed by emotion when I think of him and those twenty years of close friendship; of a time when Slava's and my life, and all our creativity, were indissolubly bound up with his.

My association with Shostakovich had a tremendous influence on me – on my musicianship as well as on my personality. Knowing him I can say, in the words of Radishchev,* 'I looked around me, and my soul was wounded by people's suffering.' I found myself witness to the tortures of a man I worshiped, before whom I bowed; and the experience forced me not only to involve myself differently in the life going on around me, but to look back and reevaluate my own childhood and youth. It was after meeting Dmitri Dmitriyevich that I, for the first time, longed to find out how Russia lived – to learn what was happening in my country. I felt driven to consider the events of the past, to realise and interpret what my people had lived through, me along with them . . .

My account in no way pretends to be a study of the life and work of Shostakovich. These are only personal impressions, and I shall write only about what he himself told me, and what I myself witnessed. But before I describe my meetings with Dmitri Dmitriyevich, I should like briefly to tell about that composer's

---

* Alexander Radishchev (1749–1802), government official under Catherine the Great and author of *A Journey from Petersburg to Moscow*, perhaps the first book to expose the oppression of the Russian peasants.

path through life, from his creative emergence as a youth to the time when I met him.

After the Revolution, many outstanding figures in the world of art who could not reconcile themselves to the injustice and inhumanity of the new regime left Russia. Among them were the composers Rachmaninov, Prokofiev, Stravinsky, and Glazunov; the writers Kuprin and Bunin; and various singers, ballet dancers, and actors.

Untrained and untalented people rushed to fill the vacancies, but soon discovered that individually their talents were insignificant, that they could never hope to fill the voids that had been left. They had to create their own organisation so as to act collectively. Such was the origin of the notorious 'Proletkult,' where dilettantes of proletarian backgrounds with Party cards in their pockets could find all kinds of support.

Unburdened with talent, and less so with culture and knowledge, the proletarian 'composers' could go no further than to produce vulgar, amateurish songs and marches. On the other hand, however, they instituted zealous programs to stifle the innovators and disembowel the classics. It was Proletkult that gave rise to the immortal idea that classical operas needed to be reworked along modern revolutionary story lines, and the repertories of the Leningrad and Moscow opera companies were soon enriched with new masterpieces. Meyerbeer's *Les Huguenots* was turned into *The Decembrists*. Puccini's heroine Floria Tosca seized a red banner and marched to the barricades to die for the radiant ideas of communism, and the opera was renamed *The Struggle for the Commune*. With Glinka's opera *A Life for the Tsar*, it was very simple; they decided to call it *A Life for the People*.

The Proletkult people did not recognise any art that wasn't proletarian, although none of them knew just what that meant; they simply obliterated everything that had been done before them. They set the future course for official Soviet art: Socialist Realism. One can imagine how much they hated not only Shostakovich's work but the young man himself, who had often been scathing in his criticisms of their amateurishness and lack of talent.

The Central Committee's decree of April 23, 1932, 'On the Restructuring of All Literary and Artistic Organisations' – that is, on the dissolution of all creative artists' associations, including Proletkult ones – was welcomed joyously by Shostakovich. He hoped that, by uniting, composers could consolidate their power, beat off the attack of the Proletkultists, and deprive them of the influence they increasingly had been exercising over all cultural spheres in the country. He didn't realise that what the Party wanted above all was to establish large-scale arts organisations, such as a composers' union, a writers' union, and an artists' union, in order to subjugate the artists completely. He did not understand that this was the beginning of an unprecedented Party dictatorship over the arts. As for the proletarian composers, they would simply move over to the newly founded Soviet Composers' Union, where with redoubled energy and their Party cards behind them they would wage a struggle for their own existence.

With the arts firmly under Party subsidy, actors', writers', and artists' 'palaces' began to be built in Moscow. Splendid estates near Moscow whose owners had either been shot by the Bolsheviks or had fled the Revolution and gone abroad, were turned over to the Bolshoi Theater, the Moscow Art Theater, the Maly Theater, the Vakhtangov Theater, the Artists' Union, the Writers' Union, and other arts organisations to be used by vacationing artists. Artists fed off the bounties of the government; they were granted 'Sovnarkom'* rations, which only high Party officials could get. And when, in the summer of 1933, half of Russia's inhabitants were swelling from hunger, people in the arts had ham, cheese, and butter on the table. The Party was fattening up a future army of propagandists for its policies and spokespersons for 'the happy life of the people.' Leading singers at the Bolshoi got 5,000 rubles a month for three performances, while a blue-collar worker got 200, and a charwoman 80. My grandmother's pension was 40 rubles a month. So much for His Majesty, the Working Class! As Russians say, 'What they fought for is what they ran up against.'

* Council of People's Commissars.

The singers, actors, writers, and artists glorying in that bonanza thanked the Party for its concern, pointing out quite rightly that in no other country in the world did people in the arts get such privileges at the expense of the whole society as in this nascent land of communism. The people in the arts did not imagine that they would soon have to pay for that generous fare not only with their creative work – with their consciences – but in many cases with their very lives. The first ones to be presented with the bill were the writers and artists. The Party demanded that they glorify the great construction projects and the happy life of the people in those frightful years when hunger had reached its apogee in the USSR.

In the Ukraine, millions were dying of hunger; corpses lay about on the streets, some of them cannibalised. For months, an endless flow of trains steamed to the Kazakhstan steppes or to Siberia jammed with peasant families, the so-called kulaks, and others who had opposed collectivisation. The heretics – with their wives and children and feeble old relatives – were thrown into the taiga in the dead of winter, where as yet there was no housing. The majority died immediately. The survivors were forced to cut down forests and build concentration camps and prisons for themselves, where they would eventually die of hunger and hard labor. Churchill wrote in *The Second World War* that Stalin had told him of the ten million kulaks annihilated during the years of collectivisation.

A wave of terror spread through the country. The murder of Stalin's rival Kirov in 1934 was followed by thousands of arrests. The mysterious deaths of Stalin's former cronies Kuibyshev and Ordzhonikidze brought more arrests and shootings. People who only the day before had been all-powerful were killed, and took hundreds of thousands of ordinary mortals down with them. In those years denunciations, even anonymous ones, assumed legal form, and did not fail to have consequences. And in that fertile soil, the basest human traits flourished like pampered flowers: lying, betrayal, envy. Settling accounts with one's competitors – removing a talented rival from one's path – became the easiest thing in the world. All you had to do was mail a little envelope

addressed to the NKVD.* The diabolical temptation was great –
all the more so since you didn't have to look far for an example. In
the top government echelon, leaders of the Revolution who had
been brothers-in-arms only yesterday were at each other's
throats; slander had become a standard method of Party struggle. The poisonous muck overflowed the walls of the ancient
Kremlin and infected the nation's soul.

To crown its inhumanity, the Party issued its April 7, 1935,
decree, 'On Measures for Combating Crime Among Minors,'
which made all types of punishment, including death, applicable to
children aged twelve and older. It stands among the most
obscene documents of our era. A normal person cannot conjure a
society bestial enough to legally allow an adult man to shoot a
child. But there had been a precedent: the Bolsheviks' cold-
blooded murder of Tsar Nicholas II and his family in the basement
of the Ipatev House in Ekaterinburg (now called Sverdlovsk). The
family included a sick boy of thirteen, the Tsarevich Alexei, who
was so weak that his father, the tsar, had to hold him in his arms
at the moment of shooting.

Now, in the thirties, any person could be made to confess
whatever the top Party echelon wanted to hear. The officials only
had to threaten to execute his children in accordance with laws in
force.

It was in that atmosphere of the Great Terror that the young
Dmitri Shostakovich was writing his music. In January 1934,
when he was twenty-seven, his opera *Lady Macbeth of Mtsensk*
was premiered at the Maly Opera House in Leningrad and the
Nemirovich-Danchenko Musical Theater in Moscow. The opera
was tremendously successful, and the public's interest unprecedented. In the course of two seasons, *Lady Macbeth* was performed eighty-three times in Leningrad and about a hundred
times in Moscow! It stirred up heated arguments and debates.
Some people were in raptures, others censured Shostakovich,
calling him a Formalist or Naturalist. But it was clear the opera
was a work of genius.

Shostakovich fearlessly beat off his attackers and openly

---

* People's Commissariat of Internal Affairs: predecessor of the KGB.

defended his position. In the April 3, 1935, issue of *Izvestia*, he wrote:

> In the past, I have been subjected to powerful attacks from critics, mainly for Formalism. I did not accept those reproaches then, nor do I accept them now. I have never been a Formalist, and I shall never be one. To defame any work as Formalist on the grounds that the idiom of that composition is complex and sometimes not immediately understandable, is to be unconscionably frivolous.

He not only snapped back at his critics but brought charges against them; in those days that demanded a great deal of courage.

I am convinced that Shostakovich would have been left alone for a good deal longer if that opera, along with his ballet *The Sparkling Stream*, had not been produced at the Bolshoi in 1935 when the reign of terror was at its height and the Party had no time for music. The former Proletkult composers who had once been ruthlessly criticised by Shostakovich were now feathering their nest in the Composers' Union – just next door to the Kremlin – and nursing their grudge toward Shostakovich. Patiently, they went about readying themselves for their revenge. They had all studied Stalin's tastes carefully, and played up to his ignorance. For Stalin had no understanding whatsoever of symphonic or any other instrumental music, and simply couldn't abide contemporary works. His amateurish, philistine tastes had become legitimised by boundless dictatorial power and were now decisive policy in art. Servile hangers-on knew how to play up to Stalin's musical predilections in order to prove their devotion to his system of lies.

Writers had already shown their colors: arrests on the basis of informers' reports had already begun in their camp. Now it was the composers' turn; and the means available to a Soviet adept at intrigue were truly unlimited.

For many years, Shostakovich had been a thorn in the side of his untalented colleagues – Party members, most often. But in Leningrad, his home, he was the pride of the city, and it was hard to take reprisals on him. It was only from the very top, from the heights of the Moscow Kremlin, that his head could be made to roll. Shostakovich's opera had been playing very successfully at Moscow's Nemirovich-Danchenko Theater for two years already (incensing the envious ones). There, it had led its quiet creative existence in the shadow of the Bolshoi; no big names played in it and no intrigue contaminated it. What his enemies needed was chance. And, indeed, a chance turned up: two of his works premiered at the court theater, the Bolshoi, in the course of a single month! The ballet *The Sparkling Stream* premiered on November 30, 1935, and *Lady Macbeth of Mtsensk* on December 26. It was an unprecedented event – two works by one contemporary composer – and it even seemed as if Shostakovich had been lured into a trap.

At the Bolshoi, a new production is kept on the boards for at least a half year, so for several months Shostakovich was the focus of heated passions on the part of the entire troupe – the ballet dancers, the opera singers, and the members of the orchestra – along with those hawkeyed observers and troublemakers, the music critics, and the group of composers who were playing politics. (When I joined the Bolshoi seventeen years later there were still many who had taken part in the ill-fated premiere of *Lady Macbeth*, and from their accounts I got an idea of what had happened.) I am all too familiar with the penchant for Machiavellianism among the Bolshoi's artists, having seen it used against me, and I am willing to wager that the ranks opposed to Shostakovich's productions were formed during rehearsals. Guided by someone's skilled hand, the artists lodged complaints with the appropriate organisations that the young composer's music was difficult to perform and, moreover, incomprehensible. Avalanches often begin with the falling of small rocks. The artists of the Bolshoi, unlike their colleagues at other theaters, have government connections and the opportunity to foster squabbles at the highest levels. After making the rounds of the Muscovite composers and critics, they have been known to take their gossip with them into the Kremlin, to banquets and drinking bouts. There, while engaging in servile banter over a glass of vodka, many have laid the groundwork for the murder of Soviet music –

perhaps without even foreseeing all the dreadful consequences for the future of our art.

Apparently, the storm came without warning. Dmitri Shostakovich was ascending the very heights of fame – young, brilliant, and recognised not only in Russia but throughout the world. His First Symphony, written when he was only nineteen, had, by the time he was twenty, crossed the Soviet borders to be performed by the best orchestras under the greatest conductors: Arturo Toscanini, Bruno Walter, Leopold Stokowski, Serge Koussevitsky. And during those fateful years especially, his music was performed often in America. In addition to his symphonies, *Lady Macbeth* premiered in New York at the Metropolitan Opera, in Cleveland, and in Philadelphia. It was also heard from one end of Europe to another – from the London radio with Albert Coates conducting, to Bratislava, Czechoslovakia. *Lady Macbeth* was conquering the world.

But how could such fame be tolerated in the land of 'equality and brotherhood'? Why is Shostakovich being performed everywhere? What's so special about him? The international recognition of that Soviet composer was bound to cost him something in his own country. He had dared to outgrow the scale the Party had been measuring him by. He had to be whittled down to size – reduced to the general level of Soviet culture, to so-called Socialist Realism. The Composers' Union – save a few outstanding composers like Sergei Prokofiev, Aram Khachaturian, Reinhold Glière, and Nikolai Myaskovsky – was made up of nonentities who packed Party cards and sucked up to the great Stalin and the Party with their worthless odes and marches. Shostakovich's genius and personality were more than out of place in that milieu. Amid that stifling mediocrity and pretense, his brilliance and honesty looked positively indecent.

On January 28, 1936, a month after the premiere of *Lady Macbeth* at the Bolshoi, the composer read about his opera in a crushing, crudely vicious *Pravda* article entitled 'A Muddle Instead of Music.' (And a few days later, on February 5, it was followed by another acerbic article, 'Ballet Fakery,' written about *The Sparkling Stream*.)

From the very first minute of the opera, the listener is dumbfounded by a deliberately dissonant, confused flow of sounds. Fragments of melody, the beginnings of a musical phrase, sink down, break loose, and again vanish in the din, grinding, and screeching. To follow this 'music' is hard, and to remember it is impossible.

. . . The composer of *Lady Macbeth of Mtsensk* had to borrow his nervous, convulsive, epileptic music from jazz in order to endow his characters with 'passion.' . . . At a time when our criticism – including music criticism – is pledged to Socialist Realism, the stage serves up to us, in the work of Shostakovich, the crudest kind of naturalism. . . .

And all of it is crude, primitive, vulgar . . . The music quacks, moans, pants, and chokes in order to render the love scenes as naturally as possible. And 'love' is smeared all over the opera in the most vulgar form. . . .

In the Party's ideological war, Shostakovich was the first musician to take a blow, and he realised it was a fight to the death for his conscience as an artist and creator. In the Soviet Union, the appearance in *Pravda* of an article like that is tantamount to a command: beat him, cut him down, tear him to pieces. The victim is tagged an enemy of the people, and a gang of worthless characters, openly supported by the top Party echelon, rushes forward to curry favor and make their careers. A fall from a big horse is bound to be painful; Shostakovich was badly wounded by that blow from the government, with which he had never had a confrontation before. But he did not accept their 'criticism'; he did not repent. For two years he wrote no response, although they fully expected him to. And however Soviet musicologists may try today, as they collect his public statements crumb by crumb, they can't find anything from those years. It was a heroic silence, a symbol of disloyalty and resistance to the regime. And very few would have been able to do as he did. Shostakovich kept quiet and to himself, not speaking his mind until two years later. He finally made his statement on November 21, 1937, in Philharmonic Hall in Leningrad with his Fifth Symphony, that extraordinary masterpiece, which, as our Dmitri Dmitriyevich told us, was autobiographical.

Listening to it, we become aware of the agonies he lived through. In that music, Shostakovich speaks on the events of those years with more passion and courage than any writer or painter who bore witness to those times. The Fifth Symphony was a turning point not only in his creative life but in his outlook as a Russian. He became the chronicler of our country; the history of Soviet Russia is nowhere better described than in his compositions.

No, Shostakovich did not betray his art. He did not repent, he did not pound his chest in public, pledging henceforth to be an ordinary Socialist-Realist mediocrity. But neither did he come out and openly defend his position. He knew that, during those years of terror, he simply would have been asking to be annihilated. He did not have the right to concede his life to the insatiable Moloch without having done another small part of what he could do best and what God had ordered him to do. Through agonising searching, through struggle and suffering, he found the only way out: the lie. He could lie if it meant the salvation of his own creativity.

Before the Fifth Symphony was allowed to be performed, it was heard by the Party *aktiv* in Leningrad. A few dozen nincompoops got together to judge a genius: to make objections, to lecture him, and in general to teach him how to write music. He had to save his newborn from their talons. But how? He tried to deceive them in the most rudimentary way, and succeeded! All he had to do was use other words to describe the huge complex of human passions and suffering that is so apparent in his music – he described his music to the Party as joyous and optimistic – and the entire pack dashed off, satisfied. The Fifth Symphony, safe from their clutches, resounded throughout the world, announcing the sufferings of great Russia that had been written in the blood of our contemporary. Yes, he had found a way to live and create in that country. In 1940 (*Shostakovich Talks About Time and About Himself*; Moscow, 1980), he said:

I remember the joy I felt when my recently-completed Fifth Symphony was auditioned by the Leningrad Party *aktiv*. I want to express my wish that new musical works should be more often presented to a Party audience. Our Party has so closely followed the growth of all musical life in our country. I have been aware of that close attention throughout my creative life. [I can literally hear the intonation of his voice. How much hatred and how many gibes in the cadence of those words!] In the compositional center of that symphony, I placed man with all his sufferings, and the finale resolves the tragically tense passages of the first parts on a joyous, optimistic plane.

In that 'joyous, optimistic' finale – beneath the triumphant blare of the trumpets, beneath the endlessly repeated A in the violins, like nails being pounded into one's brain – we hear a desecrated Russia, violated by her own sons, wailing and writhing in agony, nailed to the Cross, bemoaning the fact that she will survive her defilement.

The Fifth enjoyed fantastic success. Each member of the audience realised that it had been written for him and about him. And the people reacted. They jumped from their seats shouting and applauding, and continued for half an hour, expressing their support for the composer, their love of him, and their gladness that this great talent, far from perishing, had grown like a colossus, and that his music had taken on titanic proportions. Dmitri Shostakovich was very young, only thirty, and yet he had emerged victorious from his duel with the Party chimera, returning blow for blow with his great work. But he had learned to put on a mask he would wear for the rest of his life.

When the Party lashed out at Shostakovich it did not try to finish him off; surely it could have, but it was clear that this was not a carefully worked-out Party campaign. It was but one episode against the background of the Party's main attraction: the Great Terror.

And, indeed, the Great Terror seemed to sweep the country with an energy all its own. On June 12, 1937, the High Command of the Red Army was brought to trial. The next day they were all shot. The squad of executioners was led by none other than Ivan

Serov, whom I had met at the banquet hosted by Tito in 1955 – he was by then head of the KGB. In December of 1937, *Pravda* published Mikoyan's report on the twentieth anniversary of the secret police, the Cheka-NKVD. It was published for good reason: in that report, Mikoyan issued a new slogan that articulated the Party's goal, *'That every citizen of the USSR be an NKVD agent.'*

More than six hundred poets and writers were arrested, along with thousands of scientists, engineers, and doctors. The atmosphere of those years was evocatively described by Osip Mandelstam, who paid for his words with his life. He would read his poems to friends and fellow poets – to each one individually. They listened in terror, and turned him in.

Anna Akhmatova, too, was a victim of her times. Her first husband was shot, and her son and second husband arrested. She wrote of them in her *Requiem* (which has yet to be published in Russia), but kept that poem in her head for thirty years or so, not daring to commit it to paper. Millions of Soviet women could have signed their names to it.

By June of 1939, when the witches' sabbath was in full swing, the poetess Marina Tsvetaeva ended seventeen years of emigré life and followed her husband and daughter back to Russia. She trembled at what she saw, but there was no going back. She hanged herself two years later in Elabuga, a little town in the backwoods of boundless Russia – she was found in the dirty doorway of a wretched peasant hut. In Gavriil Glikman's portrait of her (see illustrations), we see Tsvetaeva on the brink of death. The artist has captured her spiritual state with the utmost restraint. She is, in essence, already dead and watching us from the other world. How terrifying are those hands, which we know will eventually draw the noose around her neck.

As Tsvetaeva came from Paris to meet her death, her fate overlapped with that of Vsevolod Meyerhold, the outstanding theatrical director and close friend of Dmitri Shostakovich. For several years Meyerhold had been persecuted for Formalism and barred from work in theaters. When the First All-Union Congress of Directors opened on June 13, 1939, the floor was given to only one speaker, USSR General Prosecutor Andrei Vyshinsky. No doubt he was singled out for that honor as a director with a fertile imagination in casting – it was he, you see, who had directed the last Stalinist show trials, works performed in the best traditions of Socialist Realism. Works distinguished by their dramatically effective, bloody denouements. The directors were quick on the pick-up; they took the baton from their mentor and, at the session held the next morning, vied with one another in glorifying and thanking the Party and Comrade Stalin personally for the tender, loving care lavished on Soviet drama and theater. Everything went swimmingly. But out of nowhere: 'Vsevolod Emilyevich Meyerhold has the floor.' It may even be that at the very moment Meyerhold took that fatal step, Marina Tsvetaeva was crossing the border of the Soviet Union. She had left Paris the day before. Meyerhold was the only one in that huge country who, with open visor like Don Quixote, spoke up in defense of his Beautiful Lady, Art. The act was tantamount to public suicide. He was arrested the next day and was swallowed into the torture chambers of the Gulag. The year and place of his death have never been accurately ascertained, but a few days after his arrest his wife, the actress Zinaida Raikh, was found in their home, murdered. Her body had been ravaged by seventeen knife wounds – her eyes ripped from their sockets.

When, in 1969, Alexander Solzhenitsyn moved in with us at our dacha, our friend the distinguished violinist David Oistrakh reminded us of those grim years: 'I won't play the hypocrite with you: I never would have taken him in. To tell the truth, I'm afraid. My wife and I lived through '37, when night after night every person in Moscow feared his arrest. In our building, only our apartment and the one facing it on the same floor survived the arrests. All the other tenants had been taken off God knows where. Every night I expected the worst, and I set aside some warm underwear and a bit of food for the inevitable moment. You can't imagine what we went through, listening for the fatal knock on the door or the sound of a car pulling up. One night a Black Maria stopped out in front. Who were they coming for? Us or the neighbors? The downstairs door slammed and the elevator began its ascent. Finally it stopped on our floor. We listened to the footsteps, and went numb. Whose door would they come to? An eternity passed. Then we heard them ring at the apartment across from us. Since that moment, I have known I'm no fighter . . .'

On March 2, 1938, in the October Hall of the Palace of Unions, another trial began, the show trial of the 'anti-Soviet bloc of rightists and Trotskyites.' This time the defendants included Bukharin, Rykov, Krestinsky, Rakovsky, and Yagoda – the sadist and hangman who had been chief of the NKVD. Why am I reading out the roll call of those Bolsheviks here? I have no sympathy for any of them. They all came out of the same lair and devoured one another. But their names designate those periods in the history of the Communist Party when millions of innocent citizens were tortured and killed. Few people in Soviet Russia today have any concern for the fate of those millions, but everyone still remembers the 'loyal, great sons of the Party.' Of course, it is startling and tragic when a man who only yesterday was an all-powerful marshal or member of the Central Committee is awakened at night and taken from his feather bed to the basement of the Lubyanka, where he is hit in the face, kicked in the groin, and shot. But nearly forgotten are the ordinary, illiterate Russians, the Ivans and Maryas, who were dragged out of their musty, dirty huts, torn away from their last sack of grain and their scrawny cow, and herded in prison convoys to the boundless Siberian Gulag, where they labored like beasts of burden for nothing and died on the 'great construction projects of communism.'

When Khrushchev delivered his secret speech at the Twentieth Party Congress, citing statistics and giving the names of the people who had been shot or tortured to death, why didn't he call upon all of those members of the government present – the accomplices in that unprecedented evil deed – if not to stand trial before the entire nation, then at least to die together as a lesson to posterity?

Nor did any of the members of the Politburo shoot themselves when, at the Twenty-second Party Congress in 1961, Khrushchev declared that they were guilty of crimes against their own people. At that congress the chairman of the KGB, Alexander

Shelepin, drew a frightful picture of the mass terror. And, calling out the names of the murderers – General Secretary of the Communist Party Joseph Stalin and Politburo members Molotov, Kaganovich, Malenkov and Voroshilov – he exclaimed indignantly: 'Sometimes you wonder how these people can walk the earth with no pangs of conscience and sleep peacefully. They should be haunted by nightmares. They should hear the moans and curses of the mothers, wives, and children of innocent comrades who perished.'

But they *do* walk the earth! Living on huge pensions from widows and orphans, they sleep soundly in luxurious, rent-free government dachas and shop in their own government stores – the stomachs of the leaders of the Revolution are not used to consuming slops from the public trough where the ordinary Soviet rabble feed and grunt.

At first, though, Tsar Nikita gave them a good fright. The torturers shook in their boots because they knew very well what the 'legal means of coercion' were and what awaited them in the cellars of the Lubyanka. Lazar Kaganovich, who had been Stalin's most zealous helper, couldn't restrain himself. He called Nikita at home and begged: 'Comrade Khrushchev, I've known you for many years. Please don't let them do to me what was done to people under Stalin!'

Kaganovich was given a pension. Nikita did not betray his cronies, but saddled the people instead. It was they who had to support the heavy-jowled pensioners for life, and provide remuneration for the surviving relatives of those 'loyal sons of the Party and the people.' The miserable Russian people!

After the Fifth Symphony, which the critics declared a work of Socialist Realism, Shostakovich was considered reformed, and he was no longer in disgrace. During the next decade he wrote his Sixth, Seventh, Eighth, and Ninth symphonies, quartets, a trio, and a quintet. But his ordeal was not over.

The government decree on the Formalist composers was preceded by a conference of prominent Soviet musicians and musicologists in January 1948 at the headquarters of the Central Committee. It was chaired by Andrei Zhdanov, who in his opening remarks took an unceremonious slap at the devotees of the muses: 'No doubt you still have some remembrance of a famous article published in *Pravda* in January 1936 under the title, 'A Muddle Instead of Music.' That article was published on orders from the Central Committee, and expressed the Central Committee's opinion of Shostakovich's opera.'

In Shostakovich's presence and with great satisfaction, he reminded everyone of the Central Committee's opinion of *Lady Macbeth*: '. . . the music quacks, moans, pants . . .' Then, comparing certain pieces of that music with the sounds of a dentist's drill and a mobile gas chamber, he called upon the composers to '. . . write beautiful and refined music.'

At the end of his speech, Zhdanov, the 'admirer of all that is refined' (Shostakovich was never able to bear the phrase after that), got so carried away that he came out with the following bit of idiocy: 'The new must be better than the old, otherwise it has no meaning.' Really? But why must a novel be better than *War and Peace*, or a symphony better than Beethoven's Ninth? The new doesn't have to be better, but it should be different – it should meet the needs of its own era, and strive for excellence within its own sphere. Nonetheless, the verbal diarrhea of the 'admirer of all that is refined' was often interrupted by servile laughter and loud applause. And to think that in that very auditorium sat the leading figures of musical life in Russia!

On February 10, 1948, the Central Committee issued its decree on combating Formalism in music. This time, Shostakovich was not alone. Also accused of Formalism were Sergei Prokofiev, Aram Khachaturian, Nikolai Myaskovsky, and Vissarion Shebalin. The whole thing had begun with an opera mounted at the Bolshoi, *The Great Friendship* by the talentless Vano Muradeli. His musical capabilities were on the level of a child. And yet he stood accused on the same scaffold with geniuses like Sergei Prokofiev and Dmitri Shostakovich! He tried in every way to distance himself from that honor, to convince everyone that he had been grouped with them in error; that he was not a Formalist but an honest communist. But our government, ignorant of art, tried – as in Krylov's fable – to harness a horse and a doe to the same cart. The public did not understand these nuances, and, to

Muradeli's horror, regarded him as one of a kind with the 'mercenary Formalists' Prokofiev and Shostakovich. They tore him to pieces at the meetings. Actually, he had been put in that group for the simple reason that he had bet on the wrong horse. Eager to please Stalin, he had written an opera about the peoples of the Caucasus. And not wanting to risk putting a singing Stalin on stage, he chose as the hero of his opera Stalin's best friend, Sergo Ordzhonikidze, who had died in 1937. It turned out that the 'best friend,' on orders from *his* 'best friend,' had either been murdered or had been driven to put a bullet through his own head. And the opera only reminded Stalin, the patron of all the fine arts, of how 'great' that friendship was. The sycophant Muradeli, in his confusion, had shouted 'Hurrah!' instead of 'Help!' and the mockery had provoked the wrath of the beloved Leader and Teacher.

The campaign had been planned by Tikhon Khrennikov. As a young man in 1936, Tishka had been at the beck and call of Shostakovich, whom he worshiped as a god. But he had since grown up to become Tikhon Nikolayevich Khrennikov, no longer a talented composer, but a clever, scheming courtier. He had sold his soul to the devil, had paid dearly for it with his own creative sterility, and had exhausted himself in impotent rage and professional jealousy. Figuring that after the government's reprisals against writers in 1946 the time had come to strike at the composers whom he could not best with his own paltry works, Khrennikov gathered together kindred spirits from the Central Committee and placed at their head that 'great authority on music and literature,' Politburo member Andrei Zhdanov. Former Proletkult people once again crawled out of their holes – that sturdy breed! – and joined in the campaign. All these 'gallant lads' cooked up a dish: *The Great Friendship*, served up as Formalism. Then, to vary the metaphor, the wheels of the mill began to turn, grinding the nation's best composers under its millstones. Soon, the 'rootless Cosmopolites' were also caught up in the works. This glorious campaign was concluded by the notorious 'doctors' plot' in 1952 and, finally, by the slogan: 'Beat up the kikes and save Russia!'

This baiting of the composers was organised on a nationwide

scale and, unlike the efforts of 1936, openly bore the stamp of the Central Committee. Meetings were held not only in theaters and conservatories, but at institutions that had nothing to do with art, where the speakers were uttering the words 'Formalism' and 'Cosmopolitism' for the first time and could hardly pronounce them. All enthusiastically condemned the enemies of the people, the accursed Formalists, accusing them of every mortal sin. It was an opportunity to fuel the general national fire and settle old accounts. In those years the great Russian language was enriched by two more swear words. In lines, on buses, and on the subway, in place of the cherished obscenities, one could hear: 'Shut up, you rootless Cosmopolite!' Or: 'Quit shoving, you damned Formalist!'

In February 1948 a general meeting was held in the Great Hall of the Moscow Conservatory – one to which all of the prominent figures in the world of culture were officially invited. And in order to be given a lesson on 'the wrath of the people,' conservatory students were excused from classes and herded into the auditorium. It was all quite different from 1936. By now the government had acquired a great deal of experience, and it went after the Formalist composers with a better understanding of its task. One after another, the swine mounted the speaker's platform, as if in a major competition to smear people. In one day, all that Shostakovich and Prokofiev had ever created was destroyed. After all, if someone is attacked in a one-party system, there is no hope for survival. There is no one to whom he can appeal, because there is no opposition to the ruling party. Of course there are those who stay on the sidelines and don't take part in the beating, but neither do they come to the victim's defense. So where can the victim go? To whom? The press is in the hands of the Party. If someone decides to come to his defense as an individual, that someone will never get past the tightly closed doors of government offices. If the victim demonstrates with placards in a public square, he'll be arrested in a minute. If he raises his voice at a meeting, he'll be silenced by the organised majority.

In the auditorium, so jam-packed with people that there would have been no place for an apple to fall, Shostakovich sat alone in an empty row of seats. We have that custom: no one sits next to the victim. As in a public execution. And it *was* a public execution, the only difference being that in an execution they kill you, while in this case they are magnanimous – they let you live spat upon. And for that magnanimity you are obliged to sit there and listen to all that they spit in your face, and to repent. Nor can you do it in private: you have to get up on the speaker's platform and repent aloud, publicly betraying your own ideals! And more: you have to thank the Party, the government, and Comrade Stalin personally.

In September 1948 Shostakovich was driven out of the Leningrad and Moscow conservatories where he had been teaching classes in composition, his only guaranteed source of income. He was dismissed as *professionally incompetent*; that is, for qualifications not corresponding to the rank of professor. Incalculable damage was done to all world culture by that barbarous deed on the part of the ignorant communist authorities, who deprived young musicians of the opportunity to study with the great composer. He never taught again. It wasn't until 1961 that he returned to the Leningrad Conservatory, where he worked with graduate students for a short time. Then he left of his own accord, this time for good. But Tishka Khrennikov, for services rendered, became first secretary of the Soviet Composers' Union, and holds that position to this day.

Almost all of Shostakovich's works, like those of Prokofiev, were banned for several years and not performed in concert halls; his new compositions, which did not find favor with the Party, were simply not bought by the state. He was virtually deprived of a livelihood, his morale was low, and he had lost the most precious thing – the freedom to create. Can we imagine what that genius went through in that enforced muteness, driven into a corner like a trapped beast? He had been in the full flower of his great talent: only forty-two. Just how heavy the blow dealt to him was can be judged by a list of his works over the period of five years before the death of Stalin. It is the most eloquent witness for the prosecution:

1948 – Score for the film *Young Guards*
1949 – Score for the film *Michurin*
    Oratorio, *Song of the Forests*

1950 – Score for the film *The Fall of Berlin*
1951 – Ten Choral Poems by Revolutionary Poets
1952 – Cantata, *The Sun Shines on the Motherland*

It is plain that the composer wrote these as a last resort – to get a crust of bread. In the Soviet Union, if the state organisations do not buy your new works and the government bans those written earlier, you have but one thing to look forward to: starvation. But Shostakovich could never have borne the sight of his family in such a predicament – especially his children, young at the time, whom he loved with a kind of frenzy.

He got a Stalin Prize for the oratorio *Song of the Forests*, the music for the film *The Fall of Berlin*, and the Ten Choral Poems. In that way they let him know that they were satisfied, and that they would expect the same kind of music from him in the future.

This time, for a good long while, Shostakovich was defeated. Perhaps it was only his love for his children and his hatred for his torturers that kept him going. But there's a God in heaven, and justice on earth, as Dmitri Dmitriyevich often liked to say. The great hangman Stalin died as a jackal does, cringing in his hole. And while his confederates hovered over his carcass tearing pieces of the future inheritance out of each other's teeth, his eyes, already glassy, may have caught a glimpse of the images of those victims tortured or killed under his orders. Among them he would have counted Shostakovich, whom he had persecuted, but who would now outlive him. Within a few months the Tenth Symphony rang out – the composer's tragic testament forever damning the tyrant. In the symphony's third movement, as in the finale, Shostakovich 'signed' that indictment with the melody of his musical monogram, DSCH (D E-flat C B), which he was using for the first time.

In 1954, Shostakovich was taken on at the Bolshoi as music consultant, and it was during that period of his life that I had the good fortune to meet him. Then, when Slava and I were married, my husband introduced me into Dmitri Dmitriyevich's home. I was constantly there after that, and the close friendship between our families continued until we left Russia.

In those years Dmitri Dmitriyevich was living on Kutuzovsky Prospekt. When I first entered the apartment I was amazed by the disorder that reigned within – the lack of comfort, despite the fact that two women lived there: the maid, Marya Dmitriyevna, and the old nanny, Fenya. Everything bore the stamp of neglect. Dmitri Dmitriyevich was only forty-eight when, on December 4, 1954, his wife, Nina Vasilyevna, suddenly died, leaving him to raise the two children: a daughter, Galina, seventeen years old, and a son, Maxim, who was fourteen. Dmitri Dmitriyevich transferred all his love for his wife to his children, and was a dedicated family man. I never heard him raise his voice to either of them, although their upbringing had been turned over to the maid, and they were growing up spoiled and undisciplined. He loved them with a kind of abnormal, morbid love, and lived in constant fear that some misfortune would befall them. We often had occasion to see what a nervous state he got into when one of them was late coming home. He would be beside himself with worry. He would imagine that they had been in an accident. (Both Galina and Maxim could drive, and more often than not Maxim drove very fast.) Maxim would leave the dacha for Moscow, and within ten minutes Dmitri Dmitriyevich would be on the phone to the Moscow apartment to see whether he had arrived. One didn't know how to reassure him – nothing helped, his torment was so intense.

'Dmitri Dmitriyevich, you know it takes at least half an hour to get to Moscow, and only ten minutes have passed. Calm down. Nothing has happened.'

'But I can't help it. Maxim drives fast – much too fast.'

And he would rush to the telephone every five minutes. His apprehensions proved not to be totally unfounded. Not long before they were married, Maxim and his fiancée, Lena, were indeed in an accident, and both nearly perished.

Dmitri Dmitriyevich liked to invite his close friends to his place and seat them at his table. Russians drink vodka rather than wine with their meals, and he was no exception. He didn't use small vodka glasses, and preferred to do the pouring. He would start by pouring himself half a tumbler and drinking it off right away. Then he would pour himself another half, and begin to eat – that was his 'quota.' He got tipsy rather quickly, especially in his last years; and when he did he would quietly disappear into his room for the night.

In those days he was hard-pressed for money, and there would only be sausage, cheese, bread, and a bottle of vodka on the table. But he never seemed to notice what he was eating. He had few friends (life itself had made the selection for him), and his guests were usually the same people – those whose loyalty had been proven by time. But even them he rarely visited unless it was to celebrate birthdays. (He always remembered those birthdays, and never failed to send a telegram of congratulations.)

Most often he would sit at these affairs in silence, not taking part in the general conversation. He never sat for long. After drinking his 'quota,' he would stand up suddenly and say (using almost always the same words): 'Well, we've drunk and we've eaten. It's time to go home. Time to go home.' And he would leave.

He shunned society, and the only places he frequented were the concert halls and, more seldom, the theaters. Even there, he wouldn't talk to anyone during intermissions, but would stand off to one side. Most often he remained alone in the *avant-loge*.

In his youth, Dmitri Dmitriyevich had been a joyous, gregarious man. But life had gradually forced him into retreat. When praised, he took it with a kind of painful awkwardness, as if he were hearing a lie. People felt that, and were reluctant to regale him with their impressions, their enthusiasm. A tense atmosphere seemed to envelop him. When ovations drew him on stage to take a bow, he never smiled. His very appearance was a kind of reproach, and each of us felt guilty before that persecuted Titan. The hatchet job done on him in that 1936 *Pravda* article had, like a public slap in the face, left an imprint on his whole life. He had reacted in an agonising, physical way, as if his skin were searing from the brand that had been put on him.

Nor did I see, in his family relationships, any simplicity or naturalness. It seemed to me that even his children were shy to show their love for him – for them, too, he was the great Shostakovich.

All of those in his circle were especially deferential toward him, and would be transformed by his presence. We all tried not to talk too much, to be more reserved – and we often ended up acting entirely unlike ourselves. If Dmitri Dmitriyevich offered judgments about music or the theater, and those judgments were not shared by everyone, no one dared to contradict him, so great was his authority. I must say that he knew that very well, and never abused his influence: I seldom heard him criticise anyone. More often he would praise.

It was probably his extraordinary restraint and discipline that helped him, given his finely tuned psyche, to bear up under his many trials. His mental acuity and emotional vigor stayed with him until the end, and I never saw him enfeebled, even during the worst periods of his illness. Although he was often in the hospital for extended stays during his last years, not a day would pass in idleness. Dmitri Dmitriyevich usually composed without a piano, and the fact that he had no access to one at the hospital did not hinder him in his constant creative work.

Once having seen that sensitive face, which bore the seal of genius, one could never forget it: the childlike, vulnerable smile; the eyes – light gray, wide-open, made huge by his glasses. He walked with a rigid gait – with short steps – and his restless hands appeared not to know what to do with themselves. He would often scratch the back of his head with one hand, then the other, then bring them to his chin – a characteristic gesture so familiar to us all. There was always a youthfulness about his appearance; an elusive, boyish something that he kept to the end of his life. When I look at his early photographs it seems to me he never did grow old: the same big glasses, the tuft of hair on the crown of his head, and the wide-open gray eyes. His words were never calm and flowing but always tense and lurching. He spoke rapidly, hurrying to get his thoughts out, and repeating words or entire phrases many times over, as if insisting that his listener remember. And, for emphasis, he peppered his statements with such expressions as 'don't you know' and 'you see.'

In his youth, his friends called him 'Florestan of the enchanted soul.' The poet Volodya Kurchavov, who was a friend of the young Shostakovich, wrote the following and dedicated it to him:

I love the vernal sky
When a storm has just passed by.
That is your eyes.

No doubt he had the same quick, impulsive movements as a young man.

He seemed to react to everything directly, and loved a good joke, although he himself couldn't tell one well and didn't like to. But if he heard a joke he liked, he would chuckle like a child and repeat it all evening long, laughing all over again. That very characteristic trait is often in his music: frequent repetitions of a musical phrase, or of words.

Whether at the dinner table or in general conversation, he seemed to be concentrating on – listening to – something within himself. Not that he was cut off or absent-minded; he always listened closely, and reacted quickly. But he seemed to be processing everything around him through his music. It was his wellspring, his inner 'perpetual motion machine,' and several lives would not have sufficed for him to exhaust it.

Often, in the course of a conversation, he would suddenly leave the room, go to his study, and return to resume the exchange. Without any internal shifting of gears, he would go to his desk and write down the sounds that coursed in him as naturally as his own breath – as his own heartbeat.

One day, Dmitri Dmitriyevich telephoned and asked us to come and see him. When we got there, the door was opened by a stately young woman, and Dmitri Dmitriyevich introduced her: 'This is Margarita, my wife.' We couldn't make head or tail of it. Who was she and where had she come from? Only yesterday, not a word had been mentioned. And today – a wife! It was plain to see that his children had given her a hostile welcome, and were not bothering to conceal their feelings.

As soon as a convenient moment came, Zinaida Aleksandrovna Merzhanova, Dmitri Dmitriyevich's devoted secretary for many years, took us aside and told us that Margarita had been working at the Central Committee of the Komsomol, and that when Dmitri Dmitriyevich had seen her at some conference, he had approached her and, without beating about the bush, had put the question to her simply: 'Would you like to marry me?'

At first she was stupefied. But she came around soon enough and answered, 'Yes.'

She always reminded me, in some ways, of Dmitri Dmitriyevich's late wife, Nina Vasilyevna, although I knew the latter only from photographs. Margarita was a simple, energetic Russian woman, always trying to put the home in order and to organise a more or less normal life for the family, which had not known the firm hand of a woman for a long time. But how unlike them she was! Everyone in the house rebelled against her. She never managed to endear herself to the children, and even the servants refused to recognise her as mistress of the house.

One day Zinaida Merzhanova came to me terribly upset, almost in hysterics, and simply collapsed on my sofa.

'Zinaida Aleksandrovna! What's happened?'

I had to give her a glass of water before she could even talk. 'Just imagine, Galina Pavlovna! I had said to her – to that Margarita – "You're married to a genius, and you must make an effort to understand his psyche. After all, he's a musician!" And what do you suppose she said to me? "So he's a musician, so what? My first husband was a musician, too . . . He played the accordion!" Oh-oh-oh!' And Zinaida began to wail.

A photograph of his first wife still hung on the wall in Dmitri Dmitriyevich's bedroom, but no one ever talked about her in his presence. It was a forbidden subject. Only once did I hear him utter her name. That was at the wedding of his son Maxim on October 20, 1960, when we were all sitting at the table drinking, congratulating the young couple, and shouting 'Bitter!'* as is the custom in noisy Russian weddings. Dmitri Dmitriyevich stood up abruptly and said, 'I ask you all to drink in memory of my late wife, Nina Vasilyevna.'

I remember that an uncomfortable silence descended. Everyone stood up and drank, and Dmitri Dmitriyevich didn't say a word more. No one was about to add to that toast – not even Nina

---

* When the guests shout 'Bitter!' the young couple is supposed to kiss to sweeten the drinks.

Vasilyevna's children Maxim and Galina – and the subject vanished as quickly as it had come up.

That same evening the disease that had been undermining Dmitri Dmitriyevich's health for a long time first manifested itself. I remember that he came out to the hallway landing, where Maxim and his friends were, and that everyone was making a noise and telling jokes. Dmitri Dmitriyevich was laughing along with the rest of them, and then suddenly he was sprawled on the floor. His leg muscles had suddenly given way. We all rushed to pick him up. He lay there silent, motionless, but he was conscious. The guests were shouting, wailing. An ambulance was called. In his fall, Dmitri Dmitriyevich had broken a leg, and he had to be taken to a hospital. We all crowded in the hallway, on the landing, and Shostakovich was carried past us on a stretcher. They had wrapped him in a blanket and put a cap on his head. All we could see were his glasses, and behind them his wide-open eyes. Maxim wept aloud, and the women sobbed. Shostakovich was silent. I was horrified: for a fleeting moment it seemed to me that they were taking him out in a coffin.

As his disease slowly progressed, his weakening hands would drop things more and more often. Whenever his fork fell with a clatter on his plate, all of us, frightened, would pretend that we hadn't noticed. He tried desperately to correct his clumsiness, but would only make matters worse. I would always try, discreetly, to put some food on his plate in advance so he wouldn't have to reach and feel debilitated when he couldn't hold on to the platter. He was terribly ashamed of his inexorably advancing physical feebleness – his spirit was still too strong.

Margarita's disappearance shortly after Maxim's was just as unannounced as her appearance. One fine day Dmitri Dmitriyevich fled to Leningrad, saying that he would not go home as long as that woman was there. He left all the documents for a divorce and a power of attorney with Maxim, and we never saw her again.

In 1960, Shostakovich wrote his Seventh and Eighth quartets. The Seventh Quartet was dedicated to the memory of Nina

Vasilyevna. With its subtlety and loftiness it seemed to me a hymn of love. In contrast, the Eighth Quartet was dedicated to the memory of the victims of fascism. As is well known, Shostakovich wrote it in one fell swoop, in only three days. He had written, as he told it, his autobiography.

He put into that quartet the most important events of his life, using music from the First Symphony (1924–1925); the opera *Lady Macbeth* (1930–1932); the Second Trio (1944), dedicated to the memory of his best friend Ivan Sollertinsky, who died of starvation during the war; the Tenth Symphony, written immediately after the death of Stalin in 1953; and the First Cello Concerto (1959), dedicated to Rostropovich – then the most recent of his large-scale works. Through all the movements of that quartet runs the composer's 'signature,' his musical monogram. The fourth movement resembles a requiem. In it Shostakovich borrowed from his music for the film *Young Guards* (the scene of the execution of Young Guard members), and included a melody known throughout the country – an old political prisoners' song: 'Tormented by grievous bondage you are honored by a glorious death . . .'

Shostakovich here seems to insist on the autobiographical nature of his quartet. If you carefully follow the musical material and compare it with the composer's life, the dedication 'To the Victims of Fascism' takes on still another, no less sinister, meaning.

We first heard the Eighth Quartet at Dmitri Dmitriyevich's home. Slava, stunned by the work, was burning with a desire to play it, and when we, along with Dmitri Dmitriyevich, were concertising in Leningrad, Slava gathered some friends – the outstanding Leningrad musicians Mikhail Vaiman (violin), Boris Gutnikov (violin), and Boris Kramerov (viola) – and sat down with them to play the piece.

I remember well that rehearsal in Leningrad's Maly Philharmonic Hall, done as it was in the presence of a Dmitri Dmitriyevich deeply moved by the interpretation of those splendid musicians. When Slava, with his marvelous sound, began to play Katerina's tender, plaintive melody, 'Seryozha, my love . . .' from the last act of *Lady Macbeth*, I couldn't help looking over at

Shostakovich. He sat there, his eyes staring but seeing nothing. Tears were streaming down his cheeks.

Under glass on the desk in Dmitri Dmitriyevich's study was a photograph of his favorite composer, Mussorgsky. It sat there, a constant reminder of that great man's bitter fate: his poverty and utter dependence on handouts from his friends and benefactors. When, at forty, the creator of *Boris Godunov* and *Khovanshchina* lay dying like a beggar on an army cot in the Petersburg Military Hospital, he was visited by the prosperous composer César Antonovich Cui. The latter could see that Mussorgsky's hours were numbered – that this would be their last meeting. Cui, as the story goes, reached into his pocket and drew out a scented snow-white handkerchief with his monogram. He wiped his own eyes with it, then handed it to the great composer, who was suffering from delirium tremens and dying of starvation.

That tableau haunted Dmitri Dmitriyevich all his life like a nightmare. Sometimes, when he was talking about something else, his eyes would suddenly alight on the photograph. Then, giving voice to the thought that was always with him, he would say, 'But what a scoundrel that Mr Cui was! Imagine! He gave him a handkerchief! He should have given him food, not a handkerchief! . . . He had nothing to eat . . . nothing to eat. A *handkerchief*, don't you know?'

And for a long time he couldn't get away from the thought. 'A monogrammed handkerchief, don't you know! Handkerchiefs!'

All his life Shostakovich feared he wouldn't be able to provide for his family; it was a large one, and he was the only bread-winner. Both his children – his daughter Galina with a husband and two children, and his son Maxim, still a student, with his wife and a son – were in fact dependent on him. Besides them, there was the old nanny, who had been with him all his life, the maid in the Moscow apartment, and another maid and furnace-man at the dacha, plus his chauffeur and secretary. They all counted on him for wages. If we add Dmitri Dmitriyevich and his wife, that makes a total of fifteen persons to feed.

He used to say, 'Just think. Tomorrow morning for breakfast we'll need three dozen eggs, two pounds of butter, six pounds of cottage cheese, and several quarts of milk! That's my family. What will happen to them if I stop composing?'

The wheel set in motion by Stalin and his henchmen continued to turn for a long time, and Shostakovich's music was seldom performed. At times there simply wasn't enough money for food and the daily household expenses. In such predicaments, he would call on us, and we often obliged him. He borrowed 10,000 rubles (1,000 rubles today) from us once because he had nothing to pay the servants with.

Three days later he telephoned. 'Galya, may I come over right away?'

'Of course, Dmitri Dmitriyevich.'

Within minutes he was at our place and, beaming with happiness, put a bundle of money on the table. 'There. I return it to you with gratitude. Thanks for bailing me out.'

I was astounded. 'Why were you in such a hurry? We could have waited.'

He stumbled over the words in his haste to tell us what had happened. 'Don't you know, Galya, I've had such good luck today, such good luck! I was so worried about how I would repay you. Then it occurred to me to phone the bank where my royalties from abroad are deposited. I called just in case, not even dreaming that anything would be there. But they said, "Come. You can pick it up." So I went. The money was in dollars, and I was told I could withdraw it only in small amounts and only when going abroad – $300 or $400, no more. I asked if all the dollars could be exchanged for rubles, and if I could get it all right now. They were amazed, of course, but overjoyed. The nice young lady at the teller's window just couldn't believe that I was serious and kept saying, "Good heavens! What are you doing? Go abroad and buy something! How can you exchange dollars for rubles? No Soviet has ever exchanged them. It seems such a shame!" I told her, "It's not a shame at all. Not a shame! If you want to exchange, you exchange." But that nice young lady still felt sorry even as she handed me the money. Well, I took it and dashed out, and I decided the first thing I was going to do was repay you before it all disappears. You yourselves need the money. What luck! What a day!'

Dmitri Dmitriyevich got very little of the royalties that came in from abroad; most of the money was taken by the state. But in those days even that tiny share was an important source of income – a means of existence for his large family. Shostakovich's music was performed abroad, but very seldom in the Soviet Union, so that his ruble account was often empty; prosperity came only in the sixties. We, too, borrowed money from him, and he always loaned it with great pleasure.

In his family, even the most basic necessities were often lacking; and the lines at the stores were such that it was incredibly difficult to meet those needs. The maid would show up at the door: 'Dmitri Dmitriyevich, the refrigerator is broken. We need a new one.' Or the children: 'Papa, we need new tires for the car.' In Russia, people wait for years to buy that kind of thing.

Sometimes we would tease him, saying, 'Dmitri Dmitriyevich, just call and say you're Shostakovich; you'll get everything you need, no problem.' He would laugh. He liked to tell about how once after the war, when all the Moscow movie houses were jammed, he went to see the film *Young Guards*. 'Well, don't you know, I went with a friend, and there was a long line in front of the box office, and tickets only for the last showing, although it was still daytime. My friend said, "Go to the manager's window and tell him that you're Shostakovich, that it's your film and you want to see it." But the window, don't you know, was very low – made especially that way so you'd have to bend down. *Yes, especially to make you bend down.* Well, so I bent down and looked in. The manager asked, "What do you want?" I said I wanted to see the film. And he said, "Why should I give you a ticket? Who do you think you are?" I said, "I'm Shostakovich." And he said, "And I'm Smirnov. So what?" And all that time, you see, I was standing there, bending over before him because of those windows. So I left. "And I'm Smirnov. So what?" I don't like to ask for things, don't you know? I don't like it.'

Dmitri Dmitriyevich would tell that story again and again, and he always laughed as if he were telling it for the first time.

TWELVE

In 1958 the First International Tchaikovsky Competition in Moscow was announced. Dmitri Shostakovich was named chairman of the steering committee, and the country's best-known musicians headed up the juries. Students were coached and drilled: word had come down from above that Soviet musicians had to win all the first prizes. And toward that end, everything possible was done. Young musicians who had made it through the first round of the nationwide competition were sent to the countryside to spend a few months in separate dachas. They were supplied with free board, cars, and grand pianos for practicing. The best of the professors were obliged to go and work with them. Soviet musicians were trained as if they were cosmonauts. It was a matter of building the communist state's prestige, of propagandising the Soviet system.

It cost the state no great effort to get the most brilliant pleiad of professors to teach at the Moscow Conservatory. The very conditions of life in the Soviet Union compelled the most famous musicians and singers to install themselves at the conservatory and, in addition to concertising, to teach from their early years on. They had to do this in order to guarantee themselves steady (if paltry) earnings; there was always a fear that one would have to stop concertising because of persecution, illness, a drop in popularity, or a drop in the 'demand' – a situation often artificially stimulated by the Soviet 'organs.' And to support a family by concertising alone is difficult indeed.

Soviet society has always been a closed one – it wasn't until the 1950s that artists began to go abroad. Even then, each individual case required authorisation from the Ministry of Culture. In addition, Soviet artists and musicians are restricted to performing in those places that have musical facilities: Moscow,

Leningrad, a few cities in central Russia, the republic capitals, and cities in the Baltic states. So, clearly, there is not enough work to go around for the huge community of musicians.

Even if you are lucky enough to find work in the provinces, you face a less than rewarding experience. Living conditions are dreadful in the provincial cities. I remembered the difficulties I had encountered in my youthful wanderings, and after joining the Bolshoi no force on earth could make me go on tour through the country. How well I recall my disgust at the filth in the hotels, and the restaurants with their singularly nauseating food. Little has changed since those days.

Because of such conditions, an artist on tour has to take a suitcase full of food, a hot plate, a thermos, and dishes so that after concerts he won't be obliged to eat in provincial restaurants (if any are still open!) or be subjected to people made rude and insane by vodka. One can understand why a self-respecting artist would be loath to mount that carousel even if it meant extra money. In the fifties and sixties, therefore, the best musicians in the Soviet Union had to augment their salaries by teaching at the Moscow Conservatory: the pianists Genrikh Neigauz, Vladimir Sofronitsky, Emil Gilels, Lev Oborin, and Yakov Flier; the violinist David Oistrakh; and Rostropovich. Of these only Gilels is there today. Rostropovich has been deprived of his citizenship, and the others have died.

Slava began to teach when he was only twenty, and was prouder of that than of his career as a concertising cellist. When we first met, he introduced himself as an assistant professor at the Moscow Conservatory. He didn't even mention the fact that he was well on his way to becoming the most celebrated cellist in the world. He knew too well that his entire career as a performer was in the hands of the state and that the outcome would depend not on his talent but on his relations with the Ministry of Culture. And he was proud, too, that his teaching guaranteed him at least a pittance.

The work load of a professor and his assistant is ponderous indeed: fourteen students twice a week, or a total of twenty-eight hours. It means that every week the professor must set aside two full days for teaching in addition to his main work as a performer. The highest salary for a professor is 500 rubles a month, however many students he may have. Taken together, the income amounts to about four and a half rubles an hour. In Western countries, this is little more than the minimum wage. But in the land of communism in the making, such is the highest salary for a lauded professor at a conservatory. Oistrakh, Rostropovich, Gilels, Neigauz, and their colleagues got four and a half rubles an hour in their day, and the outstanding musicians of today do not get a kopeck more.

One would assume that now that Soviet artists can go abroad with greater frequency, many might be able to dispense with teaching. But it is no secret that no Soviet artist – not even the most famous – has the right to contract personally for perform- ances either abroad or in the Soviet Union. Such arrangements are handled only by state institutions, so that throughout his career an artist is in their hands. Therefore, if the state finds it necessary, it can make any great musician teach, even if he has neither the desire nor the calling for it. And so he wears himself out mass-producing potential prizewinners, all of them as similar as twins. If he fails to cooperate, the state will simply cancel his foreign tour. The foreign impresario will get a tersely worded telegram from the Ministry of Culture informing him that artist So-and-So is ill, and the issue is closed.

So it is that at the cost of enslaving the country's leading musicians and forcibly inhibiting their careers, the conservatories annually replenish the army of well-disciplined, technically well- equipped but faceless artists. But one cannot say they are not professionals, these students. Having studied at special music schools from age five to eighteen, and having spent an additional five to seven years at the conservatory, by the end of their education, they have invested twenty years in their music and are ready for professional work.

For singers things are not the same. At the conservatories there are good voice teachers, but the young singers are on a completely different level of cultural and musical development than the instrumentalists, who begin studying music at a very early age, often coming from families in which the mother or father is a professional musician who, from the cradle, imbues the child with a love of art. Except in the few cases where talent is apparent in childhood, a young person may not discover that he has a voice until he is twenty; and the prospect of a musical career is a surprise. Suddenly two little cords in his throat, having proved themselves specially endowed with the capability of producing beautiful sounds, throw him out of his sphere and into the world of art. Of course it is the same with singers everywhere. The differences lie in the cultural development of youth from place to place.

In prerevolutionary Russia, the children in any reasonably well-off middle-class family studied music and a foreign language. Musical soirées were frequently held in the home. Quite regardless of age, a person could go to the private studio of a well-known artist for lessons in painting, sculpture, or singing, not necessarily in order to become a professional but simply to satisfy a spiritual need or to cultivate oneself generally. Such lessons often revealed artistic potential that hadn't been suspected earlier. The famous Russian singer Antonina Nezhdanova, for example, began as a provincial schoolteacher and made a career in singing only after she was thirty. And the great Russian tenor Leonid Vitalyevich Sobinov, if I'm not mistaken, was at first a lawyer.

In the villages, it was through the church that children were exposed to music. Attending services with their parents, they heard good singing and began early to manifest whatever vocal talent they had. They may have sung in the choir. Through the beauty and loftiness of the Orthodox chants, and through words addressed to God, children were enriched spiritually and could aspire toward the beautiful. Also – and this is crucial to art – at an early age they could accustom themselves to opening up emotionally without being intimidated by an audience. Almost all the great singers of Russia began in churches.

Today, you won't see a single child in a church choir in Russia: it is strictly forbidden. If adults sing in church, they are threatened with trouble on the job. It is only retired old men and women who sing in church choirs any more – those who have nothing to lose.

Today, a young person who discovers that he has a voice when he is as old as twenty has had no opportunity to ponder 'art.' Perhaps it never interested him before. He may never have been to the theater, or to a symphony concert. He may even study voice not because it is his calling – something without which he cannot imagine life – but because he may think it easier to sing than work in a factory. And with that attitude he enters a conservatory: not having to pay for the lessons and unworried by the possibility that he may never develop into an artist and that he may have wasted the best years of his life. There a singer is taught for five years, a period more or less sufficient to teach a bear to ride a bicycle or an elephant to dance the waltz. But what with the present system of teaching in Soviet conservatories, that period is insufficient to make a future artist out of a person who is narrow and culturally unprepared. The curriculum is overburdened with secondary courses that have no relation to art. I had to look in a reference book to refresh my memory:

History of the Communist Party of the Soviet Union
Political Economy
Dialectical Materialism
Historical Materialism
The Foundations of Marxist-Leninist Aesthetics
The Foundations of Scientific Communism
And – not to be overlooked – lessons in military science

Only two hours a week are given over to voice lessons – a piddling amount if one bears in mind that a beginning singer, unlike an instrumentalist, must not practice untutored for the first two years or until he has acquired the foundations of vocal technique. Conservatories consider such subjects as solfège, harmony, and piano of tertiary importance and give them almost no time. The singer progresses slowly, managing to do in five years no more than what could have been done in two years if he had studied only his own profession. As if this were not enough, in September and October, at the official beginning of every school year, students at all the educational institutions in the Soviet Union are sent to kolkhozes to dig potatoes. There they work with their hands, often in pouring rain and up to their knees in mud. The singers come back hoarse and the instrumentalists with injured, swollen fingers. If the curriculum was stripped of these Marxist-Leninist insanities which waste the students' valuable time, and larded with courses to prepare them professionally – to raise their standards of culture – the five-year program for singers would certainly yield different results.

Why not try to get out of it, then, and avoid stuffing one's head with that bilge? Why not plug up your ears with cotton at one of those 'ism' lectures and think about something interesting instead? But no! The student must take exams in his 'isms,' and as long as he hasn't passed them, he won't be allowed to take the exam in his professional course, though he be a genius among geniuses.

Slava attended the Moscow Conservatory at the same time as Svyatoslav Richter. Richter was much older, but had come to his studies late. In order to force themselves to prepare for exams in the political disciplines, the two decided to study together. But the buddy system didn't help: they both fell fast asleep over the first pages. Then Richter devised a way to stay awake while reading those 'immortal works.' The method was a stroke of genius. They got down on their hands and knees, put the book on the floor in front of them, and read it that way. As soon as one would begin to doze off, he'd hit his head on the floor and wake up. It helped! Later, Rostropovich would recommend that method to all his students.

Shostakovich liked to tell how he monitored exams on the History of the Communist Party being taken by students at the Moscow Conservatory (that was before he was fired in 1948). 'One day they obliged me to fulfill my "civic duty" by monitoring an exam on Marxism. I absolutely had to be there, don't you know. As if without me they wouldn't have been able to get along – *couldn't get along at all.* My job was to sit there quietly while the professor who taught the course administered the exam to each student. Well, I sat there for several hours, until the last students were finishing – time for soup, as they say. It was spring, the birds were chirping outside, the sun was pouring through the window, and I noticed one girl sitting there suffering. What anguish was in her eyes! She probably didn't know a thing. I

thought: what a pretty girl, no doubt a singer, and there she is
suffering, you see, in the classroom, when she should be out on
the grass . . . out on the grass! She was the last one left.
Suddenly the professor was called to the director's office. He said
to me, "Dmitri Dmitriyevich, please give this girl her examination; I'll be back right away." Well, I called her up to the desk and
asked her, "What form did you get? What questions are on it?"
She answered timidly, hardly getting the words out, "Re-vis-ion-
ism and its consequences." And there was terror in her eyes,
don't you know, and I kept thinking that she should be in the
woods, on the grass, in the sun, you see. Such a nice girl . . .
"Well," I said, "that's an excellent question, a simply excellent
question. So what *is* revisionism?" Desperately, in one breath
she answered, "Revisionism is the highest stage of Marxism-
Leninism." I was so delighted I jumped up. "That's right," I said,
"absolutely right! And what, in that case, are its consequences?"
"All its consequences come from that." "Excellent!" I said. "I'm
giving you the highest grade. I'm giving you an A – *an A!*" I
scooted her away. At that point the professor came back. "Well,
Dmitri Dmitriyevich, did she pass?" "She passed everything,
everything! I gave her an A. She spoke on the subject brilliantly."
"That's strange," he said in astonishment. "She's been way
behind all year." "But now she's caught up," I said. "She's caught
up. She spoke on it *brilliantly.*"'

Because the five years of school are not put to good use, when
a young singer graduates from the conservatory at a semi-
professional level he is not capable of working at full capacity, and
can only sing a few arias and songs. Basically, he does not master
the piano or build an operatic repertory, so that, when it comes
time to join the theater, he cannot hope to perform in productions
immediately. If he is lucky enough to be accepted into a theater,
he must begin to study all over again. It becomes obvious enough
that he is uncultured, often unmusical, and unable to act. And
while he learns the repertory – while the conductors and directors train and drill him – several years can go by. Valuable time is
irretrievably lost, and a lack of confidence inevitably creeps in. A
cultural blindness and, more important, a spiritual poverty prevent the young artists from rising to a high level of artistry. How

many talented young singers have I seen founder in their careers and never progress beyond the small parts! But Russia has, like no other country, many splendid voices, and the Bolshoi, with rare exceptions, accepts only singers with outstanding vocal gifts.

None of the graduates of the conservatory or any other institute can manage his career at his own discretion. In return for a free education, each student must pay by working for several years wherever the state sends him. Even if a Moscow orchestra or opera house has agreed to take him on, he must decline and go where the state has assigned him. Often, that post is in the boondocks where he will languish and fritter away any skills he might have had. And no student is exempt: all receive work assignments. Usually, they are to a provincial symphony, opera orchestra, music school, or concert organisation. The student cannot refuse; if he does, he won't get his diploma – and without it he will have no career. If he tries to get out of it by signing the work assignment and getting the diploma but not showing up at the designated town, he'll be hauled into court. In provincial orchestras, the pay is a mere 100 to 150 rubles a month for playing at least fifteen to twenty concerts a month in halls that are almost empty. As a rule, no housing is provided, and the young musician, for years, lives in the same room with some old woman, renting a corner behind a curtain. And he can look forward to spending the best years of his life waiting in lines for potatoes and bread, cursing the day that he decided to devote his life to art.

Let us say that he finally serves out his labor conscription. If he has left Moscow to fulfill that obligation, he loses his residence permit and can live there no longer.

And so, Moscow was readying itself for the First International Tchaikovsky Competition when suddenly, three months before it was scheduled to open, news spread through the country that Boris Pasternak's novel *Doctor Zhivago*, which had gone rejected in the USSR, had just been published abroad. It was unheard of! Moscow buzzed – people talked of nothing else. They conjectured what steps the authorities would take against the subversive writer. Under Stalin's rule, Pasternak would have been shot, period. But the Twentieth Party Congress had only recently taken place, and Stalin's bones were still happily ensconced beside Lenin's. The day had not yet come when he would be taken out of the mausoleum and, after long discussions as to where he should go, be buried beside the wall of the ancient Kremlin. Khrushchev stalled and procrastinated, and no one knew in what direction the wind would blow. Pasternak's fellow writers did not launch an open attack on him, but remained ready for combat, only waiting for a command from above. The people at the top would have strangled him gladly, but the First International Tchaikovsky Competition was to open in three months, and guests had been invited from all ends of the earth – famous musicians, many of whom spoke Russian. All the hounds in the pack were slavering, but the huntsmen had not issued the command. And then the authorities realised there was another hitch: the chairman of the steering committee for the competition was a former 'enemy of the people, the mercenary Formalist,' Dmitri Shostakovich! What to do? Throw him out? But the foreigners – that uncomprehending, inquisitive breed – might ask questions, and you can't tell some foreign celebrity to get lost or that it's none of his damned business! After all, they still don't understand a thing about the Soviet regime. They aren't our serf actors and actresses! Maybe they'll take offense, or even visit Shostakovich himself. All right, let's give Shostakovich the Lenin Prize on the great Ilich's birthday, which coincides with the days of the competition. Let the foreigners see how the liberal Soviet regime honors its Formalist! Quickly, they covered up the traces of their stampede against Shostakovich and the other Formalist composers; and for the time being, Pasternak was not touched.

The First Tchaikovsky Competition went swimmingly, except for the fact that the American Van Cliburn came from nowhere and took the first prize in piano. Shaken by that occasion, a government delegation, headed by Khrushchev, appeared at the final concert. I believe it was the first and last time that officials of the Soviet government visited a hall of the conservatory. The box seats intended for them are always empty; but the tickets are never sold to anyone else. I suppose everyone is hoping that the leaders suddenly will develop a thirst for high art and turn out for some symphony concert. I cannot remember that they ever came, except for that one time. They came to look at 'Vanya,' the tall, lanky American who had beat out all the Soviet pianists and become the public's idol – to whom, after his performance, they presented vodka, balalaikas, and pies.

Shostakovich, as chairman of the steering committee, handed out the awards, and the young foreigners were delirious with joy to see Shostakovich in the flesh and to have the honor of shaking hands with him. At that moment it must have become clear to our hot-headed leaders that they were caught in an indecent situation. There they were in the audience applauding and honoring Dmitri Shostakovich along with the rest – paying tribute to a great composer of the twentieth century, whom the Soviet regime had not quite finished off. They had long ago forgotten what he had been persecuted for – well, it hadn't been to death, had it? The result was that one morning a month later we read in the newspaper a government decree entitled, 'On Correcting Mistakes Made in Evaluating the Work of Leading Soviet Composers.' Our leaders, thoroughly plagued by awkward questions put to them by Western intellectuals, were obliged to admit that they had been wrong to persecute their own musicians – that it was something without precedent in world culture. If it had not been for the Tchaikovsky Competition, I am convinced that that decree would never have been issued.

Dmitri Dmitriyevich called us at home. 'Galya, Slava! Come right away! Right away!'

We rushed to his place on Kutuzovsky Prospekt. He was incredibly overwrought and ran about the apartment. We had scarcely managed to take off our coats as he ushered us into the dining room.

'You read it?' we asked.

'I read it. Oh, yes. I read it . . . I've been waiting and waiting for you so we can have a drink. I want to drink, to drink!'

He poured vodka into the tumblers, and all but shouted, 'Well, Slava and Galya, let's drink to the great historical decree "On Abrogating the Great Historical Decree."'

We tossed off the drinks, and Dmitri Dmitriyevich began to croon to the tune of a *lezghinka*:

> *'There must be refined music,*
> *There must be beautiful music.'*

That day's events took him back ten years to the dark days of 1948. We sat there, fearing either by word or by movement or by mere breathing to touch the wound that had opened and was bleeding before us. It was one of his rare moments of complete candor; and we were afraid lest we glance through a chink and into his soul where he harbored that boiling volcano so carefully concealed from others.

We spent the whole evening trying to talk only about other subjects, but he would come back to it suddenly: 'A historical, don't you know, decree on abrogating the historical decree . . . It's really so simple, so very *simple* . . .'

We saw him agonise over the overwhelming memories of those lost years, and tried to change the subject, but he could not control himself – could not rid himself of the memory of Stalin that obsessed him that evening. And he kept on:

> *'There must be refined music,*
> *There must be beautiful music . . .'*

He would begin a frivolous conversation, then fall silent and, as if the thought had never left him: 'Music must be refined, you see. Refined. Refined . . .'

'Dmitri Dmitriyevich, what do you think is going to happen to Pasternak?'

'It'll be bad, it'll be bad. He shouldn't have sent *Zhivago* abroad. When in Rome, do as the Romans do.'

Who, if not he, who had more than once gone through that kind of thing himself, could predict the subsequent course of events?

Finally, the storm broke. On October 23, 1958, Boris Pasternak was awarded the Nobel Prize for *Doctor Zhivago*. And what didn't begin then! One felt that a gigantic dam had finally burst. If I were a painter, I would have rendered the persecution of Pasternak by painting a sea of howling mouths and envious eyes. They smeared him all at once and with a passion. And those who tried hardest were his fellow writers, consumed by envy of their colleague's acclaim and given – at long last – all the space they wanted in the newspapers.

No one had read Pasternak's novel. I am sure that none of the members of the government had – that they had drawn their conclusions from reports drummed up by officials in the Central Committee's Department of Agitation and Propaganda. To them it mattered not at all what Soviet writers wrote, and they were not about to nourish their minds with such insignificances.

The government officials themselves have long since ceased to believe in the existing system. But they must maintain it at any cost. Thus, what Soviet writers write *about* becomes important; so important that it is a matter for the KGB and its affiliates.

In the newspaper, the 'Responses of the Workers' columns (Letters to the Editor) began as follows: 'I have not read Pasternak . . .' But they would proceed to criticise the unread book and even demand that the author be publicly humiliated, be accountable to 'the people.'

It is frightening to think that such vermin exist. But it is more frightening that the Soviet regime incites talentless, envious people and political intriguers to destroy the nation's creativity in the name of the Party and 'the people.' KGB Chairman Semichastny appeared on television and set the tone: 'We have a mangy sheep in the person of Pasternak . . . Let him get out of our country . . . A pig wouldn't do what he did . . .'

Yes. That was a member of the government speaking. In their eyes the Soviet people are just so much livestock, while they alone are the masters, the human beings. My violent desire to smash the TV screen gave way to burning self-resentment and shame for my own countrymen. Was there really any cause to place the blame on the officials? We deserve being treated like that – like docile livestock – if we can criticise something without reading it, if we can permit a belligerent cad to indulge in the public humiliation of another person. After all, I was not the only one then sitting there in front of the television feeling impotent rage: there were millions of others. But no one stepped up to defend the great poet. Where or to whom could you go? You'd only fall into the state's sticky spider web, like a sacrificial fly.

They yelled from countless podiums and from the pages of newspapers. A group of students from the Literary Institute was forced under threat of expulsion to march through the streets of Moscow to the Writers' House carrying a placard reading 'Judas, out of the USSR!' Finally, there was a general meeting of Moscow writers at which the speakers called Pasternak a 'mercenary scribbler,' an 'enemy, a betrayer of his own people,' and demanded his expulsion from the Writers' Union. Things got to the point where they quoted the rabble-rousing speech of KGB Chairman Semichastny as if it alone successfully defined the author's traits.

Oh writers, writers! What did you do to your colleague, and why? He had only written a book, a novel. But did any one of you demand that the Party bosses who physically destroyed millions of your innocent compatriots be expelled from the country? For some reason, we never read about that. (Solzhenitsyn had not yet appeared among us.) No, the whole gang of you set about to manacle your colleague because he dared tell about events of the prerevolutionary years – not as a textbook on the history of the Communist Party would have represented those times, but as he alone saw them.

The resolution, passed unanimously at the writers' meeting and published in *Literaturnaya Gazeta* under the title 'The Voice of the Moscow Writers,' ended as follows: 'The meeting requests the government to strip the traitor Boris Pasternak of his Soviet citizenship . . . No one to whom the ideals of progress and peace are dear will extend a hand to a man who has betrayed the motherland and its people!'

No, you won't extend a hand to Pasternak, but you lick the boots of those who killed millions – and, among them, hundreds of writers.

Pasternak didn't hold up: he surrendered, and refused the Nobel Prize. But for the pen-pushers that was not enough, and the baiting continued. They didn't envy him the money; their kind of writer has a lot of money in the Soviet Union. All you have to do is think carefully, lie more, and thrust your hand deeper into the pocket of the half-starved, brainwashed public. No, what they envied was his fame, which was worldwide, unstoppable. And, in their stupidity, they didn't realise that with this scandal they were making his fame even greater. But what they envied most was his honesty – the very thing they were incapable of. What had to be achieved at any price was that he repent and ask forgiveness before the entire nation – that he be gawked at in his humiliation.

Can one imagine a Tolstoy, a Chekhov, a Dostoyevsky treating a fellow-writer so shamelessly? Or the composers Glinka, Mussorgsky, Tchaikovsky? What has Russia turned into? Such a deformed society! Such perverted morals! The concepts 'honor,' 'duty,' 'conscience,' and 'decency' have long since ceased to have any meaning in that land.

After Semichastny's speech, in which he said directly that 'Pasternak can get out of the country and go to the capitalist paradise,' people began to fear that the writer would be forcibly expelled. All kinds of rumors spread through Moscow, and the Bolshoi did not remain on the sidelines.

At a rehearsal, our leading tenor, N., said to me, 'Isn't Pasternak vile? He had to go and write *that*!'

'Did you read it?'

'No, of course not. Where would I have been able to get it?'

'So maybe he didn't write anything as bad as all that.'

'What do you mean? The newspapers have articles on it. Do you think *they* didn't read it? He should be driven out!'

Then I was approached by the Secretary of the Bolshoi's Party organisation. 'Galina Pavlovna, we're drawing up a letter to the newspaper. The leading artists of our theater are signing it. You'll have to sign it, too.'

'A letter about what?'

'Condemning Pasternak and his novel *Doctor Zhivago*, of course. You know, he had it published abroad without authorisation.'

'Yes, I heard about that.'

'So you'll have to sign.'

'But how can I sign a letter criticising *Doctor Zhivago* if I haven't read it?'

'None of us has read it.'

'Well, I want it given to me to read.'

'But we don't have the book. It's banned.'

'Then I won't sign. How do I know what's in it? Foreign correspondents might ask me, and I won't be able to tell them what precisely in the book I don't like. And I certainly can't tell them you made me sign.'

They weren't bothering me too much then because people at the theater knew how Bulganin felt about me. His call to 'Vanka' Serov telling him to have the KGB agents leave me alone had not gone unnoticed. But they don't always ask your permission. They may simply forge your signature, knowing there is no place you can go to complain, and that there won't be any refutation in the press.

At a meeting of cultural figures of Moscow at the TsDRI (Central House of Art Workers) where Pasternak was to be smeared, the agenda called for a speech by Rostropovich, and he was notified to that effect by the secretary of the Moscow Conservatory's Party organisation.

Slava was indignant. 'But I haven't read the book! How can I criticise it?'

'Nobody has read it! Just say a few words – you're so quick-witted.'

As it happened, Slava was scheduled to give a concert in the town of Ivanovo, and left Moscow. After his performance – on a Saturday – he announced to the stunned management of the Ivanovo Symphony that he had long wanted to see the sights of the city and would therefore spend Sunday with them. Then on Monday he told them that he was so impressed by what he had seen that he would stay for another day. Meanwhile, the shameful spectacle at the TsDRI was going on, and many prominent cultural figures took part.

Slava flew back from abroad once in the same plane with the poet Alexander Tvardovsky. During the flight they had a few drinks and got to talking, and Tvardovsky suddenly said, 'Decent people are almost extinct in Russia.'

'I think you're exaggerating, Alexander Trifonovich. Honest people . . .'

'I'm not talking about honesty but decency. You've confused

the two. There are many honest people, but few decent ones. I'll explain the difference. Let's suppose I've told a colleague and friend – a communist – an anti-Soviet joke, or have read him a poem of mine aimed against the Soviet regime, and suppose my friend goes and tells the Party organisation about it. As a communist doing his duty toward the Party, he has acted honestly, but has not acted decently.'

The ignorance of our leaders is well-known and has long since ceased to provoke wonder. Nevertheless, when I picked up Nikita Khrushchev's memoirs, *Khrushchev Remembers*, I was surprised. To many questions about art – questions about Shostakovich and Pasternak – the same answers kept cropping up: 'I don't know . . . I never heard it . . . I don't remember . . .' And that in connection with events any halfway-educated person ought to know about and remember. You were the head of the Soviet government, after all! It was for you that your toadies and lickspittles publicly denounced Pasternak and drove him into his grave. Perhaps the heads of government of our country don't read books, but surely they read the newspapers? Or at least hear gossip in the family? The fuss over Pasternak's book was stirred up all over the world – and the book's contents were common knowledge. It's not just that they are responsible for knowing about the nation's culture; ordinary curiosity should have made those government officials pick up the book. But no. Even as Khrushchev awaited death, languishing from boredom and idleness on a pension, he never found time to read even a line or two from *Doctor Zhivago*. No doubt by the time Pasternak was already in his grave, it was reported to Nikita that there was nothing subversive in the book, so it wouldn't be particularly interesting for him. Why waste time? Better to go fishing and sit with a hook on your line, or go hunting and have fun with your little shotgun. The woodlands allotted for the pleasure of our leaders are very rich in game, and a picnic is always ready in the shade of the oaks. And if you should require some little actresses to complete the bacchanal, don't you worry, your slightest wish will be our command. So what if you tortured a man to death? Another 270 million are left. Party bosses are not going to admit that they have made a mistake once again, that they have persecuted an outstanding poet this time. Resign yourself to living spat upon if you can. Pasternak couldn't. He died on May 30, 1960.

Today, when you read Khrushchev's judgments about those events – incidents that shook not only our country but the whole civilised world – you marvel at them: 'I don't remember what Shostakovich's works were criticised for, or in what particulars . . . But I know that Shostakovich confessed, and therefore I can't say that Shostakovich was in any way persecuted in the days of Stalin. He wrote a lot, and occupied a rather prominent position among the composers.'

I can just hear the rest of the sentence: '. . . and we had many such composers . . .' But Nikita himself sums things up. 'In his day, such a fine musician and composer as [Leonid] Utyosov [!!!] was criticised . . . When people were singing Utyosov's songs to themselves, *Pravda* made mincemeat of Utyosov.' This is to say, in effect: Why take offense? It wasn't just Shostakovich who was criticised but even that famous, wonderful composer Utyosov. Good Lord! At least Khrushchev had the honesty to go on and say:

I'm sorry that the work [*Doctor Zhivago*] was not published, because the book . . . to put it in polite language, passes a sentence on the creative intelligentsia. They will tell me now that I have decided too late. Yes, it's late, but better late than never.

All that is very well, Nikita Sergeyevich. But it was your tardiness that killed Pasternak.

THIRTEEN

I have always worked on several operas and concert programs at once, setting aside first one and then another, and nurturing this or that role within myself for years. Thus, when I returned to the theater after Olga's birth, I had four parts ready: Cherubino in *The Marriage of Figaro*, Katarina (Kate) in Shebalin's *Taming of the Shrew*, Butterfly, and Aïda.

The part of Aïda occupies a special place in my operatic career. As Aïda I was taken into the Bolshoi, and in that role I first performed on the opera stage abroad. I consider the Bolshoi's production of *Aïda* the finest of all those in which I have taken part, including productions at the Metropolitan Opera in New York, the Paris Opéra, and Covent Garden in London.

The Bolshoi's *Aïda* involved the best the theater had to offer: a select cast, splendid sets and costumes by the artist Starzhenetskaya, the brilliant staging of Pokrovsky, and conductor Melik-Pashayev's unsurpassed interpretation. From the moment I joined the Bolshoi I had dreamed of singing in that opera, and I didn't miss watching a single performance. Everything about the production entranced me – everything except the image of the heroine herself, which left me cold. She lacked life, personality, a certain romantic quality. All of the audience's affection – including mine – naturally went out to Amneris. And yet the opera begins with a hymn of love to Aïda, Radames's famous aria in which he introduces the heroine to the audience:

> '*Celeste Aïda, forma divina,*
> *Mistico serto di luce e fior'.*'

Once the tenor has offered such a 'character reference,' ending on a presumably exquisite B flat in the upper octave, it behooves the soprano playing Aïda to give some thought to her appearance before presenting herself to the audience.

Aïda! That fragile, exotic creature! The great Verdi, who knew so much about the human voice and the psychology of singers, must have been madly in love with her to be so unaware that he had laid such a trap for all tenors at the beginning of the first act – an extremely difficult and awkward aria when a singer has not yet warmed up his voice or regulated his breathing. How they curse the beloved composer as they stand there, covered in a cold sweat, waiting for the curtain to rise!

Aïda! To no one else in the opera did Verdi give such exquisite *pianissimos*. Her part is the embodiment of love, of willing self-sacrifice; and her whole being must be filled with the surging tenderness heard in the orchestra when she first appears on stage. The music itself gave me a clear visual image of her. I pictured her as a black porcelain figurine come to life. I saw the elegant lines of her body, the flowing motion of her gait, the proud way in which the captive Ethiopian princess held her head.

If it sufficed to look at Egyptian frescoes to establish how Amneris should be clothed, no one really knew how the Ethiopian slave should be dressed. While the Pharaoh's daughter was arrayed in jewels, headdresses, and gowns, Aïda was customarily clad in dresses similar in style to Amneris's, but much less elaborate, thus depriving her of individuality. Yet Radames must have reason to single her out from among the many handmaidens of the Pharaoh's beautiful daughter. How striking Aïda must be, and what a magnetic and mysterious force she must radiate for the brilliant commander to renounce the hand of an Egyptian princess and face death rather than lose the love of a little slave-girl.

I wanted to free Aïda of the royal hand-me-downs so unsuited to her, and let her natural grace come into play. The wild, exotic quality of that black orchid had to be stressed. But how? As a slave-girl any adornment was out of the question and would only look like a poor imitation of Amneris.

Then I decided to start from an extreme: one dress for the whole production. But that single costume would have to evoke the entire image of the heroine so that once the audience had seen her, they would remember her throughout the opera, even when she wasn't on stage.

The dress was utterly simple: close-fitting, the left shoulder bare, slit on one side above the knee. It was red – a color not found in Amneris's gowns but which counterbalanced them – and made of a material that hugged the body to reveal every movement. The only accessories were gold hoop earrings and gold sandals. I myself drew the sketch and chose the color. And I wore that costume wherever I performed Aïda – at the Metropolitan, Covent Garden, the Paris Opéra, and many other theaters throughout the world. Without fail, at dress rehearsals the management of the theaters would give my costume a hostile reception, so unusually simple was the heroine's appearance. But that was my image, and if they didn't like it, good-bye! True, it never got to the point where a performance was canceled; and afterwards audience and critics alike would comment on the beauty and style of my costume. The critics wrote how becoming it was to me, and that I riveted attention on myself in every corner of the stage. With justification – the opera is called *Aïda*.

When working on a role, I always proceed from the music to the dramatic content and not the other way around, no matter how great the poet or writer whose work has served as a basis for the composition. I never listen to anyone else's recordings until I have my own vision of the role, until I have learned and absorbed the whole part.

To learn the music of any opera, including those of Prokofiev and Shostakovich, all I need is about ten sessions with a highly skilled rehearsal pianist. But for me the process of working on the 'musical image' of a role is a lengthy one and, if viewed from a distance, might seem tedious and boring. I go through the music for long hours, trying to penetrate the secrets of the composer's emotional state – to surmise, behind the wall of musical notes, what was tormenting or exciting him when he wrote the work. I must understand why he wrote a given phrase or interval precisely in that way, even though at first glance it may seem illogical, awkward, or even unfeasible. This is the most important stage of my work on any composition, contemporary or otherwise. It requires a lot of time, and you have to have the patience not to skip over it, not to give free rein to your emotions prematurely, and not to begin 'decorating' the work with your own embellishments before you have a clear idea of the composer's intent.

When, finally, the composer's thoughts and feelings have become my own, when I have clearly heard within me the sound of the musical image and have sketched in the contours of my prospective role, I begin to sing it at full voice, and to add color to the sketch. Then I involve my own temperament. I unleash my imagination, and it leads me to the creation of the stage image. At that point I set the part aside for a while, and as it lies dormant within me, it is cleansed of excessive emotion and takes on form.

Unfortunately, this way of working is old-fashioned in our soulless age, when human genius is concerned with inventing computers and walking on the moon. Today the experienced rehearsal pianist has been replaced by the tape recorder with headphones and pocket-size cassettes of operas. Many singers learn their parts while sitting in a train or plane. Without straining their minds, they listen to the musical material hundreds of times, quickly learn and memorise both the words and the music, and consider their work finished. But they deprive themselves of the most important thing: the creative process, 'the throes of creation' through which the musical image is gradually born; from which the personality of the singer – and not a blind imitation of a recording – gradually emerges. Can one imagine the great artists of the past – Gigli, Caruso, Chaliapin – learning a part from someone else's voice, with a tape recorder in their hands? In my view, this is one of the chief reasons why in our day so many singers, conductors, and instrumentalists are almost indistinguishable from one another, and why there is such a dearth of striking artistic personalities.

I do not especially concern myself with the beauty of the sound. For me, the voice is the means – a wonderful and most perfect instrument – which must embody and project the composer's thought as well as the artist's own feelings.

When I look at a famous Stradivarius – my husband's cello – it seems to resemble a human body. The soundboard is the singer's chest and diaphragm, the fingerboard with the strings stretched tautly over it is the throat and vocal cords, and the bow in the artist's hand is the breathing, setting the vocal strings into action. But we singers are luckier than instrumentalists: we have been given the mighty word to help us. And if to that we add the palette of colors – the various timbres we must learn to use – then the voice can express anything.

But the musical image of a role is more than its dramatic content and the necessary coloration of the sound. It is also costume, makeup, coiffure, gait, body movement, gestures . . . After mastering all this, I can then realise on stage the image of a role as I have felt and envisioned it.

Once I have done a great deal of preparatory work I can let my imagination go during the performance, and sing about the pictures which pass, like a moving panorama, before my mind's eye. I do not sing about what I actually see before me or what the audience sees. More important for me is the subtext: what I am thinking about, and what I want to impart to the audience. Often it may be pictures that bear no relation to the setting. For example, as the deranged Marfa in the last act of *The Tsar's Bride*, I see myself not in the stuffy, crowded palace tower where the action takes place, nor in a garden with my beloved Vanya, about whom I'm singing, but in a boundless, blindingly white expanse where there is no one and nothing. Not a blade of grass. Only her helpless little figure in heavy regal vestments, eagerly and hopelessly reaching out for her distant dream . . . at the edge of the world. I must have that sense of white expanse within me. It shields me from the other characters and enables me not to see or hear them. It helps me to create that indispensable, agonising tension, to hear within me a ringing silence. Then it seems that out of that silence my voice can cut like a laser through the walls of the theater to soar above the whole universe and tell of the tragic fate of Marfa, the bride of Ivan the Terrible.

In Leningrad after the blockade I would often pass a madwoman not far from my apartment building. She was always clutching a few dry branches and chips of wood to her breast, and for hours would search intently for something on the sidewalk. She never addressed or looked at anyone. I remember that the first time I saw her I was deeply affected by her intensity and the despair of her introverted gaze. It was as if she were trying to recall something, straining to make out, in the depths of a bottomless chasm, something known to her alone . . . This incident from real life helped me when I was preparing the role of Marfa.

I sang Aïda at the Bolshoi for the first time during the 1957–1958 season. As always, the season began in September and, having calculated the number of rehearsals, I planned on giving my first performance in March. But I soon realised that we were going to have another child. What was I to do? Olga was only eighteen months old, and I had just begun to work at full strength again. I had made such great plans. My husband exulted, while I tried to picture our future life. We had only Rimma – the apartment, Olga, and soon a second child would all rest on her shoulders. There was no question of hiring another housemaid, because my Leporella* simply could not bear anyone else's presence in her domain – the kitchen and the nursery. All my attempts in that direction ended in a fight, tears, and the flight of the victim. I knew she loved me, but from time to time, 'to let off steam,' she would slam the door and go off 'for good.' I loved her, too; so after a while I would call her, and she would come back and magnanimously forgive me. If I didn't call, she would come back anyway, and then I would forgive her. That was our life.

But how would she be able to cope on her own, with such a household? And the lines? I couldn't be counted on because of the theater. And my Aïda? . . . The dream of my life? Once again the sleepless nights, the breast-feeding. I unloaded all my gloomy thoughts on my husband.

'You should be ashamed of yourself,' he told me. 'There's such happiness in store for us. But instead of rejoicing, your mind is filled with calculations.'

'Who else is going to think about them? It's fine for you. You take your cello in your arms and off you go. But even as things are, my Rimessa has always had me twisted around her little finger. Every time something rubs her the wrong way, she slams

* From Leporello, the male servant in *Don Giovanni*.

the door and goes off for a week. And what am I supposed to do? Drag two little children to the theater with me? I have rehearsals every day. Are you going to baby-sit for them? Is that it?'

'We'll all help you!'

'Oh, sure. And most of the help will come from you, of course.'

'Do you want me to talk to Rimma right now? You're always complicating things. Rimma, come here!'

The response was total silence.

'Rimma!'

Silence. Nobody.

'Rimma-a-a!'

'Well, what is it? Why are you shouting? This isn't the wilderness. I'm not deaf. I hear you.' And our Rimessa appeared in the doorway like Nemesis, full of resolve to offer prompt resistance and answer 'No!' to everything.

'All I hear the whole day long is "Rimma! Rimma!" If only you'd pack up and leave! You won't let a person live! People hang around the house from morning till night, and I can't cook enough for everybody. I never leave the stove. What am I, a slave? "Rimma! Rimma!" You don't even give me time to feed the poor child. What parents!'

Having finally had her say, she crossed her arms and stared at us like a snake hypnotising two rabbits. 'Well, what is it? More guests? But my refrigerator is empty. Some of your riffraff from the conservatory were here this afternoon, and they cleaned everything out.'

'No, no one is coming. But I really don't know how to begin now. Maybe some other time.'

Right before my very eyes, Rostropovich was breaking down into his component parts. 'No, not another time!' I said. 'Right now! You were so cocksure of yourself, now talk to her! It's all so easy and simple for you.'

'You see, Rimma, when there's only one child in a family,' Rostropovich was beginning from miles away, 'he grows up self-centered. And –'

'I've already told you a hundred times that for nothing in the world will I let Olga go to a nursery school. Don't even dream of it!'

'Just wait a minute. That's not what I'm getting at. And please try not to interrupt – I'm losing my train of thought. We know that you love our family, and that you're devoted to us, and we appreciate that in you. But the thing is that a child needs company, and –'

'What? You've decided to hire a governess? Again? I won't let her cross the threshold! So, you still want to take Olga away from me. You're still not satisfied. I work for you like a slave, spend all day in lines, and don't sleep at night. And who taught Olga to sing Madama Butterfly? Who taught her "No, I don't love you"? Me, that's who!'

'Please! Let me finish! Galina Pavlovna is pregnant.'

'Oy! . . . Galina Pavlovna! . . .'

'Now do you understand?'

'I understand . . . Oy, Galina Pavlovna! . . . Dear one . . .'

'But don't you dare tell a soul. It's a secret.'

'We thought we'd warn you and ask if you'd agree to take care of both children. Of course, we'll get you a helper.'

'How can you even ask? Good Lord! Another child! What happiness! But I beg you not to hire anybody else. You know how I am. I'd only drive her out of here anyway.'

'But it will be hard on you.'

'Where did you get that idea? What's the big deal, cooking dinner and looking after two children? Have I ever complained?'

With that, the family council came to an end. Slava promised to keep everything secret until I took a leave of absence, and not to go abroad during my last month, but to stay with me.

I didn't say a word to anyone at the theater, and time flew by. I sang my repertory as always and continued working on Aïda with Melik-Pashayev and Pokrovsky. I had set myself the goal of singing the role that season, and I was not about to let my condition interfere. So I watched my weight very carefully. And when I went to rehearsals I would squeeze myself into a corset, and no one noticed a thing.

Only Vera, my dressmaker at the theater, looked at me suspiciously. 'Galina Pavlovna, you seem to have . . . grown a bit stronger.' (She never said 'put on weight,' so as not to upset me.) And once when she was changing my costume during an intermission of *Taming of the Shrew*, she grumbled, 'The dress just won't fasten.'

'I've gotten stronger . . . Pull harder on the laces and it will fasten.'

'I can do it, but I'd rather not . . .'

'Why not?'

'I don't know . . .'

'If you don't know, then pull, I tell you! The third bell has already rung.'

'All right, but look out! I'm a powerhouse.'

'I know – you could cinch the waist of an elephant.'

'That's true. Okay, here goes!'

She dug one knee into my back, and how she pulled! She fastened that dress, and the next thing I knew I was coming to on the sofa. The intermission was extended by forty minutes, but I finished the performance.

After a rest at home, I was back at the theater again, singing through Aïda with the pianist, and rehearsing at full voice with the others. Finally, the dress rehearsal – and I had come to the end of the stretch: I sang in *Aïda*. I was already six months along. Slava was in the audience, and was so anxious he didn't see or hear anything. The only thing he wanted was for the performance to be over as quickly as possible. But I was carrying the pregnancy well, and for the whole time I was in wonderful voice. If it had not been for the endless day-to-day problems of Soviet life I would have had half a dozen children.

The day after my triumph I showed up at the opera office without a corset and, not saying a word, posed in profile before the manager of the company. She looked at my belly as if she were under a spell, and didn't breathe.

'Take me off the bill for all performances. I'm going to have a baby in three months.'

Her mouth fell open, and she tried to say something. But then, dismissing the idea with a wave of her hand, she rushed to the director's office, where at that moment a meeting of the arts council was in progress. Opening the door wide, she announced in a tragic voice: 'Vishnevskaya is pregnant! She's taking a leave of absence.'

From all sides a clamor arose: 'How can that be? She sang last night, and nothing was visible. It can't be! Who told you?'

'I've just seen for myself. Six months. Big as that!'

Melik-Pashayev stood up, confused, and looked around at everyone. 'Comrades, when will this shocking business come to an end?'

I had fouled up his plans. But I still sang Verdi's *Requiem* with him. Not only that – before giving birth I managed to record *Eugene Onegin* again, this time for a film. It was the same one for which I had had the screen test in Leningrad, just after Olga was born. At that time, Tatyana was a nursing mother, and now she was very pregnant. In the film, as a result, my voice is heard but the part is played by an actress.

While pacing the lobby of a small hospital on the evening of June 22, 1958, Slava heard the deafening cry of his infant from the third floor. The old nurse on duty there stood up solemnly. 'I congratulate you, my dear. A son!'

'Really?' Slava scarcely managed to get it out.

'A son, I say. I can tell by the voice. Only boys yell like that.'

Out of sheer joy Rostropovich pulled out one hundred rubles for her.

'What's this for? It's an awful lot!' the old woman exclaimed, beaming. 'Well, thank you. God grant you good health. I'll run up and tell your wife how happy you are.'

The birth had been difficult. I was lying there half-conscious when a head appeared in the door. 'Congratulations on your baby boy!'

'Thank you. But it's not a boy, it's a girl.'

The head vanished.

From the way the nurse slowly came down the stairs and held out the hundred to him, Slava understood at once.

'What's this?'

'Take your hundred back. It's a girl.'

'No, please keep it. I'm happy anyway. Just take a note to my wife for me. I'll write it right now.'

Again the head appeared in the door. 'Here's a note from your husband. He's happy. So happy!'

Thank you for our daughter. She is of course as beautiful as you
. . . I'm terribly glad it wasn't a boy. The two sisters will grow
up together, and when I (not you!) grow old, they'll look after
me . . . If you have no objection, let's call her Elena . . . Elena
the Fair.*

---

* The name of a character in a familiar Russian fairy tale.

FOURTEEN

The minister of culture during the late 1950s was Nikolai Mikhailov, who before that had been first secretary of the Komsomol's Central Committee for many years. In his youth he had been a hoodlum, dreaded marauder of the Moscow outskirts. His appearance was as unremarkable as his intellect, and often at receptions I simply didn't recognise him among the crowd.

Slava used to poke me in the side and whisper, 'Why don't you greet him?'

'But who is it?'

'Are you out of your mind? That's Mikhailov.'

'Oh, then, hello.'

Of the blockheads in that position, I think he was one of the worst. It was he who had the brilliant idea of larding the Bolshoi's repertory with operas by composers from all the national republics. 'After all, operas by the Russian composers Tchaikovsky and Glinka are performed in Uzbekistan and Azerbaijan, so the Bolshoi, in turn, should produce operas by Uzbek, Azerbaijani, Tadzhik, and other non-Russian Soviet composers.'

Under Khrushchev's slogan, 'The next generation of Soviet people will live under communism!' ten-day festivals of the art of the national republics swept over the Bolshoi Theater like waves of an epidemic. At every one of those occasions, orchestras, choruses, and dance ensembles – thousands of performers – flooded the theater and paralysed the Bolshoi for two weeks. Productions were canceled, artists loitered about without work, collected their pay, and waited until the invasion was finally over.

It is impossible to imagine how many millions of rubles each ten-day festival cost. Hundreds of new costumes, resplendent with gold and jewels, glittered before the leaders in their loge.

The singers' barrel chests swelled in one communal and deafening roar, glorifying the Party and the government. The dance ensembles competed with one another to make splinters of the Bolshoi stage. Finally, after ten days, the most frightful of the show-offs got what they had come for: awards, titles, decorations. And the next day they were off, gone and forgotten.

But Minister of Culture Mikhailov didn't manage to realise his great plan. The powers that be wanted to get Ekaterina Furtseva out of the Politburo, and they gave her Mikhailov's job. But Ekaterina (or 'Katya,' as everyone called her behind her back) didn't care to mine the lode left by her predecessor. She had her own program, having decided that professional art was not even necessary. Her vision was to cover the country with a network of amateur theatrical groups in which, in their spare time, laborers from the fields, plants, and factories, along with what was left of the puny intelligentsia, would display their inspiration and talents to the public. At each theatrical meeting, Minister Furtseva would go on rapturously about these brilliant prospects for our Soviet art, and during the first years of her reign she devoted much effort and imagination to her idea. But seeing that artists were a hardy breed and that all her life would probably not suffice to exterminate them so easily, Furtseva shifted with real feminine fickleness to another hobby: diamonds, gold, and furs. And she gave the professional artists the job of collecting them for her, since the amateurs were not money-earners.

She preferred foreign currency, as I can testify myself. In Paris, during the Bolshoi's forty-day tour in 1969, I gave her $400 – my entire fee at $10 a day. Quite simply, I gave her a bribe so that she would let me go abroad on my own contracts. (Otherwise, it would have been the way it often was: the contract would be negotiated with my name, but another singer would go.) I was perturbed and all in a sweat when I handed her the money, but she took it calmly, offhandedly, with a mere 'Thank you.'

She had her own prospectors cum artists, who frequently went abroad on tours during her years as minister but who disappeared from the world's stages after her death in 1974. When a tour was over, the prospector – usually a woman – would make the rounds of the artists, hat in hand, and collect $100 from each 'for Katya.'

If you didn't give, you wouldn't go the next time. I was told this by artists of the folk instruments orchestra, who had been on tour in England. The tribute was collected from them by a friend of Furtseva, a singer from the Bolshoi we called 'Katya's sponge' (she would go to the bathhouse with Furtseva). The singer often traveled with that particular group. Each time she was given special instructions from her boss and knew exactly what to buy. She would stuff several suitcases with her purchases and drag them back to Moscow.

Katya had grown very attached to vodka, and would show up drunk at rehearsals and previews, especially in the last years. For all that, this simple Russian peasant woman had great charm. She had begun her career as a loom operator at a textile plant and had risen to be the only woman member of the Politburo. Having gone through hell and high water, she may have been grasping, but she was not the slightest bit stupid. She had developed her own professional techniques, and knew well how to make fools out of people. With her great gift of persuasion, she would make promises and the person would go away charmed with her warmth and femininity, thanking her.

It would soon emerge that she was doing everything wrong, but, even so, it was impossible not to yield to her charm. I had my own way of talking to her with regard to Bolshoi business. If, typically, she would begin to get off the subject, trying to fool me with fine rhetoric, I would stare into her eyes but not listen to a word. The main thing was not to yield, not to forget one's own objective. As soon as Katya stopped talking, I would try to get my objective across. She would talk about one thing, and I would talk about another.

She held on to the position of minister of culture for a long time: fourteen years, longer than anyone before her. From time to time there were rumors that she was being fired, that new candidates had been named, but she always survived. Even in the last 'dacha' scandal, when she was caught red-handed stealing rugs from the Palace of Congresses,* she managed, like a cat

* She had used them to carpet the floors of her daughter's dacha; later it was revealed that the entire dacha had been built at government expense.

thrown out of a window, to land on her feet. Katya knew all the government elite's most cherished secrets, and she used their methods masterfully.

When she died, there were rumors that it had been a suicide. And the fact that her civil funeral was held only in a branch of the Moscow Art Theater would attest that something about her death had indeed been very strange.

I already had Aïda, Butterfly, and Tatyana in my repertory, but I longed for a big, tragic role like Lady Macbeth of Mtsensk or Cherubini's Medea. The Bolshoi's repertory was limited; the same operas were shown year after year over a period of decades. These were of course the Russian operas and, among Western ones, primarily *La Traviata*, *Rigoletto*, *The Barber of Seville*, *Carmen*, and *Aïda*. I wanted to sing Mussorgsky, but there were no parts for me in his operas. Then I looked into his songs, and came upon that great treasure, *Songs and Dances of Death*. What kind of voice did Mussorgsky have in mind when he wrote that cycle? None. In the first three songs he needed a dark color, a mysterious atmosphere, and he gave them to a bass. But in the fourth, 'The Commander,' he imagined a sharp, 'trumpet-like' sound, and wrote it for a dramatic tenor. And, unworried by the consequences, he included all in the same cycle.

I had never heard that cycle performed by anyone – Mussorgsky's songs are little sung in Russia – and I decided to approach it as a new work written only recently and especially for me. I was struck by the scope of the passions and the high tragedy of the whole cycle – the tremendous possibilities for the actor's metamorphosis from one role to another. In 'Cradle Song,' death is an affectionate nanny leaning over a dying child. She manages to lull him to sleep without frightening him. Only the mother sees the nanny for what she really is and hears her soul-chilling voice. Horrified, she thrashes about, aware of her powerlessness before mighty Death. Next, beginning with the opening bars of 'Serenade,' the composer creates the atmosphere of a still white night. And I see, sitting by a window, a delicate girl, lovely in her transparent beauty – she is dying. She dreams of her fairy-tale knight, and awaits him. She whispers something, calls, and finds him there, beneath her window. Death, in the form of the mysterious knight she has long awaited, sings her a serenade and summons her with promises of unearthly happiness and love. Admiring her beauty – panting in anticipation of his imminent victory – he finally kills her with his kiss. In the third song, 'Trepak,' Death appears to a poor little drunken peasant in the form of a reckless, loose peasant woman. Seizing him firmly, she whirls with him in a howling blizzard, dragging him into the woods, farther and farther from the road. The poor fellow stomps the earth with his freezing heels and swings his arms in vain attempts to warm himself with this, his last dance. They say that a freezing person does not die in agony – he only has a sudden overwhelming desire to sleep. And Mussorgsky's dying peasant, growing numb in the cold, dreams of a warm, sunny day, of a field of ripe, golden rye, and boundless blue sky . . .

In 'The Commander,' when the din of clashing swords has died down and in the field of the recent bloody battle only the screams and moans of the dying remain, Death appears in its true form, with no masquerade: a dazzlingly white skeleton on a warhorse. Filled with majesty and exultation, Death gallops over the human wreckage, taking stock of the dead host with his sharp eye. Satisfied that he is victorious, he whirls over it in a slow, heavy, and triumphant dance.

I see Mussorgsky's musical image of Death as based on a notion of an aggressiveness and power that crushes everything. The realisation of Death's might and the inevitability of his victory must not be lost even in the most delicate of *pianos*. Death's confidence, and the implacability with which he moves toward a set goal must be maintained in the performance from beginning to end. No person living will escape him. There are no immortals.

I worked for two years on that long-awaited tragic role – it was one of the most important projects of my career. And it was then that I felt, for the first time, my ethnic identity as a Russian singer.

I came to that song cycle armed with vocal and acting skills, having behind me fifteen years of work on the stage and a rich life experience. I had something to convey to an audience about death, having myself been through the loss of a child: he had died in my arms. I would never forget how in desperation I had collapsed on the floor by his bed, crying, cursing, begging that my little child not be taken from me. How, insane with grief, I tried to breathe my own breath into his ever-colder lips.

And as I later lay dying of consumption, I was spellbound by the presentiment of a great transition from this earthly life to an eternal one. Vivid in memory were images of the blockade of Leningrad: frozen corpses sprawling in the streets; death mowing down hundreds of thousands of people. I have felt his cold breath near me more than once. Those images crowded my imagination, organising themselves, taking on the clarity of a sketch, the precision of phrasing, the idiom of the stage.

The performance of such roles demands that the artist bare himself. But how much he must have in his soul, how many riches he must accumulate within, before he can dare to publicly reveal himself! Here I can give, as an example, the art of my husband, Mstislav Rostropovich. The divine spark that made him a musician glows in him so brightly and purely that he cannot but lay it bare. And he does it as naturally and as instinctively as a sculptor hastens to unveil his work.

In the summer of 1960, during the time I was working on the Mussorgsky, Shostakovich called us to his place and asked us to listen to his new work, a song cycle called 'Satires' based on the verse of Sasha Cherny,* for soprano with piano accompaniment. Dmitri Dmitriyevich himself played and sang, while Slava and I remained rooted to our chairs, overwhelmed by the unimpeded flow of sarcasm and black humor.

'Do you like it, Galya?'

I could only whisper, 'Dmitri Dmitriyevich, it's phenomenal!'

'I wrote it for you in the hopes you wouldn't decline to sing it.'

'Decline?' I was hoarse with excitement. Dmitri Dmitriyevich got up from the piano, took the music, and before handing it to

---

* Pen name of Alexander Glikberg (1880–1932), satirical poet.

me, said, 'If you don't object, I'd like to dedicate this work to you.'
He wrote in the manuscript: 'Dedicated to Galina Pavlovna
Vishnevskaya,' and made me a gift of it.

Slava and I hurried home toting the precious gift – we were
crazy with happiness. How had Dmitri Dmitriyevich, who knew
me only as an opera singer, surmised my past career as a
music-hall singer? His cycle had been written for none other than
a music-hall singer with an operatic voice!

A few days later we performed the new work for Dmitri
Dmitriyevich.

'Remarkable! Simply remarkable! There's just one thing: I'm
afraid they won't let it be performed.'

And he was right. One of the poems was 'Our Posterity.'
Though written in 1910, it had recently been published in the
Soviet Union. Yet with the music of Shostakovich it took on an
entirely different meaning – it became an indictment of the
current Soviet regime and its insane ideology:

> *Our forebears crawled into cells,*
> *And often whispered there:*
> *'It's tough, friends, but probably*
> *Our kids will be freer than us.'*
> *The kids grew up, and they too*
> *Crawled into cells in time of danger,*
> *And whispered: 'Our kids*
> *Will greet the sun after us.'*
> *And now, as for all time,*
> *There is but one consolation:*
> *'Our kids will be in Mecca,*
> *If we are not fated to be.'*
> *They have even predicted the times:*
> *Some say two centuries, others say five.*
> *Meanwhile, lie in sadness*
> *And babble like an idiot.*
> *Obscene gestures are in disguise,*
> *The world is scrubbed, combed, nice . . .*
> *In two centuries! To hell with that!*
> *Am I Methuselah?*

> *And I'm like an eagle-owl among the ruins*
> *Of broken gods.*
> *I have neither friends nor enemies*
> *Among descendants not yet born.*
> *I want a little light*
> *For myself, while I'm still alive.*
> *Everyone from the tailor to the poet*
> *Understands my call.*
> *And our posterity? Let our posterity,*
> *Fulfilling their fate*
> *And cursing* their *posterity,*
> *Beat their heads against a wall!*

It was clear the authorities would not allow such verse to be sung on stage. The words refer to today, and could not be said better. I had an idea. 'Dmitri Dmitriyevich, instead of calling the cycle "Satires" call it "Pictures of the Past." Throw them that bone and they might sanction it. Yesterday is part of the past, too; the public will see it that way.'

He was satisfied, and snickered at the irony of it. 'Beautifully thought out, Galya! Beautifully thought out. Under "Satires" we'll put "Pictures of the Past" in parentheses, like a kind of fig leaf. We'll cover up the embarrassing parts for them.'

In that way the cycle got its name. But we were never sure, right up until the time of the concert, that they wouldn't take it off the program. The authorisation came only at the last minute.

On the evening of February 22, 1961, the concert hall was jammed with people. All of Moscow waited impatiently for Shostakovich's new work with the seditious verses. Slava accompanied me. For the first part of the program, I sang Mussorgsky's *Songs and Dances of Death.* For the second part, I sang a number of works by Shostakovich, including 'Pictures of the Past.' As I began 'Our Posterity,' I could see that the audience was taut with tension. Stalin's and Beria's crimes were being exposed; the verses were hitting bull's-eye:

> *And I'm like an eagle-owl among the ruins*
> *Of broken gods.*

Some of Russia's gods had been overthrown, but others had arrived to take their place.

When I finished, the audience did not so much shout as roar. They demanded an encore, and we repeated the whole cycle for them, but they still refused to let us go; we performed the entire work yet another time.

This work came unexpected after all of Shostakovich's tragic symphonies. It was as if he had reached back to the distant past, to the time when he had written *Lady Macbeth of Mtsensk*, feeling himself once again young and full of vital forces. The cycle – in music as well as verse – is savory and succulent, alive with dashing, youthful energy. But one quality sets it apart from the rest of Shostakovich's work. Here he scoffs – and he does so openly and maliciously. He points up the ignorance of critics, the vulgarity and poverty of life around him, the stupidity of the primitive ideology that is stuffed into our heads from childhood.

Soon after the premiere, Slava and I were invited to perform the cycle on Moscow television. We went to the studio, although I told Slava at the time that it was bound to be a fiasco – that they would never let us do 'Our Posterity.' We started to rehearse. The technicians set up the lights and got the cameras ready. Then, suddenly, stop! The producer of the show came running in, asked for the music, and read through it as frightened as if he were holding a live cobra. Without a word, he ran off.

'What did I tell you? It was pointless coming here – we're wasting our time.'

The producer came back, beaming. 'Galina Pavlovna, the cycle is very long, and our time is short. We'll have to cut something.'

Of course. Who would have doubted it?

'Let's cut "Our Posterity,"' he continued.

'What do you mean, "cut"? It's a cycle – all the pieces are interrelated. We won't cut anything. Don't beat around the bush. It's plain to see that you're afraid, but why? That poem has been published in a Soviet edition: it has passed the censors. Go wherever it is you're supposed to go and tell them that either we do the whole cycle or we won't do it at all.'

Once again he ran off, this time for quite a while. Slava and I waited a little, then put on our coats, sent them all to the devil, and went home. The cycle was never aired.

I was the only singer to perform that work. Because of 'Our Posterity,' the cycle was not published in the Soviet Union for several years, and was published only after it had appeared abroad.

The next summer, several months after the premiere of 'Pictures of the Past,' I received a big package wrapped in coarse, crumpled gray paper. 'Look at that paper!' I said to Slava. 'Stores wrap meat in it.' The return address read: Solodcha, a village in the Ryazan District, and the name 'D. Shostakovich.' He was vacationing there. I opened the package, and removed the manuscript of Shostakovich's orchestration of Mussorgsky's *Songs and Dances of Death*. On the first page, I read: 'I dedicate this orchestration of *Songs and Dances of Death* to Galina Pavlovna Vishnevskaya. D. Shostakovich.' For that, life is worth living!

Perhaps if Dmitri Dmitriyevich had not heard *Songs and Dances of Death* at my concert that evening, he might not have orchestrated them then and there. At any rate, influenced by those compositions, his Thirteenth Symphony appeared the next year, followed by *The Execution of Stepan Razin* and, finally, the Fourteenth Symphony.

On August 9, 1961, Maxim's wife, Lena, gave birth to a son, and Dmitri Dmitriyevich came to see us with the news. Of course he was glad to have a grandson to carry on the family name, but we found him especially withdrawn and taciturn that evening. It was as if some thought were tormenting him, as if he wanted to articulate it but simply couldn't.

He stayed a long time. Finally he stood up abruptly, as he always did, said good-bye, and went to the door. But there he stopped, and with his typical, curt directness suddenly said, 'They want to name my grandson Dmitri, don't you know? I'm against it. But I don't know how to tell Maxim that. And in any case he doesn't pay any attention to what I say anyway. Could you perhaps talk to him, Galya?'

I was stunned by the improbability of it: a grandson fathered by his adored son, and he didn't want the child named after him!

'But why are you against it, Dmitri Dmitriyevich? It's wonderful! Another Dmitri Shostakovich!'

He made a wry face. 'They say it's an omen – he'll drive me out of the world.' And he gave me a quick, searching glance.

'Oh, come on! Who told you such nonsense? The Jews apparently have the custom of naming a child in memory of a dead person, but we Orthodox name them in honor of the living. After all, you were named after your father; now your grandson will be a third Dmitri Shostakovich.'

He beamed, as if he had been relieved of a heavy burden. 'Really? Well, thank you. Thank you very much.'

It was plain that he was glad to take my word for it.

Shostakovich was afraid of death – you can hear that in his music. And you can feel it in his orchestration of Mussorgsky's *Songs and Dances of Death*.

Mussorgsky did not fear death. He had a believer's humility for the majesty of it, for the moment when the soul leaves the flesh behind and takes on immortality . . . Shostakovich was terrified by death – terrified by the inevitable. He hated it and resisted it with all his strength. The importance he gave to the brass and percussion instruments in his orchestration put an edge on Mussorgsky's ideas, and made them harsher. One feels death in the piercing chords of the brass. In 'The Commander,' the sinister image is portrayed by a rattling of bones, by having the string instruments play *col legno*; that is, hitting the strings with the sticks of the bows.

Shortly after his grandson was born, Dmitri Dmitriyevich came to our place looking very out of sorts. At dinner, everything became clear.

'Imagine, Galya!' Slava said to me. 'Dmitri Dmitriyevich tells me he intends to get married.'

'But that's wonderful!'

'That's what I think. But Dmitri Dmitriyevich is worried that she's too young.'

'Yes, Galya, it's an awkward situation. She's younger than my daughter, and I'm embarrassed to tell the children. There's more than thirty years' difference between us. I suppose I'm too old for her.'

'Old? But look what a stallion you are! If I hadn't been married to Slava, I'd have grabbed you for a husband long ago. Old? But you're only fifty-six!'

He was delighted and showed it. 'Do you mean that – that I'm not old?'

'I swear it!'

'Let me bring her by and introduce her to you, then. Her name is Irina.'

The very next day, Dmitri Dmitriyevich and Irina paid us a visit. It was the first time they had appeared anywhere together. She was very young, modest, and sat all evening without raising her eyes. Seeing that we liked her and approved of his choice, Dmitri Dmitriyevich grew more and more relaxed and light-hearted. All at once, like a little boy, he shyly took her hand. Never had I known Shostakovich to act out of an inner impulse like that, and touch another person – man or woman. At most he would pat his grandsons on the head.

That petite woman with the quiet voice proved to be a vigorous mistress of the household, and quickly organised the life of that huge family. It was with her that Dmitri Dmitriyevich finally came to know domestic peace. He had just moved from Kutuzovsky Prospekt into our building, to the apartment next to ours – his bedroom shared a wall with our living room. His young wife got the new apartment into shape and rearranged things at the dacha in Zhukovka so that Dmitri Dmitriyevich would be spared the noisy goings-on of the young people and their growing families. Now he had his own bedroom and study on the second floor of that house. A devoted wife, she assumed all household concerns and created the ideal atmosphere for his work. Surely, she prolonged his life by several years.

In the autumn of 1962, Dmitri Dmitriyevich invited us to his place to hear his new symphony, the Thirteenth. Also present were the composers Aram Khachaturian and Moisei Vainberg, the conductor Kirill Kondrashin, and the poet Evgeny Evtushenko. Evtushenko was still young and impulsive; he had yet to put himself on a leash. His poem 'Babi Yar' had raised him to Olympus in a single day. He felt himself on the crest of a wave, and made a show of his boldness as a rebel, seeing that he was much praised for it. But then he had a right to: it was a remarkable poem. Shostakovich had worked 'Babi Yar' into the Thirteenth Symphony, along with several other poems of Evtushenko's.

Dmitri Dmitriyevich was an excellent pianist, and always played his new works for friends himself until his illness made that impossible. On that autumn evening he sat down at the piano, played the prelude, and began to sing softly:

> *'No monument stands over Babi Yar . . .'*

I always felt I was taking part in a secret rite when, in our presence, yet one more work of Shostakovich's was being exposed to the world. Beginning with the first measures of that piece, all of us were gripped by an atmosphere of oppressive and tragic presentiment. Dmitri Dmitriyevich softly continued:

> *'Now I seem to be a Jew.*
> *Here I plod through ancient Egypt.*
> *Here I perish crucified, on the cross,*
> *And to this day I bear the scars of nails.'*

With Shostakovich's music, the poem we all knew so well grew to global proportions and burned like red-hot iron. I could imagine suddenly the blood upon his shoulders, the 'scars of nails,' and my hair stood on end . . .

> *'I seem to be Dreyfus,*
> *The Philistine is both informer and judge.'*

For a moment he paused. How frightening to be hearing those words from the mouth of Shostakovich! And he continued to play, not singing so much as shouting:

> *'I am behind bars. Beset on every side.*
> *Hounded, spat on, slandered . . .'*

He paused once more and was silent as though he had stopped breathing. Then he repeated the lines, stressing every word:

'Hounded, spat on, slandered . . .'

Yes, there was good reason why the authorities were vigilant in censoring those works that Shostakovich chose to accompany with text. They knew that he wrote only about what he himself had experienced, and hence were afraid to give him the opportunity to speak the truth through the voice of a singer. You can invent any subject matter if the music has no lyrics – even the most false – but the words of a song make their own undeniable statement.

We all congratulated Dmitri Dmitriyevich and Evtushenko, and were so joyful that we gave no thought to what torments might lie in store for Shostakovich's new symphony.

He asked, 'Galya, whom can you recommend as a soloist? I need a good bass.'

'Dmitri Dmitriyevich, for the first time in my life I'm sorry I'm not a bass. I think the lucky one should be Alexander Vedernikov of the Bolshoi. He has a good voice, but most important, he's a talented artist, a real musician. If you like, I'll tell him to call you.'

He agreed, and when Slava and I got home, I immediately called Vedernikov. 'Listen, Sanya.* Shostakovich has written an extraordinary symphony for orchestra, a chorus of basses, and a bass soloist, using the text of Evtushenko's poem "Babi Yar." Would you like to sing it?'

I could hear him choking with happiness. 'Of course I'd like to!'

'Then call Dmitri Dmitriyevich tomorrow, and arrange a meeting. I've already told him about you. If you only knew how I envy you!'

'Thank you, Galka. I'll never forget it. I'm so happy I won't sleep all night.'

The next day he went to Shostakovich's place. The composer played the whole symphony for him, and gave him the music; the grateful, exultant Sanya dashed home.

---

* A diminutive of 'Alexander.'

Excellent performers were lined up for the symphony and Kondrashin was to conduct. It seemed that everything was going perfectly. But not for long!

In the Central Committee's Department of Agitation and Propaganda, the riffraff were already poking around. The papers published a review of 'Babi Yar' in which Evtushenko was charged with ignoring the role that the Russian people played in the destruction of Nazi Germany, distorting the truth about the victims of fascism, and so on.

Vedernikov called me at home. 'Listen, Galka. I got the music from Shostakovich and agreed to sing, but, you know . . . I can't.'

'*What?* Have you gone out of your mind?'

'Well, those Jews . . . that "Babi Yar" . . .'

'Then why did you take the music from Dmitri Dmitriyevich? You knew it was about Jews. And that genius played it especially for you – for a blockhead! Aren't you ashamed?'

I could hear him squirming on the other end of the line. 'It wasn't just Jews who were killed in the war . . . Russians were killed too . . .'

'Every idiot knows how many millions of Russians were killed. But this particular work is about fascists who shot Jews in Babi Yar.'

'No, I'm not going to sing it . . . I'm a citizen –'

'You're a moron, not a citizen! All right, there's no point talking to you. It's clear who has worked on you and what side of the mouth you're talking out of. And to think that I was the one who gave your name to Shostakovich! Give me the music – I'll return it to him myself.'

When Slava and I told Dmitri Dmitriyevich that Vedernikov had refused to sing, he wasn't all that astonished: it was as if he'd been expecting it. The Party had already demanded that the text be revised or they would ban the performance. Dmitri Dmitriyevich responded by saying he would not change a single line, and would make no cuts. Either it was produced as written, or they could cancel the premiere.

Evtushenko hurried around Moscow, pulling out all the government stops at his disposal, while I looked for another soloist.

We needed not only a good voice but a man we could count on. I decided to turn to Victor Nechipailo, another soloist with the Bolshoi. He had a remarkable voice, and was a Leningrader, like me and Dmitri Dmitriyevich. Slava and I went to his place and told him the story of Vedernikov: that they had frightened him and worked him over, and that he had been so intimidated that he had returned the music to Shostakovich.

'You understand that you must think it over very carefully and decide whether you can bear up in this damned situation or not. If you don't feel strong enough, say so right now, because returning the music to Shostakovich a second time is out of the question. Will you sing it?'

'I will. Give me the music.'

He ran through the score quickly, and sang it for Dmitri Dmitriyevich, who was very pleased with him.

Interestingly enough, during those 1962 fall days when the battle between Shostakovich and the Central Committee for the Thirteenth Symphony's right to life was going on under our eyes, a remarkable event took place. On November 11 a regular issue of the journal *Novy Mir* appeared on the stands, and in it was Solzhenitsyn's novella *One Day in the Life of Ivan Denisovich*. Inadvertently, the Soviet government had let the genie out of the bottle, and however hard they tried later, they couldn't put it back in. We were bewildered that while the authorities were trying to prevent the performance of the Thirteenth Symphony, they had permitted the publication of such a powerful story about the Soviet camps. But as it turned out, Alexander Tvardovsky, the editor in chief of *Novy Mir*, had succeeded in contriving a way. He had slipped a copy of *Ivan Denisovich* directly to Khrushchev. The premier, who had not yet dismounted the soapbox of the recent Twenty-second Party Congress at which he had openly called Stalin a murderer and pronounced him anathema, read the work and ordered its immediate publication. Shostakovich, on the other hand, was being persecuted by Stalin's old gang, which had dozens of years of experience in these matters beneath its belt.

Suddenly, early in the morning on the day of the concert, before the dress rehearsal, Nechipailo called me at home in a panic to say that he couldn't sing the Thirteenth Symphony that night because he had been scheduled for a production at the Bolshoi. Here was a new one; I, who knew all the backstage undercurrents, could not have foreseen that.

A singer whose name was on the showbill – *Don Carlo*, I believe – had been ordered to 'get sick' so that Nechipailo, who would not cooperate by refusing to perform in the premiere of the Thirteenth Symphony, would be obliged that evening to fill in at the Bolshoi production. It was a well-prepared blow, and it seemed that this time the authorities had succeeded in sabotaging the premiere. But Shostakovich's persecutors had not thought their game out completely. A young singer named Gramadsky who had just graduated from the conservatory had also learned the bass part for future concerts. But since he had not taken part in the orchestra rehearsals, he had not come to the attention of the hatchetmen. Unaware of what had happened – that there was no soloist for the evening concert – he had come to hear the dress rehearsal, where the conductor Kondrashin collared him.

'Can you sing in the rehearsal right now, and at the concert tonight?'

'I can.'

That was returning a blow for a blow! And as the dress rehearsal for the evening premiere went on that morning of December 18, the people at the Central Committee conferred as to whether they should officially ban it. It was not until midday that authorisation came for the performance.

Until the first bars of the music issued from the stage, however, we were not sure that the concert would be held. Its success was tremendous. But the symphony would not have a stable life unless it got abroad as soon as possible. When Slava went on tour in America he smuggled the score out with him and gave it to the conductor of the Philadelphia Orchestra, Eugene Ormandy. The premiere of the Thirteenth Symphony was perceived by all the intelligentsia as a great victory of art over politics.

And then suddenly, literally days after the premiere – and to Shostakovich's amazement – Evtushenko published a second version of 'Babi Yar' in *Literaturnaya Gazeta* – a version obsequiously expurgated and ironed out.

What a horrible fate the poets of Soviet Russia have had!

Gumilev was shot.
Blok starved to death.
Esenin committed suicide.
Mayakovsky shot himself.
Mandelstam died in a labor camp.
Tsvetaeva hanged herself.
Pasternak was driven into the grave.
Akhmatova was hounded and didn't publish for many years.

And who survived? Those who changed their ways to please the regime – including, unfortunately, one of the most talented poets of the postwar period, Evgeny Evtushenko. He quickly learned how to pander to any taste, how to keep his nose in the wind, how to know when to bow and when to straighten up. Thus he swung from side to side – from 'Babi Yar' to the *Bratsk GES** or, even more exaggeratedly, to 'Kamaz,'† in which his toadyism is enough to make one nauseous. And when no one expected anything good from him any longer, he suddenly appeared on the speakers' platform at a meeting of the Komsomol *aktiv* in the Hall of Columns of the Palace of Unions – a meeting dedicated to the memory of the poet Esenin – and flattened everyone with his remarkable poem:

> *. . . Dear Esenin, old Russia has changed . . .*
> *. . . When the ruddy Komsomol chief*
> *Thundered at us poets with his fist . . .*

That meeting was televised live and nationwide. Judging from how soon afterward the government sent him off to some construction project to redeem his sins, he must have taken quite a drubbing.

---

* Hydroelectric Power Station.
† Kama Automobile Plant.

Many years later, when we were already in exile, we met him in London. He gave Slava a few small volumes of his poems. After reading them, I longed to talk with him and understand what had happened to him – to a man who had begun his career so brilliantly. Soon he was passing through Paris and called us. We invited him to our place. Our apartment in Paris was huge; but in accordance with the old Moscow custom, we sat in the kitchen. I served him *pelmeni*‡ prepared by a Siberian woman, thinking that as a Siberian he would like that.

I wanted to tell him what was on my mind, yet felt I should not say unflattering things to a guest in our own home. Finally I disregarded all ceremony. 'Zhenya. For a long time I've wanted to speak to you about your poems. But I'm warning you, the conversation will be unpleasant. If you don't want to hear me out, tell me. I won't be at all offended.'

He went on guard, and tensed up. 'Go ahead.' He looked on me with cold eyes, only his lips smiled.

'You gave Slava several volumes of your poems. I've read them all, and I have to tell you I'm shattered. Why? Your loss of principle, your insincerity, not to say your lying, and your cynicism toward your own people.'

'In what? Where? Show me! That's not true!'

'Just read your poems from *Kamaz Notebook* or *Monologues* – one written as if you were an American writer, another as an American poet, and yet another as an American actor! Take, for example, "The Monologue of the American Actor Eugene Shamp."'

His face lit up, and he chuckled. 'Oh, *that*!'

'Did you write that about yourself?'

'How did you know? Nobody knows that except my friends. Slava must have told you.'

'Yes, Slava. You told him that "Eugene Shamp" was your nickname. That when you were young your friends, with whom you liked to drink champagne, called you "Eugene" from "Evgeny" and "Shamp" from "champagne." But here is what you wrote as a preface to the monologue. It shook me up so much

‡ Meat dumplings.

that I remember it almost word for word. "Eugene Shamp is a young *American* actor who vigorously protested the dirty war in Vietnam. For his antiwar activities he was removed from the leading role in the film *Cyrano de Bergerac*." But in fact, weren't you supposed to play the role of Cyrano de Bergerac in a film to be made at the Mosfilm Studio?'

'Yes, and I had dreamed of it all my life. I spent several years trying to get permission from every level of the hierarchy. But just as the shooting was scheduled, some bastard banned it. But I damned well outwitted them! I exposed the whole business in "The Monologue of Eugene Shamp," and they were fools enough to publish it.'

'But whom did you outwit?'

'Whom? All those who had to be outwitted.'

'But how could anybody guess that it was you concealed under that name? You tell all those readers of yours – readers of a whopping 130,000 copies – that Shamp was an *American* actor. Is America guilty because the Soviet regime spat on you? Why don't you direct your indignation where it belongs, rather then stir up hatred toward Americans, who owe you nothing and never did you any harm? This is no clever conspiracy, it's a bald-faced lie. So that a few bottle-buddies can snicker over your inside joke, you have deceived your readers more than any KGB disinformation specialist could hope to do. And your heart bleeds for everyone: for the Cubans, Chileans, Cambodians, Vietnamese. And of course for the American unemployed, whose unemployment compensation, by the way, is more than a Soviet worker's pay. You know that very well. Why doesn't your heart bleed for your own miserable compatriots?

> '"*On the roof of Kamaz,*
> *Huge as the palm of Gulliver,*
> *The worker with his kefir and bread . . ."*

'Why don't you feel sorry for the Soviet worker, half-starved and hunchbacked from a lifetime of labor on those Kamazes? Who at fifty is already old? You've been to those gigantic construction projects, you know full well that living conditions there are murderous in the full sense of the word. In the cold of winter they sleep in tents, and the shelves in the stores are always empty. The Soviet man works hard for that hunk of bread in his hand. And after work, instead of eating, he drinks a bottle of vodka – not kefir – and returns to his barracks to bully his neighbors and beat his wife and children. But you glorify that labor-camp life in your poetry, and serve it up to the reader as something romantic. How about:

> '"*Near Slyudyanko, she elegantly hoists*
> *A bag of cement on her back.*
> *With what proud bearing does*
> *The Siberian shout "S'great!"*"'

'But a bag of cement weighs more than a hundred pounds! I've felt them on my back myself during the war, when I was fifteen. *You* should be heaving it – not that unfortunate woman who is straining her belly and will probably either remain sterile all her life or give birth to sickly, defective children. But no, you observe it in rapture! And on top of that, for your verbal whoring, you take money from that poor woman's pocket. Ironic, isn't it? It is she and others like her who pay you out of their pockets – not the general secretary of the Communist Party. And your English wife takes that money, not to stand in lines in front of Soviet stores, but to head for the Moscow market where she pays thirty rubles for a chicken and fifteen for two pounds of tomatoes – about half the monthly pay of that Siberian woman who so delighted you. Do you think she would say "S'great!" if she could read your poems? Not on your life! She'd barrage you with the three-story curses you deserve.'

And I went on, 'Could you even for a moment imagine your English wife with a bag of cement on her shoulders? Or some Frenchwoman? Or an American woman? But of course the very thought of an American sends you into a noble rage. You'd reach for your pen to blast the damned capitalists! But why does the penalcamp labor of Soviet women not horrify you? Why do you rhapsodise about their animal endurance? Do you really look upon your own people as beasts of burden?'

I was carried away and had abandoned all laws of hospitality;
but I couldn't stop. 'We all know it's hard to be an honest writer or
poet in Russia. But if you don't have the courage to speak the
truth openly, don't speak at all. Don't lie to the people. Have the
conscience not to scoff at our unfortunate people with your
romanticising.

'Surely I don't have the right to talk to you this way in my
home. You're our guest. But we may never see one another
again, and I have wanted to say it – it's been tormenting me for a
long time. It wouldn't have mattered so much, but I met you at
Dmitri Dmitriyevich's, and you were collaborating with him so
beautifully in those days.'

He sat there silently, listening with a sardonic smile. Suddenly
he laughed. 'But you're a regular Boyarynya Morozova!* That's
what you are. That's it exactly!'

I raised my hand with two fingers extended – the gesture of the
famous boyarynya as she was shown in Surikov's painting at the
moment of exile. 'Yes, in that sense I'm a Boyarynya Morozova.
And like her, I will never abandon my God for the things of this
world.'

'But you haven't lost anything in your exile. Just look at your
apartment.'

'Hasn't it occurred to you that people have higher values than
material prosperity? One's native land, for example. You cannot
imagine what it is like to have grandchildren who probably will not
understand me. That my words will be only babble to them.'

He soon left, and for a long time I couldn't calm down. His
poem was swirling in my head:

> *The intellectuals are singing jailbirds' songs . . .*
> *They sing as if by general accord,*
> *As if they all were criminals.*

---

* Boyarynya (wife of a boyar) Morozova was a prominent figure in the great
schism in the Orthodox Church in the seventeenth century. She was exiled
from Moscow and imprisoned. The schismatics crossed themselves with two
fingers instead of three.

The songs were not from criminals, but from generations of people who had known the Gulag. During the Stalinist terror, each family, each communal apartment, had its zek,* and often not just one. Millions were arrested who were not bandits, not thieves, but the flower and brains of the nation. It was Lenin who wrote to Gorky: 'The intelligentsia is not the brains of the nation but the shit . . .'

The Soviet intelligentsia returned from the Gulag singing underground songs. Those who survived Soviet concentration camps had come home after serving sentences of ten to twenty-five years and with them they brought thieves' jargon – into their families, into their social class. And since it fell on fertile soil, it bloomed copiously. Because even life 'outside' was imbued with the psychology of the zek, of a person hounded and humiliated. In a camp or in Moscow, the fear is the same. More than a half century of enslaved, censored literature and unbridled atheistic propaganda has led to spiritual impoverishment and the pauperisation of the Russian language. A person often lacks the words to express his thoughts. He flavors his speech with underground slang, sprinkles in an obscenity or two, and is understood by all. This is the language affected by students, scientists, and famous artists alike. The popularity of the sixties' artist Vladimir Vysotsky, with his underground songs of hysterical agony, was immediate and far-reaching precisely because he sang in that language. A talented man and an alcoholic, he became an idol of the people, who sank with him into the depths of drunkenness and degradation. Now, when a bunch of friends get together – whether they are teen-agers or gray-haired intellectuals – these born slaves who never knew what it is to be a free spirit, these descendants of Pushkin, Dostoyevsky, and Tolstoy, do not argue about the meaning of life but set out their bottles of vodka, turn on the tape recorder, and listen to black-market cassettes of Vysotsky's songs:

> 'Heat up the bathhouse and open the flues;
> Daylight is foreign to me.

* A word used even in English. An acronym for 'prisoner' or 'convict.'

I take in the fumes; my head aches as from booze,
And hot steam has loosened my tongue.'

Weeping drunken tears, they wail along with him. And they love him because he is so close to them, so understandable. It is heartrending:

'They've gone out wolf-hunting. Yes, they've gone out
After the gray wolves – the pups and the old.
The hounds bark till they vomit; the beaters shout:
There's red on the banners and blood on the snow!'

The Gulag has done its job: there you have today's Russian. He yells, he whines, he rails in a drunken, hoarse voice; he howls like a hounded, wounded, but thrashing beast. Yes, the people begat Vysotsky, then made him their bard and tribune, the spokesman for their despair and their hopes. But what had we gone through – what moral breakdowns had we lived through – for the zek's screams to have triggered that kind of response in us all?

In this vast, monstrous theater, with our faces twisted by underground jargon, we Soviets wriggle and squirm for one another. We are actors by compulsion, not by calling, in an amateur theater run by no one. And all our lives we perform our endless, pathetic comedy. There are no spectators, only participants. Nor is there a script, only improvisation. And knowing neither plot nor denouement, we act.

FIFTEEN

In 1959 I went with the State Symphony Orchestra on a two-month tour of the United States. Slava had just returned the week before from a triumphant two-week tour there. By that time – in addition to Slava – Emil Gilels, David Oistrakh, the Moiseyev Dance Company, and the Bolshoi Ballet had performed in America, but they had yet to hear an opera singer from Soviet Russia. I was the first.

We arrived in New York on the evening of December 31 and were met by the impresario Sol Hurok and a crowd of press people. On the plane we had all been given chewing gum, and when we set foot on the ground, a hundred pairs of jaws toiled away like machinery. I was immediately asked, 'Do you like gum?'

'No, I don't,' I answered, almost swallowing it as I spoke.

'Then why are you chewing it?'

'They gave it to us, so we're chewing.'

After that, they had no more questions for me.

Within hours we were celebrating New Year's Eve at the Waldorf Astoria, where Sol Hurok had arranged a splendid reception for the whole orchestra. He was a generous man. Above all, he realised that Soviet artists earn a miserable pittance; that all their earnings go to the embassy. So one had to feed them, to pay for luxurious accommodations for the famous soloists, to take them to expensive restaurants; otherwise they simply wouldn't come. He used to say, 'What do your Komsomol people know about anything? You have to handle Moiseyev with kid gloves!'

First thing the next morning we were taken to the Soviet Consulate for a brainwashing session. Apparently they felt that in Moscow our brains hadn't been washed enough for America.

They gave us a lecture on the accursed capitalists, warning us that provocations would be lurking at every corner, and they instructed the orchestra members to walk only in groups of four and not to pay any attention to what was in the store windows. That was all show-off, they said. Ordinary Americans couldn't afford those things, and in general, people here were dying of hunger.

After venturing out on the street and looking around without seeing any corpses swollen from starvation, the encouraged Soviet citizens explored a few stores and discovered that the accursed currency, despite the gloomy forecasts, was quite stable. And they were downright comforted when they calculated that an artist of the State Symphony, even at $10 a day, could in the course of a two-month tour buy enough stuff to sink an ocean liner. I was getting $100 a performance, so with ten scheduled concerts, and the $1,000 Slava had given me as a surprise, I felt like a millionaire.

When I went on stage to sing Tatyana's letter scene from *Eugene Onegin* for my first concert at Carnegie Hall, the audience greeted me with an ovation, although they didn't yet know what to expect of me. But I felt that they were giving me their support, and that show of goodwill thrilled me. When I finished the scene, however, the audience yelled, stamped their feet, and whistled. I was devastated. But then I saw that the Americans had sprung from their seats and were reaching out toward me and shouting. Only at that point did I understand that in America whistling is an expression of the greatest enthusiasm.

In the morning they read me the papers. The critics had ranked me among the best singers of the day . . . in an elegant black velvet gown with a plunging neckline . . . a diamond on her right hand (Interesting – a gift from her husband, or government property?) . . . without makeup . . . without lipstick . . . the best exhibit Russia can produce . . . Taubman wrote in *The New York Times*, 'Vishnevskaya is a knockout for both the eyes and the ears.'

Impressed by my success, Hurok arranged a solo concert for me at Carnegie Hall, and the tickets were soon sold out. (Interesting to see that 'communist' in a plunging neckline, with diamonds. She even sings!) Right then and there I received an invitation from the Metropolitan Opera to sing in the opera of my choice during the next season; I chose *Aïda*. I also traveled with the orchestra to several cities, and was scheduled to give a solo concert in Boston. I was to be accompanied by Alexander Dedyukhin, Slava's pianist, who had stayed behind after Slava's tour especially for the occasion.

He and I left for Boston on an evening train and arrived there at midnight. The hotel was beautiful, a great luxury for me. But on closer inspection I saw that the bathroom carpet was soaked with water. A pipe had broken, hot water had gushed out, and the room was steaming like a bathhouse.

'How can I sleep in this swamp? My voice will be ruined, and I have a concert tomorrow night.'

'We'll put you in another room for tonight, and in the morning we'll make repairs. We can't get anybody to fix it at this hour of the night.'

They took me to a tiny room, and vanished. It was like an American prison set: a bed, a night table, a chair, and a TV. A radiator ran the length of the wall, steaming and hissing like the old Broadway billboard. It was impossible to sleep. I opened the window, and in thirty seconds the room was freezing. I closed it, and it was the tropics. The phone was useless because I didn't know the language. I stripped naked, sat on the bed, and howled. After suffering until four in the morning, I threw on a dressing gown, set out down the corridor, and pounded on Dedyukhin's door. When he opened the door and saw me standing there in the middle of the night with a red nose swollen from weeping, he thought I'd been raped or robbed, as they had warned us we might be. While he looked for his pants and struggled into them, I cursed out the whole place – finally having a chance to express myself in my own language. And none of the arguments offered by the hotel personnel who came running could make me shut up.

'This is a provocation! They deliberately put me in that torture chamber so I'd lose my voice by evening! I've been maltreated, and I won't go into that room!'

As ever, I felt behind me the whole of Russia: if I sang badly, everything was finished, and Russia was done for. Abroad we go on stage as if we are baring our breasts to a machine gun. It is an indoctrination we undergo from childhood.

After shouting until I was hoarse, I told the unhappy Dedyukhin that I refused to sing that night and would return to Moscow immediately. Then I sat down in an armchair in his room and sulked. Naturally, he couldn't sleep. Early in the morning he called the manager of the concert hall and explained, in German and French, what had happened. In a panic, the manager called Hurok in New York, saying that Madame Vishnevskaya was in hysterics, weeping, and didn't want to sing her concert. Hurok, that capitalist shark, had his own way of handling such matters. When a prima donna weeps, what should be done? Give the prima donna money, only make it the right amount for the right person. Since I was a Soviet prima donna and got $100 a concert from my government (as he very well knew), the thing to do was to give me double the amount, and there'd be no more tears.

And so it was that a very nice American soon appeared before me, smiling from ear to ear, with a $100 bill in his hand.

'Mr Hurok asked me to give this to you so that you can take a stroll before the recital.'

'But why should I take a stroll?'

'You don't understand. So that you can stroll through the stores.' And he proffered the $100.

'*What?*' I bellowed. 'Money for me – a Soviet singer? It's an insult! Get out!' I grabbed the bill, tore it up, and threw the scraps after him.

I of course sang the recital that night. The next day the newspapers reported '. . . the Russian singer gave us a world of experiences we can find only in Dostoyevsky.' But it wasn't out of the blue that our great writer got his images. Russians are all of the same breed.

But as a rule the concerts went smoothly. I simply put on my best gown and gave the audience everything I had.

In operas, things were much more complicated.

The next year, when I came to the Metropolitan Opera to sing in *Aïda* with Jon Vickers as Radames, we had only one rehearsal, and in the course of it, he and I quarreled. I love to rehearse, especially with a good partner, so that during a performance I won't be preoccupied with technical details. But while going through the staging of the Nile scene with Vickers several times, I noticed that he was getting into an increasingly bad mood; it was plain that he didn't want to rehearse. We went on like that until just before the final duet, and then he got ready to leave.

'At this point, everything is clear: we stand up and sing,' he said.

'No. Let's agree on what we're going to do. If you don't want to do what I suggest, then I'll do as you wish, but we can't stand in one spot throughout a long duet. This is a show, not a concert.'

'But I'm telling you, I have no more time. I have to leave.'

'Shame on you! How rude. I'm a woman . . . I'm a guest here.'

'We're all guests here.'

'What do you mean, "all"?' It didn't occur to me at the time that that was the case, and I took his answer to be boorishness.

'Like I said, "all"! Okay? Good-bye, girl!' And he left.

I stood there with my mouth agape, and couldn't get over my indignation. I knew how we received foreign guests at the Bolshoi: often, a Soviet singer would be taken out of an opera, no questions asked, and her role given to a foreign singer – frequently a mediocre one. That was Russian hospitality – politeness toward foreigners while Vanka or Manka was getting it in the neck. And now this: 'We're all guests here.'

How dare they talk to me like that? 'If that's the way things are, to hell with your show and your theater! I'm not going to sing here! I want to go home!'

The director began explaining to me that Vickers was very nervous because his wife in Canada had given birth to a daughter instead of a son. Or maybe it was the other way around, I didn't understand exactly. 'Calm down. Tomorrow he'll beg your pardon. Everything will be okay.' And he slapped me on the shoulder!

I can't even remember how I reacted to that gesture, but whatever I did sent him reeling.

'What happened?'

My interpreter from Hurok's bureau ran up to him and began to explain that you mustn't slap Russians on the shoulder because that was deeply offensive to them.

'Why?' And he looked at me as if I were a primitive.

After that ill-starred rehearsal they took me to my dressing room, where Aïda's costumes were displayed on hangers. I didn't like them. They were heavy, and their colors were uninteresting. They were like every evening gown in the shop windows on Fifth Avenue.

'I have my own costume, and that's what I'll use.'

'*What?* Why?'

'Because that's my image – my role.'

At the Bolshoi, all visiting singers were allowed to wear their own costumes if they wanted to. But now several pairs of wide-open eyes were fixed on me.

'But there is nothing about costumes in your contract. Here, all the singers wear these.'

'That's how they see Aïda. But I see her differently. In your costumes I couldn't move or play the role as I imagine it.'

'But in your contract –'

'What does the contract have to do with it? And what difference does it make to you what I wear, provided it suits the role and is convenient to me?'

'But here everyone must be in the same position. We can't make an exception for you.'

'Then don't make an exception for me. I want to wear one simple costume throughout the performance, instead of your three.'

More and more representatives of the management came crowding into my dressing room.

'No, we can't allow it. Here everybody wears –'

'Let them, I'm not going to! Do you want me to sing in this country? Then let me be an artist, not a mannequin!'

Finally, after conferences at the highest level, it was agreed that they would make me a costume just like my own but pistachio-colored, which I would wear in the first scene only, after which I would change into my red one and wear it for the rest of the show.

Before curtain time I was fussing with my hairdo and makeup, not noticing how rapidly the time was passing, when suddenly, over the intercom, I heard the overture! I was still in my dressing gown, and my body had not yet been covered with the dark body makeup . . . hurry . . . hurry . . . And then a huge young man with a jar of makeup and a sponge appeared in the doorway.

'What do you want?'

'Get undressed.'

In front of a man? But I have to strip almost completely! What's more, my interpreter isn't here, and Radames is singing already. Help! I grabbed my hairdresser and tried to give her the jar of body makeup so she could put it on me. But she shook her head, mumbled something, and wouldn't take the jar. Radames's aria! . . . What to do? I couldn't stop the performance. And I couldn't go on stage with white arms and legs and a face painted dark. I wrapped myself up in a sheet, squeezed my eyes shut, and began to extend my extremities toward him one at a time – arms, legs. Oh, Lord! My dress has a slit clear up the thigh! And what about my breasts? Applause. The aria is finished, and I'm being called for my entrance . . . and the strapping young man, with his huge hands, is slathering on the makeup and singing my praises. 'O, Madame has some body! Legs like a ballerina!'

I scarcely made it in time for my entrance, the wardrobe woman fastening my dress on the way. I rushed on stage and ran headlong into the 'passionate' glances of Vickers, now madly in love with me for purposes of the performance. I turned brusquely away and did not once look at him during the whole scene. At the opera's start that wasn't so important, but ahead of us loomed eternal love. Vickers saw that no loving gaze would bring me out of my foul mood: I simply didn't look at him. So during the first intermission, right there on the stage, he strode over, picked me up and tossed me into the air several times. With that, peace was concluded.

After the show, Hurok came backstage to see me, and I put it to him with no hesitation: 'Solomon Izrailevich, what kind of customs do you have in this country? Why must I, almost naked, have body makeup put on me by a young man, while a woman stands there and refuses to help me?'

'Ah, Galinochka! You don't understand America. That's union.'

'What do I care who he is, union or anyone else? What kind of a name is that anyway – *union*? I want a woman to do it, not him!'

'No, you misunderstood me. "Union" means trade union. That young man works at the theater – that's his job. According to union rules, your wardrobe woman cannot do what he's supposed to do. But don't worry – I'll talk with the union people and see that they approve a woman for your performances. It's me you're dealing with. And now let's go out on the town and celebrate your triumph.'

There were more surprises in store for me in that initial acquaintance with the American opera theater. At the second performance of *Aïda*, while standing in the wings waiting to go on, I met a second Amneris. And during the fourth, it was not until I was standing on stage that I noticed that Amneris resembled neither the first singer nor the second. Again, no one had warned me, although she and I had an intense scene to do together! Each time, they tried to explain that all the singers knew their places: 'Don't worry, do your own job.' But theater is not a matter of the individual: it is a common undertaking – an ensemble. It is not just places on the stage but a community of artists – the merging of creative individualities into a single experience. But apparently that's the way things must be in a theater of wandering stars. These ways were alien to my innermost feelings – to my understanding of what opera theater should be – and I was eager to get back home, to the Bolshoi, knowing that they were as impatient to see me as I them.

The outer glitter – the packaging – of American life had little effect on me. I looked at it as if in the movies, with eyes only. Freedom? I didn't know what it was. Like a wild beast set free, I only wanted to get back in my cage.

Our people appear to be the antithesis of Americans – especially in winter, in their wretched clothing, dark and dirty-gray. But I was used to that, and didn't notice it when I returned. Something else amazed me, as if I were seeing it all only then: what tense and gloomy faces we all wore! We all had the same expression in our eyes: worry. Russians didn't walk but ran, eyes fixed on their feet. The women were all grown soft, run-down, broad-shouldered, and loaded down with heavy bags.

During the next fifteen years, I really didn't see much of anything when traveling abroad except hotels, concert halls, and opera houses. I was too busy concentrating on my performances or on not catching cold and letting the whole company down. And when Soviet artists are on tour they have such a full schedule that there simply isn't time to look around. The Ministry of Culture must squeeze everything out of them in the shortest possible time to make as much money as it can.

During my 1961 tour of America, within forty-six days I sang four *Aïda*s and one *Butterfly* at the Met, plus eleven solo concerts from one end of the country to the other. In fifty days, Slava would play from twenty-five to thirty concerts. Of course the impresario had a great deal to gain from this, but then he paid very well. Standing to gain even more were our authorities, who took our earnings and used them for maintaining our embassies and paying our spies.

For artists in the Soviet Union there is a fixed wage scale for performances, depending on one's rank and category. The theater's profits or losses have nothing to do with it. In 1978 the highest pay for instrumentalists was 180 rubles. For singers it was 200 rubles for a solo concert, even if they performed in a stadium holding several thousand people. When abroad, we got our regular pay recomputed in foreign currency, so that on Richter, Oistrakh, Gilels, and Rostropovich the state, in its magnanimity, lavished as much as $200 per concert. Singers were paid $240, on the assumption that it is harder to sing than to draw a bow across the strings or pound the ivories.

This is what is known in America as the sweatshop system: paying as little as possible and demanding as much work as possible. I have read that impresarios are hauled into court for that sort of thing. Yet in Russia, artists are prepared to slit each other's throats in order to go abroad. And even under such conditions of servitude it is profitable for them. For many – in dance companies, choruses, orchestras – foreign trips are indeed the only way to survive. For example, artists in the Bolshoi's chorus or corps de ballet get a maximum of 150 rubles per month. When they return from foreign tours they bring back the cheapest things and sell them for a profit. After several trips they can accumulate enough money to buy a cooperative apartment. It may be tiny, but it is their own. But by the time that insignificant person gets so much as a little attention from the state, he won't be needing anything at all. Six feet in the graveyard will suffice.

In our case, the material well-being of our family depended completely on our foreign tours. With both of us working for more than twenty years, we were able to amass enough money to build a dacha and pay for a cooperative apartment. But all the furniture we had at the dacha and in Moscow – all the chinaware, linen, cars, and pianos – had been brought in from abroad. We even bought the roof for the dacha in Holland. It was not until two years before we left the country that we were able to replace the furniture and finally buy antique pieces. And all my clothes as well as the children's, down to thread and hooks for our dresses, I brought from abroad.

But I got my $240 per concert only when touring alone. When the Bolshoi toured, everyone without exception – from the stage hands to the soloists – got the same pay: $10 a day. On that money you had to feed yourself well enough so as not to faint from hunger during the performances. What saved me was the foreign currency I had put aside from solo tours. In 1969 Slava was conducting *Onegin* and *War and Peace* for the Bolshoi, and went on tour with the company to France, Austria, and Japan. He got nothing extra for conducting – just the same $10 a day as everyone else. But he would play in solo concerts on the side. That was what we lived on; other artists were not so fortunate.

When our Soviet airliner landed in a foreign country, we would pour out of it like a band of gypsies, carrying our sacks and bags overflowing with saucepans, hot plates, sugar, canned goods, and other groceries, including potatoes. The objective was clear: not to spend more than a dollar a day on food. When the Bolshoi was in Paris in 1969, the company stayed at a hotel not far from the Opéra, and the smell of cabbage soup and onions wafted over the whole of Boulevard Haussmann. Within days, all the regular residents fled – 400 hot plates plugged in simultaneously had plunged the hotel into darkness, and the French had taken fright, thinking war had begun.

It was amazing how quickly our 'laboring masses' found means of communicating with the locals. The day after we would arrive, whether it was Italy, France, Canada, or even Japan, when we came to the theater for rehearsal we would be stunned to see our stagehands already talking (!) with the natives. In what language? No one ever knew. But by the middle of the day our working class and members of the chorus knew it all: where in the suburbs you could buy 200 yards of nylon tulle for $40. And, better than any CIA agent, they would produce maps that showed how to get to warehouses where for $20 you could get ten pairs of shoes, with another five pairs tossed in free. Every purchase was calculated based on a capital of $400 (forty days of work at $10 a day). Hardly needing computers, their minds quickly reckoned the profits they could make in a sale of those goods in Moscow, and lo and behold, that long-desired two-room apartment or car became a bit more of a reality. Good enough reason to burst into song!

In Paris, the Bolshoi opened its tour with the opera *Boris Godunov*. When the chorus came to the part where they chant, 'Give us bread! Bread! Give us bread!' they all fell on their knees and lifted up their hands. At that, both the opera-house management and the audience felt their hair standing on end. As a result, the management organised a mess hall in the basement of the opera house where the company thenceforward was obliged to take their meals. That would have been fine, except for the lamentable fact that the French were charging five dollars a day for the food: half of the Soviet artists' pay! Nevertheless, what efforts it must have taken to find a cook in France who would agree, for that kind of money, to try to feed four hundred hungry mouths. Slava and I were staying elsewhere, and did not once sample the cooking. But we were in the basement of the opera house one day and thought we had stumbled onto a soup kitchen for the unemployed or the homeless; the tables were loaded with heaps of bread and enormous bowls of soup.

The Grand Opéra was packed: it was impossible to buy a ticket. And the Soviet Embassy was raking in the francs – whether in checks or bags of cash, I don't know. In Italy, things were simpler. Our troupe was there on an exchange with La Scala, and because we fed the Italian company for free in Moscow, they did the same for us in Milan.

When Hurok invited the Moiseyev Dance Company or the artists of the ballet to tour in America, he fed them at his own expense. He wanted no one fainting on stage from weakness or hunger. But when our petty tyrants found out, they decided to deduct almost half of the artists' miserable pittance and tally it up for the state. I was luckier. I would sign restaurant checks in Hurok's name. After the tour, that kindhearted old man would always remind me not to breathe a word about it in Moscow, otherwise the Ministry of Culture would surely see that it was reflected in my pay.

With Hurok you felt protected. If he undertook to work with an artist, you could be sure that everything possible would be done for you – sometimes the impossible. He was a tourist attraction, and wherever you appeared with him in New York – be it a restaurant, an elegant store, or a splendid hotel lobby – you would be noticed and indulged, not because you had come in with a rich and famous man, but because if you were with Hurok, you had to be important.

At concerts he would come impeccably dressed, festive, with a boutonniere, in anticipation of the pleasure in the offing. Loving artists was his calling. What good is a great violinist if you don't put a violin in his hands? Can the violinist help loving that violin? That was Hurok's attitude toward his artists: for him, they were precious instruments. He simply loved them.

When he appeared in a concert hall, especially with a female artist, every detail was planned. Three minutes before the curtain, when the audience was seated and anticipating the spectacle, he would promenade her. He wasn't just walking with any woman: he was serving up an artist to the audience. I remember being terribly embarrassed by these little 'parades' at first, and I would strain to get to my seat as quickly as possible. But he would hold me firmly by the elbow: 'Galinochka, where are you hurrying to? Let them admire us, and the next time, they'll come flocking to your concert.'

He was humane enough to know that after the stress of a performance an artist needs to relax, to eat, and not just to accept compliments from people who have already dined well. How often it happens that some wealthy matron holds an after-concert reception in her home without stopping to think that the artist is weary as a workhorse, and needs first of all to sit down at a table and eat something. It is agonising to stay on one's feet, glass in hand, admire the collection of Renoirs or Picassos, munch on nuts, and answer (for the tenth time) such questions as 'How are you feeling?' or 'How do you like America?'

Hurok would save me in such situations. 'Galinochka, I told you you shouldn't accept the invitation. You're too tired.'

'But they insisted! They talked me into it . . . If I could only sit down somewhere! I'm so exhausted I can hardly stand.'

'We'll slip away in a minute. I've already reserved a table at your favorite restaurant.'

He enjoyed looking at beautiful women, and loved seeing them dressed to the nines. In 1967 his birthday was to be celebrated at a big banquet, and I went to buy myself an evening gown for the occasion. I was accompanied by an interpreter from Hurok's office, and he took me to Saks Fifth Avenue. With my pay I couldn't afford to shop in stores like Saks, and I asked him to take me to another that was less expensive.

'Solomon Izrailevich told me to bring you here.'

'But I don't have the money for it.'

'Don't worry. Look around, see what you like.'

But when I looked, the evening gowns ranged from a thousand to three thousand dollars (even in those days).

'What's the point?'

'But this one's beautiful! It was made for you. Solomon Izrailevich would be thrilled if you showed up in that dress.'

'But it costs two thousand dollars!'

'If you like it, Mr Hurok hopes you will allow him to make you a gift of it.' The dress was stunning – embroidered with glass beads, pearls, and precious stones. I still have it, and wear it from time to time.

Hurok was very familiar with musicians' repertories. He never interfered, never imposed his own taste; but if he gave a musician his advice, it was infallible.

'The concert must have a climax. For you, that will be Mussorgsky.'

'But it may be hard for the audience. They won't understand.'

'Don't worry. They'll understand *you*.'

And in fact, *Songs and Dances of Death* brought me huge

success. In all the countries where I sang it, the critics lavished praise on me. One went so far as to call me 'Chaliapin in a skirt.'

When an artist dies, his art disappears. He cannot be replaced. Hurok, too, will never be replaced – not because others are inferior, but because they are not Hurok.

The last time they let me out of the country to concertise in the US was in 1969, and my departure was accompanied by a huge scandal in the Ministry of Culture and the Central Committee. That year at Carnegie Hall I was supposed to sing the American premiere of the Blok cycle that Shostakovich had dedicated to me. Slava had been on tour there for two months, and I was to team up with him for several concerts.

A week before my departure I was summoned by Dyatlov, the Bolshoi's Party secretary, and for the first time in all my years with the theater, I was asked why I didn't take part in the weekly political meetings. I must admit that of all three thousand people in the Bolshoi collective, I was the only one who dared to skip those idiotic gatherings on Tuesday mornings. But they had never asked the question of me when I was a novice singer, and it was strange that I should hear it now.

'Frankly, why should I?'

'To be in touch with world issues.'

'I'm interested in my own issues: my maid has left, and I have to perform tomorrow. Who's going to stand in line at the store? Who's going to make dinner?'

'But you're setting a bad example for the young people. When they see that you don't come for the lectures, they don't come either. We have to educate them.'

'Then go ahead and educate them – leave me alone. I've never come to those lectures, and I'm not about to.'

The next day I had a call from the Ministry of Culture and was told that the Bolshoi refused to sign my 'character reference' for the trip to America, and that my tour had been canceled. According to regulations, everyone going abroad must secure from his employers a document certifying his good behavior and signed by a 'troika': the Party secretary, the chairman of the local committee, and the director. The Bolshoi was now refusing to give me that document. But the only one who could scratch me from such an important trip was Furtseva. Plainly, she wanted to teach me a lesson.

I was sick and tired of that impertinence. They steal the shirt off your back on those trips, and then they act as if they're only letting you go as a special favor. But I had no intention of going to complain. To hell with you! Go and sing yourself! I've had enough of traveling, of working for you. I'll be very glad to stay at home.

Then Slava called from New York, and I told him all about it.

'What character reference? Why didn't they give it to you?'

'Because I don't go to the political meetings.'

'Have they gone out of their minds? Go to Furtseva.'

'I'm not going anywhere. I'm not a young girl any more, and I'm not about to haunt government offices.'

'But your concerts have already been advertised here! How can they not let you out?'

'They can do anything they want to do.'

'All right. If they're going to refuse to let you out, I'll pack up my bags right away and come back to Moscow. I'm not going to concertise any more.'

'Right! Enough of our slaving for them.'

Slava called the Soviet Embassy in Washington and announced that if I didn't come for the tour he would cancel all his concerts and return to Moscow. But first he would grant an interview to *The New York Times* and explain why he had canceled his performances: that the Bolshoi would not allow its prima donna to sing in America because she had not attended political meetings . . . The Soviet ambassador, Dobrynin, saw a big scandal in the making and called Moscow. And when a Soviet ambassador calls from America, it means serious business. Furtseva got a dressing-down.

As for me, I stayed quiet and made no move to call Furtseva at the ministry. This knocked Ekaterina Alekseyevna off her pins. As always, she was set to 'explain everything and straighten out' all the damage she herself had done. One day went by, then another. On the third day, Katya swallowed her pride and called me at home.

'Galina Pavlovna. How are you?'

'Fine, thank you.'

'What's going on with you?'

'Nothing's going on with me.'

'What do you mean, "nothing"? Dobrynin has raised a big fuss, alleging that they won't let you out.'

'Oh, that! Well, no, that's true. They won't let me out.'

'But why didn't you call me?'

'Because I thought you knew everything. Who would dare to cancel my trip without your knowing it?'

'But I swear on my honor this is the first I hear of it. Who dared, and why?'

'The Bolshoi didn't give me a character reference.'

'Come see me immediately and tell me everything.'

What a show she put on then! When I entered her office, she had five men lined up: Chulaki, the manager of the theater; Dyatlov, the secretary of the Party organisation; Boni, the deputy manager; Tumanov, the chief director; and the chairman of the theater's local committee.

'Galina Pavlovna, please tell us what happened.'

'These men have probably told you everything already. All I want to say is that I have absolutely no need for handouts in the form of foreign tours. I go there to work, to glorify Russian art and the Soviet state, and to turn the money I make over to the embassy. My husband has been doing the same thing in America for two months now; he plays every day until his fingers are bloody. And here they insult me!'

'Who dared insult you, a People's Artist of the Soviet Union?'

Taking my side, Katya had begun to yell. She looked daggers at the Party secretary. The turn things had taken for him was so unexpected that he began to stammer. 'E-k-katerina Alek-seyevna, the-the th-thing is that Galina Pavlovna is n-n-not attending the p-p-political meetings.'

'*What* political meetings? How *dare* you?' And she pounded her fist on the desk. 'This isn't '37! Why are you still using those methods? It's time to forget them! What does the Party teach us?'

Her fervor was such that we all simply gawked. She bawled

them out (those recent partners in her game) as if they were little boys. They were embarrassed by my presence and reddened, but they continued to sit there as silent as stones while she scolded away as only a woman can.

And then we both began to shout, as if at a bazaar.

'Galina Pavlovna, I swear on my honor that I'll look into everything. But now I'm asking you to calm down and go on that tour.'

'What tour? First you play havoc with my nerves, and now you talk about a tour! I'm not going anywhere!'

'But Slava's over there with *his* nerves!' Katya half-screamed.

'Well, there's no point in his staying there – he can come home. The longer I stay in this office the more nervous *I* get . . . Good-bye!'

Her assistant caught up with me as I stormed down the corridor and told me that they wanted to see me right away at the Central Committee. Just to make sure I'd go, he took me himself – across the street from the Ministry of Culture. There I was met by a gray, vile creature, of whom I remember nothing more than his grayness and vileness. They pick those people carefully so that if you run into them later you don't know the difference.

'Fill me in, Galina Pavlovna. What happened?'

'I don't want to fill in anything! You yourselves know every-thing – that's why I was summoned here.'

'Do you realise the great importance of a trip to the US in terms of the national interest?'

'Yes, I realise it, even though I *don't* go to those political meetings of yours, so tell *that* to the idiots who canceled my tour.'

'We'll take care of it. But we've had a complaint that you refuse to attend the political meetings and thereby are setting a bad example for the young people. If things go on like that, it's within our power to bar you from foreign travel.'

'Bar me? But I myself don't want to go, understand? And here you are trying to persuade me! My nerves are shot, my voice has had it, and I'm supposed to sing in America – not sit at banquets! Just leave me alone!'

'But Rostropovich is upset and demanding that you come.'

'I'll call him today and tell him to come back to Moscow

immediately. He's had enough. For two months he's been over there grubbing American money for the state.'

'I hope you realise what you're saying.'

'And I hope you realise whom you're insulting. Don't forget it's me and Rostropovich here.'

'Well, if you two think you can behave like that, we'll simply create a new Vishnevskaya and a new Rostropovich. And we'll put the squeeze on you . . .'

He told me that calmly and distinctly, looking me straight in the eye. And just as slowly and distinctly, I told him, 'Too late. You should have put the squeeze on me fifteen years ago. You missed the boat. Now I am who I am, and Rostropovich is who he is, and there won't be another. A genius can't be created, he can only be killed.'

There was a long silence. He tried to bore through me with his tiny eyes, but he swallowed the pill and refrained from discussing the dangerous subject any further. It was clear that he had remembered my government connections, and had decided to be more cautious and step on the brakes.

'Please calm down. I understand: you're an artist, a temperamental woman. This whole business has upset you. And I don't blame you one bit. We ask that you make the trip. In the meantime, we'll look into things here, and put them in order. We'll call Mstislav Leopoldovich so he won't go on worrying, and you, too, can reassure him when he calls. One last thing – I beg of you – when you're in America, don't talk about these things in your hotel room with your husband. Over there, all the hotel rooms are bugged. Talk on the street if you have to.'

Idiot! Was he so nervous that he had confused my tour with a trip to Leningrad? 'We'll create a genius!' Specialists in the creation of geniuses! Just cover any Brezhnev with decorations from ear to navel, and there's your genius! I know the process well enough. And I daresay I even remember Brezhnev when he had not yet been presented to the world as another 'great and eternally living Ilich.'*

I made his acquaintance when he was chairman of the Presi-

* Brezhnev, like Lenin, had the patronymic Ilich.

dium of the USSR Supreme Soviet and came with a government delegation to East Berlin to celebrate the fifteenth anniversary of the German Democratic Republic. It was October of 1964 and Slava and I were on tour there. We had been staying at the Soviet Embassy at the invitation of Ambassador Abrasimov (he and Slava were on friendly terms), who told us very significantly that he wanted to introduce us to Leonid Ilich Brezhnev, a man with a great future. At that time, Khrushchev was head of state, and the name Brezhnev meant nothing to me. On the evening of October 8th or 9th a dinner was given at the embassy – not in the main dining room but in a small room for a select group of people. Other than Brezhnev, Abrasimov, Slava and me, there were perhaps only six more. I was seated next to Brezhnev; and like a charming dinner partner, he tried his best to amuse me. He was, as they say, in the swing of things. A well-dressed, dark-haired man of fifty-seven, he was energetic and sociable – he was good company. He enjoyed showing off his knowledge of poetry, especially of Esenin:

> *'I've grown more miserly in my desires.*
> *Is this my life? Or did I dream of you?*
> *As though on an early, resonant morning*
> *In spring, I were galloping on a pink horse.'*

In the course of the evening, he recited it several times: it must have been a favorite. He didn't drink much. He told jokes, and even sang funny songs, beating time with his heels, pretending to play the balalaika, clicking his tongue, and singing in dialect. He surprised me with a rather pleasant voice and a performance that was not untalented.

Someone proposed a toast. 'To you, Leonid Ilich!'

'No, why me? Let's drink to the artists. What's a politician? Here today, gone tomorrow. But art is eternal! To the artists!'

Then he asked me to sing something, and I sang from *The Tsar's Bride.*

I viewed him dispassionately, having no idea of the post he would come to occupy in the government. Slava and I enjoyed his company that evening. For us, his position as chairman of the

Presidium of the USSR Supreme Soviet was not such a high one –
those were the people who signed decrees and gave out awards –
and I found it strange that all the others were fawning on him.
They seemed tongue-tied, and altogether too giggly. I don't
remember who those people were, only that they were members
of the government delegation; but they must have been close
to him to have been included at such an intimate dinner. There
may have been good reason why they were all meeting in
East Germany, a good long distance away from Moscow and
Khrushchev; perhaps the plot was already coming to a head.

A few days later, in Moscow, the telephone rang. 'Hello,
Galya? This is Abrasimov.'

'Hello. Where are you?'

'In Moscow.'

'How so? We only saw each other last week and you didn't say
anything about coming home.'

'We were summoned urgently for a conference. Have you
seen today's papers?'

'Good God, what's happened?'

'Your new acquaintance has just taken a high post.'

It would be interesting to know what flashed through Leonid
Ilich's memory when, many years later, he signed the authorisation for us to leave Russia for two years, and subsequently, when
he signed the decree stripping us of our citizenship . . .

I toured the United States five times – in 1960, 1961, 1965, 1967,
and 1969 – the first two times with the pianist Alexander
Dedyukhin, and the rest with Slava.

After my first American trip, I began to go abroad more often,
and Slava and I wouldn't see each other for several months out of
the year. He would be coming back from one tour, just as I was
leaving for another; and in Moscow, each of us had his own
professional life. When we were first married, Slava had wanted
to accompany me on the piano, and we did perform together, but
not often – only a few times a year and mostly in Moscow and
Leningrad. But eventually we worked up a whole repertory for
foreign tours, in order to be together more often. Surprisingly

enough, most of my concertising was done abroad, and this unquestionably left its mark on my way of performing. Wanting to be understood by an audience that didn't know Russian, I tried to paint musical pictures by emphasising the phrasing, using voice color more boldly, and varying the shade and nuance.

It wasn't easy for us to work together. Slava was always away – in addition to his 100 to 120 concerts a year, he had his teaching at the conservatory – so he didn't have enough time to rehearse for my concerts. It would be interesting to know if there has ever been another pair like us that never truly rehearsed. I would prepare my programs with a pianist from the theater, Margarita Kondrashova, and working with her for long hours day after day, I created my entire concert repertory.

Since I would prepare my new opera parts at the theater, Slava would not see me in my new roles until performances, and what he would hear was the finished product. It was a different story in our concerts. Slava would come back from some country or other three or four days before we were scheduled to perform. His twenty students from the conservatory and I would immediately pounce upon him, demanding rehearsals. But before rehearsing with me he had to learn my whole program by heart, because he has always insisted on accompanying from memory.

'When are we finally going to rehearse together?'

'Go ahead and sing while I learn the music.'

'But that's of no use to me. I want you to listen to the way I sing it, and at some point I have to hear how you're going to play it at the concert!'

'Be patient. We still have time.'

And he would go on learning the difficult passages, while I paced back and forth in the apartment like a caged animal. Fine, he was learning the music. But what I needed was to sing the program in full voice several times with him. (I wonder if that day will ever come!) More often than not it wasn't until the eve of the concert that we'd finally work together. But before we'd gone through half the program we'd be fighting like cats and dogs.

The next day we'd be furious with each other. Without exchanging a word, we'd go to the concert hall, each of us vowing never again to perform with the other. We would appear on stage

. . . and, with the very first bars, we would merge into an indissoluble whole and lose ourselves in the music . . . Why it worked that way for us, I don't know. With the audience looking on, we couldn't quarrel, or try to prove our point to one another, or walk out and slam the door – so we would start a dialogue. And, speaking in the language of music, we would 'clarify' our relations. Without interrupting, we would ask questions and get answers. Essentially, our concerts provided the human contact we longed for in everyday life – living apart from each other for months at a time. That's why our concertising worked so well. At our concerts, the audience would be moved by Rostropovich's tender regard for his wife – the way he picked up her every nuance. 'What a duo! How much work it must take to achieve such blending!' And no one suspected what battles had been fought the day before, that we had sworn at each other all during for one rehearsal, and that I hadn't slept all night. I might stand on the stage, joyous and smiling, as my husband kissed my hand, but I wouldn't speak to him during intermission, nor the next day. Slava may have the fortunate trait of being able to forget quarrels and insults, but I can't get over them for months.

Over the thirty years I have worked with my dear, brilliant husband, I have made it a practice to arrive at the concert hall two or three hours before a performance and run through the whole program with him on stage. That is the only place where the telephone doesn't ring a thousand times and where no one can approach him with endless questions about upcoming tours or requests to audition such-and-such a musician. Nor can his students come by. That is the only place where it finally sinks in that in a few hours we will in fact be giving a concert.

Those concerts with Slava brought me great happiness: I was engaging in artistic interplay with one of the unique musicians of our time. It was a privilege that I, like an addict, could never give up. But when, in 1968, he told me he wanted to start conducting *Eugene Onegin* at the Bolshoi, I sank into despair. I wept and threw tantrums, begging him not to intrude in my life at the theater. I didn't want to mix my theater with my family. The Bolshoi had been my special world for sixteen years, and I had categorically forbidden my husband to enter it. If he wanted to conduct, he could go to another theater, not to mine. It was so important to me! I pleaded with him not to do it. But he did.

Knowing Slava's gregariousness and the ease with which he befriended all sorts of people, I was horrified at what would be in store for me at home. I was not mistaken: singers and members of the orchestra dragged all the latest scandals into our home. They hung on Slava's neck, hugged and kissed, and drank vodka. My relations with the management and with other singers became open topics of discussion for the family. And our personal relations, which I so carefully had kept from the eyes of outsiders, were exposed to observation and gossip.

He conducted *Eugene Onegin* and *War and Peace* at the Bolshoi for three years, and he did it brilliantly. But that was not the happiest phase of our life. And for a long time I resented the fact that he had not taken my feelings into account in a matter of such importance to me.

SIXTEEN

Alexander Shamilyevich Melik-Pashayev – my first conductor!

After my successful debut in *Fidelio,* Alexander Shamilyevich began to cast me in all of his new productions; and during his last years it was usually I who sang the title role in his favorite opera, *Aïda.* He said that in me he had finally found a singer capable of interpreting the music as he wanted it – that only I allowed him to be faithful to the Verdi score with its divine *pianissimos.* In addition to *Fidelio* and *Aïda,* I sang under his baton in *Falstaff,* the Verdi *Requiem, The Queen of Spades, War and Peace, Madama Butterfly,* and *Onegin.* And I took part in his symphonic concerts.

In 1952, when I joined the Bolshoi, Alexander Shamilyevich was only forty-seven years old. Of medium height, he cut an impressive figure, and was always smartly dressed. He was reserved, and incredibly tactful and polite. An Armenian, he began his career at the Tbilisi Opera Theater, joining it at sixteen as a rehearsal pianist. Even at that age, he knew thirty-five operas, and so was assigned to rehearse the theater's leading singers. Within two years he was a conductor. In 1931, when he was only twenty-six, he made a triumphant debut at the Bolshoi with *Aïda.* And in his first month there he conducted six operas: *Tosca, Aïda, Carmen, Faust, Rigoletto,* and *Madama Butterfly.* Then, five months later, he mounted the first of his own opera productions at the theater: *Otello.* He was never a novice conductor. From his first days at the celebrated court theater with its splendid orchestra, he confidently took his place alongside such outstanding conductors as Suk, Golovanov, Pazovsky, and Samosud. For the next thirty-three years, until his death on June 18, 1964, he worked only at the Bolshoi. On rare occasions he conducted symphonic concerts, but his true calling was that of an opera conductor.

When it came to his art, Alexander Shamilyevich made absolutely no compromises: he was extremely demanding of everyone without exception. He was no less demanding of himself – every performance he conducted was an event.

We who took part in those performances knew he would not forgive us any musical sloppiness. So in the days preceding a performance, all of us took lessons with rehearsal pianists and reviewed our parts carefully, even though some of us had been singing the same roles for fifteen or twenty years. During that time, it never occurred to us to accept singing engagements elsewhere: everyone was sparing his voice and strength. Two days before each performance, Alexander Shamilyevich would schedule a run-through, and every soloist felt an obligation to sing at full voice, wanting to test his abilities once again, to sense the support of the conductor in the difficult passages of the opera, and to attune his voice to the part. After a run-through Alexander Shamilyevich could gauge each singer's form, and adjust the musical and dramatic accents in the upcoming performance accordingly.

The day before a performance he never showed up at the theater, and would not come to the telephone. Then, on the day itself, he would arrive at the theater before everyone else – elegant and solemn, as if filled with the sense of an impending religious rite. His mood would affect everyone, even the messengers and the ushers. And hours before the curtain, the soloists were applying their makeup and warming up.

During the performance, nothing escaped his attention. The slightest roughness of voice, whether from a singer in a lead role or a member of the chorus, would catch his ear. Carried away by the moment, you might permit yourself too much portamento, or hold a note too long. Two little errors in an entire performance, but he would never miss them! For the next few days you would try to avoid him in the hopes he'd forget. No such luck! At the first opportunity, he would be reminding you of all your mistakes. 'Your part, my child, seems more and more overgrown with "effects." That's not good. And why, suddenly, that portamento? For some reason you held that high B flat too long – you have to know where to stop. And by the way, in that same phrase you sang an eighth-note instead of a quarternote. Where are you getting these novelties?'

He could rest assured that I would never again in my life permit myself those 'effects.' And the quarter-note that I had not held long enough would pound in my mind like a hammer. How lucky I was during my years of development to have had at my side a mentor and friend who could lead me through the sacred fire of art! Since those years I have been uncompromising with myself and intolerant of any form of shoddiness on stage.

From his youth Alexander Shamilyevich had loved singing to the point of obsession. Not only did he know vocal literature inside and out, but he cherished his singers with all their virtues and foibles. And no one was more considerate of them than he.

Shortly after *Fidelio*, I wanted to sing in his production of *The Queen of Spades*, but he wouldn't let me. 'Don't even think about it! Sing the Italian repertory for a few years.'

At the time his refusal offended me deeply. Yet how right he was! In Russian operas, the vocal and emotional load falls in the middle register. Inexperienced singers are compelled to force and bear down on their voices. They lose much of their upper register, develop a heavy, wide vibrato and, as a result, limit their repertory. Having lost the lightness, the high placement of the sound, they can no longer sing the operas of Mozart, Verdi, and Puccini.

I think it was precisely for this reason that by the time I joined the Bolshoi there was a tradition that a soprano who sang Aïda didn't sing Marguerite and Butterfly; that one who did Tatyana could not sing Marfa in *The Tsar's Bride*; and it was unthinkable for one who sang Liza in *Fidelio* to sing Violetta in *La Traviata*.

Within a few years, however, I broke through the iron barriers, and sang all these parts, as well as operas by Prokofiev and Shostakovich. This became artistically possible for me only because Alexander Shamilyevich had taken me under his wing. And, no less importantly, because I had heeded him without question. He literally pampered the voices of his favorite singers. Little by little, sometimes over a period of several years, he would prepare them for such difficult operas as *Boris Godunov*, *The Queen of Spades*, and *Prince Igor*. In return, the parts crafted with his guidance were distinguished by clarity of vocal phrasing and impeccable technique. Each became an event not only in the life of the artist but for the whole theater.

Despising amateurishness in singing, Alexander Shamilyevich selected the soloists for his operas with great care. To get cast in one of his operas was exceedingly difficult. But if an artist had the good fortune to sing with him, he gained in the conductor a friend and well-wisher. Melik-Pashayev's attention never strayed from the singer for an instant. He was absolute master of the perform-ance, and yet there was always a desire in him to subordinate himself – a quality shared by few conductors. When giving a cue, he would look the singer in the eye, measure that singer's feelings and communicate his own. At the podium, he was aglow with an inner light, able to awaken the creative impulse without imposing his own will. There was always a sense that music was being made freely.

Western music was his element. Among his masterpieces were *Carmen*, *Madama Butterfly*, *Aïda*, *Falstaff*, and *Traviata*. The first time I performed in *Madama Butterfly*, with the conduc-tor Evgeny Svetlanov, Alexander Shamilyevich was in the audi-ence. And although he had not conducted that opera in years, he wanted to do it again with me. We did indeed give several performances together, one of which Slava attended. I left such an impression on him – one of the strongest in his life, he said – that he couldn't contain himself and raced off in the middle of the night to see Alexander Shamilyevich and express to him in person his rapture and admiration.

In the company I was regarded as his favorite; when I came on stage all the musicians in the pit waited for Melik-Pashayev's face to dissolve in a smile. I knew that he was fond of me, but I also knew that what he was in love with was my art. And his was the most devoted love in my artistic career – the truest and most enduring.

I feel sorry for the singers of today, especially the young ones. The age of great opera conductors is over. Generally speaking, the best conductors now prefer to work with symphony orches-tras. For them, conducting an opera is often but a minor episode, just another feather in their maestro's cap. I have sung with many maestros both in Russia and abroad. And I have never experienced that harmony and oneness with any other conductor, for none has been as sensitive to my artistry as Melik-Pashayev. I shall never forget the ecstasy of singing Aïda with him. And no matter where in the world I sang that opera, I would rush home to Alexander Shamilyevich and be renewed. I worked with that outstanding musician virtually every day for twelve happy years. After his death, I sang Aïda at the Bolshoi several times, but realised to my despair that I no longer wanted to sing that role. It was as if he had taken all my inspiration to his grave. It was his production; and when he died, my Aïda died along with him.

The last role I worked on with Melik-Pashayev was Violetta in *La Traviata*. I might never have sung it if at one point our famous tenor, Sergei Lemeshev, had not asked me to record duets from *Traviata* and *Werther* with him. I agreed joyfully. The part of Violetta was somehow surprisingly easy and natural for my voice, and I bathed in its sound. But I hadn't intended to sing Violetta on the stage. *Traviata* had long been a staple at the Bolshoi, passing from one conductor to another. The reason I wasn't interested in it was that I had never found the right partner. Lemeshev had all but retired, and I was not burning with desire to perform *Traviata* with anyone else. So after we finished the recording I set the part aside.

Some time later, Sergei Yakovlevich [Lemeshev] ran into me at the theater. 'Galya, have you heard our recording?'

'No, it's not out yet.'

'But my admirers already have it. I gave a concert in the provinces recently and they followed me there. They came to my hotel with our record in hand. How wonderful it turned out! We spent the whole evening listening to it. I recalled my life, my youth, my favorite performances, and I wept. They wept, too. I looked at them and thought: Lord, how time flies! I've known that one for thirty years, and that one for twenty. How old they all are, how old I am!'

'Stop it, Sergei Yakovlevich! You look younger than any of our young tenors. Just look at their stooped shoulders and sad faces.

They even walk like old men, dragging their feet. Everybody adores you, me included.'

'If that's the case, I have a favor to ask of you.'

'Anything – whatever you wish.'

'Sing *Traviata* with me.'

'At the theater?'

'You already know the part. And you just promised to do whatever I asked. Sing it, Galya! The role is made for you.'

'Yes, but I'd have to work on the aria, and there's no time now – the season is coming to a close. Maybe next year . . .'

'You'll sing the aria, too – your technique is good, and with a little work, you'll have a splendid role in your repertory. As for me, I haven't sung Alfredo for years. But I want desperately to perform it again, if only once, but only if you'll do it with me. We have three months until the end of the season. That leaves us enough time to rehearse and perform it before vacation. Don't forget that I'm sixty-three. If you refuse, I'll never sing *Traviata* again. Please do it. My admirers will go mad with joy, and you and I will knock 'em dead all over Moscow. Is it a deal?'

'It's a deal! They're as good as dead! But I won't sing without Melik. Do you think he'll agree? He conducts *Traviata* so rarely these days.'

'We'll persuade him!'

Violetta was the first role that did not hold me prisoner of age, as did my young heroines Natasha Rostova, Tatyana, and Liza, or of ethnic traits, as did Aïda or Butterfly with their Eastern submissiveness. It seems to me that no other operatic role – except Tosca, of course – demands of the actress such a full-blooded display of temperament and voice, such boldness of feeling, beauty and femininity, such elegance in carriage and dress. In my opinion, singers with a lyrico-dramatic repertory – for example, Aïda or Leonora in *Il Trovatore* – should not be afraid of *Traviata*. The part of Violetta is a real treasure. True, the first-act aria requires a great deal of work. But for a singer with a free, light upper register, it should not present any insurmountable technical difficulties. Because of a certain heaviness in Russian voices, the Bolshoi had an age-old tradition that Violetta was to be sung only by coloratura sopranos. But if they could sing the first-act aria brilliantly, with embellishments and spectacular high notes, for the rest of the part they plainly lacked the voice, the incandescence of sound, to express the passion and high tragedy of the heroine's feelings.

I threw myself into work on the part and on the aria in particular, singing it at full voice several times a day. Before approaching Alexander Shamilyevich, I decided to listen to a recording of the opera with Renata Tebaldi, whose work I admired. As I listened I was enraptured by the lightness and brilliance with which she sang the fast passages. Then suddenly, in the recitative before the aria, I heard her shift to a different key – a half-tone lower! She did it so skillfully that I jumped for joy, and decided that if the famous Italian soprano could sing the aria a half-tone lower – then it was God's will – so could I. The very next day I announced to Melik-Pashayev that I was preparing *Traviata*, and I asked him to work with me and conduct the performance.

'O-o-h, so you've decided to sing Violetta! Well, the part is right for you in every way, and you're a natural for the role. You and Lemeshev will make a wonderful pair!'

He scheduled a class for the next day. When I was taking leave of him, I mentioned in passing that I was going to sing the aria a half-tone lower.

'*What?* Why?'

'Tebaldi sings it that way, as do all Italian singers with voices like mine.'

Alexander Shamilyevich looked a little crestfallen, but said nothing. That evening, however, he called me at home and said that he would not conduct *Traviata*.

'But why? What happened?'

'Please don't be offended. I thought it over for a long time before calling you. It isn't easy for me to decline to take part in a performance that is so important for you.'

Everything went dark. 'Alexander Shamilyevich, dear friend, why are you doing this to me?'

'You want to change the key of the aria. I consider it disrespectful to the composer, and I can't go along with it. You know how much I care for you, and how happy I always am to work with you. But even for your sake I can't forgo my principles as a musician. It's painful for me to tell you this, but I feel that if you can't sing the aria in the original key, it would be better not to do the performance at all. In art, one must be honest. I'm convinced that you can sing it the way it was written – you've just gotten a bit lazy. If, however, you insist on doing it your way, you'll have to sing it with another conductor.'

'With another? How can I appear on stage in such a part without you? I'll do whatever you think is necessary. It never would have crossed my mind if it weren't that the Italians –'

'The Italians aren't the authority for us in this case. Come to the theater tomorrow. I want you to sing the whole part for me.'

I was so agitated I didn't even notice that for the first time in all those years, Alexander Shamilyevich had used the familiar form of 'you.'

When I came to class I could see that he was nervous; he understood that if I missed the high D flats it might affect me psychologically – a common enough occurrence among singers – and that I might never risk appearing in *Traviata* on stage. And he would be to blame because he had insisted that I sing it in the original key. Throughout the aria he did not once raise his eyes and he did not conduct. When I finished, he sprang from his chair and laughed happily. 'I knew you could do it, lazybones! But you had to make a big production of it, and force an open door.'

Elated, I dashed to the scheduling department and drew up my rehearsal schedule with Lemeshev, then hurried to the wardrobe department to order new costumes.

There the news was greeted with great enthusiasm: the dressmakers loved to sew for me. First, because I had a good figure; and second, because I always knew what I wanted and didn't quibble over trifles. We created all my costumes in close collaboration, and I must say that no one else at the Bolshoi had anything comparable. There were few materials available to them: chiffon and crepe de chine, which are lost on the stage, tulle . . . Of all their 'goods' I preferred the satin from which they made slippers. With their magic hands and imagination they could create miracles out of it. They dyed it, sketched something on it, hand-embroidered it with silver, gold, and jewels, and the result was a work of art. People would congregate from all the departments to look at my costumes when they were finished. I would model them, to everyone's delight. On such a day I would bring a case of champagne, and we would christen the fruits of our labor. On this occasion, armed with French magazines of the period and the inevitable slipper-satin, we racked our brains trying to come up with at least a minimally decent wardrobe for the 'dame aux camélias.'

'Come along with me, Galina Pavlovna. I want to show you something,' whispered the seamstress standing next to me. We went into a small storeroom, and when she turned on the light I saw on the floor a heap of priest's vestments! There were old brocades and heavy silks with stunning hand-embroidery.

'Where did it all come from?'

'They sent it from the cellars of the Kremlin, thinking it might be useful to us. Those cellars are overflowing with that stuff. They don't know what to do with it all.'

'But these are museum pieces!'

'Who needs them now? Think about it – perhaps we can sew your gowns out of them. We have to use them for something.'

'But how can one cut up such beautiful things?'

'See those pieces of silver brocade in the corner? We're patching them together for scenery. Take my advice. These things are beautiful, all right, but they'll just go to waste!'

'No, we're not going to clothe a courtesan like Violetta in them! But I'll be singing Marfa in *The Tsar's Bride* soon. You can make my costumes out of these things then. I suppose people should have a chance to admire them. In the meantime, keep an eye out and don't let anyone else have them.'

'I won't, don't worry. You're the only singer I've shown them to. It's just a pity I wasn't on the lookout sooner. So much as already been cut into pieces. Well, now, what are we going to do about *Traviata*?'

'What choice do we have? We'll use slipper-satin. White for the first act, with silver appliqué. Red for the third, embroidered with red jewels. But what am I telling you for? You yourself know perfectly well . . .'

'We won't let you down, Galina Pavlovna. We'll make you dresses the likes of which have never been seen.'

Before rehearsals began, I asked Pokrovsky what he thought of the image of Violetta.

'Play the whole first act so that it won't occur to anyone that you are dangerously ill and doomed to die in the last act. For all those around her, Violetta is a seductive mistress. And she wants to be seen only as such. Consumptive courtesans are not valued very highly.'

He didn't have to say another word. The entire image of Violetta immediately took on distinct form in my mind.

My beloved teacher for twenty-two years, Pokrovsky directed me in the creation of every one of my roles. With me he staged *Fidelio*, *War and Peace*, *Falstaff*, *The Snow Maiden*, Prokofiev's *Semyon Kotko*, *Tosca*, and *The Gambler*, and revised the productions of *Onegin*, *The Queen of Spades*, and Rachmaninov's *Francesca da Rimini*. He also helped me prepare Aïda and Butterfly.

Whenever this outstanding director and wonderful man got carried away by his work, he would shout and swear, and many singers resented him for it. I didn't. He could call me a blockhead or a cow – I didn't even hear the words. I saw only that he was fired up, and I wanted to reap as much as I could from him at those moments.

Using amazingly simple methods, he was able to trigger a singer's imagination and fill him with ideas. 'You must fall on your knees before her with such despair that the audience will think you'll never get up – that you'll die there – if she says No. Now look into her eyes. You've never seen such eyes! And they're looking at you! Can it really be that she loves you? Now she's walking away. Follow her, follow her with your eyes . . . Here comes the culmination of your aria . . . she's a goddess! Such women don't exist! A diva! Do you hear what's going on in the orchestra? Now soar, soar to heaven with your high note! Bravo!'

A few days later, breaking off the rehearsal, Pokrovsky would take me aside. 'What have you done to him? You're ruining everything for me.'

'What do you mean?'

'He looks at you like a goddamn calf! What are we going to do with him now?'

'But you're the one who drilled it into him . . . "Goddess! Goddess!"'

'Lord knows what's gotten into him! . . . Let's go on. Listen, you're a man, damn it! Little feet . . . pretty eyes . . . big deal! You've seen them before! Be a tenor on stage, and *basta*! The hell with prima donnas! I want you to sing that last phrase with such passion that at least a dozen of your admirers will faint dead away . . . Galya, embrace him on your *pianissimo*. Hold him tight, don't move, and draw out the *fermata* . . . Squeeze harder, I'm telling you! All the men in the audience have got to envy that numbskull! There! Now I'd say it's beginning to resemble a love duet.'

He never demonstrated what he wanted a singer to do, but, proceeding from each artist's potential, helped him to find his own way into a role.

In 1971 he directed *Tosca* at the Bolshoi, an opera I had never liked and didn't want to sing. The piling up of passions seemed exaggerated to me then. True, in 1963 I had heard *Tosca* in Vienna, with von Karajan conducting and Leontyne Price in the title role. I was stunned by the sound of the orchestra, and Price's singing left me with the strongest impression I have ever gotten from listening to opera. But I still couldn't imagine performing all those 'bloody' passions myself.

So in 1970, when Pokrovsky asked me if I wanted to do *Tosca*, I was reluctant. 'I don't know. I'll have to think about it.'

'No, give me a definite answer. I'll direct it only if you're in it. Otherwise, I won't include it in the repertory.'

'I'll tell you frankly, Boris Aleksandrovich – I just don't see myself in the role.'

'*What?* Galya, you're a fool.'

'Why!'

'Because you were born to sing *Tosca*.'

I don't know if that's the case, but Tosca became one of my favorite roles.

At the first rehearsal, I was sitting next to him on the

proscenium wondering how he would handle my entrance. Would it really be the same as I had seen in many theaters? I looked at him, and it struck me as suspect that he hadn't directed me to my place in the wings. Yes, he definitely had something up his sleeve . . .

'Well, why aren't you making your entrance?'

'From where?'

'From wherever you want.'

'I don't know what I should do. I can't rush out and do a jealous scene to that slow love music.'

'You don't have to. Who's asking you to?'

'But that's the way everyone does it.'

'But you're Galina Pavlovna, "our empress." A prima donna. So make your entrance accordingly.'

'Oh, stop being malicious, Boris Aleksandrovich! I really don't know. I can see the whole role clearly, but not the entrance.'

'But I'm serious. Take your position upstage and center. There will be a black velvet drop there. As soon as the orchestra begins to play your love theme – Tosca's portrait – the spotlight will pick you up. In your left hand you'll carry a bouquet of roses – hold your hand out to the side – and in your right a long walking stick, as was the fashion at that time. Don't place it in front of you, but extend your arm to the right . . . Then walk toward the proscenium as slowly as possible, scarcely touching the floor, as if on air. Now that's the entrance of a singer, an actress . . . Mario must freeze at the appearance of such a picture: he's a painter, after all. You're Tosca, a prima donna, the favorite of the queen and the public. Keep walking. You love and are loved. You're the happiest woman on earth . . . You smile, and as if in passing, over your shoulder, you ask, "Why was the door locked? Who were you talking to?" . . . Don't stop! . . . Pace yourself so you don't reach the proscenium too soon. Be slightly jealous, to please the man in love with you . . . Men like it when a woman is jealous . . . Not seriously . . . Real jealousy will come later, in the scene with Scarpia. That's good. Mario, admire her. Now you make haste to paint her portrait. She's your inspiration, your muse. You're both artists – you live in another, imaginary world . . . Now, just as slowly, approach the Madonna with the bouquet. You must feel with your back the painter's enraptured gaze, and kneel as prettily and elegantly as possible. Mario is watching you! That's it . . . All your rivals have been destroyed. Now stand up just as slowly . . . Oh, hell! Don't lean on the Madonna as if she were a wall!'

'But I can't stand up without holding on to something! My knees wobble. I'm not a ballerina!'

'Damn! The whole scene is ruined! . . . Mario, help her! No, not that way. Don't pull her by the arm – she's not in a hospital bed . . . Galya, without getting up, reach out your arms to him as if you want to kiss him. You feel sorry for him – you've just refused him a kiss . . . Mario, grab her hands! But she won't let you kiss her near the Madonna. Lift her up from her kneeling position and lead her off to one side so the Madonna won't see . . . Faster, faster! You're young lovers, and life is beautiful!'

That entrance gave me the impetus for the development of the whole role.

Many male opera singers, especially those who do the dramatic, 'bloody' roles, have a great need to impress the audience with their masculinity. They throw themselves on their unfortunate partners, enacting burning passion, and think that in this way they have demonstrated exceptional virility. To express love, they'll grab at their partner all over her body and squeeze her until her eyes pop out of her head. To express jealousy, they'll twist her arms until the bones crack. If such a singer has not left several healthy bruises on his victim's body, he feels he hasn't given his all to the performance. The perpetrators are usually tenors – the lover's repertory is their domain. But baritones are even more dangerous. They have few roles as lovers, and when their shining hour comes – as Scarpia in *Tosca*, for example – watch out, prima donna! And pray to God.

In the second act, after his declaration of love to Tosca, Scarpia does not have much left to sing. Knowing that he will soon be murdered, he doesn't waste a minute of his precious time and pounces on her. He'll rough her up, shake her, throw her on the sofa or the floor, as his imagination dictates. Moreover, he fully expects her to resist, fight him off, and flee from him, or else . . . or else, what? He can't really rape her in front of all those good people! And it doesn't occur to him that although his part is over, Tosca has yet to sing her aria.

Once I was on tour in East Berlin at the same time as the Bolshoi's leading baritone. I don't remember what opera he was performing in there, but they asked him to sing Scarpia as well, and he joyfully agreed. The Bolshoi was not doing *Tosca* in those years, and he was, you might say, hungry for love; he decided to give all those foreigners a real taste of Russian temperament. Even at rehearsals the soprano playing Tosca – a big, hefty German woman – complained that she couldn't sing with him, that her arms were already bruised. I thought to myself: You haven't seen anything yet – just wait until the performance.

The rehearsals ended with her running in tears to the management, telling them she refused to perform. But a contract is a contract, and somehow everything was straightened out. As for our baritone, he declared that he wouldn't touch her at all during the performance, since the Germans were incapable of understanding passion anyway.

Everything went smoothly until the fatal scene in the second act. Then all hell broke loose. Forgetting all his oaths and promises, he chased her around the stage until she collapsed flat on her back on the sofa, barely breathing. Ardently, he flung himself on her, covering her with his burning body. Then a miracle happened. Working one mighty leg free from under him, Tosca mustered all her strength and kicked him in the stomach so hard that he rose into the air like a feather and, before the eyes of the dumbfounded audience, flew into the wings. But not all sopranos have such Valkyrian strength.

Whenever I sang Tosca, I would forewarn Scarpia at rehearsals not to touch me during that scene until the very last moment.

'But what am I supposed to do? I have a passionate temperament!'

'You can do whatever you want – even gnaw the back of a chair – but don't touch me: I have to save my breath so I can sing the aria. Otherwise, you'll have only yourself to blame. I have a passionate temperament too, you know!'

What I value in a partner is, above all, mastery of his art. All that forced passion is simply a lack of acting skill and control. Temperament is the ability to exercise self-restraint, as our great artists of the past used to say.

For dozens of years Sergei Lemeshev was the public's idol. Lensky, Romeo, Alfredo, the Duke of Mantua, Fra Diavolo, Almaviva . . . In these roles he was unique, and in Soviet Russia there has not been – and will not be for years to come – an artist to equal the enchantment of his voice, his irresistible charm, and his mastery. Everything about him was artistic: his movements, his inspired facial expressions, his disarming smile. Every emotion he portrayed – from love to hate – was genuine and artistic. Always elegant, with beautiful manners, he had a keen sense for the costumes of any era. On the stage, until the end of his career, he was a youth, beloved and vulnerable. Even at seventy he still drove his admirers into ecstasies every time he sang Lensky at the Bolshoi. In women he roused not passion but tenderness and pity – the most primordial and enduring of feminine feelings.

Sergei Lemeshev! Singer of love, singer of sadness!

Never had I had a partner who so brilliantly expressed the masculine charm of the romantic hero. Some lacked talent, others mastery, and still others physical appearance. I felt that on the stage they were a little afraid of me and shy; that we did not relate to each other as equals. At one time or another, almost all of them would let slip something like, 'Will you permit me to put my arm around your waist, Your Majesty?' But in his domain, Lemeshev was himself 'His Majesty'; and with a largesse worthy of a king he gave the public passion, jealousy, and tenderness. We understood each other without words, with but a glance. No doubt that is why Violetta was the role I created the most easily and quickly.

I had already been with the Bolshoi for twelve years, but this was the first time I understood what it meant to work with a real partner. When I sang abroad, my encounters with even the most splendid of singers had a chance quality about them. We would perform together several times, and even if we wanted to, there would not be enough time to become fully acquainted with one another, to probe each other's personalities before we would go our separate ways – more often than not, never to meet again.

We had a total of three rehearsals for *La Traviata*: two offstage and one with the orchestra. Virtually the entire company showed up for the orchestra rehearsal. It was the first time a soprano with a lyrico-dramatic repertory was singing Violetta at the Bolshoi. What happened on the stage could hardly be termed a rehearsal. As soon as Melik-Pashayev took the podium, the musicians, chorus, and soloists began to play and sing with a fervor seldom heard even at a performance. That morning rehearsal may have been one of my best performances.

All through the first act I sang with such relish that I forgot about the ordeal I had yet to face – the aria. I was reminded of it only when I felt the watchful eyes of the chorus members trained on me. They could not conceal their curiosity ('Something's bound to happen now!'), and hurried off the stage to take seats in the hall. At that moment, something in me faltered. 'What is this feeling I've never experienced before? Can it really be fear?' I glanced at Alexander Shamilyevich, saw his smile and his open arms reaching out toward me – You can do it! Suddenly it all seemed like child's play. I sang like a bird set free.

After the rehearsal, Alexander Shamilyevich came in, beaming. 'I haven't conducted *Traviata* with such pleasure for a long time! What a wonderful opera it is! You did a superb job at the rehearsal. And what a good thing that you finally took on Violetta. I can't understand why you didn't do it earlier. Take a rest now. I'm sure your performance will be a triumph. What else can I say? You already know I can't listen to you without tears coming to my eyes.'

It had already been a year since Melik-Pashayev had been removed from his post as chief conductor. How did it happen? He and Pokrovsky felt that the Bolshoi should eliminate 'command' positions such as chief conductor, chief stage director, and chief artist. The system was obsolete, they thought, and each conductor should bear full responsibility for the quality of his own performances. In short, everyone should work rather than command. Knowing their own value, and confident that it would be impossible to replace them, they were convinced that the authorities would have to accept their plan, and they presented their proposals to Furtseva. She was quite amiable, asked them to draft a statement outlining their suggestions, and promised to report to the government. All appointments to top posts at the Bolshoi are made in the Central Committee of the Party. And so far as Central Committee members are concerned, no one is irreplaceable: where there's a swamp, there'll be devils to live in it. Within a few days a decree was posted in the theater office announcing that Melik-Pashayev and Pokrovsky had been discharged from their positions at their own request, and that Evgeny Svetlanov and Iosif Tumanov had been appointed chief conductor and chief stage director, respectively. For the Bolshoi it was an utter catastrophe. Melik-Pashayev found himself the subordinate of a novice conductor, an uncouth and irrational man. And Pokrovsky was under the command of the least talented stage director I have ever met, but a most crafty and unctuous courtier. For the next five years he filled the Bolshoi with his artistic excrement. The effort it took to get rid of him – for which I can take credit with pride – was incredible, but it finally paid off and Boris Pokrovsky was reinstated as chief stage director of the Bolshoi.

Regardless of his artistic potential, the conductor who is appointed to the post of chief conductor at the Bolshoi is immediately proclaimed the first and incontestably the best, and must conduct performances of the theater's 'treasures': *Boris Godunov, Prince Igor, The Queen of Spades, Aïda*, and so on. This repertory had belonged to Melik-Pashayev but was now claimed by Svetlanov, a young petty tyrant who had greedily fallen upon power and, in his high post, was able to punish or pardon others at will. With the support of the Central Committee and Furtseva he elbowed his way onto the pedestal, trying to shove Melik-Pashayev aside, and gradually deprived the venerable conductor of the productions he had created. The situation became unbearable for Melik-Pashayev, and he only looked forward to the day he would turn sixty and could retire. Yes, he must have had a bellyful if, at the height of his powers, he was counting the days until he could finally give up the work he loved so well.

Arriving at the theater the day after my rehearsal, Alexander Shamilyevich stopped in front of the poster listing the events of the next ten days to jot down the performances he was scheduled to conduct. He had already put down *Boris Godunov*, an opera that no one but he had conducted at the Bolshoi for over ten years, when his glance happened to fall upon the names of the performers and – in place of his own name – he saw someone else's.

The blow had been perfectly calculated, and it hit the bull's-eye. That renowned conductor at the height of his fame – that highly cultivated and educated man – could not recover from the sheer crassness of it, from the realisation that after giving the Bolshoi more than thirty years of his life, he had not even merited a respectful conversation, but had learned from a poster that he would no longer conduct *Boris Godunov*.

He must have remembered how they had settled accounts with his predecessor, Golovanov, simply by taking away his pass and not permitting him to enter the theater. It had turned out that Stalin's methods were still very much alive, and were being continued by worthy successors. Like Golovanov, Melik-Pashayev was fully aware that he was a serf without rights; and again like Golovanov, he could not bear the humiliation. Deeply offended and shaken, he walked out of the theater at once. Shortly thereafter his wife, Minna Solomonovna, called to say that she had returned home to find Alexander Shamilyevich lying unconscious on the floor, and that he was now in the Kremlin hospital.

Aghast at the news, I hastened to call the doctors I knew at the Kremlin hospital to find out what had happened. They said that Alexander Shamilyevich had had a stroke, but that it was a mild one and he would soon recover and go on working at the theater. And it turned out that it was in fact a mild stroke. The next day Alexander Shamilyevich himself called from the hospital and asked the conductor Boris Khaikin to replace him in *Traviata*.

Three days later I sang Violetta on the Bolshoi stage for the first time. During each intermission a messenger from the main office came running to my dressing room with the news that Alexander Shamilyevich had called from the hospital to find out how the performance was going. 'We've been telling him every-thing, Galina Pavlovna – how many flowers there are, and how marvelous your costumes look.' In the lobby it was being rumored that my costumes had been made in Paris. We had indeed knocked 'em dead in Moscow.

After the performance, when the applause had died down, Lemeshev gave me a big hug. 'I'm so happy tonight, Galya! How I regret that we didn't meet on the stage twenty years ago. The things we could have sung together!'

I, too, was infinitely sorry. We sang *Traviata* a few more times after that; and I will always cherish the memories of that remarkable artist.

Late that night Alexander Shamilyevich called me at home. I was deeply touched by his attention and concern. His voice trembled with excitement. 'So you've finally come home! I know everything. I called the theater, and they told me what a brilliant performance it was. If you only knew how tormented I was that I had let you down because of this stupid illness. After all, you had to sing with Khaikin without a rehearsal, which must have added to your anxiety. But thank God it's over with. You'll do the next performance with me. I congratulate your splendid work. I'm proud of you, and so happy for you!' Those were Alexander Shamilyevich Melik-Pashayev's last words to me. He was back on his feet, taking long walks in the garden – we were expecting his return to the theater from one day to the next. But when I came to rehearsal on the morning of June 18, I learned that he had died in his sleep during the night. He was only fifty-nine.

For me, his death was not a misfortune or a sorrow – those are the wrong words. They cannot begin to express the feeling that came over me like an avalanche that early morning of the darkest day in my life. A friend and beloved conductor had died; and with him died that Bolshoi Theater he had so selflessly served and which would cease to exist without him.

His body lay in state in the main lobby, but there was no civil funeral as is the custom in such cases, because Minna Solomonovna, his widow, had not given permission for speeches and music. Furtseva summoned the management of the Bolshoi and raised hell, demanding that there be a 'normal' funeral. 'What do you mean, no music? What kind of a spectacle do you intend to put on?'

It didn't occur to that moron of a woman that a pompous concert, complete with 'wedding generals,'* at a funeral *was* a spectacle.

'The deceased's widow said that she didn't want to hear speeches read at the coffin by the people who had killed her husband. You must understand her – she's in such despair . . .'

'If that's the way things stand, I'll see to it that the body doesn't lie in state at the Bolshoi Theater.'

'But that would be a scandal, Ekaterina Alekseyevna! The former chief conductor and People's Artist of the USSR – what will people think?'

There was nothing Katya would not stoop to. She threatened that the widow would not receive her pension, and that Melik-Pashayev would not be buried in the Novodevichy Cemetery. But Minna Solomonovna stood her ground. 'I won't let them mock my dead husband!'

Finally, three days later the great theater threw open its doors to divest itself forever of one of its most devoted servants, the last of a vanished breed. The crowd, including delegations from various cities, flowed to the upper foyer. There were representatives of opera theaters, orchestras, the armed forces, and industrial plants, all of whom had come with prepared speeches and were at a loss that there would be no opportunity to speak.

Furtseva did not appear at the funeral: she sent her deputy. In the oppressive silence, disturbed only by the shuffling of footsteps, I stood near the open casket, and a single thought throbbed in my head: we were all to blame for the death of that extraordinary man and artist, who had become the victim of scoundrels and careerists. Despair and irredeemable guilt tore at my heart. How was it that we, his pupils, had not been able to protect our mentor and friend, the honor and conscience of the Bolshoi Theater, against humiliation and blatant disregard?

The mezzo-soprano Irina Arkhipova, pale and out of breath,

* A reference to the custom of inviting, as wedding guests, high-ranking persons who are total strangers to the family.

clutched my arm and whispered in my ear like a madwoman: 'Don't cry. Don't cry. I've avenged him . . . I've avenged him . . . I've just come back from the Central Committee . . . I've avenged him . . .'

'*Avenged him?* Do you realise what you're saying? Alexander Shamilyevich is gone, the theater is gone. You've avenged him . . . We should have saved him, not avenged him . . .'

Alexander Shamilyevich's face was sorrowful and stern. Death had not stamped him with its seal of serenity.

Before the coffin was carried out it was placed for a few minutes in the dark hall of the theater, in front of the spotlighted podium on which the famous conductor had stood for more than thirty years, bestowing his art and inspiration upon the public. One corner of the curtain was raised; from the back of the stage the chorus of priestesses from *Aïda* began to sing; and to the accompaniment of their quiet singing, Alexander Shamilyevich Melik-Pashayev left the Bolshoi Theater forever.

In 1976, when I was already living abroad but was still a Soviet citizen and officially a member of the Bolshoi company, a book about Melik-Pashayev was published in the Soviet Union containing reminiscences of him by singers, composers, and music critics. They all recalled his jewel, *Aïda*, saying it was his best opera at the Bolshoi, and that in recent years it was almost always performed by the same cast, each of whom the great conductor had fostered: Andzhaparidze as Radames, Arkhipova as Amneris, Lisitsian as Amonasro, Petrov as Ramfis, and . . . others. In all the articles about the opera *Aïda* there was simply no mention of Aïda herself. And in the section entitled 'Opera Productions at the Bolshoi Theater Directed by A. Sh. Melik-Pashayev' the names of my understudies were given – to commemorate all the premieres I sang with him.

In that same year of 1976, 'by imperial order' of the Central Committee, my name was deleted and my photographs removed from the jubilee album issued on the occasion of the 200th anniversary of the Bolshoi. In order to avoid squabbling among the prima donnas, the empty spaces in the book were hastily filled with photographs of young, beginning singers. I imagine they were shocked beyond words, and of course overjoyed, to find themselves featured so prominently. Well then, with all my heart I hope that some day they will occupy a similar place, not only in an album but on the stage.

In their attempt to eradicate all trace of me from the history of the Bolshoi, they went so far as to collect all my photographs from the theater's archives and throw them out. My admirers retrieved them from the trash heap and sent them to me in Paris. But before the trash-heap incident took place, how many conferences, secret exchanges of letters, and government decrees there were on the subject! For shame! Well, it certainly wasn't the first time our rulers demonstrated – to the public's amusement – their mental deficiency. They act in accordance with a mold stamped fifty years ago, and it's impossible to expect anything new out of the dense stagnation of their sclerotic brains.

Fyodor Chaliapin, who left the Soviet Union with the consent of the authorities in 1922, was soon damned by his dear countrymen as an enemy of the people, and was pronounced anathema. For decades his name was never mentioned, as if the great singer had never existed.

I have before me Chaliapin's book *The Mask and the Soul*, published in Paris in 1932. As I read about the reasons he was deprived of his title, First People's Artist of the Republic, I can't believe my eyes: financial assistance to White Guard organisations, contacts with enemy centers in California and Paris, et cetera, et cetera. In a word, exactly the same things Slava and I would be accused of. What poor imaginations the authorities have! So many years have passed, and still nothing new. And yet, for the sake of fairness, it must be acknowledged that there *is* something new. Chaliapin had the honor of learning from London reporters that the Soviet authorities were *about to* take away his citizenship, whereas Slava and I, while watching television in Paris, learned from the late news that our Soviet citizenship *had been* taken away.

The 'White Guards' to whom Chaliapin offered money were starving Russian children in Paris. As for Rostropovich, he donated the proceeds from two of his concerts: in Paris, to needy

Russians; and in California, to disabled Russian veterans of World War I – eighty- and ninety-year-old former soldiers who had been wounded defending the honor of their fatherland when the future Kremlin elders were still in diapers.

At one point in his book Chaliapin describes his encounter with some Russian women in the courtyard of the Orthodox cathedral on the rue Daru in Paris: 'They were in rags and tatters, and so were their children. The children's legs were crooked, and they were covered with scabs. The women asked me to give them something for food.' The famous singer gave 5,000 francs to a priest and asked him to distribute the money among the poor. It was for this noble impulse that the Soviet authorities anathematised the great Russian artist. But then they had a very different understanding of helping hungry children. It was not long thereafter (April 7, 1935) when the decree 'On Combating Crime' was issued, extending the death penalty to include children twelve and older.

Chaliapin continues:

Moscow, which once caught fire from a one-kopeck candle and burned, was again ablaze from my meager donation. The newspapers printed articles stating that Chaliapin had joined the counter-revolutionaries. Actors, circus performers, and other servants of art issued protests proclaiming that I was not only a bad citizen but worthless as an actor. And the 'popular masses' held meetings and excommunicated me from my native land . . .

After reading these bitter lines, I remembered how in 1973 – almost fifty years after his disgraceful excommunication – the whole country celebrated the 100th anniversary of the birth of 'our dear, great Fyodor Ivanovich.' At the Bolshoi there was a gala concert in which I participated. As I stood on the stage it of course never entered my mind that in a few months the same fate would befall me: that like that great artist, I would find myself in exile. Behind me, stretching from one end of the huge stage to the other, was a portrait of Chaliapin, who seemed to be eyeing his worshipers – those who had once reviled and cursed him –

who now, as if nothing had happened, were vying with one another to sing the praises of 'the great Russian singer, the great son of the Russian people.' A command had been given from on high, and the people lamented on cue.

SEVENTEEN

In October 1964, four months after the death of Melik-Pashayev, the Bolshoi went on tour to Milan for the first time. The preceding summer, the La Scala company had performed in Moscow.

Our month-long engagement met with great success. I sang in *The Queen of Spades* and *War and Peace*. After hearing my performances, the management of La Scala invited me to sing the part of Liù in *Turandot* with them when the season opened in December. I agreed; and however hard the new management of the Bolshoi tried to thwart me, I got permission to do it.

After the tour, the rest of the Bolshoi returned to Moscow, and I remained in Milan alone. The director of La Scala, Ghiringhelli, thoughtfully provided me with an interpreter – a young Ukrainian woman by the name of Tatyana who had been living in Milan since the end of World War II – and I immersed myself in work on my new part.

November and December are the foulest months in Milan: constant rain, cold, and fog. Yet December is when the opera season opens at La Scala and when, of course, singers are most likely to catch cold. Although I tried to stay indoors as much as possible, I came down with acute bursitis in my right shoulder. Tatyana took me to the doctor, who prescribed various procedures including heat treatment, but nothing helped. The pain was especially severe at night, and sometimes prevented me from getting any sleep at all. In the morning I would gulp down strong, black coffee and hurry off to the theater.

On the eve of the dress rehearsal, the pain increased sharply. Seeing that I was in for a sleepless night, Tatyana decided to stay over with me so that she could at least be of some assistance, if necessary. Before long, she dozed off. But I, wrapped in electric heating pads, tossed about in bed half the night, tormented by the persistent pain. The one thing I prayed to God for was a few hours of sleep. Neither sleeping pills nor sedatives helped. Closing my eyes, I mentally counted to a thousand, then back again . . . I repeated the Italian text of my part hundreds of times . . .

I was seized with a sensation of terrible cold. A light was on in the room, and Tatyana was sleeping. 'I have to get another blanket,' I thought. I tried to get up, but couldn't stir. Through my body, suddenly heavy as lead, crawled a chilling, deadly cold – it crept from the tips of my toes and fingers higher and higher toward my heart. It had gripped my entire body, and I felt that my face was growing cold. . . 'What a strange state! This is probably the way people die . . . It's not at all painful, and it's not frightening . . . Yes, I'm dying, I'm dying . . . Now my heart will stop, and I'll be no more . . .'

Sinking into oblivion, I only managed the thought that I should call Tatyana. But I could not open my stiff, benumbed lips . . . Then, with a desperate effort, I screamed, 'Tanya! Tanya! I'm dying! I'm dying! Help me! Help me!'

As if from the other world, I saw her dash about the room, quickly throw on some clothes, and run out. And I saw myself lying flat on the bed, immobile.

I don't know how much time had passed when the door opened slowly and a middle-aged woman came in. She was wearing a white smock and a kerchief wrapped around her head like a Russian peasant woman. She stopped at my bed and peered at me.

'Who are you?' I asked her.

'Death,' she answered calmly.

She had a plain, tired-looking peasant face, and everything about her appearance reminded me of our Russian nannies. I wasn't at all frightened. She walked around the room as if she were looking for something.

'Go away!'

She stopped and turned around.

'Go away, do you hear me? Come back in thirty years!'

She came up to my bed, once again looked me over closely, and then left the room. As soon as the door had closed behind her I added thirty to my thirty-seven: sixty-seven years . . .

The light was on in the room. Turning my head, I saw Tatyana peacefully asleep on the sofa. It was unbearably hot, and my body, warmed by the electric heating pads, was burning like an iron. I got up to open a window, and retraced the steps of the woman in white.

'Tanya, wake up! Wake up! Listen. Did you leave the room?'

Half-awake, she looked at me with uncomprehending eyes.

'You didn't see anyone here just now?'

'Who was here? What – is it time to get up?'

'No. Go back to sleep.'

I left her in peace, and she promptly went back to sleep. I tried to open the door, but it was locked. Had it been a hallucination?

As I was getting back into bed, my body suddenly felt unusually light, almost weightless. At first I couldn't understand the cause of that sensation. Then it dawned on me – the pain in my arm was completely gone. Yet for two weeks it hadn't given me a minute's relief.

I sank into long-desired sleep, but in my haze I kept hearing: 'In thirty years . . . In thirty years . . . In thirty years . . .' How infinitely many!

At La Scala I had no run-through rehearsals with the other soloists. I was merely shown the staging, and told that the others would arrive in time for the orchestra rehearsal.

I had heard Birgit Nilsson as Turandot when she came to Moscow with La Scala, and I knew the unlimited possibilities of her big, splendid voice. I had never heard or seen Franco Corelli, however. At the one rehearsal with orchestra, soloists, and chorus, after singing my first phrases, I was standing on the proscenium concentrating on what I had to do – trying to commit the staging to memory and estimate how well my voice would carry. Suddenly from behind I heard a voice of such beauty and power, with such a phenomenal high B flat, that I went numb and couldn't sing my next phrase. Turning around, I saw Franco Corelli standing far (!) upstage and I became rooted to the spot. I had never encountered a tenor so endowed by nature: hand-some, tall, well-built, with long legs and a big, flowing voice of extraordinary beauty. Italian tenors generally have brilliant high notes – their voices seem to bloom in the upper register. But Corelli's were altogether special: full and undulating, even his high C, which he sang with such ease that it seemed he must have a D and E of equal quality in reserve.

I relished singing the part of Liù. Her vocal image is a natural continuation of all Puccini's heroines. Indeed, it was to her that the composer, in his last opera, gave his heart; and, having written her death scene, he died along with her, without finishing the work.

The theater's splendid rehearsal pianist coached me in the part with painstaking care, and did such a fine job of teaching me how to pronounce the Italian words that after the premiere one critic wrote that in contrast to the other singers, including the Italians, I had a special, aristocratic pronunciation (!). He even named the Italian province where this pronunciation originated. Yes, there are wonders in this world!

At one of the sessions with the rehearsal pianist, I came to the end of the first-act aria, singing the high B flat *piano* as usual, and holding it there. He asked me if I could crescendo to a *fortissimo* on that note and then break it off sharply.

'Of course I can,' I replied, and showed him.

'Brava! You absolutely must do that in the performance.'

'Why?'

'Because the audience knows that it is very hard to do, and not every singer has the technique.'

'But what's the point of such tricks? Producing an hysterical scream may be very effective, but it's not at all in character for the shy, withdrawn Liù.'

'But the audience expects to hear it. If you don't sing it like that, they'll think you're simply unable to.'

'Let them think whatever they want! I have to retain a consistent stage image through the whole performance – that's the main thing. In her aria at the beginning of the opera, Liù must not reveal so much emotion.'

'But I'm telling you that you're cheating yourself. However

beautiful a *piano* you may sing, it will not take the place of what the audience is expecting. This is Italy!'

'I just don't know. In my opinion, it's unmusical.'

I knew that my opponent in this disagreement would be in the audience during the orchestra rehearsal, and just to spite him I disregarded his advice and sang the last note of the aria in a very beautiful and long *piano*. After the rehearsal he came to see me backstage and said that it was the first time in his life he had seen a singer who didn't want to show the Italian audience what she was capable of. 'It's just as if you had a large diamond in your hands and deliberately tossed it in the garbage.'

'But it's against my principles!'

'Save your principles for another time and place, and don't try to prove anything to anybody here. You should grab success, and *basta!* Go ahead and use all the effects you can. Forget that the rehearsal went so smoothly. You'll see what goes on during the performance, when the critics are there.'

I couldn't understand what significance the execution of one particular note in an entire production could possibly have. Why should I have to do something just because the audience expects it? For me the original music is paramount, and must be executed faithfully. As for the audience, three thousand people cannot all have the same taste. An artist has an obligation to present his own point of view, and to be a dictator on the stage.

Naturally a conflict arose about the costume, as always. The one they brought me was heavy, embroidered in gold, and I felt it was too elegant for a humble adolescent girl serving as a blind man's guide. I asked for something very simple and unadorned. And again it began . . .

'Everyone wears it. There isn't any other.'

'Then make me one. The costume should consist only of tight-fitting pants and a simple tunic. It would cost almost nothing. Or, better yet, buy it ready-made at a Chinese store.'

Seeing that I was getting worked up and that red spots were beginning to appear on my face, they called Nikolai Benois, the designer of the production, and told him that I refused to wear his costume. Nikolai Aleksandrovich [Benois] asked them to put me on the phone. It was easy for me to communicate with him – he spoke Russian beautifully. But having already had endless arguments on the subject, I controlled my temper and tried to explain in an angelic voice that the elegance of the costume disturbed me and I'd prefer something simple – the kind of thing that Chinese women wear on the street. To my delight, Nikolai Aleksandrovich said with complete equanimity that he himself didn't like the costume; originally a different one had been made, but later someone wanted to replace it, having found it too plain.

'Call somebody to the phone and I'll tell them to find it and bring it to you. I think it's just the thing you need.' As if by magic, the very costume that I had imagined soon appeared before my eyes. I almost wept for joy.

I did not regard my performance as a debut at La Scala, and I was not at all nervous about it, since I had just performed on that stage in the familiar company of other artists from the Bolshoi and had had great success and rave reviews. I must say that of all the countries where the Bolshoi Opera has performed, it has enjoyed the greatest recognition and success in Italy. But it was not until I appeared with an Italian company in an Italian opera that I learned what success at La Scala was.

My partner singing the role of Timur, the old blind man to whom Liù is tied throughout the performance as his servant and guide, was the splendid bass Niccolo Zaccharia. He had sung in *Turandot* at La Scala many times. At rehearsals he kept reassuring me: 'Don't bother memorising the staging. I know it, and I'll steer you in the right direction.' And indeed, it wasn't hard for him to do, since his hand was resting on my shoulder all the time. Standing in the wings before my entrance and running through the staging in my mind, I suddenly noticed that the old blind man at my side was rather suspiciously standing up straighter and straighter, and looking everyone over with an eagle eye, like a general before a battle. I had hardly taken a few steps on the stage in the called-for direction when my blind man, puffing out his chest and firmly squeezing my shoulder, steered me in the opposite direction. He pushed me through the crowd formed by members of the chorus and, waving his cane like a marshal's baton, confidently led me along what was apparently an oft-trodden path. Where? To the proscenium, of course, where he planted himself firmly. And when in the course of the action he had to fall, he stretched out his legs across the space remaining between us and the edge of the stage, so that not one inch of the conquered territory was left to the 'enemy.' Satisfied with this maneuver, he opened one 'blind' eye and winked at me as if to say, 'With me you won't get lost!' Scarcely were we in position when Corelli as Calaf appeared. But now, after singing his opening phrase from the very back of the stage, he rushed forward to take the hall by storm; and covering fifteen meters in three steps, he belted out his brilliant B flat from the edge of the proscenium, where we had all come together.

And now the three Chinese, Ping, Pang, and Pong, were stealing up closer and closer. With each minute the bridgehead dwindled, until all the troops were concentrated in a narrow zone along the line of the defense. They were stopped only by the orchestra pit, yawning like a chasm at their feet and preventing them from throwing themselves on the enemy in the audience. Well, I thought, look out! This is only the beginning of the performance. If it continues like this, then I, with my concern for the psychological development of the character in the Stanislavsky tradition, will get so battered in this brawl that, as they say in the song, 'nobody will find my grave.' And when the time came for my aria I realised that I would have to put into it all the skill I was capable of to control my voice. Remembering the advice of my rehearsal pianist, on whom I had heaped so much mockery, I made my way to that damned B flat at the end of the aria and deliberately sang it *pianissimo* long enough for the audience to think that that was all. But at the last moment I crescendoed to such a *fortissimo* that, as Ghiringhelli said later, one had the impression of a locomotive sounding its whistle as it emerged from a tunnel. After I released the note and fell sobbing at the feet of Calaf, the audience broke into a roar and stopped the show for a long time. Frankly, I wasn't expecting anything like it, although I was already used to the stormy reactions of Western audiences.

Calaf's aria followed immediately after mine. When the applause began to die down, I looked at him. From the way he set one foot in front of the other and squared his shoulders, from the flashing of his eyes, I realised that the time had come 'to open one's ears and one's soul.' And indeed, I had never heard such singing before, and probably never will again. He was a tremendous success, and the first act ended brilliantly. In the second act, Birgit Nilsson, with her huge, powerful voice, finished off the audience. Our *Turandot* was a triumph.

After that, Ghiringhelli offered me an open-ended contract with excellent terms. 'We need you! Callas has retired. We'll stage whatever productions you want.'

'But I live in Moscow. It doesn't depend on me.'

'But you can live here, and travel the world. Don't go back to Moscow now. Stay here and work for a few years. I know you have an excellent position in your theater. But you don't realise what kind of career is waiting for you in the West if you could work freely here.'

Oh, I knew that very well! But to stay there for several years? It was so bizarre for me to hear his offer! After all, Slava and the children were waiting for me in Moscow . . . I simply changed the topic of conversation.

The three of us – Francesco Siciliani (the artistic director), Ghiringhelli, and I – met on several occasions. They had me listen to various operas so I could choose the ones I'd like to sing at La Scala: *Manon Lescaut, Luisa Miller, Don Giovanni, Adriana Lecouvreur, Faust* . . . Three months later I received a letter from Siciliani offering me those parts.* But alas! It was not fated to be. The Ministry of Culture barred all access to La Scala for me.

Before my return to Moscow, Ghiringhelli wanted to present me with a gift in honor of my success and asked me what I'd like. Since I adore dogs, I said, 'A female black toy poodle!' I named her Joujou and brought her to Moscow with me. She died in 1973.

But if I had come to know what success at La Scala was all about, I also learned the meaning of failure when I attended a premiere of *Traviata*. The production was a flop, despite the participation of a renowned cast and the co-direction of none other than Herbert von Karajan and Franco Zeffirelli.

My first performances of *Turandot*, December 7, 10, and 12, coincided with the final days of rehearsal for *Traviata*, the

* See Appendix, p. 500.

premiere of which was scheduled for December 14. Since I was not accustomed to singing so frequently, I confined myself to my hotel room between performances, trying to avoid conversation and the out-of-doors as much as possible, for fear of an inflamed windpipe on top of my ailing shoulder. So, unfortunately, I did not catch even a glimpse of a rehearsal, though I badly wanted to observe those two celebrated men at work together.

But backstage, during my own performances, I could sense the uneasiness growing with every passing day and spreading through the theater. Some people cursed the co-directors, while others praised them; and the nearer it came to the premiere, the more the arguments spilled beyond the walls of the theater. In the course of a few days, storm clouds had gathered over Milan; and after the dress rehearsal, the whole city was in a frenzy. Everyone was preparing for a scandal, and tickets were impossible to come by.

Coming into the hotel restaurant on the day of the premiere, Tatyana and I could already detect all the signs of the approaching storm. The level of noise and excitement in the room was extraordinary. Waiters with a warlike air were gathering in groups, shouting something and gesticulating vigorously. Our waiter came up to us at once, his black eyes flashing threateningly, and inquired: 'The signora plans, of course, to be at the opera this evening?'

He was simply bursting with indignation. He had to let off steam and share his deliberations and predictions about the upcoming premiere.

'The signora absolutely must come! There'll be a scandal the likes of which we've never seen at La Scala. We're all going to be there,' he explained, taking down our order and then shouting at the top of his lungs to someone at the other end of the room: 'We won't let him mock our Verdi! He came to teach *us* how *Traviata* should be sung? But tonight we'll give him something he won't forget all his life! And if that's not enough for him, we'll bring tomatoes to the next performance!' And he hurried off to see to our order.

Before we had a chance to look around, several people had gathered at our table and were vying with one another, trying to explain to me – a Russian singer, clearly taken aback by all the shouting – just what was going on.

'We'll teach him to respect our Verdi! We already know what he's been up to. The tempos are all wrong!'

'What do you mean, "wrong"?' I asked, trying to get a word in edgewise. 'In the first place, you still haven't heard the perform-ance. In the second place, he is a great conductor, and it wouldn't hurt you to hear his interpretation. His very name is a guarantee of a high-quality performance.'

'*O Madonna!*' howled our waiter, returning to our table. Instead of the steak I had ordered, he plunked down a plate of spaghetti with tomato sauce, which I can't stand.

'Do you know what you're saying, Signora? He's strangled all the singers. He doesn't let them hold the high notes! O, *mamma mia!* He wants to kill our Verdi!'

Unable to go on, he fell silent . . . and wept.

I tried to console him. 'Why are you sobbing? Give the performance a chance.' But around my table the shouting con-tinued. Someone, waving his arms, was singing an aria, trying to prove to me that some note or other must not be cut short, while someone else was explaining how the orchestra should play this or that phrase. Numbed by this unbridled outpouring of emotion, I gloomily ate my spaghetti with the despised tomato sauce.

That night the audience came to the theater armed with their preconceived notions and determined to wreck the performance. Throughout the opera I kept wondering why the new production of *Traviata* had provoked such a hullabaloo. The conductor had merely purged the score of long-standing clichés and followed the composer's instructions in both tempos and nuances – which sounded boldly innovative in an opera that has been played and sung to death. The staging was completely traditional, as were the sets. The only thing that surprised me was that before Violetta's and Alfredo's duet in the first act, the stage suddenly revolved to reveal a bedroom. Alfredo sang his declaration of love against the background of a huge bed, which seemed to be inviting him to jump right in. But the orchestra intervened just in time; and singing 'until tomorrow,' the future lovers parted.

At that point, the entire chorus thronged into the bedroom to take leave of their gracious hostess. She, however, dashed off into the wings. I thought she perhaps needed a drink of water before singing her aria. But it turned out that she had exited in order to throw off her dress, for she returned to sing the magnificent aria in her underclothes – emphatically unfeminine and inelegant ones at that – a plain chemise and, over it, a crude, suspiciously dirty corset with lacings. This attire might have been fitting for a regimental canteen-keeper but hardly suited the appearance of a woman at whose feet the most prominent social lions had thrown their fortunes.

Apart from everything else, the coarseness and vulgarity of the costume were antithetical to the delicate lyrical gift of the soprano singing Violetta, so out of keeping with her tender, light voice! And by giving the scene a boudoir character, the director reduced the all-absorbing transport of the heroine's first love – for which she paid with her life – to the level of a banal, routine affair.

But the audience was not irritated by these vulgarities. Everyone was too busy concentrating on the singing and on the conductor, who, in not permitting the singers to hold the high notes until they were blue in the face, deprived the audience of its usual pleasure. Vociferously expressing their opinions, shouting back and forth between the orchestra and the loges during the singing, reacting stormily to each imperfect note, the audience grew more and more inflamed. Yes, the famous maestro had stepped on the Italian's tender corns and it was clear that he would not take his foot off of it until the end of the performance. The audience was thirsting for blood. When the curtain finally went down on the first act, people hissed, booed, and swore. Fights even broke out in the gallery. And so on throughout the performance, and then late into the night on the public square in front of the theater.

Whether anything like it had ever happened at La Scala before, I don't know. It was the first time in my life – and I hope the last – that I witnessed such indecent behavior by an audience. I was sitting in the center box, my head hunched between my shoulders, my teeth chattering with fear. As soon as the howling started, I closed my eyes. I couldn't look at the stage. If I had attended this premiere before my first performance in *Turandot*, I doubt that the experience would have encouraged me to feel free on stage or bolstered my confidence in my vocal skills.

The next day the scandal carried over into the newspapers. The critics assailed the performers and the co-directors, and tore the whole production to pieces. But what exactly did the audience and the critics achieve as a result of the scandal, the defamation, and the insults? For many years one of the greatest conductors of our day would not cross the threshold of La Scala, no matter how he was beseeched. One may presume that he was not left without work. But did the Italian theater find even an approximate replacement for such an outstanding personality? What the singers were deprived of goes without saying.

In the course of any career, there have been few times when I could complain about unjust treatment from the critics. Clearly, God has shown mercy on me. But I have often witnessed completely undeserved attacks by the press, when some famous singer was ground to dust for muffing one high note.

I gradually came to understand the mentality of singers in the West. It became clear to me why they dislike rehearsing so much. Why should they rehearse if their main concern during performances is to maintain an even sound and to hold the high notes as long as possible without breaking? They do not want to give the critics any reasons to pick on them. But, by holding renowned singers at penpoint, the critics deprive the audience of the artists' full emotional output and creative daring.

But are the critics themselves so invulnerable in their knowledge of opera and theater that they can categorically tell conductors, directors, and artists how a certain opera should be sung and played? A curious incident took place in Canada when I was on tour there with the Bolshoi in 1967. The mezzo-soprano Irina Arkhipova and I were singing in *The Queen of Spades*. At the beginning of the second scene, there is a beautiful duet with harpsichord accompaniment which is very well known in Russia, and great importance is attributed to it in performances. Before this particular performance, we sang it through several times, striving for the perfect purity and blending of our voices.

We had both sung in *The Queen of Spades* for many years. The usual staging called for Polina (Arkhipova) to sit at the harpsichord pretending to play, and for Liza to stand at her side as they sang the duet, 'It's already evening, the edges of the clouds have darkened . . .' A moonlit night, young ladies melting with rapture all around (the members of the chorus) – in short, an idyll.

Just before the second scene, when we were on stage waiting for the curtain to rise, I got the idea of changing the staging. 'Irina, let's stand side by side. That way our voices will blend better. One of the girls in the chorus can sit at the harpsichord.'

And that's what we did. We put our arms around each other, like shepherdesses in old engravings, and brought our heads as close together as possible in order to blend our voices, and hear every nuance. The harpsichord began to play, the curtain rose, and we began to sing. I don't know what happened to Irina – perhaps it was the change in staging, or the close range of the soprano part – but she started to sing in a different key. Boris Khaikin was conducting. His jaw dropped, and the baton fell out of his hand. The members of the chorus all went into a state of shock. The harpsichord was never loud enough for us on stage, but now it was as if it weren't there at all. I understood only one thing: come what may, I had to stand my ground, keep the key, and not listen to the foolishness Irina was up to beside me. During the whole first verse she fumbled up and down two octaves, trying to hit the mark. And I, having affected an expression of languorous bliss, decided: To hell with you! You can sing 'Moscow Nights' or 'Dark Eyes' if you want to, but you won't get me to budge. Finally, after realising the utter futility of her search, Irina began to sing my part, but an octave lower. It gave me a start, for it seemed as if a bass had joined us.

Somehow we managed to get through the first verse, after which the harpsichord had a solo. And I thought: Now she'll come to her senses, and in the second verse we'll finally demonstrate 'the perfect purity and blending of our voices.' But she whispered to me as though from the grave, 'I'm dying!' Tightening my hold around her waist, and stretching my lips into a broad smile, I whispered back, 'Stop panicking! Everything's all right.' But apparently something had become firmly wedged in her brain, and she sang the entire second verse with me – an honest, perfect, and pure octave lower – bellowing her bass into my ear like an archdeacon.

Everything must come to an end, however; our duet was no exception. The chorus, faint from the horror of it, then had to pick up the action and sing, 'Entrancing, charming! Ah, marvelous, wonderful!' They even had to beg us to sing 'More, more!' – but this Peter Ilich Tchaikovsky did not permit us to do, and rightly so.

Irina was of course hysterical during the intermission. When I came to her dressing room she was sobbing and rolling on the couch. The doctors who had been called in were giving her sedatives.

'I've ruined the production! It's all my fault! I've let the whole theater down! What a disgrace before the whole world!'

'Stop crying! What do they understand? It can happen to anybody.' I tried to console her, but in my heart I was sure that the next day the critics would rip the two of us apart. Who would miss such an opportunity? I myself had never heard anything like it in my life.

We hardly slept that night. When the papers came in the morning, we pounced on them as if expecting a declaration of war. Some liked *The Queen of Spades* more, others less. But the music critic of *The New York Times* simply abhorred the production. Without mincing words, he stingingly criticised the director, railed at the soloists for the shrillness of their voices, ridiculed the sets, and went to great lengths to be witty on the subject of the falling snow in the 'winter canal' scene. Apparently, our Russian snow had brought the venerable critic to the boiling point. But . . . we had half a dozen newspapers in our hands, and could not get over our astonishment. Not a *single* critic had caught what was not so much the faking – the word doesn't even come close – as the total catastrophe in the first half of our duet, or the subsequent singing in octaves for three minutes! And all that without orchestral accompaniment, when not only each of the soloists' notes but their slightest breath could be heard! . . . But the snowflakes, and of course the notorious accusation 'old-fashioned.' Too bad no one wrote that Tchaikovsky had pirated the brilliant idea of scoring Liza's and Polina's duet in octaves from the 'Agnus Dei' in the Verdi *Requiem*. Now that would have been amusing!

EIGHTEEN

One day in the summer of 1965 Dmitri Dmitriyevich told me that Lenfilm (Leningrad Film Studio) was planning to make a movie of the opera *Katerina Izmailova*,* and that he was hoping I would agree to play the lead role. He needn't have hoped. I had dreamed of playing the role of Katerina for so long that it had become a kind of obsession for me. Had I been told that it would be my last role and that I would never sing again, I would have done it anyway.

At the time I was passing through a difficult phase of my life. Melik-Pashayev had died in 1964 and for a long time I had lost all interest in the Bolshoi. The invitation of Lenfilm was, therefore, a kind of creative salvation for me. I took the whole season off from the Bolshoi and eagerly plunged into work on the long-desired role.

Dmitri Dmitriyevich gave me the piano score into which he had written a part above the printed line. He said nothing, and never asked me to sing those passages in place of what was printed, but I learned that handwritten version. I had no idea that these were passages he had resurrected from his original version. For me the musical authority of Shostakovich was so unshakable that if he had told me black was white, I would have agreed. I knew that he saw better than I what was at the heart of my art, and I had learned to take what he gave me and follow it to the letter.

Shostakovich did not like to talk about his compositions, and never explained the significance of given musical phrases to the performers of his works. It was as if he were afraid of words – afraid that words might destroy his inner musical vision. He

* The main character in Nikolai Leskov's 'Lady Macbeth of the Mtsensk District' – the story on which Shostakovich's opera was based – is named Katerina Izmailova, hence the title of the second version of the opera and of the film.

always granted artists the right to interpret his works and so put the responsibility squarely on their shoulders.

I was very familiar with Leskov's story, and already had my own attitude toward that willful creature, Katerina. It was with much excitement that I looked forward to meeting her operatic version. But when I opened the piano score a wave of pity overcame me. There was no room for condemnation in that flow of passion and girlish tenderness that flooded the musical idiom of the murderess-heroine. Shostakovich, a man deeply repelled by any and all violence, not only had not condemned Katerina for the murder she committed, but, with all the intensity of his temperament, had empathised with her. Katerina possesses all the beauty of feeling that he himself is capable of, and we become infected with his love for her.

On the first page of the piano score I noticed the dedication, 'To Nina Vasilyevna Shostakovich.' So that was it! Of course! Nina had been his fiancée at the time, and Dmitri Shostakovich was twenty-four and madly in love. His opera was a direct reflection of his relationship with his future wife. But then why did he use this 'sketch of a courtroom chronicle' by Leskov? He had been thinking about writing that particular opera for a long time; had he not met Nina, I am convinced the image of Katerina would have been different, for Shostakovich always wrote about himself – about his own feelings and his own sufferings. Since his first real love had swept in and overwhelmed him as he wrote, he could not help but endow the heroine of his opera with the things he wanted from the woman he loved. He wanted Nina to love him without hesitation, to be ready to do anything for his sake, and so he justified all the crimes of Katerina. He justified her murder of an obstinate husband and father-in-law, because they interfered with her love. Sweep it all away! For the sake of love, one could do anything . . . He wanted to pluck his heroine from the dreary quagmire of a merchant-class existence and give her wings to fly . . . to *him*. It is the recklessness and elemental power of her passion that make us identify with that strong young woman and forget all her evil deeds. 'Kiss me so the blood rushes to my head, so the ikons fall out of their cases! Oh, Seryozha!'

And how Shostakovich hates and despises her lover Sergei!

That vulgar drugstore cavalier of a lover with a 'sensitive' soul irritates him, and like a boy, he envies him. From Sergei's first appearance, Shostakovich suggests to his Katya that, compared to her, Sergei is nothing: as what dregs, what slime, does the composer portray him in the penal-camp scenes.

Before *Lady Macbeth of Mtsensk* there had been no women in Shostakovich's works. Katerina is an original Russian woman. She is not the heroine of Leskov's story, she is Shostakovich's Nina. I realised his violent passion for her immediately. She must have been a woman of strong, uncommon character to have provoked such an explosion within him. And he, with his own overpowering temperament and sensitivity, was seeking just such a passion from his heroine. We hear that in all the love scenes of the opera.

Lady Macbeth seems to me the most lifelike and vivid portrait of the composer during the happiest time of his life. Here we see him as God made him: the young genius, who embodies an amazing combination of intellect, well-honed talent, and unbridled temperament. Here he wrote heedlessly and from the heart. Everything in the opera is open – the tremendous scale of passions and the brilliant humor. He did not yet have that cudgel hanging over him; he had not yet developed that malicious wit. I often told Dmitri Dmitriyevich that he had an obligation to write at least one more opera. His answer to this was always the same: so long as *Lady Macbeth* was not being performed in Russia, he would write no other. Shortly thereafter it was staged in Moscow, and after the premiere I again asked Dmitri Dmitriyevich to write another opera for me.

'But where can I find a libretto? It must have a big female role.'

'What could be better than Tolstoy's *Resurrection*? Actresses dream of playing Katyusha Maslova.'

He started as if frightened. 'No, no! Not another Katerina! It's an ill-starred name. No. Anything but that!'

Dmitri Dmitriyevich never showed the rough drafts of a new composition to anyone. No one knew what he was writing until the work was finished; and he never rewrote anything. The only time he departed from that rule was when he produced a second version of *Lady Macbeth*. The people in the Central Committee's Department of Agitation and Propaganda (a fitting name for the department that decides all questions involving art in the USSR!) told him that if he agreed to reword the opera and change the title, they would allow it to be produced at the Stanislavsky-Nemirovich-Danchenko Musical Theater in Moscow. But if not, well . . . It was important for the authorities to get a new version so they wouldn't have to acknowledge their banditry of 1936, so that they could show everyone that the 'criticism' was just – that even the composer had accepted it as such.

In the revision the orchestration was simplified. The overture to the second act was done away with, as was the musical epilogue to the love scene in the second act. And the vocal parts were simplified. Almost half of the libretto was reworked, which gave certain scenes different meanings from the original. A case in point is the scene with Katerina's father-in-law, Boris Timofeyevich. In Shostakovich's original he was a husky muzhik of about sixty, a widower, who was still strong enough to toss bags of grain around. Men like that could have children up to the age of seventy, and in the villages it often happened that such old men, when their sons were not around, would crawl into bed with their *snokhi* (daughters-in-law) and breed little *snokhachi*. Shostakovich sketched the father-in-law as that sort of man so as to emphasise the worthlessness, the weakness of Zinovy, Katerina's husband. In the original, the father-in-law sings, 'Such a healthy woman, and no man . . . Zinovy doesn't take after me. If I were his age . . . I'd take her and . . . A woman is bored without a man . . . No man . . . No man . . . No man . . . No man . . .' And repeating that phrase he expresses his lust for Katerina. He paces outside her door, and finally: 'All right! I'll go to her. She'll be glad . . . I'll go to her . . . I'll go . . .' And he goes in to her room to crawl into bed with her.

But since no Soviet woman is allowed to be bored just because she has no man, the text of that aria had to be rewritten, and the father-in-law ceased to burn with carnal desire. The same happened with Katerina's aria in the second act. In the original, the heroine, lying in the hot feather bed and growing faint from passion and yearning, sings:

'But no one comes to me at all,
No one puts his arm around my waist,
No one presses his lips to mine,
No one fondles my white breasts,
No one wears me out with his ardent love . . .'

In the new version of that scene, Katerina dons (up to her very ears) the decency proper for a Soviet woman, and sings, 'Under the roof I saw the little nest and the little birds flying to it. How sad she doesn't have her beloved dove . . .' Now that's a horse of a different color!

There are many such reworkings in the score and libretto, and it was using the revised text, unfortunately, that the opera was filmed.

In Shostakovich's music all the characters are so vividly and graphically sketched that, as I sat at the piano and learned the part of Katerina, I could imagine how to act it out. Even the very high tessitura in so many of the phrases, which Dmitri Dmitriyevich had reinstituted for my role in the film, became easily surmountable, because I had discovered the psychological key. True, when I first saw the very high phrases that Dmitri Dmitriyevich had written into my copy, both in the dramatically tense scene of Sergei's flogging and in the scene of the old man's poisoning, I confess that my head swam, it frightened me so. But I stopped myself: Don't panic. Analyse why it's written that way. The great Shostakovich must have had his reasons. Why is such a high tessitura used for the phrases 'Ah, Boris Timofeyevich! Why did you leave us? . . . For whom did you abandon me and Zinovy Borisovich? What will now become of me and Zinovy Borisovich without you?' And the answer is simple. It is because she is not singing, but 'lamenting,' as peasant women lament over the dead. It is their custom. And she poisoned – murdered – the old man; so she had to 'waste away with grief' and the more fervently because people were watching her. Shostakovich's conception of Katerina's part was true genius. I immediately understood the technique this particular phrase called for: a whiteness of sound. What had seemed insurmountable was now simple and clear.

There are quite a few such passages in the opera. In the first aria of the first act, for example, there are two leaps from B flat in the middle octave to B flat in the upper, which must be executed without changing the tempo or the *piano*: 'Only I am languishing, only for me is the world not fair.' Here one must think in terms of phrases, not of individual notes. There is much hopelessness expressed here, but if it is sung as an exercise in vocalisation, none of it will come through. What is needed is the psychological 'lining,' the subtext of the role. It's not important what the heroine is singing about, but what she is thinking about. Her thoughts give the clue to the necessary coloration, the technique.

A completely different coloration of the voice – dead, without vibrato – is needed in the aria in the penal camp. Insulted by Sergei, Katerina is beside herself with despair; she has a premonition that he will betray her. In that oppressive silence, when time seems to have stopped, one suddenly hears the melancholy sound of the English horn and the voice of a solitary, unhappy woman mechanically uttering: 'It's not easy, after having been bowed to and honored, to stand in front of a court . . .'

When insight comes, and she understands what she has done, the avalanche of the orchestral prelude to her last monologue brings the heavens down on her. Here is the resolution to the whole of Katerina's character: her loneliness and the road to her private hell. She walks along it and moans and wails . . . She cries out not to people but to all of space. Here, for the first time, are her horror at what she has done, her self-condemnation, and her only salvation – death.

Shostakovich's opera is realistic and thoroughly Russian. And its vocal idiom is logical and natural. I don't know any other opera with such emotional openness. In terms of complexity, of vitality of the characters and range of passion, it can be compared only to the operas of Mussorgsky. The plot development is so capricious at times that the audience gasps for breath. Scarcely do they have time to experience one event before others rush at them. The musical interludes are more eloquent than any words. That is no doubt why, in the filmed opera, one does not feel the *length* that plagues all film versions of classical operas. One gets the impression that *Katerina Izmailova* was written especially for the screen.

As in the works of Mussorgsky, the minor roles are sketched just as vividly and graphically as the main characters. How rich is that single, two-minute magical scene of the disheveled peasant who reels from complaints about his unhappy fate and a desire to get dead drunk, to his chance discovery of a terrible crime – a murder – to his headlong dash to the police. Dmitri Dmitriyevich used to say, 'The bastard ran to the police, overjoyed that he could inform on her. A hymn to informers . . . That's a hymn to all informers!'

That summer Slava, Benjamin Britten, Peter Pears, and I were vacationing in Dilizhan, in Armenia. With us was our friend Aza Amintayeva, Slava's rehearsal pianist at the conservatory. Several hours a day for an entire month, I worked with her on Shostakovich's opera. I sang it through dozens of times from beginning to end at full voice. I realised what Katerina had meant to Dmitri Dmitriyevich in his time, and I wanted to bring her alive again for him with all the brilliance I could muster.

Aza was a fine pianist. Slava called her Osya. She was from Daghestan, had jet-black hair and a faint moustache. Slava glanced into her room one day in Dilizhan, saw her sleeping, and shouted: 'Iosif Vissarionovich!' She bounded up in bed, too sleepy to understand, and he chuckled. 'Ioska! Osya! You resemble Stalin frightfully!' After that, we all called her Osya.

Eventually, after enough practice, Osya and I felt ready to perform for Dmitri Dmitriyevich. We walked from our dacha in Zhukovka to his. I was so nervous I couldn't talk. Beside me, Osya kept whining, 'Oy, Galya. I'm afraid! I'm so scared my stomach is killing me.'

'Hush! I have a stomach-ache too – my insides are trembling.' With reason: I had to sing, and she to play, an opera as difficult as that in front of Shostakovich himself! We may both have been friends of Dmitri Dmitriyevich's, but work was work. Before Shostakovich everyone was intimidated. Even Slava became nervous in front of him as with no one else. When we performed Shostakovich's Blok cycle for him, the hands of that great artist David Oistrakh shook from nerves.

I began to sing. Dmitri Dmitriyevich didn't stop me once, but as soon as I approached the difficult passages, he would either gnaw on his fingernails or get up and pace the room. He would take a cigarette, then remember that he wasn't supposed to smoke, and sit down again. His nervousness communicated itself to me. It was a good thing that in such situations I sing even better than when I am calm.

Finally he sat down, hung his head, covered his face with his hand, and simply listened: the scene of Sergei's flogging with its high tessitura; Katerina's lamenting over the dead old man. When I lamented at full voice, Dmitri Dmitriyevich sat up straight in his chair and opened his eyes wide. The appearance of a ghost . . . The scene of Katerina's arrest with a final high C sharp. 'Oh, Sergei, forgive me!' And silence. The quiet was unbearable. My heart was beating wildly. Dmitri Dmitriyevich's face was twitching and I was afraid to look at it. Why wasn't he saying anything? Was something wrong?

'Galya,' he began, 'much of what you sang just now I have never heard before.'

'I don't understand, Dmitri Dmitriyevich.'

'Today, for the first time, I heard many phrases in my opera sung for the first time. Forgive me, but that's why I'm so nervous.'

'But that's impossible, Dmitri Dmitriyevich.'

'When I wrote it, all the sopranos refused to sing it. They said they were afraid they would ruin their voices. So I had to rewrite the vocal part. But in your piano score I wrote it in its original version. I wasn't counting on your singing it, but I hoped that you'd try. And now I know it can be sung. It can be sung! So that's the way it sounds! Thank God! Thank God! That's the way I imagined it. Thank you, Galya. Thank you.'

He was leafing through the score, his hands shaking. He asked me to sing the scene of Sergei's flogging again, and to lament. I repeated it all. And he broke into his radiant, childlike smile. So that was it! For the first time in more than thirty years he was hearing, in a woman's voice, the incandescence that had filled his soul when, as a youth and torn by passions, he had written that scene – the most powerful in the opera. And it had now fallen to

ABOVE: Alexander Solzhenitsyn and Alya, his second wife, at our dacha in Zhukovka. BELOW: With Rostropovich, Shostakovich and David Oistrakh in 1967 at Zhukovka, where Shostakovich also had a dacha.

BELOW: With Dmitri Shostakovich, Benjamin Britten and Irina Shostakovich in 1971. RIGHT: My voice teacher, Vera Nikolayevna Garina, without whom I would never have become an opera singer. Painting by Krill Doron.

ABOVE: *Matryona's Funeral* by Gavriil Glikman, inspired by Solzhenitsyn's story "Matryona's House". Clockwise from left: Solzhenitsyn, Rostropovich and me. LEFT: Gavriil Glikman's portrait of Marina Tsvetaeva (see page 226).

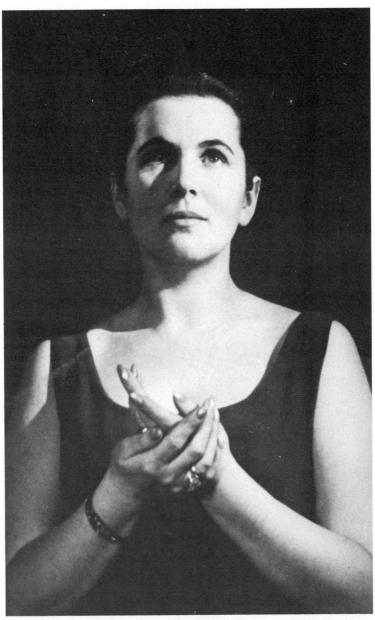
Britten's *War Requiem* at the Albert Hall in London in January 1963
(Photograph: Lotte Meitner-Graf).

Foreign travels. LEFT: In New York in January 1960. I was the first opera singer from Soviet Russia to perform in America. BELOW: In Prague in 1965.

ABOVE: As Tosca in 1971. BELOW: In concert together, Carnegie Hall, New York, in 1975 (Photograph: Myra Armstrong).

ABOVE: Press conference in London in 1978 after our Soviet citizenship was revoked (Photograph: AP/Wide World).
LEFT: "Dear Mama! Love us! We can't live without you! We miss you, are waiting for you and love you. Papa, Olga, Lena." December 31, 1959.

ABOVE: Together in Rio de Janeiro in 1979 (Photograph: *Manchete*/Pictorial Parade). BELOW: After farewell performance of *Eugene Onegin* in Paris in 1982. Elena on the left and Olga on the right (Photograph: Francolon/Gamma Liaison).

me to give him, already a mature man, the opportunity to hear the embodiment of his young passion.

I didn't dare look at him: I was afraid to frighten him, to embarrass him with my presence. But he was entirely under the sway of his memories. It seemed that during those minutes, all his life passed before him. Osya and I remained silent, looking the other way and trying to conceal our agitation.

I choked back tears and, afraid to show him that I was crying, began to cough, pretending that something was caught in my throat. I desperately wanted to run to his side and console him – to utter the words with which my heart was bursting and which he so needed to hear. But he was the great Shostakovich! I didn't dare. All I could do was remain silent, love him devotedly, and defer.

Slava and I arrived in Leningrad the day before the shooting was to start, and it was only then that I saw the actor who was to play the role of my lover, Sergei: Artem Inozemtsev. (All the roles in the film except mine were to be played by actors rather than singers.) The director, Mikhail Shapiro, had decided to start the shooting with a sequence in the middle – with the bedroom scene – so that the leading man and leading lady would overcome the psychological barrier and get to know each other quickly. When I arrived on the lot in the morning, I found myself in front of a huge double bed and under the curious stares of the young technicians, eager to see how, in plain view of everybody including her own husband, the respected Galina Pavlovna would submit to embraces and kisses.

I had armed myself from head to foot for this 'first acquaintance.' I had donned a long skirt, two pairs of thick trousers, and woolen stockings and, wasting no time, I boldly crawled in under the quilt onto the warm feather bed. My lover Sergei, who was in full uniform – only the boots were missing – crawled in after me. I put a thick blanket between us, and announced that we were ready to shoot. They turned on the klieg lights. The first shot was a close-up, and the director, his assistants, and representatives of the Lenfilm Studio's management crowded around the bed.

They all wore serious, worried expressions and labored visibly over the basic problem: how to show less sex, less of the body, in an opera dominated by bedroom scenes.

I was wearing a nightgown that left my forearms bare, and Sergei had on a long-sleeved shirt. We stuck our arms out so that the filmgoers would not think – God forbid! – that we were embracing under the quilt.

'Ready? . . . Galina Pavlovna, your shoulder is bare. Cover it up with his shirt . . . Pull the quilt over your breast . . . Yes, that's good . . . Artem, don't touch her . . . What's that he's got on? What kind of shirt is that? The sackcloth makes him look like an animal! We can't afford to offend the people's sensibilities! Change into another shirt . . . Yes, better . . . Ready? Artem, move off to the side a bit . . . Galina Pavlovna, your shoulder is bare again. Cover it! . . . Lights! Sound! Camera! . . . Stop! Stop! Where is the assistant director? What's the matter with you? His shirt is unbuttoned . . . That take is no good . . . Why? . . . His chest is all *hairy*! Awful! Shave it immediately. We're making a film for the laboring masses, not for sex maniacs!'

Inozemtsev was hauled out from under the quilt and shaved. Once a week thereafter they shaved the bristles from his chest. And later, when it came time to shoot the flogging scene, they shaved his back. When the hairs grew in, they bristled from beneath his shirt as if he were a hedgehog. In order not to debauch the builders of communism – in order that their gazes would not be averted from that blinding vision of the radiant future, not be tempted by earthly lust – Katerina and Sergei were taken out of the warm bed to shoot the longest love scene under a blooming apple tree in the garden. There we proceeded to have a warm, friendly talk in the moonlight, where the huge mosquitoes did not so much bite us as simply gnaw.

At that same time, Mosfilm was shooting *Anna Karenina*, and our directors told me about a near-tragic incident. They were doing test takes, and the director got brave and decided to shoot Anna in the nude – from behind! – in the scene where she is seduced by Vronsky. The actress agreed to strip. Everything was to be done in the greatest secrecy, late at night, when the Mosfilm studio was almost empty and only the director, the cameraman, and two actors were present. The scenery was in place, the lighting had been set up, and it remained only to close the knife-switch for the spotlights. Everyone took his place. The lights came on, the actress threw off her peignoir, and Vronsky took her in his arms. Suddenly there was a crash and a scream, and from somewhere up above a matronly Soviet citizeness came barreling down on the set. It seems she had been up on a high ladder cleaning a spotlight and had not heard the four come on the lot in the semi-darkness. When the glaring lights were switched on without warning, illuminating a naked woman in the arms of a man, she decided that Judgment Day had come. Screeching 'Lord have mercy on us!' she plunged down, and the ladder toppled after her. It was a miracle she didn't break her neck.

Unfortunately, the director and producer of *Katerina Izmailova* were obliged more than once, while shooting the film, to give thought to such Soviet citizens and citizenesses falling from the rafters. This involved scrupulous attention not only to how many centimeters of the actress's bare neck should be shown but, most disastrously, to the sound track. The orchestra – the main feature of the opera – could scarcely be heard. It was muffled deliberately so as not to work up the audience. As the sound engineer explained to me, the music must not interfere with the words. The chief concern of the producer and director was to avoid stimulating the appetite of the monster (which, one would have thought, was already well-satisfied and dozing), to avoid stirring up the stagnant swamp waters, to avoid inciting the 'angry masses' to start up yet another campaign of harassment because of the opera: 'Whose bread are you eating, after all, Comrade Composer and you other Comrade Representatives of Soviet culture?'

When the film finally premiered I began getting a lot of letters, many of them expressing indignation that the people of the Soviet Union were being subjected to a film that shows a woman in bed with a man. One day, thinking I would amuse Shostakovich, I told him of a letter I had received from an engineer. He had written, 'How could you, a famous artist and the mother of a family, have permitted yourself to behave so shamelessly?' To my amazement, Dmitri Dmitriyevich flinched, and his faced reddened. One would have thought that such idiotic blather would have meant nothing to the great Shostakovich.

I was sorry I had told him.

For my work on the film I was paid at the highest rate a Soviet film star can get – a flat fifty rubles a day – even though I'd often put in as many as twelve hours a day. Not exactly Hollywood!

It took about eight months to shoot, but when it finally was finished in early September, they couldn't find the film of the last scene – a close-up of Katerina and her rival, Sonetka, drowning. Originally, we had filmed that sequence on a wide, warm river near Odessa. But now I had to dunk myself in the Gulf of Finland, where the water was a chilling 46 degrees. Although that episode – so vivid in Leskov's story – had been omitted from the screenplay to play down the original heroine's cruelty, I insisted that it be included in the film. Now I was paying for my convictions with an icy bath. The scene begins with a shot of the placid water; suddenly the surface is broken by the emergence of Sonetka and Katerina, who supposedly had already drowned. Seeing her rival swimming away, Katerina catches up with her, throws her whole body over her, and drags her under.

The scene was filmed where the water was very deep, and on the special raft, along with the cameras, there were four professional divers ready to come to our aid if an emergency arose. They greased our bodies, and we donned thick woolen underwear. When both of us, wearing the heavy clothing of prisoners and with kerchiefs on our heads, jumped into the icy water, the cold pierced us to the bone. The thick, sodden overcoat dragged me toward bottom like a rock.

We needed to rehearse the action several times. Sonetka and I had to immerse ourselves in the water; she had to count to five, then surface, and I had to count to ten. Then I had to swim like a woman possessed, pull her under the water, go under myself, and count to ten. For an opera singer, the episode was not so easy.

Finally, they made the first take. 'Come out, we have to reload the camera!'

'If I come out, nothing in the world will make me go back in! We'll wait in the water. Hurry up!'

We clung to the raft, trying to be as still as possible so that the water wouldn't flow through our clothing. Finally, after more than forty minutes, they got the second take, and the filming of *Katerina Izmailova* was over.

Right there in the bus we stripped and were given an alcohol rubdown. I gulped down a half-bottle of vodka on the way home, and slept round the clock. I never even sneezed.

The film was fine. Herbert von Karajan, after viewing it, said at the time that he considered it the best of all filmed operas. Unfortunately, it is not shown in Russia – nothing that bears my voice or likeness is. But the Soviet agency Eksportfilm sells it abroad, and Slava bought a copy for me. In the credits, opposite the name of Katerina Izmailova, there is *nothing*. The name has been removed. For the Soviet authorities, that singer-actress never existed and never will. Orwell's *Animal Farm* is no fantasy. It is a reality, and above it the Kremlin stars shine brightly. I lived there . . . I survived. I know.

In the summer of 1966, between shooting sessions at the film studio, I performed with Shostakovich for the only time in my life. It was at a concert in his honor at the Maly Hall of the Philharmonic in Leningrad. One day, quite unexpectedly, and as if between parentheses, Dmitri Dmitriyevich asked me, 'Do you mind if I accompany you?' He had not performed in public for many years because of his disease – the muscles of his hands had grown too weak. This concert would turn out to be his last public performance.

The day before the concert, we rehearsed. We had already gone through the arias from *Lady Macbeth of Mtsensk* and the song cycle based on Sasha Cherny's verses, and finally we came to Shakespeare's Sonnet no. 66: 'Tired with all these, for restful death I cry . . .' In the middle, there is a change of key. I had sung the 'Sonnet' many times before, and had never had problems with it. But in the rehearsal it was clear that the piano and I were in different keys. I stopped. Strange . . . I was sure I had made no mistake.

'Dmitri Dmitriyevich, I'm sorry. Can we try it again?'

We started over, reached the same place, and it happened once more. It was bewildering. It seemed to me that Dmitri Dmitriyevich had forgotten to change keys, but I couldn't very well tell Shostakovich himself that he had made a mistake! On the other hand – was I going mad? – perhaps I had made the mistake myself.

'Forgive me, Dmitri Dmitriyevich. I don't understand. Maybe I'm overwrought . . .' The shame of it! *Before Shostakovich!* And the hall was full of musicians who had come to hear the rehearsal.

'It's all right, Galya, it's all right. Let's try it again.'

But it was plain that he was distressed. We began a third time, and again it happened! I got hysterical. 'I just don't know what's happened to me!'

Suddenly Shostakovich jumped up from the piano stool and ran to me, waving his sheet music. 'Forgive me, Galya! For the love of Christ, forgive me! It's not you – it's me! It's my fault. The change of key! I'd entirely forgotten – entirely. The music was right there, but I was so nervous I didn't see anything. I didn't see anything at all, don't you know? How awful! Please forgive me!' I hadn't even dared to think that Shostakovich could make the same mistake three times in a row in his own composition.

He was a splendid pianist. But on the evening of the recital, waiting to go on stage, he was not only nervous, he was afraid – terrified that his hands would fail him. In the wings he paced this way and that, not knowing what to do with himself.

Wanting to distract him, I said some silly things, no doubt making myself look like an idiot. 'Oh, Dmitri Dmitriyevich! How good you look in that dress coat! You're positively handsome! I've never seen you in a dress coat before. You look like an English lord.'

'Thank you, Galya . . . I'm so nervous . . . so nervous . . .' And he was back rushing from room to room.

The recital went off brilliantly. Never had I seen Shostakovich so joyous. 'Oh, Galya! I've never been this happy before!'

But hours later, during the night he had a heart attack. He was in the hospital for several months.

In the summer of 1967 he invited me to his dacha and played a new work he had just written for me: a song cycle based on poems by Alexander Blok for soprano, violin, cello, and piano. It is one of the most beautiful and most inspired of his compositions. 'I'm dedicating this to you, Galya, if you don't object . . .'

This work of agonising beauty occupies a unique place in Shostakovich's oeuvre. He wrote it in the hospital after his heart attack, after his confrontation with death and return to life. He seems to survey his life journey as if from the vault of the heavens, and he addresses himself to those spiritual values for whose sake alone life is worth living.

NINETEEN

I first met Benjamin Britten in the summer of 1961 when I came to England for the Aldeburgh Festival. Slava, who had met him the previous year, was already waiting for me there. I had been to London before, but the bustle of the capital, my nervousness about my debut in that splendid city, and the shortness of my stay had given me no opportunity to get to know the English themselves. So I consider this second visit my real introduction to a people I had been very fond of since childhood, when I shed many tears over the novels of Dickens, still one of my favorite authors.

I met Ben the day I arrived, and my heart opened to him instantly. From the beginning I felt at ease with him; I'm sure that everyone who was lucky enough to know that charming man must have felt the same sense of simplicity and naturalness in his company.

We met at a garden party at his Red House. Looking at him, friendly and gracious with everyone regardless of rank, dressed in one of his favorite checked suits (he told me he'd worn all of his suits for at least twenty years!), I thought that he had probably once been David Copperfield and had walked along the roads of Suffolk in search of Miss Betsy Trotwood. And now he was living in Aldeburgh, that enchanting nook on the seashore where the spirit of Old England is still preserved – where people are so friendly and simple.

It was at my solo concert, with Slava accompanying me, that Britten heard me for the first time. He must have thought I was a madwoman. Indeed, thinking back, I can't believe such a program was possible. In addition to songs by Prokofiev, Tchaikovsky, Richard Strauss, and Schumann, plus arias from *Norma*, *Manon Lescaut*, *La Forza del Destino*, and *Lady Macbeth of Mtsensk*, for dessert I sang Mussorgsky's *Songs and Dances of Death*.

After the concert Britten came up to me, showered me with compliments, and said he was particularly glad he had heard me right at that moment because he had begun to write his *War Requiem* and now wanted to write in a part for me. He added that this composition, which was a call for peace, would bring together representatives of the three nations that had suffered most during the war: an Englishman, Peter Pears; a German, Dietrich Fischer-Dieskau; and a Russian, myself.

'Have you ever sung in English?'

'No, of course not. Only in Italian.'

'Then I'll write your part in Latin. Do you know Latin?'

'Yes!' I exclaimed, and joyfully threw my arms around his neck.

That winter, Britten sent me the music for my part in installments, and I learned it right away. When Slava first looked at the part, he was stunned – and not just by the greatness of the music. 'Even if I hadn't known that Ben had written it for you, I'd have said it was you – he's drawn your portrait.'

And in fact my part in the *War Requiem* bears no resemblance to anything Britten wrote before or since. The world premiere was scheduled for May 30, 1962, in Coventry Cathedral. The timing was perfect for me, because I was supposed to be in London before then to sing in six performances of *Aïda* at Covent Garden (for the first time), and I could work concurrently on the *War Requiem* with the composer himself.

Then one day Ben called me, quite upset, and told me his request for my participation had been refused. I couldn't understand why – since I was going to be in London at that time anyway – so I rushed to the Ministry of Culture to see Furtseva. While I was sitting in the reception room, a woman I knew who worked in the foreign department stealthily handed me, as a keepsake, a letter she had retrieved from a wastebasket. It was from Britten, and addressed to Vladimir Stepanov, the head of the foreign department in the Ministry of Culture. I have kept it as a precious relic.*

A few minutes later I was sitting in Furtseva's office and, as I listened to her, I tried to figure out what was going on.

* See Appendix, p. 499.

'The Germans destroyed Coventry Cathedral during the war, and now they've restored it,' she began.

'How wonderful!'

'But people may lose their vigilance and forget that West Berlin . . .' She was spouting some sort of nonsense, while I was racked by the thought that I was being deprived of the right to sing a remarkable piece of music. What on earth was she rambling on about?

'Ekaterina Alekseyevna, the work is a call for peace. Don't our papers tell us every day that we are struggling for peace throughout the world? And here we have a simply wonderful opportunity: Russians, Englishmen, and Germans all joining together in the name of world peace!'

'But how can you, a Soviet woman, stand next to a German and an Englishman and perform a political work? Perhaps on the issue in question our government isn't in complete agreement with them.'

'But what is there not to agree with? It's not a political work but an appeal to all people for peace.'

'But it's the Germans who've restored Coventry Cathedral.'

Still puzzled about whether we were for war or for peace, but realising there was no way out of that vicious circle, I said good-bye and left.

Slava asked our acquaintances in London to tell Britten he should write again and try to obtain permission; the correspondence went on all winter.

It is my hunch that neither Furtseva nor the officials of her ministry really understood what was going on; otherwise, they would simply have stopped me from going to England. And so, when I arrived in London for *Aïda*, I was sure that Britten would write still another letter, and permission would finally be granted. It was unthinkable that they would obstruct him – a foreigner! – in so noble an undertaking, one so advantageous, it would seem, for our government, which was propagandising its own struggle for peace throughout the world with such zeal that Khrushchev even took off his shoe and banged it on a table at the General Assembly of the United Nations.

But shortly after my arrival, Britten and Pears came to see me in my hotel room and, greatly distressed, told me that Britten had received a final refusal.

'We don't understand why. What can we do now? Her Majesty is expected at the premiere.'

What could I say in the presence of my Soviet interpreter? For that matter, I really couldn't make any sense of what was going on. My heart was bursting with shame at the crassness of our government. A great English composer had written a part for a Russian soprano in a major work; I couldn't understand how the Soviet authorities could refuse the honor. It was an honor not only for me but for my people! I felt deeply ashamed that involuntarily I had put a person so dear to me in a terrible position. For with so few days left before the premiere, he would have to find a singer to replace me who could learn the part on such short notice.

I kept hoping up until the last minute that the rulers of our destinies would come to their senses and I would sing at Coventry. But a week before the premiere, after my last performance at Covent Garden, I was ordered to fly back to Moscow the next day. They made me tell the reporters that I was urgently needed at home . . . to do a television show!

While I was singing at Covent Garden, Slava was running about Moscow trying to secure permission for me to sing at Coventry. Finally Vladimir Stepanov told him, 'Don't bother knocking on any more doors. We won't change our minds.'

'But why?'

'Because the cathedral was restored by the Germans. It would have been better to leave it in ruins as a monument to the brutality of fascism. A former enemy should not be transformed into a friend. Do you understand? It was rebuilt with German money. We do not agree with the English on this issue, and we're not going to take part in their celebrations.'

'But in a few years everyone will forget who provided the money to rebuild the cathedral. Yet it will go down in history that a Russian soprano sang the premiere of that extraordinary work. Who remembers today under what emperor or president or king Bizet wrote his *Carmen*?'

'Never mind. The Soviet authorities will remember.'

Yes, and I shall always remember why and by whom I was forbidden to sing, at Coventry Cathedral, Britten's *War Requiem* – one of the greatest works of the century, as Shostakovich told Slava and me.

Another thing I shall never forget is the date of the premiere: May 30, 1962. On that day, instead of experiencing the thrill of taking part with all the others in that solemn event, I was sitting at home in Moscow, weeping bitter tears. But a few months later, in January 1963, I did sing the *War Requiem* on the stage of Albert Hall, and while in London I recorded it with Peter Pears, Fischer-Dieskau, and Benjamin Britten.

The *War Requiem* was not performed in the Soviet Union until May 1966, after it had triumphantly made the rounds of almost every country in the world.

In later years I visited England often – more than any other country. On three occasions I sang a series of performances of *Aïda*; I gave solo concerts; and I came to the festival in Aldeburgh annually. One year Slava couldn't come for some reason, and Ben had to replace him as my accompanist at the last moment.

It goes without saying what kind of pianist Britten was. He is renowned for his accompaniment of the incomparable tenor Peter Pears, whose art is the very embodiment of the culture, beauty, and elegance of vocal chamber music. Their rendition of Schubert's *Winterreise* is unforgettable. And will anyone play Schubert's Sonata for Piano and Arpeggione or Cello with such magical simplicity as Britten in his recording of it with Slava?

That evening I sang a selection of songs by Tchaikovsky, whose music Ben loved so much. (Can it be true that no one has that recording?) The song 'A Fearful Minute' concludes with but a few bars on the piano, which seemingly offer little to reflect upon. Yet after Britten played them, one wanted to hear nothing more and let the unearthly purity of that brief ending live on in one's soul.

At a subsequent concert Peter and I sang Tchaikovsky's love duet from *Romeo and Juliet*, written for soprano, tenor, and orchestra – it is the only part of that opera the composer ever completed. The way Ben played the long prelude, which is quite unsuited to the piano, could not be called piano playing at all – it was a unique, unparalleled moment. Is it possible to convey the feeling that life has suddenly come to a halt? 'Stay on, moment, you are so beautiful!'

Standing by the piano on stage I was listening with such rapture that I missed my entrance. The ensuing silence brought me to, but at first I didn't realise where I was or what I was supposed to do. Ben waited a moment as if nothing had happened, then repeated the last bars of the prelude.

In the summer of 1965, Slava persuaded Ben and Peter to spend their vacation with us in Russia. To be frank, I didn't encourage the invitation because I was beset by an insoluble problem: How would I feed those gentlemen for a whole month? Where could I find edible steak for them, and fresh fish?

For gala receptions of foreign guests I had worked out an emergency fail-proof menu: bliny [Russian pancakes] and a four-pound can of caviar (it could still be bought in those days) into which I stuck a big soup spoon for a touch of extravagance. The effect was fantastic! The foreigners came away thinking that in Russia people ate caviar instead of soup. But the main thing was that four or five hot bliny, each smothered in butter and sour cream and topped off with a heaping spoonful of caviar, lay like a ton of bricks in their unaccustomed foreign stomachs. After consuming them the guests staggered away from the table and could only gaze at the delicacy left in the can, unable to swallow a bite more. Then I would announce that dinner was about to be served, and lie brazenly that a succulent roast beef was in store. The response would always be a general groan and a plea for mercy. The hot bliny never let us down.

While I was racking my brains trying to figure out what I was going to feed Ben and Peter, Shostakovich gave me a wonderful piece of advice. He had recently been in Armenia, where he had vacationed at the Composers' House in Dilizhan, located high up in the mountains, and he was greatly impressed by the Armenians' hospitality. So he suggested we take our foreign guests there, assuring us that the Armenians wouldn't disappoint us, whereas in Moscow we'd hardly manage on Russian grub. And indeed, when Slava called the Composers' House and said they might have the honor of playing host to Benjamin Britten himself, along with us, they were so overjoyed they were ready to declare a national holiday. I should think so! Britten was going to vacation in the Soviet Union for the first time, and not in some Kremlin sanatorium or other, but with the Armenians!

The first thing Ben did when he and Peter arrived in Moscow was to show me a little book of Pushkin's poems with English prose translations, and say that he was planning to write a song cycle for me during the vacation using the Russian text! Such was the happy beginning of our journey. Aza Amintayeva – Osya – joined us and soon we were breathing the pure mountain air of Dilizhan. The Armenians assigned us two separate cottages, and even a cook! They had obviously prepared to receive their guests in a grand manner. Slava had told them that if we were not completely satisfied, we would just go to their neighbors, the Georgians. After that, we didn't have a thing to worry about. The Armenians would have moved their mountains not to forfeit the honor of hosting Britten – and to the hated Georgians at that. They hauled cases of wine, cognac, Eastern sweets, and fruits up to our house. Lamb, chicken, trout, and other food appeared on our table every day. How they got it all was beyond our comprehension, but we felt we were living in paradise.

There was only one crisis. One of Ben's shoes wore through, and he wanted to buy a new pair. It was a good thing that Slava managed to round up the discarded shoes, otherwise what would we have done? One couldn't buy shoes for any amount of money: there simply weren't any in the stores. Slava called a 'council of elders' – the Armenian composers who were taking care of us – and, holding up the pair of gentleman's shoes, said, 'What are we going to do? Britten doesn't have another pair. Right now he's sitting at home in his slippers and writing – in Dilizhan – music that will bring you fame. I can hold him off for a few more hours, but what then? Will I have to call the Georgians? They always have everything.'

Then the oldest got to his feet, clutched Britten's worn-out shoes to his chest, and, rolling his eyes ferociously, said that only over his dead body would a damned Georgian touch them. 'Faust and Othello will repair them so they're better than new. It is a matter of honor for the Armenian people.' (Apparently, almost all the shoemakers in Armenia are called either Faust, Othello, or Caesar.)

And indeed, after Ben finished working for the day and asked Slava when they could go to buy shoes, Slava placed before him a beautifully repaired pair, polished and gleaming like new. 'Why buy a new pair? You're used to your favorite shoes. Just look how Othello knocked himself out for you. You must admit that you have never had your shoes repaired by Othello before!'

Ben was delighted.

What didn't our kind hosts think up to amuse us! Neither Ben nor Peter ever knew what heroic efforts it took to arrange all those wonderful picnics, those trips high up into the mountains, where as far as the eye could see there was not a single human dwelling, and where we were always greeted by friendly people and a table laid as if by magic. As for me, knowing the difficulties of day-to-day living in our country, and the eternal shortage of groceries, I couldn't believe my eyes when I saw all that abundance. And yet there was nothing in Armenian stores.

Slava and I were greatly surprised at how unassuming both Ben and Peter turned out to be; how undemanding they were; and how little attention they paid to bothersome inconveniences or the lack of comforts they were used to. On one occasion we were supposed to fly to the mountain village of Goris, where some old Armenian churches have been preserved. The only plane we could take was one small enough to land on the short airstrip in the mountains. When I saw our means of conveyance, I felt faint. 'If you ask me, Slava, that vessel is nothing more than an old boiler from an army kitchen with wings and a motor. We'll all perish!'

To my amazement, our Englishmen – wearing shorts and hats, equipped with cameras and, of course, flasks at their sides – were the first to jump into that oil stove. There was nothing we could do but follow them. I need not describe how we pitched and tossed during that hour-and-a-half flight. Miraculously, we ended up alive on the ground in the village of Goris. Within ten minutes we were shown to tables literally sagging beneath the load of food. And again it began . . . I must say honestly that never in my life had I eaten such butter, sour cream, and honey; and the same went for Ben and Peter. They served us a special kind of vodka made from grapes. In the course of two weeks we had already gotten used to drinking cognac by the glassful, and here, too, we were drinking with abandon. Peter really let himself go. He proposed toast after toast, and everything was fine. But then we decided to take some pictures.

'Petya, take one of all of us together with the mountains in the background!'

With perhaps too steady a step, Petya walked off to the bushes and aimed his camera at us. We all said 'cheese.' And then suddenly there was no Petya! We could have sworn that he had just been with us; his hat lying on the ground was proof of it. Seeing no sign of his ascension to heaven, we rushed over to the bushes and found him flat on his back among the burdocks, fast asleep.

Our hosts kept dreaming up new ways of entertaining us lest we get bored and – God forbid! – take it into our heads to go off to the hated Georgians. One day they decided to make *khash* for us. Even after trying it, I had only a vague idea of what it was. All I know is that it is a mutton dish, cooked for a very long time with great ceremony, and that it has to be eaten in the daytime. (So that one won't die of it during the night?) They took us up a mountain, where tables were already laden with all kinds of food, bonfires were burning, and in the very center, on coals, a huge vat stood, with something gurgling inside. For several hours we kept ladling the *khash* into our bowls, eating it, and washing it down with glasses of cognac, as endless toasts were proposed. By evening we were feeling so merry and carefree that we decided to dismiss the car that had brought us and go back home on foot. Down below, our cottages could be seen in the light of the setting sun: they seemed to be within arm's reach. And, rejecting the idea of walking home by way of the road, we took off through the woods straight down the steep mountain slope – which turned out to be as slippery as ice because of the thick layer of dry pine needles covering it. Taking a fall from time to time, we proceeded at a snail's pace. But the farther down we went, the more distant our cottages seemed. It began to get dark. Fearing that we might have to spend the night in the woods, Ben made a bold decision: he sat and went zooming down the slope on his rear, deftly maneuvering between the trees. We all followed his example, and it saved us: in the last, fading rays of the sun we braked to a halt near our settlement. Of course our pants were torn to shreds and I had lost a shoe.

But usually our orgies were held in the evening; the mornings were devoted to work. Slava practiced a new piece; Ben composed; and, after closing all the windows so as not to disturb them, I went over and over Shostakovich's opera with Osya, singing at full voice, in preparation for the shooting of the film. As for our dear Petya, he wrote in his diary.

One morning at breakfast he and Ben exchanged mischievous glances and began to conjugate the Russian verb *pisat'* (to write). Petya was the more talented and diligent student, and Ben seemed to acknowledge his superiority. But at critical points, fully convinced of his own authority, Ben would come to Petya's aid.

'*Ya pishu pis'mo* (I write a letter),' began Peter. But what came next sounded strange, and Ben attempted to correct him, triumphantly uttering something that verged on obscenity. Slava, Osya, and I burst out laughing, but just what transformation the word *pisat'* had undergone on their lips, the English gentlemen never knew. And with that, it seems, their study of the Russian language came to an end. From time to time, still wondering why we laughed at them so much, they would stubbornly begin all over again: '*ya pishu pis'mo . . .*' hoping to perfect their pronunciation. We assured them that they were making great progress, but begged them never to demonstrate their achievements to anyone.

I don't know how we managed to communicate. Slava and Ben conversed in German – Ben called it 'Aldeburgh Deutsch.' To be sure, anyone who knew German could not tell what they were talking about – whether it had been, was, or would be – but they understood each other perfectly. As for me, at the time I didn't know more than two dozen English words; but, as Peter said, my pronunciation was decidedly Oxfordian. Osya, however, never got beyond 'Let's go!' Ben and Peter, in addition to *'pisat' pis'mo,'* had learned the Russian equivalents of 'let's go,' 'darling,' 'dear,' 'I love,' 'mushrooms,' 'delicious,' 'bread,' 'good,' and 'bad.' Our stock of words was enough for us to talk every night until the wee hours. And then words did not suffice to express all our emotions, we simply threw our arms around each other's necks.

But our stay with the hospitable Armenians was coming to an end. On the eve of our departure, Ben invited us over to show us his newly completed song cycle.

. . . 'Echo' . . . 'Angel' . . .

From the very first pages, we were struck by how accurately he had captured the feeling of Pushkin's verse without any knowledge of Russian.

. . . 'I thought my heart had forgotten' . . . 'The Nightingale and the Rose' . . .

He had not set the poems to music which was intended to stand on its own. Rather, he had succeeded in penetrating the very heart of the verse, in grasping the secret of the poet's genius. And that's what the music is about, though Britten's own inimitable mark is clearly felt.

. . . 'Half-milord, half-merchant' . . . 'Insomnia' . . .

As I listened to him play that exquisitely beautiful music, it seemed to me that I could even pinpoint the day he had been working on this or that song. In my mind's eye I saw the harsh, wild Caucasian landscape: the bottomless, rocky gorges and the high mountains reaching up into the boundless sky; the paths in the woods we walked along every day; the wildflowers Ben loved so. And I saw Ben walking off to stand alone some distance from us, gently smiling at something . . . 'I thought my heart had forgotten / How easy it is to suffer. / I said: "What is past / Shall not return . . ."' Whenever I sing that enchanting song, I always see him, standing in the shade of the huge trees and smiling at something deep within himself.

When he had finished playing, Ben wrote the dedication in Russian: 'To Galya and Slava.'

When we got back to Moscow, Ben and Peter had only three days before leaving for London, and a mad scramble began. We had to cover more than 1,000 kilometers in the car, from Moscow to the village of Mikhailovskoye, where the Pushkin House Museum is, then drive back to Moscow in time to see our dear friends off. I begged Slava to consider going by plane, but in vain. 'No, we must show them Russia.'

'But what will they see? We'll be driving like mad, because we have so little time. And where are we going to eat along the way? You'll starve us all to death!'

'We'll take a basketful of food and have a picnic in the woods. It'll be wonderful!'

We left at noon, and by nightfall we had reached Novgorod, where we slept over. In the morning we made a hasty tour of the churches, then jumped back into the Mercedes and drove on at top speed. Any plans for a picnic in the woods were out of the question. To sustain us during this race against time, Slava thrust flasks of whisky and sandwiches into our hands. Finally, late in the evening, rattled from the trip but still alive, we appeared before the curator of the museum, a kind and highly cultured man named Semyon Geichenko, who was waiting for us. He had expected us to arrive in the afternoon, so that we could visit the house and the park while it was still light. Electricity had not been installed in the house to prevent fire, and as soon as night fell it was securely locked up. But for the sake of his dear guests our host flung the doors open wide, and we immediately found ourselves in another world . . . 'Greetings, sequestered nook . . . Refuge for work, serenity, and inspiration . . .' How many magical poems Pushkin wrote here!

And here, not far from the estate in the Svyatogorsky Cemetery, he lies buried. Holding candles, trembling with emotion, we walked in semi-darkness from room to room. Through the gloom of night, the great Russian poet looked down at us from the walls . . . A guest from overseas, the Englishman Benjamin Britten, was bringing him his inspired work. Outside, a clock struck the hour hoarsely.

'What a strange sound! As if someone were beating a tin can.'

'It's an old clock,' Geichenko explained in a whisper. 'It's been there in the courtyard since Pushkin's day. I've been here for almost twenty years, and never once has it needed repair. Only it's gotten a bit hoarse.'

Then we went into the house next door, which in the past had probably served as an office for the steward of the estate, and where our host now lived. We made ourselves comfortable in the little living room, and Ben sat down at the piano to play his song cycle. Peter stood next to him. The room was cloaked in semi-darkness – only two candles burned. They reached the last song, 'Insomnia': 'I can't sleep, and there's no fire / Dull dreams and darkness all around / All I hear is, next to me, / The ticking clock's monotonous sound.'

The moment Ben started to play the prelude, which he had written to suggest the ticking of a clock, Pushkin's clock began to strike midnight, and the twelve strokes chimed in exact synchrony with Ben's music. We all froze. I stopped breathing, and felt my scalp prickle. Pushkin's portrait was looking straight at Ben . . . He was shaken and pale, but didn't stop playing . . . *The Poet's Echo* . . . Not daring to speak, we silently dispersed to our rooms.

The next night, Britten played the cycle for Shostakovich. That brief interlude, unforgettable for all of us, marked the beginning of the friendship between the two composers, which was later crowned with Britten's dedication of his opera *The Prodigal Son* to Shostakovich, and Shostakovich's dedication of his Fourteenth Symphony to Britten.

And yet, how different they were! With Ben I could be open from the start. I could even tell him when I had a stomach-ache. How often I ran my hand through his wiry hair! He would purr with pleasure, laugh, and say that in a past incarnation he must have been a horse. I would stroke his face, and could kiss him.

But did I ever hug Dmitri Dmitriyevich when we met or parted? Today, straining my memory, I can recall embracing him only once: when we parted forever. For him, an outward demonstration of feelings – even toward the people closest to him – was unnatural.

In 1974, after we had left Russia, we went to see Ben who had had a heart operation, and were shocked by the change in him. Dear Ben! Now he often sat in an armchair with a plaid blanket around his legs. Gone forever was that look of a mischievous boy up to pranks, and the seal of suffering was stamped all over him. But he accepted his illness humbly and from time to time even laughed at himself. At the table, he gratefully accepted help from those close to him.

Poor Ben! On that day he soon got tired, and was taken to his bedroom. We had to leave, and came in to say good-bye. He kept trying to explain to us how awkward he felt that he could not be the hospitable host he always was.

'Dear Ben, nothing irreparable has happened. But you have always worked so much and done things so fast that you can't get used to another pace. Now, for a while, you're going to have to do half as much, and at half-speed. For you that won't be easy, but you must be patient.'

And, like a child, he gratefully accepted that transparent lie from his loving friends.

We last saw Ben in the summer of 1976 at his annual festival in Aldeburgh. He was rarely able to attend the concerts. And at dinner – sitting to his left, as always – I heard with horror the heavy, hollow beating of his heart, and saw the pronounced throbbing of his shirt on the left side of his chest.

That evening – the first anniversary of Dmitri Dmitriyevich's death – Slava conducted, and I sang, his Fourteenth Symphony. Ben was in the audience. I recalled the first time Dmitri Dmitriyevich played that symphony for us at his place, and the time I had sung it here at Aldeburgh with Ben conducting. 'Dedicated to Benjamin Britten.' What exalted love is heard in Shostakovich's words, now from another world, to a friend and brother: '. . . What is persecution? Immortality is equally the lot of bold, inspired causes and of sweet singing. So, too, our alliance – free, joyous, and proud, firm in fortune and misfortune – will never die . . . The alliance of favorites of the eternal muses.'

Dmitri Dmitriyevich was already dead; his widow, Irina, was in the audience; Slava and I, exiles, were standing on the stage;

looking at us from a box to the left were Peter and the disease-racked Ben, with death already hovering over his head.

Three months later, on December 4, 1976, we learned that Benjamin Britten was dead.

But all that came later – what seems like a century later. Then, in the summer of 1968, I premiered Shostakovich's Blok song cycle with Slava in London and Aldeburgh, sang the *War Requiem* with Carlo Maria Giulini at the Edinburgh Festival, and gave solo concerts in a number of English cities.

Slava had bought a Land-Rover. He liked the fact that when he raised the top, two beds emerged, while below there was a table, chairs, a refrigerator, and a gas stove – in general, everything to suit the whims and sporting activities of a gentleman. Just where in Russia he intended to go in it, I couldn't imagine; and I tried in every way to dissuade him from acquiring yet one more superfluous burden. But the thing was that in Munich Slava had once heard a car horn that gave out a deafening cow moo, and since that time he had been consumed by a desire to install the same thing in one of our cars. But you couldn't very well put it in an elegant Mercedes; and our little Volkswagen probably would have fallen apart from such a loud blast. So he bought the Land-Rover, and finally installed that horn of Jericho.

Then, equipped with maps, a teapot, mugs, knives, and forks, he announced to me that we were going to drive all the way across Europe: we'd sleep in the car, prepare meals on our own stove, take our time, and have a delightful trip and vacation. He loaded the car to overflowing with wallpaper for our Moscow apartment and crates of furniture for the kitchen. We could hardly close the doors. And there was no question of getting into the back of the car. The only free space left was the two front seats. He put soft pillows on mine so I wouldn't complain about the hard seats. Having decided that all the free space had not yet been utilised, he filled a huge iron trunk with cans of paint for the dacha and put it on top. Last but not least, he hooked a boat on wheels to the back. After all that, a beaming Rostropovich declared that he was ready.

All the people who had come to see us off were gathered on the lawn at Red House. We were faced with the problem of what to christen our ship before it set sail on its maiden voyage. Ben thought up the name 'Buttercup,' the cow's favorite flower, and then mysteriously vanished. In the meantime, Peter fashioned a white pennant, sketched a yellow buttercup on it, and fastened it to the body of the car. Soon Ben returned and solemnly handed Peter, Slava, and me our parts in his just-completed cantata for soprano, tenor, and cow, entitled *Buttercup*, as a blessing for the trip ahead of us. Everyone assembled around the car, Ben waved his baton, Peter and I began to sing, and Slava climbed into the car and started 'mooing.' All the rest joined in as best they could. Then Ben smashed a bottle of champagne against the car, we broke into another round of our cantata, and drank one down for the road.

Finally, accompanied by the shouts and singing of the guests and hosts of Red House, with the cry of 'Onward to Moscow!' we were on our way.

PART FOUR

TWENTY

In our Land-Rover Buttercup, we made our way leisurely across Western Europe in the summer of 1968: through France, Austria, and Switzerland. Slava was amusing himself with his new toy. As we drove through Switzerland's tidy countryside, our Buttercup's horn would issue forth a deafening moo, and the cars on the road would move aside. But the cows grazing in the meadows would take off after us at a headlong pace and, eyes bulging, would trot behind us for miles. It seemed Buttercup spoke their language.

We made a side trip to Basel to see our friends Paul and Maja Sacher, and rested for two days in their wonderfully hospitable home. A few years later, when we left Russia impoverished, Slava had the opportunity to buy a Stradivarius cello – the one he plays now. Upset because he couldn't afford to pay the astronomical sum, he told Paul about it, and got a shock when Paul pulled out his checkbook and wrote out a check for the amount in question. Slava hadn't dreamed that one could get that much money on the basis of a little piece of paper. He was happy to become the owner of that cello, and he was no less excited when, after working for himself rather than the Soviet government for a year, he was able to repay the debt.

Carefree, we reached the border of Eastern Europe. Only then did we know how serious the political situation there was. After the first few miles in Czechoslovakia it was clear that it wouldn't do to talk in Russian: the Czechs could not hide their hatred of us, and simply would not answer. We decided that if we had to ask directions of someone, we would speak in German. They answered us then, and that fact alone was shaking: how much must the Czechs resent us Russians to have come to the point that they would prefer to hear German! We remembered the Prague of 1955, when we had met. How the Russians were loved then! Any Czechoslovakian house would open its doors to a Russian as to a brother. But now we were trying our best to be on the road only during the daylight hours. We were haunted by a sense of danger, especially at night; if they recognised us as Soviets, they might kill us then and there.

The British license plates on our car turned out to be a help to us. We were making our last crossing – through Poland – when near a wooded, uninhabited area, the huge, heavy trunk full of cans of paint jarred loose from the top of our car and fell onto the road. Cans rolled along the highway. Some came open, and oil paint flowed from them. We stood there in desperation, not knowing what to do. Then a car driving in the opposite direction stopped, and some Poles asked if we needed help. What? Help us? Soviet citizens? But we soon realised that they had taken us to be English because of our license plates. We thanked them in English, said we didn't need anything, and they drove off unsuspecting. Somehow, we gathered up our cans of paint, smearing ourselves thoroughly, and drove at top speed so as to reach the Soviet border before dark. We knew that come nightfall it would be closed, and no amount of talk would get us through.

That was precisely what happened. We spent the night in the car, before the locked gate that leads into the great expanse of our motherland. It wasn't until morning that they let us through.

Finally, Brest. We were home, and could cast off the tension we had been under. But what was this we were seeing? All day, as we drove along the Belorussian Highway, we were met by an endless stream of military vehicles with soldiers, tanks, weapons . . .

'Good Lord, Slava! What is this? A war?'

'No, no. It's just maneuvers.'

It never entered our heads that our country was preparing to occupy Czechoslovakia.

We spent only a short time in Moscow. Three weeks later we were on a plane back to London to take part in the Festival of Soviet Art. We arrived on the evening before the opening day of the festival, August 21, 1968. Slava was to perform Dvořák's

Cello Concerto with the USSR State Symphony Orchestra for the opening.

In the morning, after breakfast, we went for a walk. The streets were thronged with people carrying placards reading: 'Russians are Fascists!' 'Russians Out of Czechoslovakia!' We couldn't bring ourselves to believe that this had happened – it seemed the most disgraceful act in the history of the Russian state. We ran back to the hotel and turned on the television. On every channel the Soviet tanks rolled through the streets and squares of Prague. It was true, plainly visible. The confusion on the faces of Soviet soldiers . . . the thousands of Czechs on the sidewalks . . . They did not resist, but with what despair they regarded their former brothers! Many wept. Others shouted, pushing at the steel monsters with bare arms.

The television camera moved to the other end of the square. There several women linked arms and suddenly threw themselves on the ground before the tanks. I cried out in horror.

Slava flung himself about the room like a madman. 'Galya, what are we going to do? How shameful! Criminals! I'm ashamed to go on stage tonight. We're Russians, aren't we? Soviets!'

There could not have been a sadder coincidence: in London, on a day that was tragic for the whole world, a Soviet festival was opening, with Dvořák's concerto at the head of the program!

A few hours later, Slava walked onto the stage of the huge Albert Hall. A tumultuous demonstration was churning in the street just outside. In the hall, six thousand people greeted the appearance of the Soviet symphony musicians with prolonged shouting, stamping of feet, and whistling. They would not allow the concert to begin. Some yelled, 'Soviet fascists, go home!' Others yelled, 'Be quiet! The artists aren't to blame!'

Slava was pale, and stood as if on an executioner's block, taking on himself the shame of his government. I closed my eyes and, not daring to raise my head, shrank into a far corner of the loge.

Finally the audience quieted down. Dvořák's music poured forth like a requiem for the Czech people; Rostropovich, with tears in his eyes, began to speak through the idiom of his cello. Rapt, the audience listened to the confession of that great artist as he merged himself through Dvořák's music with the very soul of the Czech people, suffering with them, praying for them, asking their forgiveness.

When the last note had died away I rushed to Slava backstage. He had not recovered from that public suffering. Pale, with trembling lips and tear-filled eyes, he grabbed me by the arm and pulled me to the exit. 'Let's get back to the hotel. I can't bear to see anyone.'

We went out on the street. There the demonstrators still yelled, lying in wait for the musicians to emerge so they could vent their rage at the criminal actions of the Soviet government. When they saw the two of us, they suddenly fell silent and parted to let us pass. Afraid to look at anyone and feeling that we ourselves were the criminals, we quickly passed through to the car that awaited us.

When we got back to the hotel, we could finally express our anguish to each other. But what could we do? We did the only thing within our power: we drank.

Without our suspecting it, the events in Czechoslovakia had slammed shut the book on what had been our good life. Within a year, Alexander Solzhenitsyn would move in with us at the dacha.

Slava met Alexander Isayevich Solzhenitsyn in the spring of 1968 when he was in Ryazan for a concert. Before going on stage, he learned that Solzhenitsyn was in the audience. He was delighted with this opportunity to meet the famous writer, and assumed that Solzhenitsyn would come to see him backstage after the concert. But Alexander Isayevich went home. Slava was determined, however; he found out his address, and simply showed up at his place the next morning.

'Hello. I'm Rostropovich. I wanted to meet you.'

Solzhenitsyn lived in a small apartment on the ground floor, and Slava was surprised at the cramped conditions, the poverty that the famous writer endured. Living with him and his wife in that apartment were two of her aged aunts. Outside, day and night, trucks roared past so loudly that the windows rattled. Their casements were locked tight against the poisonous fumes of Ryazan's chemical plants.

Shortly thereafter, Alexander Isayevich came to Moscow and was at our place, but I did not have occasion to meet him then – I was on tour abroad. Slava saw him several times after that at the home of mutual friends. He learned from Lydia Chukovskaya's daughter one day that Solzhenitsyn was very sick, and that he was now living in the village of Rozhdestvo, where he had his own little cottage. Slava got into his car immediately and went to pay him a visit.

When Khrushchev was in power, people were allowed the private use of small bits of land for growing fruits and vegetables. On those garden plots they were permitted to build little one-room shacks as shelters from the summer rains and to keep their gardening tools in. But the Soviet people, who had learned not to be choosy, lived in the shacks during the summer months – whole families at a time – and remembered Tsar Nikita with gratitude. It was in such a shack, on the Kiev Highway, that Slava found Solzhenitsyn when he came to see him one cold, rainy autumn day. It was the only place the writer could find that was quiet enough for him to work in, and every year he lived there from early spring until the cold set in. (Later, assisted by KGB lies, the shack grew into a fine, privately owned dacha near Moscow about which we learned from *Der Stern* and *Literaturnaya Gazeta*.)

Alexander Isayevich was afflicted with acute sciatica, which he had contracted while living in that damp, unheated place. He had to get out of there right away. But if he went back to Ryazan, he could kiss his work good-bye. Moreover, his expulsion from the Writers' Union was imminent, and after that he would be defenseless, with no rights. It was only natural that Slava, seeing his new friend in such straits, propose that he move to our place in Zhukovka for the winter.

We had just finished building a small guest house on our grounds. In one half was a garage, and in the other a little two-room apartment with a kitchen, a bathroom, and a porch. The heating came from the main house.

Excitedly, I looked forward to Solzhenitsyn's appearance at our place. As luck would have it, I was once again without a housekeeper; and, aided by the girls, I carried the bed, the kitchen furniture, and the dining-room furniture from our house to the future home of the famous writer. The curtains gave me particular trouble. There was no place to buy them, and I had no time to sew any, so I took down the curtains from the third floor of our house and hung them in his study. I had brought them back with me from a trip to America. They were white with an abstract blue pattern, and I kept asking Slava whether it was all right to hang such curtains in Alexander Isayevich's place. Weren't they too modern; wouldn't they make him nervous? What was his taste? Maybe he liked old-fashioned things? But all Slava could remember from Ryazan was Solzhenitsyn's reddish beard and the two old ladies in a corner of the crowded apartment. When you have spent your youth fighting a war at the front, and then ten years in prison and labor camps, such banalities probably don't enter your head.

One morning I looked out the window and saw an old Moskvich car on our grounds. Slava reported that Alexander Isayevich had come at six in the morning, left all his things, and gone back to Moscow on the train. He would be back in a few days to settle in.

'Well, was he satisfied? Did he like the house? Maybe he needs some help – maybe another piece of furniture.' We went into the guest house, and I looked about with the sharp eye of a household mistress. Nothing had changed. There were no new belongings except for a strange bundle on the bed in the bedroom. I went into the kitchen, and there was nothing new there either. Perhaps he hadn't unloaded his car yet? I went back into the bedroom. What was that bundle? I looked closer and saw that it was an old, black quilted jacket like those issued in labor camps, so worn out it had holes. It was wrapped around a thick pillow in a patched pillowcase. One could see that the patches in both jacket and pillowcase had been sewn by a man – they were pieced together with big, awkward stitches. All was neatly tied with a cord from which hung a dull aluminum teakettle. It was as if a man had just returned from a concentration camp and was getting ready to go back. The pathos of it stabbed me like a knife.

'Slava, that's from *there*, isn't it?'

We stood staring at the bundle, which in every lived-in fold and patch carefully preserved one man's torment and suffering. So, Alexander Isayevich carried that precious property with him from place to place, traversing the world as a penal-camp inmate – not allowing himself to forget.

Thus it was Solzhenitsyn's fate that presented itself to me first; and it wasn't until a few days later that the man himself showed up. He was a light-haired, thickset man of middle age with a reddish beard, clear gray eyes that harbored a feverish glint, and a nervous, resonant voice.

'Well, let's get acquainted, Galina Pavlovna. I am Sanya.'

'Forget the formalities, then, and call me Galya.'

'Thank you. I'm infinitely grateful to you and Stiva (his nickname for Slava) for your generous invitation. But I'm afraid I'm crowding you.'

'Not at all. The guest house was empty, and we're glad you agreed to live in it. But I'm worried that it's not comfortable enough for you. The house is small.'

'Galochka, I've never before lived in such luxury. For me it's the realisation of a dream. It's a marvelous place: the garden, the silence! A house and work – that's paradise – Lord above! I have but one favor to ask. Is it all right if I put a table and a bench for my work somewhere far down in the garden? I know an old carpenter who will come and make them, if you don't object. And I must bring my desk – I'm accustomed to it.'

'Bring whatever you want. Settle in, I want things to be pleasant and comfortable for you.'

Shortly afterward, I met Solzhenitsyn's wife, Natasha Reshetovskaya, a frail woman with a large head. I didn't see much of her, since she lived at our place only during the first winter. But I remember my first impression of her when the two of them came to our house for tea. 'What a strange couple,' I said to Slava. 'When did they get married?'

You find that type of woman in Russia – the old maid from a provincial nest of gentlefolk. She and Solzhenitsyn were the same age. They had had no children. As a girl she had written verse and played Chopin, but she had never outgrown her role as the little, coldly proper young lady. Now, thirty years older, she struck me as odd indeed.

The evening we met, we were sitting at the table engrossed in conversation with Solzhenitsyn when suddenly Natasha flitted away from us and into the next room. She sat down at the piano and began clumsily to play some Rachmaninov and Chopin, stabbing ruthlessly at the keys. Alexander Isayevich winced and dropped his eyes. Then he looked at Slava. 'She might have refrained from playing in your presence, no?'

I thought at the time that it wasn't really so deplorable for a woman wanting to be 'interesting' to sit down at the piano and make music in the presence of a famous musician. But if she knew it was going to be embarrassing for her husband, that was another matter.

Solzhenitsyn's first novel, *One Day in the Life of Ivan Denisovich*, first published in the journal *Novy Mir* as early as 1962, brought him worldwide fame, and received great acclaim. For several months, the Soviet newspapers printed only laudatory reviews, comparing him with Dostoyevsky and Tolstoy. The book was even proposed for a Lenin Prize. But at that point the writer's success with the Soviets, which had started off so suspiciously, came to an end. Seeing the effect that *Ivan Denisovich* was having on the people, the authorities beat a quick retreat.

For them, the danger did not lie in the facts set forth in the novel. The Twentieth and Twenty-second Party Congresses, which exposed Stalin's cult of personality, had come and gone, and the people knew about the millions who had perished in Soviet concentration camps. But the figures already had been buried by the sediment of time – by the Party's new slanders and slogans that people so wanted to believe. The danger for the authorities lay in the author's talent, in *Ivan Denisovich*'s power over the reader. The image of the village muzhik rose up from the pages of the book as a symbol of the people, riveting attention, appealing to human conscience, tormenting the mind and soul, and demanding repentance. Can one forget the book's last sentences, so terrible in their simplicity? 'His term amounted to three thousand six hundred and fifty-three days, from reveille to lights out. Leap years accounted for the three extra days.'

And now Solzhenitsyn's second novel, *Cancer Ward*, was lying securely in the bottom of a safe belonging to Alexander

Tvardovsky, the editor of *Novy Mir*. With all his connections and influence, he could not get it into print. I myself read it in original manuscript, when Solzhenitsyn was staying at our place.

Cancer Ward's brilliantly realised Party bureaucrat Rusanov, with his simplicity of character and utter self-righteousness, made a terrifying impression. It was clear why the authorities were so much against the book's being read in the Soviet Union. It is the Rusanovs, the millions of them, who hold the Soviet regime together. Every official, from lowest to highest, would have recognised himself in that collective image.

Neither Slava nor I could have imagined what would flow from the appearance at our house of such an 'odious' individual. When we offered him shelter, it was not for the writer's 'struggle for freedom,' nor was it in the name of saving Russia. Far from that. We had simply offered a roof to a man whose lot had been hard, and we did not think of helping one's neighbor as heroism but as a normal human act. That regard for him as a Christian brother filled my soul before I ever set eyes on him, even as I looked at his eloquent bundle in what was then my happy and beautiful home.

But in that country you cannot simply be a human being who has his own view of the world and lives by the laws of his own God. On the contrary: you must drive Him out of your soul, and fill the vacuum with Marx, Engels, Lenin, Stalin, and all their nonsense. That must be your religion. As the eternally living Ilich said, 'He who is not with us is against us.' In sheltering Solzhenitsyn at our place, it seems we had shown ourselves to be *against*.

The first winter passed rather peacefully for us. Slava often went on tour abroad as before, and continued to conduct at the Bolshoi. Nevertheless, the authorities had begun to 'nibble.' They started with a recording I was to do with von Karajan. When the Bolshoi had gone on tour in East Berlin in 1969, von Karajan heard me in *Onegin* and proposed that I sing Marina Mniszek in a recording of *Boris Godunov*. I of course agreed enthusiastically, and asked him to send an invitation – as is standard procedure – to the Ministry of Culture. Shortly thereafter I went off to London, where I was called by von Karajan's secretary. His invitation had

been refused. I asked her to forward the letter to me, and to
assure the maestro that I would sing with him even if I had to blow
up the Kremlin in the process.

I soon had my hands on that eloquent document signed by the
chief of the foreign relations section, Kalinin. When I got back to
Moscow I rushed to the Ministry of Culture and marched straight
into the office of Deputy Minister Popov. 'Who dared to prohibit
me from making a recording with von Karajan?'

Popov and Kalinin answered in one voice, 'This is the first we
hear of it. Calm down.'

'The first? And whose signature is this?' I thrust the letter in
their faces. It was addressed to von Karajan and read in black and
white: 'Vishnevskaya does not sing the part of Marina Mniszek,
and cannot sing it; at the Bolshoi Theater it is sung only by a
mezzo-soprano. Nevertheless, in her place we can offer you any
other singer from the Bolshoi Theater.'

Popov got all red in the face and pounced on Kalinin. 'You son of
a . . . Are you trading in a Persian bazaar, or are you working at
the Ministry of Culture?'

'But we were of the opinion –'

'To hell with your "opinion"!' I snapped back at both of them. 'I
have to sing! You might have listened to von Karajan's opinion –
he understands music no less than you.'

To make a long story short, a telegram was dispatched to
Berlin authorising my participation in the recording of *Boris
Godunov*.

I was always amazed by Solzhenitsyn's optimism; and I had never
met a person more undemanding in day-to-day existence. He
often lived at the dacha alone, especially in winter.

We dropped in once and found him about to have dinner. On the
table was a piece of bread, a plate of noodles, and some bouillon
cubes. Obviously, he was getting ready to cook. Glad to see us,
he began bustling about. 'How nice that you dropped in! Now
we'll have some tea.'

I couldn't tear my eyes away from that wretched 'dinner' he
was about to prepare. The minute he went into the other room, I

sneaked a quick look in the refrigerator: a bottle of milk, a jar of sauerkraut, a boiled potato, eggs. That was all.

'But what do you live on here? What do you eat?'

He was surprised by the question. 'What do you mean, "What do I eat?" I go into Zhukovka, buy what I need, and eat it. I'm living very well!'

'Do you really call that food? It's terrible!'

Seeing my reaction to his supplies, he laughed. 'Don't worry, Galochka, I'm used to living like this. I don't need anything more. The main thing is that I'm warm, there is silence all around, the air is pure – it's such a good place to work!'

As I later learned from Slava, Alexander Isayevich lived on one ruble a day. Thus he spread over many years his rather large royalties from *Ivan Denisovich*, having set himself the goal of writing all that he had planned – all that he lived for – before the funds ran out.

After the Nobel Prize his life scarcely changed. The only thing I noticed was the appearance of gin, bottles of tonic, and nuts from a hard-currency store. (They were for guests: he himself neither drank nor smoked.) And, naturally, the dinners improved a bit.

In the spring of 1970 I went off to Vienna to record *Boris Godunov* with von Karajan. The fee was turned over to the embassy, as always; and the magnificent 'honorarium' I ended up with sufficed only to buy a pair of white shoes and a white polar fox cap. It was during that time, when I was working on *Godunov* and enthusiastically anticipating my collaboration with the famous conductor, that the events occurred which radically changed the course of our lives.

Solzhenitsyn had been awarded the Nobel Prize, and a campaign of open harassment was launched in the press. It was as it had always been, the only difference being that no one had openly supported Pasternak, nor Shostakovich nor Prokofiev in their day. Rostropovich took a stance – he registered a protest in favor of Solzhenitsyn. I well remember that cold morning in Moscow when Slava, coming into town from the dacha, told me he had decided to speak out in defense of Solzhenitsyn. He showed me a letter he had written, to be sent to the editors in chief of *Pravda, Izvestia, Literaturnaya Gazeta,* and *Soviet Culture.**

'But no one will print your letter – no one will publicise it. What good will it do?'

'Solzhenitsyn lives at our place, and I must make my views known.'

'You're absolutely right! And if I were told that your letter would appear in the Soviet press, I'd be the first to add my signature though they threatened to tear me into tiny pieces. But it's stupid to hand yourself in to them – to give your life over to some secret strangulation.'

'But times have changed. I know the letter won't be printed, but there are those who will learn about it from the editorial staffs of the papers.'

'You have to realise that you're not alone in this; you will affect the fate of many – your sister the violinist, for example, may be fired from the orchestra; don't forget she has a husband and two children. You can't fail to realise what's in store for them, and for me. I have my theater – everything I've worked to create will be destroyed.'

'Nothing will happen to my sister. As for you and me, we can get a fictitious divorce. Nobody will touch you.'

'A fictitious divorce? But where will you live? And what do you propose we tell the children?'

'We'll live together. And I'll explain it to the children – they're old enough to understand everything.'

'But if the purpose of the divorce is to clear me of any association with you – we'll have to live apart. What do you expect to do – crawl in through the window at night? Is that it? But that's ridiculous! I suppose if we live together, all I have to do is hang a placard around my neck saying that I'm not sleeping with you, then they can't expect me to answer for you. Is that what you have in mind? Don't make yourself a laughingstock, Slava. Keep your opinions to yourself.'

'But if I don't speak out now, nobody will.'

'Nobody will speak out openly in any case. You're opposing an

* See Appendix, pages 496–9.

infernal machine single-handed, and you have to see all the consequences clearly and soberly. Don't forget what country this is. The first thing they'll do is quietly throw you out of the Bolshoi. That's not hard, you're a guest conductor. And of course you can say goodbye to your foreign trips. Are you ready for that?'

'Don't panic! Nothing like that will happen. I've thought about it a lot, and I must do this. You have to realise –'

'I understand you very well. And you know I'll stand by you whatever you decide. I have a very clear notion of what's in store for us; I strongly doubt that you do. But you're an important person and a great artist – you have a right to speak out.'

'I knew you'd understand.'

'Now give me the letter. Let me revise it a bit.'

Slava agreed with my corrections, and rewrote it. A few days later, on his way to the airport on a trip to Germany, he dropped four copies of the letter in a mailbox. I was supposed to go to Vienna to finish the recording of *Boris Godunov* with von Karajan, but I worried that because of the letter they might not let me out. My hope was that, with half the recording already made, von Karajan would use his prestige to ensure my departure. And that's what happened. Although two weeks later all the foreign radio stations were broadcasting the letter several times a day, the powers that be let me go to Vienna to finish the recording.

The first thing I learned when I got back to Moscow was that a film about my life and work, which had been completed long before at the Moscow television studio, had been banned. The film would never be shown.

It had begun . . .

To get to our place in Zhukovka, you would take the Belorussian Line, get out at a station called Ilinskoye, and, after crossing the railroad track, turn right and follow a high, long fence behind which lie dozens of acres of woods: the estate of the Council of Ministers. At the end of the fence, if you turned left, you would soon reach our residential area, about sixteen houses belonging to members of the Academy of Sciences. Beyond it was another stretch of the Council of Ministers' zone, with its government dachas, and along the sides of the thoroughfare the small village of Zhukovka.

The houses in our area were built on personal orders from Stalin for nuclear scientists after the war; Stalin himself gave them to the scientists, although most of them wondered why, since they all had fine dachas of their own in various areas near Moscow. After Stalin died, two of the academicians sold their houses: Shostakovich bought one, we bought the other. Of course one cannot assume that the Soviet monarch made that magnanimous gesture merely because of his love for scientists. By settling the very flower of Societ science in the middle of the forbidden government zone – an area vigilantly guarded by the regular police and the secret police – he could maintain total surveillance on them. Also, he could use that opportunity to addict them to the unreal life of the Soviet elite – one unburdened by day-to-day cares. The scientists were given permits authorising them to use the stores in the Council of Ministers' zone, to buy at the special government stores in Moscow, to be treated at the Kremlin hospital, and so on. Once a person becomes accustomed to privileges that are fabulous in comparison with the way the rest of the people live, it hurts to lose them.

Unlike Slava, I had always been a private person, and even after living in Zhukovka for almost fifteen years, there were still some of our neighbors I didn't know. I didn't meet Andrei Sakharov for a long time, although he lived across the road from us, and his son Dima was a friend of my two daughters and was often at our house.

Once when we were driving back to the dacha, we met up with two men out for a stroll. Stopping the car, Slava exchanged greetings with them. He invited them to drop by the house, and we went on. The face of one man struck me for its intelligence and spirituality, for a lucidity in his eyes. I remarked to Slava later, 'Good Lord, what eyes! Who was that?'

'Sakharov.' The next day he and his wife, Elena Bonner, came to see us.

They lived in a two-story brick house that only seemed big. Seen from the outside, it gave the impression of having many spacious, light rooms. But inside it was surprisingly cramped and inconvenient. On the ground floor there was one medium-sized room and an unheated summer porch; upstairs there were two or three small rooms. It was as if there were large unfilled spaces between the walls of the house and the walls of the rooms. It was incomprehensible how he found space in it, especially in the summer, for his huge family: the children from his first marriage (his first wife had died), a son and married daughter with her family; the children of his second wife, Elena Bonner, a son and again a married daughter with her family; Elena's old mother; Elena and himself. There was almost no furniture in the house, and for that matter there would have been no room for it: several beds crowded each room.

The great scientist did not even have his own study, but slept downstairs in an adjoining room. He never let this irritate him, never complained of anything; it seemed even the household bedlam had no effect on him. Good-hearted Andrei Dmitriyevich!

We tried to persuade him to add another room to the house so he could at least sometimes be alone behind a closed door. Each time he would agree and, with an embarrassed smile, try to change the subject quickly. Later I realised why: he had no money. When he came into conflict with the Soviet authorities, that supremely honest man with the crystalline-pure soul had returned 150,000 rubles of his earnings – his life's savings – to the state.

He soon was deprived of the right, extended to all academicians, to use a government car with a chauffeur. His own car was being used by the children, and so he commuted to and from work on the train. One could often see him, toward evening, plodding from the railroad station to the dacha – lugging heavy bags of groceries from Moscow.

When Solzhenitsyn moved into our place, he was fated to find himself between Sakharov on one side and Shostakovich on the other. It was natural that, as such a close neighbor, Solzhenitsyn would see a good deal of Sakharov. But Slava made it a project to bring Solzhenitsyn and Shostakovich closer together. Dmitri Dmitriyevich had a very high opinion of Solzhenitsyn's art, and wanted to write an opera based on his story 'Matryona's House.'

They got together several times, but it was plain that they wouldn't strike up a friendship: different life experiences, different temperaments. Solzhenitsyn was an uncompromising and natural-born fighter, willing to demand justice and public exposure, eager to throw himself against cannon with his bare hands if it meant the struggle for creative freedom. But Shostakovich had been an introvert all his life, and had no stomach for the fight.

'Tell him he shouldn't take on that Kremlin gang. He has to work. A writer has to work. He should write – he is a great writer.'

Although Shostakovich knew he was considered a leader among musicians, he could not fail to see that he was being reproached by those who felt he had declined the political struggle. He saw that people expected him to speak out openly, to fight for his soul and creative freedom as Solzhenitsyn had done. Such is our custom: that one person must sacrifice himself for the rest. But why is it that the rest don't mobilise to save one person, particularly if that one is the pride of his nation?

Poor Dmitri Dmitriyevich! It was probably in 1948, in the crowded Great Hall of the Moscow Conservatory – as he sat alone like a leper in an empty row of seats – that he decided on what he must do to survive. He often told us when we erupted over yet another injustice, 'Don't waste your efforts. Work, play. You're living here, in this country, and you must see everything as it really is. Don't create illusions. There's no other life. There can't be any. Just be thankful that you're still allowed to breathe!' He felt that we were all participants in the farce. And having agreed to be a clown, one might as well play that role to the final curtain.

Once he had made his decision, Shostakovich unabashedly followed the rules of the game. He made statements in the press and at meetings; he signed 'letters of protest' that, as he himself said, he never read. He didn't worry about what people would say of him, because he knew the time would come when the verbiage would fade away, when only his music would remain. And his music would speak more vividly than any words. His only real life was his art, and into it he admitted no one. It was his temple: when he entered it, he threw off his mask and was what he was.

If in today's Russia the human consciousness is being more and more liberated, a great share of the credit must be given to Dmitri Shostakovich, who in his music, from the beginning of his career to the end, called upon people to protest against the coercion of the individual. He called on us with more frenzy, more passion, than any other composer of our time. But in order to do that, he had to brush aside the extraneous – the things that interfered with his creativity. From time to time, he would throw a bone to the pack of hounds – to his harassers – and buy time to compose in peace by signing his name to articles and letters. They were a form of promissory note. He knew that, even so, they wouldn't leave off; that sooner or later they would circle him again, and keep him from embodying in sound what was tearing his soul asunder. He would speak at various meetings and plenums that had no real meaning for him, and, having bought more time, would hurry back to his desk. But those who forced his words attributed great importance to them. Within months after his death, the Soviet government presented his promissory note for payment. An album called 'Shostakovich Speaks' and consisting of recordings of his public statements was issued in the Soviet Union. How the authorities hastened to cover up the traces of the gradual murder of that great man! But they deluded themselves if they thought that by presenting Shostakovich in their package, by palming a Party card off on him, they had made him the very image of a loyal communist. Those statements, which run counter to his art and his life, constitute nothing more than a damning document – a searing testimony to the communist regime's perversion and suppression of the individual.

And yet, through all the jeers his art was forced to suffer, and despite all the times his countrymen handed him over for immolation, he remained true to his people. Why didn't he commit suicide? What force saved him from that step? Can it be that he feared God? In the soprano part of Shostakovich's Fourteenth Symphony are the words 'Three lilies. Three lilies on my grave without a cross . . .' I remember with what deep self-absorption, with what apparent agony, Dmitri Dmitriyevich listened to that passage during rehearsals. He never talked about faith, but often said, 'God disposes.' And in his mouth, it was not an empty phrase. Shostakovich bore his own cross. He staggered under its weight, but did his duty to the end.

In all his works he angrily exposes, he grieves, he suffers deeply. In his symphonies, those wordless monologues, there is protest and tragedy, pain and humiliation. If music can be anti-communist, I think Shostakovich's music should be called by that name. Without the name of Shostakovich there would be no Soviet art and no twentieth century. And the more time passes, the better we realise it.

When I hear people simplemindedly attribute this or that action of Shostakovich's to his fear, I am indignant. Everything within me protests. A man whose spirit was crushed by fear could never have written such powerful music – music that deeply shakes even those who are uninitiated in the politics of terror. Shostakovich's music is the soul of the twentieth-century Russian people. Drawing upon the musical heritage he has left us, following his Sisyphean journey with all its contradictions, future generations will be able to study the moral foundations of the society he lived in. And so long as culture lives, so long as people have not been forced down on all fours, Shostakovich's art will serve forever to unmask the false, base, and cynical communist ideology, which is metastasising through this earth and destroying all spiritual values in its path.

Shostakovich's Fourteenth Symphony, dedicated to Benjamin Britten, was premiered in the autumn of 1969 by the Moscow Chamber Orchestra and its conductor at that time, Rudolph Barshai. Dmitri Dmitriyevich had written the soprano part with me in mind, and I was the first singer to perform in that work – on September 29, 1969, in Leningrad, and on October 6 of the same year in Moscow. To give some idea of the way Soviet artists work, it suffices to say that there were sixty rehearsals before the first concert!

At a rehearsal open to select musicians in the Maly Hall in

Moscow, we witnessed a meaningful event: the death of Aposto-lov, one of the ideological 'leaders' of art in the Soviet Union, who had devoted a good part of his vile life to harassing Shostakovich. As the rehearsal wore on he began to feel ill, and was assisted from the hall. Passing through the lobby, I saw him propped up on a sofa – such a no-account, despicable little man! His dull eyes, which no longer saw anything, darted around in his head, and then he gave up the ghost. Would it fall to God or the devil to receive his soul?

Our children were growing up. They were attending the music school of the Moscow Conservatory with a view to becoming professional musicians. Olga was studying cello, and Elena piano. I spent more time with them than Slava did, but the theater demanded all my strength and attention. Every day, I would leave the children in Rimma's care and go off to work with an accompanist, rehearse, or sing in a production – off to my other world.

From time to time I would come down from my heights and discover to my amazement that my husband had returned from one of his regular tours. Like a hurricane, he would storm into our women's domain, pry into everything, interfere, give orders and, finally, after turning the house upside down, disappear again.

During the first years of our marriage the mad pace of his life and his furious energy drove me out of my mind. I would quarrel with him, demanding that he not play so many concerts, that he organise a normal family life and spend more time at home with the children and me. He would agree to everything, promise to cut his work load by half, and make plans for all of us to go on vacation . . . His good intentions would last for a month at most, after which everything would start whirling again, faster than ever.

As before, he would walk in from a long tour, and tear through the apartment, flinging his jacket, shirt, shoes, socks behind him. And first from one room, then from another, he would call out questions that never required an answer. 'Why are the girls wearing jeans instead of dresses? How are they doing in school?

Where have you been? Who were you with? Why does Elena
have such long hair? Is it to please the boys? Rimma, where is my
baton? Rimma, where did you put my tie? The one I just took
off . . .'

And my meteor-husband would flash past me for the hundredth
time. Finally, having had enough of dashing about, he would
suddenly stop in front of me, as though he had just discovered
that I was in the apartment, and collapse on the sofa.

'Oof! I'm tired. Let's sit a bit, all right?'

'I've been sitting here for a long time.'

'Yes . . . Well, how have you been getting along without me?
What's new? Lord! Am I really home? How wonderful!'

'And who drove you out, pray tell? Why do you work like a
madman, catapulting yourself all over the world?'

'For our family.'

'Oh, enough of that! We don't need one thing more. You've
bought a third car; one is plenty. Slow down. Stay home and
spend some time with the children. No one can help them in
music the way you can.'

'You're right. I'll start right now . . . Olya, get your cello.
We're going to practice. Elena, come here!'

Then the children would show up. Elena was something of a
crybaby then, and Slava took it easy with her. But Olga, a cellist
like him, was prepared to pay him back with ten words for his
one. All three would disappear into the music room with great
ceremony. Fifteen minutes later, the shouting would begin. Then
Rostropovich would shoot out, clutching at his heart, followed by
the children howling. The fact was that he would work with them
once every three months, and demand that they grasp everything immediately. Of course he was worn out – exhausted. With
someone other than his own daughters, he would have restrained
himself, and as for Olga, with another teacher she would have
held her tongue. But not with her father: she gave him tit for tat.
He wasn't used to that, and before long they would be off and
running. I came to object to these lessons: I wanted him to leave
the teaching to someone else.

The master of the house! The *only man* in the house. He
adored his daughters, and was a jealous father. At the dacha, so

that boys wouldn't crawl over the fence to visit them, he planted a hedge with big thorns all around the yard. He went about the important business with great seriousness. He consulted specialists until he arrived at the perfect hedge so that, as he explained to me, all the boys would leave pieces of their pants behind on the thorns.

He simply couldn't bear to see his daughters in jeans. He didn't like the fact that they fitted their rears so closely, that they made them seductive to boys, and he reprimanded me for bringing them back for the girls from abroad. Once when I came back to the dacha from a performance, I found the place plunged in total darkness. A layer of thick, black smoke was suspended above the ground, and a pile of ashes lay on the open verandah of our wooden house. The three of them were standing around it: the triumphant Rostropovich and the bawling Olga and Elena.

'What happened?'

'Those damned jeans won't poison my life any more! I poured gasoline on them and burned them, period!'

It was a good thing the autumn rains had set in. Without them, our house surely would have gone the way of those ill-fated jeans.

Solzhenitsyn could not have dreamed up a better hostess for his next four years. My personality – my tendency to be withdrawn, which is often mistaken for haughtiness – was just what was needed. I, like Alexander Isayevich, am not much inclined toward intimate friendships; like him, I am fond of my solitude. In that sense we were an ideal pair, and lived in harmony. In the summertime at the dacha, I could go for weeks without exchanging a word with him: I simply didn't go to that part of the garden where he was working, and he didn't come to our house.

He lived only to write. He would get up at dawn, work until evening, and go to bed at nine or ten. He maintained that schedule for those four years, and lives by it still. Eventually, he brought his huge, old desk to Zhukovka. (It is with him even now in Vermont.) And in a corner of our garden, under the trees, an old man (obviously a former zek) built him a table with birch legs and a bench so that he could work outside when it wasn't raining.

Solzhenitsyn worked there from early spring until the cold spells set in. The window of my bedroom looked out on that same corner of the garden, and when I woke up in the morning, the first thing I would see was Solzhenitsyn pacing off the kilometers like a tiger – walking alongside the fence, back and forth, back and forth. Then he would go to the table quickly and write. After that, he would go back to pacing again for hours. The bonfire he kept going beside his house almost never died out; he stoked it constantly with all the rough drafts and other papers he didn't need. I had never seen such tiny, exquisite handwriting as his, and when I told him that he laughed. 'It's a habit I acquired in camp: to put as much as possible on tiny scraps of paper. They're easier to hide.'

At first we urged him to come and take his meals with our family, and from time to time he would. But he was as taut as a string. One felt that his ideas obsessed him, and pulsed feverishly within. He could not let go of them, he could not relax. It was a burden for him to sit at the table and waste precious time eating. And, after thanking us, he would make haste to leave.

I soon learned from Slava that another woman had come into Solzhenitsyn's life, and that he had filed for a divorce from Natasha Reshetovskaya. No divorce was granted at the first hearing, because Natasha did not give her consent. But on December 30, 1970, Solzhenitsyn's first son, Ermolai, was born. His new woman was another Natalya, whom we all called Alya. Although I was rarely at the dacha that winter, I met her when we picked her up on the way to the church where Ermolai was to be christened. Slava was his godfather. After the christening at the Nechayannaya Radost Church on the Obydenka, we celebrated with a lunch at our house, and it was only then that I got a good look at her. She was thirty, in full bloom, a strong woman and the personification of a good wife and mother. Indeed, in three years she gave birth to three sons, each one more handsome than the next. In a conversation with us once, Solzhenitsyn had said, 'What I've set out to do I'll do. It's impossible to frighten me. I was dying in the war, I was starving in the camp, and I was dying in the cancer ward. I'm not afraid of death, I'm ready for anything.' I looked at Alya as he spoke, and I realised that such a woman would follow him into the fire without thinking twice.

By profession she was a mathematician, and had taught at an institute in Moscow until the birth of Ermolai Solzhenitsyn, at which time she was fired. Her mother, Katya, was also fired and expelled from the Party. For what? Because she hadn't looked after her daughter?

But Alya, who was devoting her life to Solzhenitsyn, was actually glad she was now free to be his assistant and give all her time to his work, to his ideas. She followed him without question and without making any claims for herself. I remember what she said to me one day, during all the twists and turns of the divorce, which took place before my eyes. She was in her last weeks of carrying her second child, and I went to see her to reassure her after another court hearing at which a divorce was denied. With circles under her eyes and pains in her belly, she said, 'But why all this fuss? I've told him already that we can just go on the way we are. I don't need anything. It can't be easy for her. I understand.' Yes, they could live like that for the time being. But what about the children? And what would happen to them all if he were expelled from the country?

When Solzhenitsyn finished *August 1914*, Slava advised him not to send it to the West right away. 'First you should inform the Soviet publishing houses that the novel is finished.'

'But they won't publish it. They'll just tear it up.'

'Don't let them have it. You can send a notice to all the editorial boards informing them that the novel is finished, and telling them what the subject is. Let them reject it officially, then you can assume you have the right to send the manuscript abroad.' Solzhenitsyn heeded his advice and wrote to seven publishing houses. There was not so much as a single word from any of them.

Slava then asked Alexander Isayevich for a copy of *August 1914*; he had decided he himself would blaze the trail. This was still during the time that Slava felt he could do anything. He had a host of friends he drank vodka with and for whom he played free concerts; he was sure they all liked him and would go to the block for him, as he would have done for them.

'I'm sure it's all because of the cautious ones – the small fry at the publishing houses. They're scared to death of the fuss being made over you abroad. But they don't realise there's nothing dissident about this novel! I'll go to the Central Committee. Let them read it – I'm sure I can convince them. If not, I'll be the first to tell you to send it abroad.'

He put in a call to the Central Committee – to Pyotr Demichev, the secretary of the Ideological Commission. Demichev was happy to hear from him. He asked about Slava's health, and invited him to drop by. 'I'd be very pleased, Pyotr Nilovich – how's today? I have to pass something on to you. You know, of course, that Solzhenitsyn is living at our dacha. He's just finished an historical novel, *August 1914*.'

'Oh? It's the first I hear about it.' This in a completely different voice, coldly official.

But Slava did not catch Demichev's intonation and went on enthusiastically: 'I've read it, Pyotr Nilovich. It's great! I have it with me now, and I'd like to bring it to you. I'm sure you'll enjoy it.'

The pause that followed brought Slava back to his senses. 'Can you hear me, Pyotr Nilovich?'

'I'm listening.'

'I'll bring you the manuscript in half an hour.'

'No, don't bring it. I don't have time to read it right now.'

'Then maybe one of your assistants will?'

'No, they don't have time either.' Slava realised that the conversation was over.

It was a bad beginning. But not one to be daunted, Slava called on Ekaterina Furtseva, the minister of culture. Having learned from his telephone conversation with Demichev, he decided to go in person to see Ekaterina, and announced to her secretary that he was on his way. She told her boss, and Slava appeared in Furtseva's office.

Ekaterina Alekseyevna greeted him warmly, as if she were his own mother. 'Slavochka! How glad I am to see you! How are you? How are Galya and the children?'

'Everything's fine, thank you, Ekaterina Alekseyevna. We're all in good health.'

'And *that one* – is he still living at your dacha?' She never called Solzhenitsyn by name in conversations. He was always and only 'that one.'

'Of course. Where can he go? He has no apartment, and he can't very well live in the woods! You should pull a few strings for him, get them to give him an apartment in Moscow.'

'But why doesn't he live in Ryazan?'

'Because he's separated from his wife, not to mention the fact that he can't work there. But that's not important. Galya and I are glad that he's living with us; it's no trouble for us at all. The main thing is that he is healthy, is working a lot, and has just finished a new book!' Slava conveyed this last bit of news joyfully, hoping he could coax a happy smile onto Furtseva's face.

'*What?*' she exclaimed in fright. 'A new book? What's he writing about now?'

'Don't worry, Ekaterina Alekseyevna. It's an historical book about the war in 1914.' And thinking that in her fright she might confuse history itself, he hastened to assure her: '*Before* the Revolution.' Then he added, 'I've brought it with me. It's in this package. You really must read it. I'm sure you'll like it very much.' And he tried to put the manuscript on her desk.

At that point Katya, forgetting all ministerial dignity, let out a shriek. '*No!* Don't put it on the desk! Don't put it on the desk! Take it out of here immediately. And remember: I never saw it.'

So ended Slava's second attempt to bring Solzhenitsyn's manuscript to light. For a long time afterward he kept trotting around to various offices with it, like a peddler. We knew a number of ministers well – people with whom we often shared a bottle of cognac – and Slava asked several of them to read it. But not a single one of them would so much as touch it with his hand. Each of them wanted to be able to say, if need be, 'I didn't read it. I don't know.'

Finally, Slava returned the manuscript to Solzhenitsyn. 'Nothing worked, Sanya. Send it abroad.'

On tour in Vienna, Slava and I met Vladimir Semyonov, head of
the Soviet delegation to the disarmament commission. His was
the kind of job that makes for a good feeding trough. The lucky
delegate stays abroad for years and keeps the wheels in motion,
the longer the better. Everyone fawns on him – takes him to the
best restaurants, and his wife is lavished with gifts of jewelry.

While in Vienna, we went with Semyonov and his wife to a
restaurant. At a certain moment I was drinking champagne alone
with him at the bar, and it occurred to me: Why not talk to
him about Solzhenitsyn. With his sort of connections, he might
have a chance to explain that shameful state of affairs to the
right person. One more intercessor would never hurt, in any
case.

'Listen. You're a man with influence – talk to the right person
and have this hounding of Solzhenitsyn stopped. How can the
newspapers publish such outrageous articles about books nobody
has read? It shames us before the whole world! Foreigners are
laughing at our stupidity. They think of us as a nation of sheep,
and they're right. For months the official press has been thundering and damning the books that have yet to be published anywhere. They don't even quote the passages an author is being
damned for. And then, even more ridiculously, they publish
'responses from the workers'! It's embarrassing to talk about it
with Europeans – I feel like some kind of idiot. You, you've been
living abroad for several years now. You've probably read every
one of Solzhenitsyn's books published here and know there's not
a single word of falsehood in them.'

'Ah, Galina Pavlovna! That's a complex question . . . He was
foolish to deal with foreign publishers. All that BBC, Voice of
America . . .'

'But what was he supposed to do? I know for a fact he offered
all his new works to Soviet publishing houses first. But after *One
Day in the Life of Ivan Denisovich* and the collection of short
stories, the censors banned everything. And the press has
published only spiteful reviews of his books not published in the
Soviet Union. They even slander him personally. How could
Solzhenitsyn defend himself? The Soviet newspapers haven't
printed a single word from the many letters he has written them.

So it's only from foreign radio stations that we know what's really happening.'

Semyonov listened very closely, nodding his head in silence, and it seemed that he was agreeing with me in many respects. Then suddenly he threw back his head, gave me a long, significant look, and his ardent whisper reached me like a blow to the solar plexus. 'But does he love Lenin?'

Had I heard right? I had been prepared to expect almost anything from him, but not such an idiotic question. *'What?'*

'I asked, "Does he love Lenin?"'

I went numb. And as in a dream, I heard the drone of that self-righteous voice continue: 'So-o-o! You're not saying anything! That's it then! He doesn't love Lenin . . .' But he himself knew perfectly well what Solzhenitsyn had gone through: ten years of prison and hard labor, and nothing but a rehabilitation paper in his pocket. He was no fool, that glorifier of Lenin. He understood everything. He even had a reputation as a liberal; and unlike most high government officials, was well-educated and cultivated. He knew literature well, went to concerts, had an extensive collection of paintings in his home, and was said to be an admirer of modernistic, unofficial art. But Goering, too, was an admirer of painting – it didn't stop him from being a monster.

Some liberal! He had sprung the mousetrap so skillfully that it even provoked my admiration. 'But does he love Lenin?' And the conversation was over.

TWENTY-ONE

Once in the summer of 1971 Solzhenitsyn announced to us that he and a friend were going to an area near Rostov-on-the-Don to gather material for one of his books. He hoped to find some old men who had fought in World War I and could serve as eyewitnesses. His decision to drive his old Moskvich terrified us. 'But how can you? It'll fall to pieces on the road. And the trip is a long one. A round trip of several thousand kilometers is no joke.'

'Don't worry, we'll take it easy. We'll stop in villages along the way. If something happens to the car, well, my friend is a mechanical engineer. Between the two of us we can repair it.'

'Listen, Sanya. Be careful. God looks out for those who look out for themselves. Who knows? The KGB may set up a highway accident for you, and no one will be able to prove that they murdered you. You'd better take the train. Or, better yet, why don't you just stay here at the dacha – it's the safest place.'

But it was an inborn trait of his to ignore danger to his life, regardless of warning. So off he went, promising to come back in two weeks.

Three days later, early in the morning, I was standing at the kitchen window waiting for the coffee to boil when I suddenly saw Sanya. He was back! But what was the matter? He wasn't so much walking as dragging himself along. His whole body collapsed against the wall of the porch, and he hung on to it with his hands.

Inside me, everything froze. I flung open the door. 'Good Lord, Sanya! What happened?'

He staggered into the kitchen, his face distorted with pain. 'Don't worry, Galya. I have to call Alya in Moscow right away. Then I'll tell you everything.' At the time, the only telephone was in our house. After that incident, we insisted that an extension be installed in the guest house.

Exactly what happened on that occasion is still a puzzle to me. His legs and body were covered with huge blisters as if he had been badly burned, but he had not been in the sun. He had only left the car a few times to eat in a lunchroom. Had they perhaps put something in his food . . . ? Naturally, he had turned back immediately.

Summer was hot and humid that year. We set up a cot for him in the shade, and he lay there for several days. Slava called a friend of ours, a well-known oncologist. Alexander Isayevich had been to his clinic before for an examination. At the time, our friend had advised Solzhenitsyn to register under another name, just in case.

He came to the dacha promptly in response to Slava's appeal, examined Alexander Isayevich, and told us that he had to be hospitalised right away. But he could scarcely be taken to a hospital when feelings about him were at a fever pitch and he could well be poisoned. No, it was better for him to stay where he was. Here there was someone to take care of him.

We asked the doctor what was wrong with him, and he said that it looked like a strong allergy. I simply could not imagine that such an allergy existed: his body was covered with huge, watery blisters which broke at the slightest movement and were excruciatingly painful. My grandmother had had blisters like that when the stove had set fire to her dress and burned her from head to toe. Looking at Solzhenitsyn's blisters, I couldn't imagine how he could have managed to sit, hunched over, in his little car.

And then, literally the day after Alexander Isayevich's return to the dacha, Katya came running to us in a panic and asked us to go in to him. 'Hurry! Something's happened! He's beside himself, and I don't know what to do.'

Here is what had happened. After returning so unexpectedly from his trip, Solzhenitsyn had asked an acquaintance of his, Alexander Gorlov, to go to the village of Rozhdestvo and get a spare part for the car from his cottage there. Gorlov left right away. As he approached the cottage, he saw that the lock had been broken and the door was ajar; voices came from within. He threw open the door, and saw nine men in civilian clothes rummaging through papers and belongings. The KGB.

Having been informed through Solzhenitsyn's estranged wife that he had gone south for two weeks, and not knowing about his sudden return, they were looking for his manuscripts. They had to be idiots to think that Solzhenitsyn would keep his papers in that empty shack.

'Who are you and what are you doing here?' Gorlov demanded. They slammed the door behind the unwelcome witness and ordered him to be quiet. But he wouldn't be intimidated. He demanded they show him a search warrant and explain why they had broken into the cottage. Tempers flared, and there was a scuffle. They beat him, pinioned his arms, and dragged him out, face down, to a car parked nearby. He instantly realised that he needed witnesses. Without them, he might be beaten to death somewhere, and no one would find any traces. So he began to shout and call for help. People came running from neighboring plots of land, and blocked the road. Then the man in charge of the group produced his KGB credentials, and Gorlov was shoved into the car. They told the neighbors that they had caught a thief: that they had been tipped off that Solzhenitsyn's place would be burglarised (!) and had staked it out.

Gorlov was taken to the district police station, where they demanded that he sign a written promise not to divulge what had happened. He flatly refused. They threatened that if Solzhenitsyn found out about it, Gorlov would never defend the dissertation he was working on and his son would never enroll in college. Eventually, they simply told him that if need be they would put him in prison. Not only did he continue to refuse, but he even said that he would tell everyone what had happened. After detaining him at the police station for several hours, they let him go. He came straight to the dacha, all bruises and scratches and in torn clothes, to see Solzhenitsyn. And of course when the latter found out what had happened, he flew into a rage.

Alexander Isayevich recounted the outrageous incident to us and showed us an open letter he had written to Andropov, then head of the KGB, in which he demanded an immediate explanation as to why, and by what right, the KGB had made a search of his house in his absence, and had beaten and blackmailed a man who was guilty of nothing.

That very day Katya took the letter to Moscow. We were sure that, as always, his statement would go unanswered. But to our collective surprise they answered. And they did so rather promptly – not by letter, of course, but by telephone.

I picked up the phone and heard a man's voice. 'Is this the Rostropoviches' dacha?'

'Yes.'

'To whom am I speaking?'

'Vishnevskaya.'

'Hello, Galina Pavlovna. This is KGB Colonel Berezin. I'm calling at the order of Comrade Andropov.'

My reaction to those words was sheer reflex: a sharp pain in the pit of my stomach. But the voice was polite. Perhaps they wanted me to do a concert . . .

'We received a letter from Alexander Isayevich Solzhenitsyn. Can you ask him to come to the phone?'

(Impossible! Had they finally decided to discuss things?)

'Sanya!' I shouted. 'Come to the phone! They're calling on behalf of Andropov.' Unfortunately, Alexander Isayevich was still ailing and couldn't get out of bed.

Alya came to the phone. They explained very politely that Solzhenitsyn's complaints had been completely misdirected, that Comrade Andropov personally had asked them to assure him that the KGB was not to blame, that it had had nothing to do with what had happened, and that he advised Solzhenitsyn to contact the police in the area where the incident had taken place.

In the summer of 1972 in Ryazan a second divorce hearing was held, and once again Solzhenitsyn was denied: 'no grounds for divorce.' Ermolai was already eighteen months old, another child was due any day, and still no grounds for divorce! Sanya came back frightfully upset and overstrained, and sat down immediately to write to the Supreme Court and request a review of the case.

One evening soon after, as we sat together on Solzhenitsyn's porch, the telephone rang. I picked it up. A woman asked me to call Alexander Isayevich to the phone.

'Who's speaking?'

'I'm Alekseyeva, his wife's new attorney. I have to talk to him about an important matter.'

I handed the receiver to Alexander Isayevich. 'I don't know you, and I have nothing to say to you.'

'Please. I beg of you. The matter can't be put off. Can you come to Moscow tomorrow?'

'No.'

'Then I'll come to you at the dacha. I repeat, it's a very urgent matter. It has to do with your divorce.'

'Then tell me on the phone.'

'No, it's not something we can talk about on the phone. I must talk with you in person.'

Alexander Isayevich turned and asked if she could come to the dacha.

'Of course.'

'Well, all right. Come tomorrow.'

'How will I find you?'

'I'll meet the three-o'clock train.'

The next day Alexander Isayevich went to the station to meet Alekseyeva, but he came home alone. 'It's strange. She didn't come. I waited for the next train, but she wasn't on that one either.'

A few days later I was strolling in the garden, and some old woman called out to me, 'Citizen, a man just handed me a letter and asked me to give it to you.' I took it from her. It was from Alekseyeva and addressed to Solzhenitsyn. There was no postmark on the envelope, and no stamp. I showed it to Slava, and together we called Alexander Isayevich. He opened it, read it, and reddened.

'What's happened now?'

'Here. Read it. I knew she was a KGB agent.'

The same Alekseyeva who had so insistently implored Solzhenitsyn to see her had written him a letter that made Slava and me go numb when we read it. We had heard how she had pestered

Alexander Isayevich to see her, and now, among other slanders, we read more or less the following:

> Stop your grimy proposals – I want nothing to do with you . . . Knowing full well that as your wife's lawyer I did not have the right to meet with you under unofficial circumstances, like a provocateur you tried to lure me to the dacha . . . You wanted me to fall into the trap you had set, and you would have advertised to the whole world that there had been another scandal . . . Your true identity as an intriguer will be recognised by all your friends, to whom I am sending a copy of this letter . . .

And so on, in the same spirit.

Indeed, during the next few days several of Solzhenitsyn's friends received her nasty concoction in the mail, and not long afterward, Natasha showed up at the dacha in a new Moskvich. Alexander Isayevich had bought it for her with the first money from the Nobel Prize. (He himself continued to use his old heap.) She pulled up at the gate and called out, 'Galya, I have to talk to Alexander Isayevich.'

It was a good thing she hadn't gone directly to the guest house. There Alya lay in bed, scarcely stirring, with pains in her stomach and grief in her heart. I was afraid that if she were subjected to an emotional scene she would give birth prematurely. She was a strong, healthy woman, but she had had a hard time with her pregnancies.

I went to the guest house and quietly called Alexander Isayevich. 'Sanya, Natasha is at the gate. She wants to talk with you.'

'I'll be right there.'

'I'll invite her in. Just don't say anything to Alya. Everybody's nervous – if she starts to give birth, no one will know what to do.'

Natasha came into the house. I felt terribly awkward and didn't know what to say to her. Suddenly she was at me. 'Galya, what do I need to do to keep Alexander Isayevich from divorcing me? Give me some advice.'

I could only tell her the truth. 'Natasha, you shouldn't do

anything. Alya will have her second child in two months. You have no children.'

'I won't give him a divorce for anything in the world.'

'But you know that if it doesn't happen now it will in a year or two. There will be a divorce. Why are you poisoning your own life and Alexander Isayevich's too? Why are you storing up hatred?'

'I must remain Solzhenitsyn's wife. Let him live with her – I'm ready to recognise his children. But I must be his wife.'

'But he won't agree to that. And how can you want such a humiliating position for yourself? Why?'

'Because if they send him out of Russia, I'll go with him.'

I kept quiet. Fortunately, Alexander Isayevich arrived. I stood up to leave, but he asked me not to. 'Galya, I want you to stay and be a witness to our conversation. I no longer trust my former wife.'

'How dare you say that? On what grounds?'

'I know what I'm talking about. The last time you and I agreed on everything before the hearing. You said you would no longer oppose the divorce, but in the courtroom you acted out a farce. Now you've hired a lawyer, and she's sent me a letter. Here, read it. Now will you go on saying you're not connected with that den of scoundrels? How did you come to know Alekseyeva? Did the KGB give her to you? She's only just graduated from the institute, and it's her first case. If you'd picked a lawyer yourself, you'd have found someone with a reputation, not a novice. But they gave you a guarantee that the case would be decided in your favor, and you fell for it. I'd like to be your friend, not your enemy. But if you want to take sides against me along with the KGB, I want nothing more to do with you.'

'I didn't know anything about a letter. It's the first I've heard of it.'

It was hard for me to listen. I could see that she was abandoning all feminine self-respect and forcing herself to play a role that had been foisted on her. But the role was too much, and she was playing it badly. It seemed to me that in fact she hated him, that at any moment she would lose all self-control and fling out everything she had been holding back with such effort. It would have been the more honest thing to do. She was not a bad person. It was simply that he wasn't for her, just as she wasn't for him. And I think that in the depths of her soul, she knew it.

She knew very well that divorce was unavoidable: they had been living apart for almost three years. But she was trying to drag out the process as long as she could. And that fitted perfectly with the KGB's program: to pressure Solzhenitsyn by not allowing him to register a marriage with the mother of his children. In the event he were exiled, the threat seemed a terrible one indeed.

'You're forgetting what we suffered through together, how I waited for you to get out of prison.'

'No, *you're* forgetting that you went and married someone else while I was in penal camp. I never held it against you, I'm simply reminding you, since you mention the subject.'

'Forgive me!' And she fell on her knees before him.

I could no longer bear to see or hear any more. I excused myself and left.

But the day's events did not end there. At eleven that night, Natasha showed up with some woman. 'Pardon me for coming so late, Galya, but we have to see Alexander Isayevich right away. This is my lawyer, Alekseyeva.'

Well, I thought, now it's getting serious! I showed the two women in and hurried to the guest house. It was dark: they had already gone to bed. I knocked softly so as not to alarm them. Like a specter, Alexander Isayevich's head appeared in the window.

'Sanya, come right now. It's important. Natasha has come with Alekseyeva.'

I returned to our night visitors. Natasha was pale and tired, she didn't say a word. The other one also remained silent, staring at the floor. Her appearance struck me as very strange: she was short, with a big head and no neck – a humpback without a hump. Drab, straight hair, a broad face with a muddy complexion. Very young, about twenty-three.

Alexander Isayevich came in and walked slowly across the room to the table. Both women got up and greeted him. He did not answer nor look at them, but took a seat and said nothing.

He had been living at our place for several years now, but it was at that moment, seeing him make his way slowly across the entire living room, that I understood what he had been through, and I was flooded with pity for that great man. He must have entered like that, I thought, every time he was called into an investigator's office to be interrogated. They summoned him, and he came. He had sat down and said nothing, in just that same way. And he had waited.

Natasha was the first to break the silence. 'This is my lawyer, Alekseyeva. I've brought her because this morning you accused me of knowing about her letter to you. I'm telling you once again that I knew nothing about it. Alekseyeva can confirm that. And she has something else to tell you.'

She looked confused, pathetic, and didn't say a word more. Alexander Isayevich was calm and not in the least surprised that they had come. 'I'm listening.'

Never looking at us, Alekseyeva began in a toneless, weak voice: 'I'm asking you to forgive me for the letter you received, and I want to tell you why I didn't show up when you came to meet me. I came on the three-o'clock train, as we had agreed. But as soon as I stepped out onto the platform two men grabbed my arms from both sides and pulled me back into the train – KGB agents. They brought me back to Moscow, to the Lubyanka, where they detained me for six hours and forced me to write that letter. They made me come back the next day and the day after that and finally got me to promise to do everything to prevent you from divorcing your wife for as long as possible, and to discredit you in the eyes of your friends. If I didn't obey, they said, I would lose the right to practice law. What could I do? What should I do *now*?'

Alexander Isayevich calmly heard her out. 'But that's not the first time you visited that institution. It was they who recommended you to my former wife. I'm only saying that for what it's worth. You ask me what you should do now. Here's a sheet of paper. Write down everything you've just told me.'

To my amazement, she began to write. It was as if she had been prepared to do just that. I was shaking like a leaf. I felt as if I had been dreaming, and I wanted to pinch myself, to awake from the nightmare. Never in my life had I been present at such a conversation. Seeing that my teeth were chattering, Sanya smiled. 'Yes, Galochka. It wasn't for such scenes that Slava built this room.'

When she had signed the letter, Alekseyeva handed it to Alexander Isayevich, and he read it aloud: '. . . I was wrong. I misunderstood the invitation to the dacha. . . . I ask forgiveness . . . Alekseyeva.'

'No, that doesn't serve my purposes. If you wanted to wriggle out of it, this sort of letter wouldn't mean a thing. Write what you told us just now.'

And again, without resisting in any way, she wrote on another sheet of paper: '. . . At my insistence, Solzhenitsyn agreed to see me at his place, but I was arrested by KGB agents at the Ilinskoye station . . . They interrogated me for several hours, and made me write a slanderous letter and send it to Solzhenitsyn and his friends . . .' In general, she recorded everything she had told us. And she signed it: 'Alekseyeva.'

As she put the letter into Alexander Isayevich's hand, she asked what he intended to do with it. 'Precisely nothing,' he replied. 'But if the first letter, that vile concoction of yours, appears in *Literaturnaya Gazeta*, then this one will be read by the whole world. Tell that to the people who sent you here tonight, and consider that once again you have fulfilled your obligation to them.'

She sat quietly. I wanted to smash that drab face of hers and throw her out of my house. Alexander Isayevich rose, apologised to me, bade me good night, and left. The two of them went into the night.

It was only after the third hearing that Solzhenitsyn was granted his divorce. Alya was already pregnant with their third child when they were married in April of 1973 in that same church on the Obydenka where their son Ermolai had been christened.

Several months later Solzhenitsyn was sent into exile.

Today I ask myself why the authorities put up with Solzhenitsyn's staying at our place for such a long time. They simply could have evicted him on the grounds that he was not a registered resident on our property. Under Soviet law that alone is a serious violation, and under its cover they could have moved in on Solzhenitsyn boldly. No protests from famous artists would have helped him then.

All those visits from time to time by the police, all those talks, all that pressure from the authorities demanding that he leave us, now strike me as mere games. In the Soviet Union no opinions, including world opinion, are persuasive: they just don't count. The authorities could have concocted an 'opinion' of the academicians living in our area demanding that Solzhenitsyn be thrown out. Andrei Sakharov was thrown out of his own home and, without so much as a trial, exiled to the city of Gorky. For several years now, the world has voiced its indignation, but for our rulers the noise is like water off a duck's back.

Most likely they figured that Solzhenitsyn would feel obligated to hosts who until shortly before had been total strangers; that he would be more restrained in his declarations; and that, living in a prohibited government zone, he would be more isolated from society. But they overlooked the most important thing: for the first time in his life, Solzhenitsyn had an opportunity to live and work in quiet surroundings, under normal living conditions, building up the physical and spiritual strength he needed to do battle.

But to some extent they did not miscalculate. Not wanting to subject us to the responsibility for what might happen, he demanded that we tell no one he could be reached at our address, that we never meet with foreign correspondents in Zhukovka, and if they did show up unexpectedly, that we simply not open the door to them. During those years we received no foreigners at the dacha, so as not to give the authorities any grounds for suspecting that Solzhenitsyn was using us as a channel to publish his manuscripts abroad. Solzhenitsyn lived like a hermit, and apart from his closest friends, saw no one.

Near our house, and making no attempt at concealment, the KGB set up an observation post: a black Volga commandeered by a number of people. As he drove past, Slava would honk his horn at them as if they were old acquaintances.

As for the house itself, it was not difficult – through our maids, whom we changed often – for the KGB to install any number of listening devices.

Shortly after we left Russia, five men in civilian clothes came to the dacha gate. A friend of ours was staying there.

'Good morning. We need to come in the house.'

'I can't let anyone in without approval from Veronica Leopoldovna, Rostropovich's sister, and she's not here right now.'

'We're from the KGB. We need to come in.'

'Show me your papers.'

They produced their KGB identification. To that mighty institution no Soviet citizen bars the door.

'Come in. May I accompany you?'

'Please.'

Thinking that they wanted to take a look at the rooms, she started to lead them to the main house.

'No, no – we only need access to the porch of the guest house.'

She took them there. Not at all deterred by her presence, they pulled back a rug in the corner, pulled up a few of the floorboards, and dragged out a big iron box with some mysterious apparatus in it. And they did it with such cynicism, without the slightest embarrassment. In a businesslike way they set to work, did their job, excused themselves, and left, taking their property with them.

After Slava sent his letter, the authorities naturally began to put the squeeze on us – especially on Slava – and continued that noble enterprise for three and a half years. First they removed him from the Bolshoi, then, gradually, they canceled all his foreign trips. Eventually the time came when Moscow orchestras would be forbidden to invite Rostropovich to conduct. And finally they wouldn't even let him use a hall in Moscow or Leningrad for his solo concerts. It was then that Slava got a call from Moscow University asking him to come to Lenin Hills to play a concert for them. He joyfully agreed.

On the morning of the day of the concert, there was another

call. 'I'm sorry, Mstislav Leopoldovich. I know you were supposed to play for us tonight, but an unexpected conference has
come up, and the hall is needed for the evening. We apologise.
But perhaps you will agree to play for us another time? We'll call
you.'

Late that night some students from the university called.
'Mstislav Leopoldovich, how are you feeling?'

'Just fine, thank you.'

'But they posted an announcement here that you are ill, and
that's why the concert was canceled.'

'But I was told that the hall was going to be used tonight for
some urgent conference!'

'No. The place is empty.'

'So, they lied to both you and me.'

A group of BBC staffers came to Moscow and called us at
home. 'We're shooting a film about Shostakovich, and of course
we hope you'll take part in it.'

There had been so many refusals already. We were tired of
asking and fed up with the games of all the small-time bureaucrats
in the various ministries – this one we would refuse on our own.
'We don't have the time.'

The next day there was a call from the Novosti Press Agency
tearfully begging us to do the film. 'Mstislav Leopoldovich, we're
making a film about Shostakovich jointly with the BBC. Since you
and Galina Pavlovna have performed so much of his music,
without your participation there can't be any film.'

'But they'll only ban it again!'

'No, we have permission. This our *official* invitation.'

'All right, then, let the firm's representatives come and see us
at home.'

They came, those dear sweet Englishmen, and we agreed that
Slava would play a movement of the Cello Concerto for the film,
and I would sing an aria from *Lady Macbeth* and something from
the Blok cycle. On the day we were to shoot, we rehearsed at
home and got ready – the car was coming at three. It never came.
Not at three nor four, nor even six. Nothing; no phone calls; no
letters. We weren't about to call anyone ourselves – we were
sick of the whole thing. That night Maxim Shostakovich came and

told us that the Central Committee had banned our appearance in the film.

It so happened that within days we were dining at the British ambassador's residence, along with guests from other foreign embassies. Slava couldn't restrain himself. In front of everyone at the table, he declared, 'Mr Ambassador, I have always considered England a land of gentlemen. But a few days ago I was disappointed – stunned – by English impoliteness.'

A deathly silence fell over the table. The ambassador straightened in his chair, and went a little pale. 'Pardon me, I don't believe I understood you . . .'

'A British firm asked us to take part in a film. We agreed. They were supposed to come for us at a certain time. We waited for them for several hours – I in tails and Galina Pavlovna in a concert gown. Not only did they not come, they didn't even call to apologise or explain what had happened.'

The ambassador went from white to red. Then, without so much as uttering a word, he jumped up from the table and hurried into another room to use the telephone. He was soon back with the following story. The day before the shooting, someone from Novosti Press Agency had called a BBC representative and said that Rostropovich and Vishnevskaya had left Moscow on urgent business; the story had it that we had refused to take part in the film. We learned later that the film came out anyway, and that in the English version they spliced in some old footage of Slava and me.

Another time, Yehudi Menuhin called from London. 'Galya, where's Slava?'

'Giving a concert in Erevan.'

'And how's his health?'

'Good.'

'He was supposed to come and give some concerts here, but they sent a telegram saying he's sick. What should we do?'

'You can tell everybody that you talked with me, and that I told you that the Ministry of Culture is lying. Rostropovich is fine. They just won't let him out.'

TWENTY-TWO

In general, my warning to Slava was proving to have been well-founded. He was no longer conducting in Moscow or Leningrad. He began to tour the provinces – for the time being, at least, that road had not been closed to him. He was often in Yaroslavl, a town about 200 kilometers from Moscow; and he would persuade me to go along and sing with the orchestra.

Yaroslavl is a beautiful, ancient city, once a center of Russian culture and home of the oldest Russian drama theater. Its waterfront is lined with handsome private homes that still preserve the spirit – and seem to reflect the lives – of those who lived there in centuries past. Though the façades are maintained, however, the communal apartments inside are falling to pieces.

The old churches of Yaroslavl are breathtaking. Each is affixed with a plate stating that this particular monument of architecture is being preserved by the state. Locks hang from the doors, but the windows are often broken. We would often peer in through the broken panes to find only desolation and darkness within. Once in an abandoned church we saw hundreds of ikons lying face down on the floor. The snow was blowing in through the broken windows and blanketing them all. With the coming of spring and the thaw, we knew they would be ruined forever.

What struck us was the contrast between the city and its tired, embittered inhabitants. With all its dying splendor, Yaroslavl seemed to be saying it was not built for them and not for that wretched, gray life.

On one of his trips there, Slava took Olga and Elena – teen-agers by then – to show them the Russian antiquities. By evening, the question of food came up. But room service in the hotel was prohibited, and he couldn't very well take two young girls to a restaurant which might have been full of drunks by that hour of night. He went with the children to a store and asked the woman behind the counter to weigh out some cheese, butter, and bread. Nothing else was on the counter.

'Let's have your coupon.'

'What coupon?'

'What do you mean, "what"? For butter.'

'But I don't have a coupon.'

'No coupon, no butter.'

'What do you call that sitting on the counter?'

'What are you, a tourist or something? Where are you from?'

'Moscow.'

'It's plain as day you're from Moscow. Here, butter has been rationed for ages.'

'So that's it! Well, if there isn't any, there isn't any. Let's go, girls!'

Seeing the customers who had blown in from the capital shuffle off so downheartedly, the saleswoman relented. 'Hey, Citizen! Come back! Okay, I'll give you a hundred grams of butter, just don't come in here again without a coupon.'

Ration coupons for butter! And where? Two hundred kilometers from Moscow, and we who live there know nothing about it.

Almost every musician in the Yaroslavl Symphony Orchestra is a Muscovite – a former student at a Moscow music school, if not the Moscow Conservatory. They work with only one hope: to get out as soon as possible and go back to Moscow, back to the familiar bustle of that city's life.

The pay for artists in the provinces is paltry, ranging from 100 to 150 rubles a month; and unlike Moscow, there is no chance for outside work. At best, the wind instrumentalists may be asked to play at local funerals, for which they are paid five rubles apiece. There they can drink themselves senseless at funeral feasts. When the orchestra goes on tour, they are all glad to go, because they are given a daily allowance of two rubles and fifty kopecks. If they can feed themselves with that, they can save their salaries for a pair of shoes at least.

In Yaroslavl, the quota of eighteen concerts a month must be fulfilled, even though it is only a small provincial city in which mustering enough symphony-lovers for one concert a month is hard enough. As a result, if the program doesn't feature a well-known musician from Moscow, the concerts are played to an empty hall. One can imagine the mood of the orchestra and the conductor when they walk out onto the stage under those conditions.

Is a permanent symphony orchestra really needed in this sadly decayed city, wallowing as it does in its insoluble daily problems? Of course not, no more than in any other small city. Perhaps if one touring orchestra were made out of ten orchestras, and one good opera company were made out of ten provincial ones, they could tour throughout the year, play to full houses and make more money. But what would the others do then? Here is the ticklish question of Soviet employment itself. The fact is that in the Soviet Union – especially where high skills are not demanded – in order to avoid the appearance of unemployment one real job is filled by two or three employees who actually share one person's wages. A brilliant solution? Perhaps it's not important that the pay is so low it doesn't feed the wage earner – that in America a person who collects unemployment earns more than the Soviet worker. Perhaps it's not important that the work ends up being done helter-skelter. Russians have long said, 'The state pretends to pay us for work, and we pretend to work.' But the Communist Party is always ready with its trump card: There is no such thing as unemployment in the Soviet Union.

I continued to sing at the Bolshoi as often as I liked. In that regard no restrictions were placed on me, and in 1971 I received the highest award in the Soviet Union – the Order of Lenin. I was even permitted to go abroad. The last trip I made was to Vienna during the 1972–1973 season, where I sang *Tosca* and *Madama Butterfly* with the Vienna Opera. But the major newspapers simply stopped writing about me, and my voice could no longer be heard on radio or television. I was singing into a void. In this way the authorities were trying not only to humiliate me but to exclude me from the cultural life of the country.

Yet I still had my privileged place on the stage where I could express my art. I still had my former status – the theater in the capital, the splendid orchestra – so my artistry did not suffer. And, bathing in undiminished success and the love of the public, surrounded by my fans, I could have tried not to notice the vicious intrigues going on around me.

But Rostropovich was in a completely different position. After performing with the major orchestras of America, England, and Germany, and after associating with the outstanding musicians of our day, he had to sink into the mire of Russian provincial life and perform with conductors and orchestras incapable of expressing the ideas of such a musician no matter how hard they tried. He was forced to make artistic compromises, gradually lower his level of performance, and adapt himself to mediocrity. It is an old Russian tradition that under such circumstances, vodka comes to one's aid, and Rostropovich was no exception. More and more often after concerts he would turn to the bottle. And more and more often he would clutch at his heart. The time had come for me to step in, to keep him away from his drinking companions – to swallow the bitter pill of provincial life once again.

They called me from the Saratov Theater and begged me to sing *Tosca* with them. 'Please help the theater, Galina Pavlovna. Attendance is way down and only guest artists keep us going.'

Seeing how Slava was wasting away in enforced idleness, I decided to accept and asked him to conduct the performances. He jumped at the chance, and left for Saratov a good ten days ahead of me to rehearse the orchestra. The work itself was of interest to him: it would be the first time he had conducted *Tosca*. And so, for the first time in many years, I went on tour within the Soviet Union.

Saratov is a large, once-prosperous city on the Volga. It has a concert hall, an opera house, a dramatic theater, a symphony orchestra, a conservatory and music schools, a university, various institutes, and so on.

The manager of the theater greeted me with flowers. 'Galina Pavlovna! What a pleasure it is to see you in our city! Mstislav Leopoldovich is already at rehearsal, and he's expecting you at the theater at eleven.'

Everybody at the hotel was also accommodating. 'You're in room—on the sixth floor.'

'But where is the elevator?'

'Unfortunately, it's out of order.'

'Oh, I see. Can I order coffee in my room?'

'In your room? Our snack bar was closed down for repairs ages ago.'

'Then where can one get breakfast in the morning?'

'There's a cafeteria across the street.'

So that's the way it was! For the moment it didn't matter. But what about after a performance? Was I supposed to crawl out of bed in the morning, get dressed, fix my hair, and go out on the street? Well, okay, we'd see. In any case it was only for two weeks.

Even though it was still morning, the cafeteria was already pungent with the smell of food gone sour. The tables were covered with grimy oilcloths. Despite the early hour, a few characters were already downing beer mixed with vodka. Obviously, they were getting their hair of the dog. No, this was not Paris, it wasn't even Moscow!

I waited silently for someone to come to the table. The manager of the theater, who had accompanied me, despaired to see the prima donna sinking deeper into gloom with each passing minute. Finally a strapping matron came to the table and, seeing that I was wiping the filth off it with a napkin, struck a 'ready for labor and defense' pose, though it was not so much for labor as for defense.

'Well, what will you have?'

'Coffee with cream, please.'

'Cream? Never in all my born days! Only milk.'

'All right. Milk, then.'

Under her eagle eye I felt myself begin to shrink. As politely as possible, I asked her to bring the coffee and milk separately. Her amazement knew no bounds. 'How can I do that? What will I bring it in?'

My mouth dripped honey. 'In whatever you want. But please don't mix them.'

'Well, all right. What else will you have?'

'That will be all.'

'You're from Moscow, right?'

'Yes, from Moscow.'

She brought some sort of reddish fluid in a sticky glass, a teaspoon of granulated sugar in a saucer, and another saucer with something smeared on it.

'But where is the milk?'

'What do you mean, where? There, in the saucer. You asked for it separately.'

'But that's sweetened condensed milk, isn't it? I asked for milk. And I don't take sugar.'

Oh, how she let me have it! 'How dare you! Our kids never see milk, and you want it then and there! What a princess! Imagine, condensed milk is not to her liking while our women stand all day in line for it. And no sugar for her. Go ahead and eat it! You won't choke.'

Oh, Galina Pavlovna, 'our empress'! You've traveled to foreign lands, you've nestled into your Zhukovka with two refrigerators. And you've deigned to forget that you yourself once ate bread with chaff and washed it down with boiled water. Come down a notch, take a look around, and see how the people live . . . But I don't want to remember. I don't want to 'come down a notch.' Why are they living like that? It's not wartime, for God's sake!

That evening at the theater, after rehearsal, I looked in at the audience. A performance was going on, and there were fifty people in the hall at best. Yet the voices were quite good. And the tenor, Vladimir Shcherbakov, simply had a remarkable voice.*

I don't remember which opera it was, but it involved a corps de ballet, and I was horrified by the ballerinas, they were so fat. And again revealing my Muscovite mentality, I said to the director of the theater, 'But it's a disgrace! Why have they fattened themselves up like that? You should make them get into shape.'

She looked at me patronisingly and took time to explain. 'Galina Pavlovna, those overfed girls are paid eighty rubles a month by the theater, enough only for bread, potatoes, and macaroni.

---

* Afterward, I arranged an audition for him at the Bolshoi, and he's been singing there ever since. (G. V.)

That's why they put on weight. They have to save something for clothes besides, you know. After all, they're artists, too, even if only members of the corps de ballet.'

I wished the earth would open up and swallow me, I had been so tactless.

That summer the Saratov Theater went on tour to Kiev, and asked Slava and me to join them, if only for two performances of *Tosca*. This time I refused, and all of Rostropovich's attempts to persuade me were in vain. I needed to rest and prepare for the new season, so I ensconced myself at the dacha. Slava agreed to go, and worked out a fine plan: he would take Olga and Elena with him; they would go by car all the way to Kiev, stopping at various interesting places en route. Of course the girls were overjoyed. They had not yet been to Kiev, but more than that, their father was going to conduct, so they would be able to sit in on all rehearsals and performances.

They left at dawn, well-equipped with clothes, food, and maps. The first night they stopped in Bryansk. But the next day, toward evening, they returned to Zhukovka with despondent faces. It turned out that when they arrived in Bryansk, a telegram was waiting for them from Kiev saying that because of a change in the program, the performances of *Tosca* had been canceled.

We found out later that the Kiev authorities had simply prohibited an appearance by Rostropovich in the city, and had announced to the public that he had gone abroad and refused to conduct in Kiev. The performances of *Tosca* went on as scheduled – with a different conductor.

But while in Saratov, I *did* sing in the performances of *Tosca*, though I nearly slit the throat of the baritone singing Scarpia, right on the stage.

I always rehearse the murder scene very carefully, because Scarpia and I have little to sing toward the end of the act, so we can let ourselves go and act up a storm.

I explained to my partner that I was going to stab him in the throat near the collarbone, rather than in the back or the heart. 'When you embrace me, I'll put my left arm around your neck, and I'll strike from above with my right hand.'

'Oh, how effective! We simply must do it that way!'

Then I realised that I was holding a real knife – with a sharp blade! I almost fainted. 'Have you gone out of your mind? Where's the stage director? Replace it with a prop knife immediately, and don't forget to check it before the performance. I pick up the knife from the table while I'm standing with my back to it. I can't see it, and I grab whatever is at hand.'

'Don't worry, Galina Pavlovna. I'll see to it.'

'Now, please let's get this straight. Once I've put my arm around your neck, try not to make the slightest move. Otherwise I might stab you in the face. It's a wild scene, and I'm not thinking too clearly by that time –'

'But these are such trifles they're not worth talking about. I'll have no trouble remembering.'

During the performance he of course forgot everything and decided to ham it up before his 'death.' Wailing 'Tosca, you are mine!' he grabbed me in his arms. As we had agreed, I threw my left arm around his neck. At that moment he tried to kiss me, and I slashed his ear . . . with a real knife! They had forgotten to switch it.

Carried away by the drama of the scene, I wasn't even surprised to see blood pouring down Scarpia's face. It was only when I saw the 'corpse's' eyes rolling wildly that I came to my senses.

How did he endure it lying there until the curtain went down?

Shortly after this incident, I sang *Tosca* in Vienna, and in the very same scene an absolutely terrifying thing happened. It's a miracle I survived.

Two splendid singers – Placido Domingo as Cavaradossi and Kostas Paskalis as Scarpia – were performing with me in that production. In the second act, set in Scarpia's study, huge candelabras stood on the table and in two or three other places. The candles were lit and so big that their flickering flames could be seen even from the gallery. At the Bolshoi real fire of any kind was forbidden on the stage. We couldn't even light a cigarette when the action called for it because striking matches was not allowed. So naturally there was no need to fireproof the costumes and wigs, as is the practice in all theaters in the West. I of course knew nothing about it. And the management of the Vienna Opera permitted me to wear my own costumes and wigs, unaware that they had not been fireproofed.

I was standing near the table as always, having completely forgotten that candles were burning behind me. After stabbing Scarpia, I pushed him away from me forcefully, then fell back. And my nylon (!) chignon was drawn into the flame. In all the commotion of that drama-packed scene, I was unaware of what had happened and, with the knife in my upraised hand, I ran around Paskalis, who was writhing in his death agony. Suddenly a woman's scream pierced the air. (The first to cry out was my Austrian friend, Lyuba Kormut.) At that same moment I heard a crackling above my head, as if fireworks had gone off, and I felt my entire chignon rising up. A blinding light flashed before my eyes, and through it I saw that Scarpia, whom I had just 'murdered,' had jumped to his feet. Shouting *'Feuer! Feuer!'* he rushed toward me and, grabbing me by the arm, threw me to the floor. The thought crossed my mind like lightning: my dress is on fire! Instinctively clutching at the rug, I tried to bury my face in it. The flames reached my hands. My hair was on fire! Grasping the burning chignon with both hands, I tugged at it with all my might and finally tore it off, along with some of my own hair. Jumping to my feet, I saw people running toward me from both wings. 'Why don't I hear the music? I haven't finished the second act yet. Why are they taking me off the stage?'

Later the newspapers reported that after I had killed Scarpia I was running around him, when suddenly the audience saw my long chignon rise up in flames, while I stood in the center of the stage like a human torch.

After Paskalis threw me to the floor, they lowered the curtain. The audience panicked and screamed, thinking I had burned to death. But, seeing that I was on my feet, the director of the theater dashed out in front of the curtain and explained that there were no serious burns. As for me, my only thought was that I had to put on a new chignon immediately and go on with the show.

'Bring me another chignon right away! The performance is being held up too long.'

The manager looked at me as if I were an imbecile. 'You mean you intend to sing?'

'Of course. Bring me a chignon right away.'

I hadn't noticed that a doctor had bandaged my hands – that my nails on both hands were burned. During a performance, everything I do on stage is a matter of life and death. Only if my head had been cut off would I have been unable to finish singing my part.

After a ten-minute delay I was again standing by the table, the same candelabra burning behind me. The orchestra began to play, and the curtain went up. What went on in the hall defies description. There was no need for me to sing, they were shouting so. I killed Scarpia a second time, and we went on with the show. When Domingo sang '*O dolci mani*' in the third act he wept real tears as he held my bandaged hands.

After the performance I was in a strangely giddy state. Lyuba and I went to a restaurant for a good meal and lots of wine. Then I returned to the hotel and fell into a sound sleep. I was in shock, of course, which prevented me from realising the full horror of what I had been through.

The next morning I ordered coffee and then took the bandages off my hands. Only when I saw the blisters and my blackened, burned nails did I clearly understand what had happened to me the night before. My legs felt like jelly. I had indeed almost burned to death in front of the audience! What had saved me was that the dress I was wearing was not nylon. Otherwise, I would have been lying in a hospital with a burned, disfigured face.

The telephone rang. 'Hello.'

'To whom am I speaking?' It was a familiar woman's voice, speaking Russian.

'It's me.'

'Who?' From the voice, I gathered that it was the secretary to the director of the Bolshoi.

'This is Vishnevskaya.'

'Galina Pavlovna, my dear! Is it really you? You're alive? What happened?'

'Why are you calling, Nina Georgiyevna?'

'Someone was listening to the BBC today and didn't understand whether Vishnevskaya had been burned, or had burned to death, and just called us at the theater. I was afraid to call you, and couldn't believe my ears when I heard your voice.'

I told her exactly what had happened, and asked her to call Slava at home before any rumors reached him.

And then other calls started coming in: from London, Paris, America. Acquaintances, friends, even complete strangers. They all asked me if there was anything I needed, and expressed their joy that I was alive – that they were hearing my voice. The media throughout the world reported the nightmarish incident. It was only from the Soviet Embassy that no one called. For all of them without exception, I was already an outcast. I felt disgust to the point of loathing. What kind of people were my compatriots? I understood that they might have been afraid to call me from home. But could it be that no one from the huge Soviet colony in Vienna was willing to make an anonymous call from a phone booth on the street and ask a woman – an artist – how she was feeling after the horror she had been through, to say a few words in our common Russian language? That omission couldn't be ascribed to fear. What is it then that has come to replace the celebrated breadth and kindness of the Russian soul?

When La Scala came to Moscow a year later, in the summer of 1974, one of their productions was *Tosca*, with Raina Kabaivanska and Domingo in the lead roles. As a rule, the Milan troupe tours with only one cast, so when Kabaivanska took ill, there was a threat that the performance might be cancelled. Domingo suggested asking me to sing the role, and the Italians approached our management.

'Unfortunately, that's impossible. Galina Pavlovna isn't in Moscow.'

'How can that be?' exclaimed Domingo. 'I've talked to her on the telephone, and I'm having dinner at her place tomorrow.'

'Really? Well, that's not the point. She doesn't sing *Tosca* in Italian.'

'But she does!' the great tenor persisted. 'I sang it with her just last year in Vienna.'

An hour later they informed the Italians that they had called me at home, and I had refused to perform in *Tosca*.

Domingo told me all this over dinner in my Moscow apartment. 'Can it really be that they didn't call you or ask your consent?' 'Of course they didn't. Don't forget, this is the Soviet Union.'

In your youth, you can find the strength to laugh off the raps on the knuckles and the boxes on the ear. But with time, as your inner vision becomes mercilessly sharp, life reveals itself to you in both its ugliness and its beauty. And you inevitably realise that your best years have been stolen from you, that you haven't done half of what you wanted to do and were capable of. You become tortured with shame for permitting the criminal abasement of what was most precious to you: your art. And it becomes impossible to remain a marionette eternally dancing at the will of a stupid puppeteer, to endure the endless interdictions and those degrading words 'You can't!'

The provincial concerts soon began to leave a bitter residue of creative dissatisfaction in Slava's soul. But to sit in Moscow doing nothing while his colleagues performed was even more unbearable. Here he was, a great musician in his prime, and he could only attend performances as a member of the audience. A surer, slower punishment for Rostropovich could not have been devised. The only question was how long he could hold out.

A friend of ours had a fine collection of Russian porcelain. Slava suddenly took an interest in it and, for something to do, began to buy a few pieces. These treasures had long since disappeared from antique shops in Russia, and acquiring them was an arduous process: one had to cultivate the collectors and pursue all leads. Since Rostropovich never did anything halfway, he quickly decided that we had to have the finest collection in Russia. He set himself that goal, and threw himself into the search.

While learning his way around in these matters, he encountered many an embarrassing occasion when he would be sold daubed-over pieces of junk passed off as museum pieces. But only by making mistakes does one become a real connoisseur, and Rostropovich was not in the least daunted. I welcomed this new hobby and tried to encourage his enthusiasm, realising that it was far better to have broken, badly mended cups on the shelf than all-night drunken parties with their idiotic conversation about the meaning of life.

Upon his return from one such 'expedition,' he told me with breathless rapture of a picturesque old man he had met – Uncle Vanya.

'Will I ever meet him?'

'Oh sure. He and his wife, Aunt Masha, are coming tomorrow. I'm going to help her get into the hospital for treatment. Uncle Vanya will be spending the night with us. You'll see what a handsome old man he is!'

The next day, when I came home after rehearsal, the first thing I saw was a pair of feet in felt boots propped up on my Empire furniture in the dining room. Then I saw Uncle Vanya, a tall old man with a long beard. He really was handsome – right out of a picture.

In the kitchen, Slava and Aunt Masha were drinking tea. They had just come from the hospital. In the evening he would take her back, and Uncle Vanya would stay the night with us, then go back to his village. But first Slava would go all over Moscow with him, so that he could return with as many groceries as possible. Uncle Vanya, dignified and handsome, condescendingly chalked Slava's enthusiasm up to his own charm. He was thanking Slava when suddenly he seemed to remember something.

'You know, Slava, there's an old woman not far from us in the village, and at her house I've seen plates with the tsar's crest.'

'Really?'

'I've seen 'em.'

'Then give me the address.'

'No, I can't tell you the address exactly. But come to my place and we'll go see her together. It's not far – about thirty kilometers.'

'Good. Galya and I will make the trip together. How's next Sunday?'

In our Land-Rover, we traveled about 200 kilometers from Moscow. Slava had forgotten the address, and we meandered through small villages for a long time before we found Uncle Vanya's place. No sooner had we crossed the threshold than he began ushering us out the door so we would get there before dark. Rapidly, he loaded big bags into our car. They were full of dry bread crusts. He filled the car with them, so that there was scarcely enough room for us. Did he intend to take all that to the old woman?

We drove for an hour, and finally stopped in a little village.

'Well, is this it?'

'No. Wait here while I unload the bags. My son lives here. I've saved this up for him for the winter. Then there are cookies and candy from Moscow for the kids. Want to come in and have some tea?'

'But where does the old woman live?'

'The old woman? Not far. We'll make it in plenty of time. There are a lot of old women with that kind of stuff around here . . . about another thirty kilometers.'

We set off. We went up to one house, and a toothless old peasant woman came out, quite unable to understand what we wanted of her. We went to another house, but only children came to the door. After the third house I began to shake with laughter. I understood everything.

'Slava, do you suppose your Uncle Vanya merely needed our car to take the dry bread crusts from his place to his son's?'

The embarrassed Rostropovich saw that he had been had. I never let him hear the end of it.

Later I realised why the old man had to transport his dry bread crusts in secret. In Russia, it is against the law to feed bread to livestock. But what can you do if you can't buy cattle feed anywhere? He was probably afraid he'd be denounced if he asked his kolkhoz for a car. So, when he came across a madman from the capital who was willing to drive all over the country to buy broken cups, he saw his chance and dreamed up the plates with the tsar's crest.

Slava's hobby soon became a passion. Just to get his hands on some statuette, he would drive hundreds of kilometers along virtually impassable mud roads. Our house gradually became filled with broken crocks. Rostropovich would lovingly glue them, then place them in a display case. Soon he would be off again on another 'expedition.' Getting home in the middle of the night – tired but happy – he would drag me out of bed to show me some glass knickknack that had been palmed off on him by some Uncle Vanya or Aunt Masha. I would squint at the monstrosities he brought home, listening to him tell about the fascinating people and how he was off tomorrow for such-and-so place where, he had been told, manuscripts of Mussorgsky's were hidden. That passion of his was a kind of salvation in his idleness. But could it really replace his music, for which he was born? I looked into the future with great trepidation.

The San Francisco Symphony, under Seiji Ozawa, came to the Soviet Union on tour. Their concerts had been planned long in advance, and according to the contract, Slava was supposed to take part in them. However hard the authorities tried to remove him from the Moscow program, the Americans would not give in; and – wonder of wonders! – the authorities had to let Rostropovich perform the Dvořák concerto in the Great Hall of the Conservatory. Of course 'all Moscow' attended the concert. Slava played splendidly, but I was shaken by the way he came on stage, the way he sat, the way he bowed to the audience. With what gratitude he looked at Ozawa, who was just beginning his career; how grateful he was to each member of the orchestra since it was because of them that he was playing in that magnificent hall. And suddenly I realised with horror that deep within Rostropovich a fatal fissure was beginning to open up, and that he could very soon be torn asunder.

The rejoicing that went on in the concert hall, and then at home until late at night! Friends, admirers, musicians: 'Brilliant . . . phenomenal. . . .' They were all hugging and kissing one another. But Rostropovich hadn't been given a concert hall in Moscow for years and wouldn't be given one in the future. The audience should have been staging a revolt.

Finally everyone left, and we were alone. Seeing Slava so radiant and happy, I hesitated a long time before speaking my mind. 'Slava, no one else will tell you what I'm going to tell you now. You're not going to like it, but nobody can hear us. Tonight you played –'

'What are you trying to say? That I played badly? To the contrary, I played well.'

'Yes, you played beautifully. You *can't* play badly. But you need a large audience. You must be able to travel abroad, otherwise it's all over for you. Playing in the boondocks all these years has left its mark on your soul. You're losing the special quality of a great artist, who must be above the crowd, not with it. You're losing the loftiness of the spirit. Don't say anything, and don't respond. I'm an artist too, and I know how painful it must be for you to hear all this, especially after such a triumphant concert. But I'm your wife and I feel it's my duty to tell you.'

In the spring of 1973 we were invited to take part in a music festival along the Volga with the symphony orchestra of Ulyanovsk. Slava agreed, and for his sake I accepted the invitation, too.

Rostropovich's candidacy was discussed at a special meeting at the Ministry of Culture, the question being whether he should be permitted to conduct an orchestra that hailed from the city where the eternally living Lenin had been born and rocked in his cradle. After fierce debate it was decreed that Rostropovich could go, but without too much publicity. When Slava arrived in that 'world capital,' the first thing he saw as he walked down the street was a poster of an important upcoming event: an exhibit of rabbits. Sticking out from under the announcement was the beginning and end of his own name: Ros.....ich. A certain Skachilov, the First Secretary of the District Committee, had issued an order to paste over the concert announcement so that people would think it had been canceled. But Rostropovich's name turned out to be very long – there weren't enough rabbits to cover it. Lenin had a shorter name – they'd have sufficed in his case.

After seeing only his head and heels sticking out from either side of the rabbits, and after finding an empty concert hall that evening, the indignant Rostropovich sent off a telegram to Brezhnev demanding that he put a stop to the sabotaging of his concerts – to the humiliation – and give him an opportunity to work; otherwise, he said, he would be obliged to give up his profession.

When he told me about it, I asked, 'Just whom are you trying to scare?'

'Nobody. But they won't forfeit a musician like me! They'll realise they should call me in and talk with me.'

'Well, I always knew you were naïve, but I had no idea to what degree. Who are you for them, that they should want to talk with you? For them, you're the same kind of scum as everyone else. Imagine! You thought you could frighten Brezhnev by threatening to give up your profession. Well, go ahead and stop playing. Go ahead and guzzle vodka by the glassfuls – the quicker you'll drink yourself to death or die of a heart attack. That's what they're waiting for. You'll only give them great pleasure.'

'But what a swinish trick! I come to this godforsaken place to play a concert, and that snake has the nerve to paste another poster over mine!'

'Just wait and see. You remember how they boxed the ears of Shostakovich, Prokofiev, and Pasternak as if they were naughty little boys. Now that you've threatened them, they'll do everything they can to reduce you to a cipher. I warned you before, but you didn't believe me . . . The only reason I'm tolerated at the Bolshoi is because they can't simply fire a People's Artist of the USSR, and I still have a few years to go before retirement. They can't find fault with me professionally: I sing better than the others, I look better than the others. But every time I go on stage I have a feeling deep down that people are watching, hoping that my nerves will finally snap, that I will fail, and then they can settle accounts with me. Just how much tension this costs me, what a burden it all is, and how insulting, nobody in the world can know – not even you. But I was aware of what I was getting into, and so I don't complain. I walk with my head held high to spite those who envy me. I want to be the bone in their throats.'

But despite that letter and despite the rabbits in Ulyanovsk the festival tour along the Volga went ahead. A small steamer was made available to the orchestra. The itinerary began with the city of Gorky, then Kazan, Kuibyshev, Saratov, Volgograd, and Astrakhan. We were given a 'luxury' cabin. Tiny, like all of them, it was different from the rest only in that it had a small washbasin in the corner. There was no toilet, no bathroom, and of course no 'luxury.'

What struck us most was that in none of the Volga cities, neither in the stores nor in the restaurants, did we ever see any fresh fish. Nor did we see any red meat. What did people eat? Going through Kazan at dawn, I noticed that there were already lines in front of several stores. I thought the women were getting up early to do battle for some kind of imported goods; but when I raised my eyes a bit and read the sign on the storefront, I was stupefied. It read: MILK.

The tour lasted about a month, during which time we gave about twenty concerts. Our names were on all the posters, so people flocked to hear us. And the reviews were many, always rapturous. They praised the orchestra and expressed thanks for the lofty art of the cellist and the singer, not sparing the exclamation points. It was all there – all except the names of the cellist and the singer. The oversight couldn't be blamed on any senile idiot. It was clear that the Central Committee had issued a nationwide order.

That fall the Bolshoi was to go on tour to Milan. Not wanting to give the authorities the chance to destroy my self-respect, to publicly show their disdain for my art, I decided to decline the tour, and went to see the Bolshoi's recently appointed director, Kirill Molchanov.

'Kirill Vladimirovich, you're a decent and intelligent man. I don't have to give you a long explanation about the situation I've found myself in. You know that in accordance with orders from the Central Committee, I've been driven out of radio and television like a leper, and that to mention my name in the press is prohibited.'

'Yes, I know that, and I sympathise with all my heart.'

'Then what do you think of my situation now that the Bolshoi is going to Milan? Of course my name will be deleted from all the Italian reviews when they're reprinted in the Soviet press. I have no intention of undergoing such humiliation in front of the whole company, and I can't answer for what I might do. So to avoid a scandal – one abroad, at that – I'm asking you to release me from the tour.'

'But I'll never agree to that! Besides, the Ministry of Culture won't go along with such an outrageous proposal. The Italians will think that you weren't let out of the country on account of Solzhenitsyn.'

'Frankly, I couldn't care less what the Italians say. I'm up to here with everything. I'm tired of all the petty intrigue.'

'But maybe it would be worth your while to go and have a talk with Furtseva.'

'Why? I don't want to go to Milan, and you can tell her that. If she insists that I go, tell her that I want her guarantee that there will be no repetition of what happened on the Volga – when they managed to leave my name out of every review. And I don't want any lies! If there are any, I'll call in the reporters in Milan and give them an interview that'll make the very devil green. As you know, I have a great deal to say. And I'll keep my promise! Tell her, too, that if she's worried about what the Italians will think if I don't come, I myself will send a telegram saying I have a bad cold and can't go.'

The next day Molchanov called me and said he had been to see Furtseva and told her everything, and that she had begged me to go to Milan and not worry about a thing more. She added that she herself would go to the Central Committee to discuss the situation, and had said reassuringly, as always, 'I swear on my honor – I'll straighten the whole thing out!' And in fact she did try to straighten it all out, though in the most peculiar way.

Late on the eve of my departure for Milan, a woman who worked in the Bolshoi's financial department came to see me at home. She had brought $400 in American money with her, and asked me to take the money to one of the management people who was already in Milan and with whom I was on very friendly terms.

'But why didn't he take it himself? He only left two days ago.'

'I don't know. He asked me to pass the money to you.'

'But both he and you know very well that, of the entire troupe,

I'm the one most likely to be searched at the Moscow customs office. They're sure to suspect that I'm taking Solzhenitsyn's manuscripts abroad. If they find dollars, I'll be in big trouble – that's a criminal offense.'

'But who would dare search you?' She was trying hard to persuade me.

'No, I won't take the money.' She seemed to shrink into herself, and hurried off.

They had figured, of course, that I would take the dollars; that I would be searched at the customs office; that I would, with a scandal, be eliminated from the tour and charged with illegal dealing in hard currency. I wouldn't be able to prove that the money had been given to me because there were no witnesses; and they would howl to the world that the dollars had come from Solzhenitsyn, who had 'sold out his people for gold.' Had they wanted to they could even hold me up at a show trial for 'hard-currency operations.'

The authorities' contempt for Solzhenitsyn had reached its apogee: they had read a manuscript of *The Gulag Archipelago* which his acquaintance, E. Voronyanskaya, was keeping for him in Leningrad. How they picked up the scent, I don't know. But Solzhenitsyn told us that Voronyanskaya had been interrogated by the KGB around the clock for five days and five nights. She ended up producing the manuscript for them; when she got back home, she hanged herself.

Thank God I didn't fall into the trap that Furtseva had set for me! It was a clever one: I had been tempted by the opportunity to do a favor for my friend. But interestingly enough, when I arrived in Milan he didn't even ask me about it. He didn't know, and they had forgotten to do anything about warning him. To make a long story short, Furtseva complied with my conditions and made haste to haunt the thresholds of the higher-ups. The press boycott was lifted for the tour. Soviet newspapers reprinted the Italians' rave reviews of our *Onegin*, and *Izvestia* even had this to say: '. . . a photograph of Galina Vishnevskaya was in all the Italian papers, and the reviewers called her the best singer of our time.' That was the last the citizens of Russia read about my singing in the Soviet press. Since then I have been mentioned only once in *Izvestia*: on March 16, 1978, when Slava and I were stripped of citizenship by ukase of the USSR Supreme Soviet.

One fine day two singers from the Bolshoi came to see us. They didn't so much walk in as burst in, joyous and excited. No sooner had they greeted us than they dragged Slava into his study for a secret conference.

A short time later Slava rushed out of the room and called me.

'What happened?' I asked.

'Let them tell you themselves . . . Well, boys, so long. I have to leave. And don't count on me. I'm not going to sign.'

'Listen, Galya,' one of them said to me. 'You must persuade Slava. It's all turning out so beautifully! We've come from some very important people, who sent us here specifically to have a serious talk with Slava. A letter against Sakharov is being drawn up now. If Slava signs it, he can start conducting at the Bolshoi tomorrow. He'll be able to conduct any performances he wants.'

'*What?* You want me to persuade him? No! If he signs, I'll strangle him with my own hands. How dare you propose such a thing to me? Just what kind of person do you think Rostropovich is?'

'But what's so unusual about it? Who pays any attention to those letters? Everybody does it.'

'But Slava won't do it.'

'Why?'

'So our children won't be ashamed of their father and call him a bastard some day. Now do you understand?'

'But you yourself can see that he may be ruined as a musician.'

'It's all right. He won't be ruined.'

'Such a great artist as he, wasting his time in the boondocks playing with God knows what kinds of orchestras, when he's so badly needed at the Bolshoi. Things are falling apart, and only Rostropovich can save the cause to which you and I have given twenty years of our lives. Now there is a real chance for him to become head of the theater. But if he doesn't sign the letter, the doors of the Bolshoi will be closed to him forever.'

'Well then, he'll never conduct at the Bolshoi. But he'll remain a decent man. He'll remain Rostropovich!'

The noose was pulling tighter and tighter.

TWENTY-THREE

Things got to the point where we accepted an invitation from the Moscow Operetta Theater to take part in a production of Johann Strauss's *Die Fledermaus*. Rostropovich put all of his talent into it, everything which for so long had not found an outlet, and would hurry off to the theater early every morning. I didn't even go to the rehearsals. I couldn't help but feel that it was labor lost, that something would happen to prevent him from conducting in Moscow, even if it were a circus orchestra. But, not wanting to dampen his enthusiasm, I of course did not tell him why I couldn't bring myself to rehearse. Sometimes I would sit in the hall and observe as he tried to turn a group of near-invalids into a first-rate orchestra. It goes without saying that with him they played as they never had before, and never would again. But however hard they tried, their music was on a low level. The great musician had stooped, and to see that was more than I could bear. He himself realised that he was falling to the bottom, but he never admitted it to me, perhaps because his masculine pride would not permit him to acknowledge that my predictions had been right. He merely began to withdraw into himself, which was not at all like him; a perplexed look appeared on his face and his shoulders sagged. Above all, he didn't want me to see him in his humiliation.

The theater in which the Moscow Operetta company performs used to belong to the Bolshoi, and is located only a few hundred yards from it. One day, after a rehearsal of Prokofiev's *The Gambler*, I stopped by to pick up Slava so we could go home together. His secretary met me at the door.

'Galina Pavlovna, I'll call Mstislav Leopoldovich right away. He asked me to tell him when you arrived.'

'Don't trouble yourself. I'll go get him myself.'

'But he told me to have you wait for him here.'

'Where is he? What happened?'

'He's in the snack bar.'

'Then I'll go there. Show me the way.'

'But Mstislav Leopoldovich asked . . .'

Of course Rostropovich didn't want his wife to see him in such squalor: a windowless, dingy little room in the basement, dimly lit from the ceiling by a lamp covered with flies; dirty tables, a long line, and at the end of it, Slava. He wasn't even talking to anyone, and though there were quite a few people in the room, it was quiet as the grave. When I saw his stooped shoulders and absent gaze, I was terrified. What had become of the brilliant Rostropovich I had known all these years, and where would it all end?

'Ah, so you've come . . .'

'Yes, my rehearsal's over. Let's get out of here and go home.'

It was hard to predict the subsequent course of events, but something happened that was completely unforeseen. At the Bolshoi, some of the musicians clustered around me and asked, 'Galina Pavlovna, why did you refuse to record *Tosca*?'

'A recording of *Tosca*?'

'We're taping it now. We were told that you didn't want to, so Tamara Milashkina is doing it. But it's your best role!'

'I never did refuse. This is the first I've heard about it!'

Hardly had I gotten home when one of the producers at the recording studio called. 'Galina Pavlovna, please don't refuse to make the *Tosca* recording. You know there won't be another one during your lifetime or mine. After all, Milashkina recorded it several years ago, and this will be her second. Trust me: a third recording of *Tosca* in the Soviet Union is unthinkable.'

'But I never refused!'

'But we were told . . .'

And then it began. A stream of phone calls from soloists and members of the chorus . . . If it hadn't been for those endless calls and questions, I never would have gotten so worked up about it. The hell with the recording! At the time, I had other things on my mind. But the whole company was seething with indignation, and my prestige had become involved – my position as prima donna of the Bolshoi.

Slava and I went to see Furtseva. Although it was only two in the afternoon, she was already well under the influence, and her speech was slurred.

'Ekaterina Alekseyevna,' I said, 'I'm asking you to intervene. I'm not demanding that you cancel Milashkina's recording, although she recorded the opera a few years ago, and I haven't yet. But I would like your permission to make a parallel recording of *Tosca* with a different cast.'

'All right. I swear on my honor . . . I'll take care of everything . . . How are you doing, Slavochka?'

'Ekaterina Alekseyevna, do you realise the position I'm in? It's because of me that Galya is having all these troubles. It's very important to me that you help.'

'I swear on my honor,' she mumbled. Then she hiccuped and dozed off.

'Galya, she's dead drunk! She's sleeping!'

'Not so loud, Slava.'

'But she doesn't hear a damned thing! . . . Ekaterina Alekseyevna!'

'Uh? What? Oh, yes. Of course you must record *Tosca*. I understand, and I swear on my honor . . . I'll take care of everything.'

With that, we left her. But two days later she called me at home and said that she couldn't authorise two recordings of *Tosca* because it went against all the rules. Furious, I hung up on her. Slava immediately called the Central Committee to speak to Pyotr Demichev, who was head of the commission dealing with ideology, but he was in a meeting. So Slava told his secretary it was a very important matter, and asked her to have Demichev call me as soon as he was free. Whereupon Slava flew off to Moldavia to give a concert.

Late that afternoon Demichev called me. I was already so keyed up that I burst into tears.

'Galina Pavlovna, what happened?'

'Pyotr Nilovich, for the first time in my career I have to ask for help.'

'Please calm down and tell me what happened.'

'They won't let me record *Tosca*.'

'*You?* Who won't let you? A singer of your caliber, in tears!

They should consider it an honor that you want to do the recording at all.'

At these words, I wailed even louder and told him the whole ill-starred saga, asking him to authorise a parallel recording.

'But what nonsense! Did you talk to Furtseva?'

'Yes, I did, and she wouldn't permit it.'

'I just don't understand this. Please stay at home – don't go anywhere. Furtseva will call you soon.'

He must have really given it to her, because she called me within five minutes. My tears had already dried, and I was malicious as a witch.

'Galina Pavlovna, what happened? How are you feeling?'

'Bad.'

'But why?' she asked in surprise.

'You have the nerve to ask me why? Because they won't let me record the opera.'

'But who's stopping you?' she asked in complete astonishment.

'*You* are! Or have you forgotten?'

'But you misunderstood me. I didn't prohibit it. You can work to your heart's content. Don't worry, I'll make all the necessary arrangements right away.'

No sooner had I hung up than I got a call from Vasili Pakhomov, director of the Melodiya recording studio.

'Galina Pavlovna! So we're going to record *Tosca* after all! We have to decide on a cast. Who should sing Cavaradossi?'

'Sotkilava. And for Scarpia we should ask Klenov.'

'Ri-i-ght. Fine. When do we begin?'

I realised that the machine had started to function, and it was essential not to let it stop. We had to begin the recording right away. It was Friday, and over the weekend my dear colleagues wouldn't be able to trip me up – all the offices were closed.

'Monday, the theater's next day off.'

'But a taping session with the other group is already scheduled for Monday evening.'

'Then we'll record in the morning. We won't interfere with them.'

'But Ermler can't conduct both in the morning and in the evening.'

'We don't need Ermler, Rostropovich will conduct.'

'*Rostropovich?* Terrific! But he'll need rehearsal time. He's never conducted *Tosca* at the Bolshoi.'

'He and I have done it several times on tour. He won't need any rehearsals.'

'Wonderful! Rostropovich conducting, and Vishnevskaya as Tosca. It'll create a sensation the world over!'

And on that exultant note, our discussion was over.

I immediately called Slava in Kishinev and told him how kind Demichev had been to me. I also let him know that the recording session was scheduled for the following Monday, and that he would conduct. Slava, delighted that everything had turned out so well, sent Demichev a telegram as loving as those he had sent me during the first days of our marriage.

On Monday morning we didn't answer the telephone for fear of learning that the recording session had been canceled. At ten o'clock we arrived at the studio. The members of the orchestra greeted Slava with bear hugs, and congratulated one another on having a musician of such rank in their midst once again. In three hours we had recorded almost all of the first act.

Of course everyone regarded Rostropovich's return to the Bolshoi orchestra as a sign that he had been completely rehabilitated; and that's probably what would have happened. But man proposes, and God disposes.

That night Alya Solzhenitsyn came to say good-bye: she was leaving for Switzerland to join Alexander Isayevich in a few days. More than a month had passed since he had been shamefully deported from Russia under KGB escort. I didn't have the feeling that we were parting forever; and she, too, was convinced that after a while they would all come back home. We were sitting in the kitchen, communicating mostly through gestures, noiselessly forming words with our lips. Alya had brought a blackboard. She used it to ask questions or answer us, erasing the words as soon as she had put them down. Suddenly she wrote: 'Are you planning to go?' Slava and I replied with one voice: 'Where?' She wrote again: 'There.' It had never entered our minds. 'Of course not!' Then Slava told her that apparently he was no longer in disgrace, and that he was again conducting the Bolshoi orchestra.

At that very time a group of singers – Tamara Milashkina, Vladimir Atlantov, Yuri Mazurok – had assembled for the evening recording session of their *Tosca*, only to learn that a different cast had begun a recording of the same opera that very morning. One would think they'd just go ahead with their job and sing as best they could; no one was depriving them of work, after all. But there is no escape from envy. It was essential to get rid of dangerous rivals by any means. As if grasping at a lifeline, they seized upon the exiled Solzhenitsyn and his *Gulag Archipelago*, and went to the Central Committee to see Demichev. Sensing a windfall, Evgeny Nesterenko and my former pupil Elena Obraztsova joined the noble mission. Early the next morning, when Demichev found the 'three musketeers' and the two 'ladies' in his waiting room keeping watch for his arrival, he was amazed beyond words.

'To what do I owe the honor of such an early visit from artists of the Bolshoi?'

The first to speak was the tenor, Atlantov, who began on a high, false note. 'Pyotr Nilovich, we have come to see you on a matter of the utmost importance – and not as artists but as communists. We ask that Rostropovich be removed as a conductor of the Bolshoi orchestra.'

'Do you think he is a poor conductor? Do you have anything against him as a musician?'

And he asked that question of each one individually. They all replied that he was both a great musician and a great conductor.

'Then what's the problem?'

The tenor, the baritone, the bass, the soprano, and the mezzo-soprano, with no attempt at harmony, all began speaking at once, each one trying to make his voice heard above the others. 'By writing a letter in support of Solzhenitsyn, he acted against the Party line . . . And now, when Russian radio stations in the West are broadcasting *The Gulag Archipelago*, we, in the name of the collective and communists of the Bolshoi Theater, demand that Rostropovich not be allowed to conduct the theater's orchestra.'

Even the ideology secretary of the Central Committee, who had seen much in his lifetime, was left agape by the show. When he came to his senses he realised that he couldn't ignore the denunciation, because the magnificent five would run to the next office, their ace of trumps in hand, and denounce *him*, saying that he lacked vigilance if he would permit an enemy of the people to conduct the Bolshoi.

We heard the whole story the next evening from a friend of ours who was also a secretary of the Central Committee. He ended by asking me, 'And what about your protégée Elena Obraztsova? What did she want?'

I'd like to go into somewhat greater detail about that woman in order to show how, under the Soviet system and with the encouragement of the authorities, all the vileness concealed deep in the human heart can come to the surface and bloom like a gaudy flower.

I met her in 1961 at the Helsinki Youth Festival. By that time a singer of some renown, I was on the jury of the voice competition. She, a twenty-year-old student at the Leningrad Conservatory, was one of the competitors. Her beautiful mezzo-soprano voice had one shortcoming, an exaggerated vibrato; and she came to me in tears, asking for help.

'But you have a teacher in Leningrad.'

'She can't do anything with me. I don't understand her.'

I was only thirty-four. I was singing a great deal at the theater and traveling abroad, and it wasn't easy for me to find time to work with her. But I liked the timbre of her voice and knew how to rid her of such a blatant defect, so I promised to coach her.

Not long after that she came to Moscow for the Glinka Competition, where I was also serving on the jury, and I was surprised at the deterioration of her voice. The vibrato had widened, and her voice had become more shallow and sopranolike. She made no impression on the jury, and received one of the lowest scores in the first round. During a break she came to see me, and broke down.

'I know I sang badly. Help me, I beg of you! I'll be eternally grateful.'

I felt terribly sorry for her, that lanky girl from Leningrad – sorry that she was unable to bring out the possibilities of her voice, which I, with my experienced ear, could hear so well. I remembered the troubles I had had with my voice at the outset of my career, and how Vera Nikolayevna had literally saved me. I knew how rarely the chance came along in a singer's life to understand even the most splendid teacher.

'All right. Come with me.'

I took her into a classroom right there at the conservatory, where the competition was being held. And from then on I worked with her twice a day: during the break after the four-hour audition in the morning (skipping my lunch), and again after the afternoon audition. Half-dead from fatigue, I would drag myself into a classroom to coach her. Naturally, I didn't charge her anything. I restructured her whole repertory, giving her arias and songs she had never sung before so that, by concentrating on new feelings, she could free herself of her old habits, which hindered her from bringing out her voice and her musicality. I rid her of her wide vibrato by correcting her breathing; its shallowness had caused the problem. I must give her credit. She instantly grasped whatever I taught her, remembered everything the first time, and was able to bring to the stage every bit of what she had learned.

When she sang in the conservatory's Great Hall a week later, she was literally unrecognisable, and she came out first in the third round. One more week of lessons, and she won first prize. I was happier for her than for any of my own accomplishments. She didn't have an evening gown for the final concert with the orchestra, so I gave her mine. Inspired by success, against my advice she dashed off to the Bolshoi for an audition, but disappointment awaited her there. After hearing her sing a selection of mezzo-soprano parts with the orchestra, they told her that the Bolshoi had no need of sopranos.

From that time on she came to Moscow regularly, and would stay for months. I would work with her after my own rehearsals. I trained her for the roles of Marina Mniszek and Amneris –

working not only on her singing, but on her acting as well – until she had mastered everything down to the smallest detail. Wanting to help her as quickly as possible, I would often sing her parts, not sparing my own voice, so that she could simply copy me. And two years later, through my connections with the Ministry of Culture and Furtseva, through my friendship with Melik-Pashayev and Pokrovsky, I made it possible for her to make her debut (!) at the Bolshoi as Marina Mniszek in *Boris Godunov*. It was an unprecedented case: she was still a student at the Leningrad Conservatory. Does she remember that the night of her first performance I stood by her side on the stage right up to the last second, trying to boost her confidence and transfer all of my own strength to her; that, with tear-filled eyes and trembling with fright, she clutched my hand and begged me in a whisper not to leave her; and that I let go of her hand only when the curtain started to rise?

Actually, it was a most risky venture, especially for me. If she had failed, it wouldn't have cost her much: she was only a student, after all. But I had staked my prestige on her. Everyone knew that I was coaching her and had used my position to bring her into the theater, skirting the requisite auditions. But I knew that at an audition, if they had wanted to they could have eliminated her early, for though her voice was beautiful, it was fragile and not yet fully opened up. In the performance, however, in the brief but effective scene at the fountain (the other scene with Rangoni was not included in the Bolshoi production), she was able to demonstrate the sum total of her artistic gifts. The mezzo-sopranos of the Bolshoi hadn't had time to come to their senses before she was signed up as a soloist, bypassing the youth group. She was twenty-four.

Ten years later, the same Elena whom I had rescued like a drowning puppy, whose eyes were always ready to fill with tears, to whom I had given the most precious thing I had – my art – denounced Slava and me.

Of all five, the only one whose behavior I could understand was Milashkina. For her sixteen years at the Bolshoi, she had been second to me. When we sang the same roles, I was always given the premieres – she the second performances. It was only natural for her to hate me. But Nesterenko had nothing to do with the recording of *Tosca*; he was not competing with either me or Slava. What's more, he had professional ties with Shostakovich, and was the first to perform several of his works. Yet, just a few days before denouncing us, he had gone to the Central Committee to report that the Bolshoi was losing its vigilance: Pokrovsky was staging Prokofiev's worthless and socially harmful Formalist opera, *The Gambler*. The following morning he showed up at a rehearsal of the opera as if nothing had happened, and walked up to his teacher, Pokrovsky.

'What a wonderful production, Boris Aleksandrovich! I congratulate you with all my heart, and I hope I'll have the good fortune to sing in it one day. Please accept this little souvenir as thanks for the unforgettable impression it has made on me.' And he handed Pokrovsky a toy roulette wheel.

'Oh, Zhenya, Zhenya!* Yesterday, when you betrayed me at the Central Committee, you said something entirely different. When were you telling the truth – just now, or yesterday?'

The normal reaction, upon hearing such words from one's teacher, would be to freeze in horror. But those people aren't affected by anything they hear. They know what they're after.

What had compelled Nesterenko to denounce his teacher, who had given him a career on the stage? Or Obraztsova to turn against me? From early childhood these two had seen people awarded decorations, apartments, and the good life for denunciations. And they realised that the time had come when they could earn enough political points to ensure prosperity for the rest of their lives and gain the trust of the Party. The traditions of betrayal were still very much alive; Nesterenko went to the Central Committee along a well-worn path – 'against Formalism in music' – while Obraztsova demonstrated her patriotic vigilance by shouting 'Down with Solzhenitsyn!' at the opportune moment. Such a perfect occasion might not have come again in her lifetime, and she took advantage of it brilliantly.

But none of the world's material comforts will help her forget the moment in New York several years later when she came

---

* Zhenya is the diminutive of Evgeny, Nesterenko's name.

backstage at Carnegie Hall to see me, an exile, during my
performance in *Eugene Onegin* with the Boston Symphony and
American singers. In front of everyone I called her a Judas,
showed her the door, and ordered her out of the greenroom.
She'll never forget turning pale with the fear that she might also
get a slap in the face. Like a snake with a broken spine, she
crawled past the amazed Americans, who stood aside to let her
pass.

For that matter, the Nesterenkos, Obraztsovas, Atlantovs,
Mazuroks, and others like them are typical products of the Soviet
regime; ever since they were young children, the communist
ideology has magnanimously liberated them from the chimera of a
conscience.

But let us return to that 28th of March. Having no idea what
had happened that morning in the Central Committee's offices,
we were getting ready to go to the recording studio when the
phone rang, and I picked it up.

'Galina Pavlovna? What a good thing that I caught you at home.
You were supposed to have a recording session today –'

'What do you mean, "supposed to"? We're on our way to the
studio now.'

'Don't go. There's not going to be a recording session. The
room is taken.'

'Who am I speaking to?'

'You don't know me. I was asked to inform you.'

Slava called the studio. 'What happened with our recording
session? Has it been postponed?'

'No, it has been canceled altogether.'

Slava went pale, and the blood rushed to my head, as if I'd been
doused with boiling water. He hurriedly put in a call to Furtseva.
Her secretary answered.

'Ah, Slavochka! How are you? Yes, Ekaterina Alekseyevna is
in. I'll tell her you're on the phone. She'll be glad to talk with you.'

After a long silence, she again picked up the phone and
whispered in confusion, 'Uh, Slavochka, Ekaterina Alekseyevna
is in conference. As soon as she's finished, she'll call you.'

'Tell Ekaterina Alekseyevna that I'll make it a point not to leave
the house and I'll be waiting for her call any time, day or night.'

After waiting two hours, Slava called again.

'No, Ekaterina Alekseyevna isn't in. She was urgently summoned to the Central Committee. When she comes back, she'll call you.'

An hour later, Slava called a third time.

'Ekaterina Alekseyevna has gone to the airport to meet a delegation.'

Ekaterina was obviously hiding out. The whole day went by like that. When Slava called her again the next morning, he was told, 'Unfortunately, Ekaterina Alekseyevna is not in.' Then he went to the recording studio and walked into the office of the director, Pakhomov.

'Tell me, please, why was our recording canceled?'

Sprawled brazenly in his armchair, Pakhomov replied, 'Because we don't need it.'

'Do you mean to say it wasn't going well?'

'No. Everybody says you did a wonderful job.'

'Then give me hope that we can resume in a month or six months, whenever you want.'

'No, I can't promise you that.'

'Then perhaps somebody has forbidden you to do it?'

'Why should I tell you?'

'Because our recording was authorised by the Central Committee.'

'But now I'm telling you that we don't need it.'

Beside himself, Slava slammed the door and hurried home. Clutching at his heart, nearly losing consciousness, he collapsed in an armchair.

'You can't imagine the humiliation I went through just now – I was told to my face that there was no need for me! And I gave him the option of simply lying – of saying that we could record a year from now, or two years from now. But that bastard didn't even have the decency to lie to me!'

Who had dared to cancel the recording when it had been authorised by a secretary of the Central Committee? When the first act had already been taped? Who had dared to disgrace us publicly, in front of the whole theater?

Knowing how defenseless my husband always was in the face

of outright boorishness, I visualised the scene of his humiliation, and the blood pounded in my temples so, I thought my head would explode . . . Away from here! . . . Away from here! . . . And as soon as possible, never to see those obscene mugs again! . . . But my theater? Damn the theater, my whole family was in mortal danger! If the noose was drawn that tight, it had to be cut in one fell swoop. There was no time to think things over.

'Slava, there's no point going to see anyone else. Enough! I have no intention of pretending any longer that nothing is going on. Sit down and write to Brezhnev requesting permission for the whole family to go abroad for two years.'

Slava was taken aback with surprise. 'Are you serious?'

'More serious than I've ever been in my life. Even if I'm able to swallow the stinking pill and continue working at the theater, your end has come. And you're bound to follow the path of other Russian geniuses – either you'll end up lying drunk in the gutter or you'll pick out the sturdiest hook you can find and tie a noose around your neck . . . All we can do is pray to God that they'll let us out.'

We went to the ikons and swore to each other that neither of us would ever reproach the other for our decision. At that moment I felt a sense of relief, as if a heavy slab had slid off my chest. A few minutes later, our application to Brezhnev was ready.

(What a strange coincidence! It was on that very day, March 29, that Alya Solzhenitsyn left Russia with her mother and the children. I found out about it only ten years later, in a chance conversation when we were visiting them at their estate in Vermont. At the time it seemed to me that she had left the day after her visit to us. That's how overwrought we all were.)

To avoid the possibility that the application would get bogged down at some intermediate bureaucratic level, I advised Slava to inform two people who didn't trust each other; they would thus be forced to report it to Brezhnev. And that's what we did. Slava wrote to Demichev explaining what had happened and asking him to forward our application to Brezhnev. He added that we had also informed Abrasimov, head of the Central Committee section in charge of foreign personnel, about it. Then Slava went to the

Central Committee's offices and left his letter with Demichev's secretary.

'Pyotr Nilovich will be free in a few minutes. Perhaps you want to talk to him?'

'No, it's not necessary. Just give him the letter.'

It took no more than fifteen minutes to walk from the Central Committee building to our place. Nonetheless, when Slava got back to the apartment, I was already talking with Vasili Kukharsky, the deputy minister of culture, who had called us.

'Galina Pavlovna, I have to talk to Slava.'

'He's just come in. I'll put him on.'

Worn out and pale, Slava picked up the phone. 'Hello? No, I won't come to see you. I'm fed up. I don't have anything to talk about with you.'

Kukharsky asked him to put me on the phone. 'Galina Pavlovna, I'd really appreciate it if you'd come with Slava to the Ministry of Culture right away.'

'I'm not going. I have a dress rehearsal of *The Gambler* tomorrow morning, and I don't want to strain my nerves any further with useless conversations.'

'I know that. But it's a very serious matter . . . Ekaterina Alekseyevna is not here now, and I've been instructed to talk to both of you.'

From his unusually beseeching tone I realised that it had begun. 'Is it about our application by any chance?'

'Yes.'

'All right. We'll be there right away.'

We were amazed at how quickly the state machine could crank itself into action.

TWENTY-FOUR

Our calculation had proved to be correct: vying with each other, Demichev and Abrasimov had made haste to report to the highest authorities. Only slightly more than half an hour had passed since the application had been turned in, and there we were sitting in Kukharsky's office. Also present was Popov, the second deputy minister of culture. He took no part in the conversation, being only a witness.

'Come in. Unfortunately, Ekaterina Alekseyevna isn't here. We can't seem to find her anywhere.' It was clear that by that hour of the day Katya was probably in her usual drunken stupor and didn't want to risk entering the arena.

'Please tell us everything in detail.'

Slava was surprised. 'Why? You already know it all.'

'We have to report to the Central Committee, so it's important that you yourselves explain the reason for your application.'

'Years of insults and humiliation; the cancellation of Rostropovich's concerts; the lack of work for him in accordance with his rank as an outstanding musician . . .'

'So why didn't you get in touch with us before?'

'Get in touch?' Slava cried. 'I personally sent Brezhnev several telegrams and letters asking him to save my life! Get in touch? Nobody deigned to answer me.'

'You canceled all his foreign trips,' I snarled. 'You leave him to rot in the boondocks, and sit there coldbloodedly waiting for that brilliant artist to become a cipher. He has put up with your tricks for a long time. But unfortunately for you, in that incident with the recording of *Tosca* you ran up against me, and I'm not about to tolerate that sort of thing.'

'What happened with *Tosca*?'

'Oh, nothing much. We were only driven out of the studio. And

Pakhomov, that toad, told Rostropovich to his face that there was no need for our art. That's all. You realise, of course, that if he dared to speak that way to artists of the highest rank in this country, it was only because he was authorised to do so by the government. I don't want to talk about it any more, but you can be sure I won't let anybody insult me a second time.'

'I'll give orders right now to find that idiot Pakhomov! We'll make it rough on him for doing that.'

'No, don't bother – don't try to pin the blame on just another idiot. There's no need for me to explain to you that canceling a recording personally authorised by Central Committee Secretary Demichev was something that only could have been done by him or by his superior. There's no need to look any further.'

'All right, we'll look into it. But tell me, Mstislav Leopoldovich: you *did work*, didn't you?'

'Yes, in the provinces. But I haven't conducted at the Bolshoi for several years now. In Moscow and Leningrad my concerts have been blocked many times, and recently they have simply banned me from the concert halls or from working with Moscow orchestras.'

Then Kukharsky played a trump card that he had obviously kept up his sleeve for a long time. 'So! You're complaining that you're not working with the best orchestras?'

'Yes, I am.'

'But what can we do if the orchestras don't want to play with you?'

Those words so stunned Slava that he went completely dumb, and I jumped out of my chair. It cost me tremendous effort not to punch that good-for-nothing. 'Well, that's just fine! Here they don't want to play with him, but the orchestras of Paris, London, and New York are longing to do just that! We have no choice then but to get out of here and go to them.'

'Well – don't hope for too much from the foreign orchestras.'

'That's not your concern!'

'You've become used to people standing on ceremony with you here. But that application! Just look at whom you threaten – Brezhnev himself!'

'Who else could we turn to?'

'For such things there's Ovir.'

'Who is Ovir? I don't know him. Slava, who is this Ovir?'

'Not who, but what. Ovir is the agency that takes care of emigration questions.' It was the only time Popov opened his mouth. He fell silent again.

'But we're not emigrants. You yourselves are compelling us to go abroad temporarily and wait until they again allow Rostropovich to play here. Let's go, Slava. They have to draw up a report for the Central Committee, and I have to sing in a dress rehearsal tomorrow morning.'

'This better not turn out to be blackmail.'

'*What?*'

'You heard me. Once you've filed an application, you can't go back on it. And don't harbor any hopes that anyone will try to persuade you otherwise.'

'I can see that you have no idea whom you're dealing with here. Persuasion might have made sense before, but now none of your persuasion can help. We'll wait two weeks for an answer.'

'We don't see any reason why the authorities would object to your departure.'

'Thank you. That's all we need.'

We wasted no time getting out of that stinking hole, and went to the dacha to get the children. When I walked into the house I had the strange feeling that nothing there was mine any longer. For that matter, it never had been mine. I went through all the rooms without feeling the slightest regret that I would not be seeing that place for a long time.

Slava was standing alone in the living room so absorbed in his thoughts that he didn't hear me come up to him.

'Slava, don't be sorry about anything.'

'I put so much love and so much effort into this house.'

'Don't think about the house: think about saving your life.'

We called in our two daughters, Elena (sixteen) and Olga (eighteen). Very gently, so as not to frighten them, Slava told them of our request to spend two years outside Russia. They could see how depressed and anxious we both were, and tried to conceal their great joy, but the smiles began to spread over their faces. Finally, the delighted girls could contain themselves no longer and threw their arms around us.

'How wonderful! Will they really let us out?'

For them, it was a heaven-sent ticket for a two-year pleasure trip around the world.

The next morning, with my vocal cords red from nervousness, and risking the loss of my voice altogether, I sang in the dress rehearsal of *The Gambler*. The news that we had filed an application to leave the country had already spread through the theater, and everyone had their own reason to be horrified. The 'gang of five' was envious and angry that suddenly we were being allowed to go abroad: that wasn't what they had had in mind when they denounced us to the Central Committee. They themselves would have liked to have been in our place. And my friends and well-wishers were saying that under no circumstances would the authorities let us go abroad. But they would make it so unbearable for me that I would have to leave the theater.

As for me, I now had but one goal in life: to leave at any price and by any means.

On stage I don't usually look out into the audience – I don't see the public. But in *The Gambler*, during the scene at Igor's house, the director had me in my own room high above the gamblers, and I spent the entire fifteen-minute scene in a frozen pose. Snuggled comfortably in the corner of a sofa, I could look directly into the audience.

Strange . . . It was a morning dress rehearsal, but there were many men in black suits and white shirts – a disturbingly large number. Had it always been like that? I simply had never studied the audience before. The selection committee from the Central Committee, officials from the Moscow City Soviet, the KGB, the Ministry of Culture . . .

'She quarreled with the great Bolshoi – that singer sitting in that room up there. She disrupted the order: nothing like it has ever happened before. A People's Artist of the USSR is supposed to leave the Bolshoi only when he or she retires, with an anniversary show and a decoration . . . or else feet first, in a funeral service in the great foyer with a chorus and orchestra – with a burial in the Novodevichy . . .'

Looking at their stupid, puffy faces turned toward me, I was all too aware how much they would have enjoyed dragging me off the stage by the feet, throwing me on the floor, and stomping on me as was their way. 'Take that, slime! And let it be a lesson to the others!'

But if I, with their one kick, was feeling the blood rush to my head so that I was ready to smash it against these walls, then what had Prokofiev felt, who for many years had suffered public abuse? The genius Prokofiev, whose *The Gambler* was only now – sixty years after it had been written – being presented to the Soviet public . . . No, not even to the public just yet, but to those thugs who thought themselves capable of pronouncing sentence on that brilliant work: to clear it or ban it, to punish or grant mercy.

Red spots swam before my eyes as my 'room' was lowered: my final scene with Alexei was beginning. When in the course of the action the time came for my 'hysterics,' it was as if a dam were breaking within me. My shouts were desperate – I wanted to bring down the hall and swallow all those I hated so much at that moment. And I longed to be destroyed with them, because I was of one flesh and bone with that people.

Alexei, with trembling hands, proffered me, Polina, a heap of money. But could he really save Polina from that soul-wrenching humiliation – not before others, but most importantly before herself? Humiliated again, and by such a worthless person! Not for anything in the world! Throw the money in his face, and may you all be damned! I want to see nothing, flee quickly, burrow into a hole . . . 'Here! Take your money!'

On the verge of collapse, I stood in the wings. Someone touched my shoulder: Larisa Avdeyeva, who had sung the part of Babulenka in the performance. 'Galya, what's the matter with you? You shouted so loudly I was frightened for you. Calm down. You're lucky they didn't throw you in prison long ago.'

I had hardly walked through my door at home when Furtseva called. 'Galina Pavlovna, what's this I hear? Why did you file an application without talking to me first?'

'Ekaterina Alekseyevna, I'm tired. I've just come from a dress rehearsal. I don't want to offer further explanations of something you know very well. I have just one thing to say to you: let us go on friendly terms. Don't make a scandal and an uproar out of it; neither my husband nor I need any publicity. And be kind enough to give us an answer in two weeks, we have no intention of waiting any longer. We've decided to go, and go we will. You know me well enough by now – I'm capable of anything.'

'We could have a quiet discussion. I'll go to the Central Committee and settle everything. What is it you want?'

'Ekaterina Alekseyevna, we don't need anything – neither Slava nor I. I want only one thing: to get out of here quietly and without a fuss.'

She tried several times to lure Slava into having a talk. 'Slavochka, please come. Without Galya.'

'No, I won't come without her. This situation involves both of us.'

During those tension-filled days, when the fate of our entire family was being decided, we received a call from the US Embassy. 'Mr Rostropovich? This is Senator Kennedy's secretary calling.'

'I'm listening.'

'Surely you know that the senator is in Moscow. He has asked me to tell you that he met with Mr Brezhnev today, and that among other things he talked about you and your family. He told Mr Brezhnev that people in America are very upset about your situation. The senator expressed the hope that Mr Brezhnev would facilitate your departure.'

'Oh, thank you! Please tell Mr Kennedy that our whole family is grateful, that his support is so very important to us in these difficult days.'

For the first time a fresh breeze had blown in on us from afar, and Rostropovich's eyes shone. Later we learned that our friend Leonard Bernstein had played a large part in our fate. When he had heard that Kennedy was going to Moscow, he had talked with him personally and asked him to help us.

In a few days the two weeks elapsed, and Furtseva called us. 'Well, I can inform you that you have been given permission to go abroad for two years – you and the children.'

'Thank you.'

'You should bow at the feet of Leonid Ilich [Brezhnev]. He made that decision personally. We'll designate your trip as travel for artistic purposes.'

It was essential to see Slava off as quickly as possible. Although Brezhnev had authorised the departure, there was no guarantee that he wouldn't block it at any moment. Slava was worried that if he left alone they might keep me from leaving later, but I absolutely had to stay in Moscow for another two months: Olga was taking the entrance examinations for the conservatory, and I didn't feel I had the right to cut off such an important step in her life. If she passed the examinations she could consider the next two years a leave of absence and return after that to begin her studies.

Now I realise what an enormous risk I was running in staying behind. I should have rounded everyone up and fled without so much as a backward glance. But I persuaded Slava to leave alone, taking with him our huge Newfoundland dog, Kuzya. 'If something happens to us, you can protest and make demands from there, but you must leave now. Who knows what could happen within a week. Somebody may take it into his head not to let any of us out.'

What I feared above all, knowing how depressed Rostropovich was, was that they would persuade us to stay. For me, all doubts and worries had ended when they issued our permission to leave – from that moment I had slept soundly at night. But as Slava admitted to me much later, he would go quietly into the kitchen and weep. That most intelligent of men, that brilliant artist, was still expecting them to call him in and beg him to stay – he would have agreed to it joyfully. He was tortured by the realisation that nobody needed him in his own country – that they were letting him go so easily.

The time was drawing near for another Tchaikovsky Competition. Slava had always headed up the jury of cellists, and he hoped that now they would ask him to delay his departure. No one called.

He decided to call Furtseva himself. 'Ekaterina Alekseyevna, the competition will begin soon, and some of my students are playing in it. If necessary, I could remain in Moscow during that time and work with the students.'

'No, it's not necessary. Leave as planned on May 26.'

In spite of my attempts to dissuade him, he went on rehearsing *Die Fledermaus* at the Operetta Theater. He was still trying to prove what he was capable of. How naïve did he have to be to go on hoping they would let him conduct the premiere in Moscow!

But as if he had not already had enough slaps in the face, there was yet another in store. During an orchestra rehearsal a few days before the premiere was to take place, he was called into the office of the Operetta Theater's artistic director, Georgi Ansimov. Only a month before, Ansimov couldn't address Slava without weeping tears of joy and tender emotion; as he sat in the hall listening to the rehearsals, he would repeat, 'Marvelous! Marvelous!' Now that talentless opportunist lounged in his armchair, and didn't even stand up to greet Slava when he came in.

'You know, Slava, I must have a serious talk with you.'

'Why? What's happened?'

'We can't let you conduct our orchestra.'

'Did they tell you you couldn't?'

'No, nobody said we couldn't. But, well . . . how can I put it to you gently? As a musician, you've degenerated much too much, and we simply can't entrust you with a premiere for our theater. Yes, yes – now, don't take offense – as a musician you've gone downhill.'

Slava had only strength enough to walk out of the theater, cross the street, and hide in the first doorway, where he burst into sobs.

After we were abroad, he told me that two days before his departure from the country, he went to see Kirillin, deputy chairman of the Council of Ministers, who lived in a dacha near ours. He asked Kirillin to talk with other members of the government. 'Explain that I don't want to leave. If they consider me a criminal, let them send me into internal exile for a few years; I'll serve out my sentence. But then let me work in my own country, for my own people . . . If they'll only stop blacklisting me, denying me permission . . .'

Kirillin promised to talk to them. The next day he came to see Slava at the dacha, and called him into the garden. His expression was very sad. 'I did as you asked, but things have gone too far. You have to leave. Go ahead and leave, and then we'll see.'

Then they both got dead drunk.

Yes, Rostropovich was right in thinking that it wasn't a good idea to tell me that story in Moscow!

Slava's friends and students came to the airport to see him off. Hovering around were some suspicious-looking plainclothes-men. The send-off was more like a funeral: everyone stood outside the building silently, glumly, and time dragged on end-lessly . . . Suddenly Slava seized me by the arm, his eyes full of tears, and pulled me into the customs hall.

'I don't want to be with them any more. They look at me as if I were a corpse.' And, without saying good-bye to anyone, he disappeared through the door. Irina Shostakovich and I were allowed through with him.

'Galya, Kuzya won't go!' I heard someone shout behind us.

Our huge, splendid Kuzya was lying on the floor, and no amount of persuasion could make him get up. So it is with Newfoundlands: if he didn't want to, he wouldn't get up for anything in the world. But at two hundred pounds, he would be impossible to lift! I had to lie down beside him and explain at great length that he was going with Slava, not alone; that he wasn't being given away to anyone. Finally he believed me. He got up and let himself be led into customs, where he joyfully threw himself at Slava.

'Open the suitcase. Is this all your luggage?'

'Yes.'

Slava opened the suitcase. On top lay an old, tattered sheep-skin coat that the furnace man at the dacha would wear when he went down to the basement. When had he managed to put it in?

'Why did you pack that rag? Give it here, I'll take it back with me.'

'But winter will come.'

'Then we'll buy something! Have you gone out of your mind?'

'Ah, who knows what will happen there? Leave it.'

Rostropovich was leaving for the West with his morale totally destroyed, fearing that there, too, nobody would need him, and he might find himself destitute.

One customs official began rummaging through the suitcase. Another went through Slava's pockets. He got a hold of his wallet, and took out my love letters, which Slava always carried with him as relics. He pored over them as we watched. I felt as if I were in the hands of the Gestapo; it was only in the movies that I had seen such thorough searches. Yes, there had never before been such 'travel for artistic purposes.'

'What are those little boxes? And why so many of them?'

'They're my awards.' Gold medals from the Royal Society of London and the London Philharmonic, a heavy gold medal from Israel, more and more engraved gold medals, and decorations from foreign countries . . . They were all opened and laid out on a big table. Slava had no decorations from the Soviet government: just medals – the State Prize and the Lenin Prize. He also carried medals for 'the development of the virgin soil' and 'the 800th Anniversary of Moscow,' which were given to all Muscovites.

The customs official pushed those last two pieces of tin toward Rostropovich. 'You can take these with you. But not the rest – they're gold.'

Slava began to shake all over. 'Gold? That's not gold, it's my blood and life – all my art! I won honor and fame for my country, and for you it's gold! What right do you have . . . ?'

Seeing that he was growing hysterical, Irina Shostakovich and I pulled him into a corner. I noticed that one of the customs officials had gone off somewhere.

'Be quiet, hear me? Be quiet, or I'll strangle you!'

'I can't. I just can't bear it any more!'

'Shut up! I don't want to hear one more word out of you! Remember that your two children are standing over there, and that I'm staying here. Do you realise what you're doing? Calm down. In a few minutes you'll take your seat in the plane. You'll close your eyes and open them in London. And there you'll see very different faces. Remember how many friends are waiting for you there. Soon you'll be seeing Ben and Peter.'

I went back to the table, took a pair of pajama bottoms out of the suitcase, tied them into a knot, and put all the little boxes in it. The confused customs official started to explain to me that his buddy had gone to make a phone call; that perhaps they might still authorise, might make an exception . . .

'There's no need, I'm taking all of it home. Slava, let's say good-bye. Call as soon as you've landed.'

Carrying two cellos, and with Kuzya on a leash, Slava went through passport control. And I, throwing the pajama bottoms over my shoulder like a bag, went back to the people who were seeing him off.

'What is that you have there, Galina Pavlovna?'

'I'm taking Rostropovich's awards back home. The only decorations and medals you can take out of the Soviet Union are those made of pure dung.'

Three hours later, on the BBC, we heard Slava's voice coming from the London airport: '. . . I am grateful to the Soviet government for seeing our position and permitting us to go abroad for two years . . . My wife and children are still to leave.'

In the theater's office, for everyone to ponder, they posted an excerpt from a decree stating that 'People's Artist of the USSR G. P. Vishnevskaya is being sent abroad by the Ministry of Culture for two years of travel for artistic purposes.'

But after the premiere of *The Gambler*, because of my name not a single newspaper published a review – not even the one Shostakovich wrote for *Pravda*. Critical articles on that brilliant opera did not appear until six months later, until I had long been abroad and replaced by a new singer.

During those last two months in Moscow, I often heard radio broadcasts of my operas, but my name was never mentioned as one of the cast.

Those stings had ceased to bother me. I was counting the days for the moment when, finally, I could get away from that country I had once loved so much, away from my own people.

TWENTY-FIVE

I have a lot to do today:
I have to kill my memory,
I have to turn my heart to stone,
I have to learn to live – again.

Anna Akhmatova

I put on a red dress and arranged my hair carefully, as was only fitting for a rendezvous with one who could claim so many years of my life. I crossed Gorky Street, passed the Moscow Art Theater, turned into Pushkin Street and, walking beyond the Operetta Theater, turned left. There he stood: the sovereign Bolshoi Theater.

I stood at the door for a long time and knocked, until finally it was opened a crack and a watchman I knew showed his head. 'Is it really you, Galina Pavlovna? But nobody's here – everybody's on vacation.'

'I know, I don't need to see anyone. I have to pick up a few things from my dressing room.'

'Then come on in, come on in . . .'

How fortunate to find the theater empty. For the last time I could walk the path I usually took before a performance alone and unhurried, and imagine all the people I'd have wanted to see. First to the office on the first floor to announce my arrival and to complain that I wasn't feeling very well. Are there any singers who feel fine before a performance? I used to know one, a tenor, but he was a fool. Rewarded with sympathetic looks, I would go to the second floor, to my dressing room – the best witness of all my anxieties, raptures, and doubts. I always arrived several hours before curtain time, and there I would find my three trusty partners: the makeup artist, the hairdresser, and the dressmaker. With them, the invisible spectators and unseen performers, I would spend my hours of greatest tension. I had been lucky. These three had been at my side from my first day at the Bolshoi until the last – their very presence gave me a feeling of confidence. They liberated me from what was trivial and enabled me to concentrate on what was important. I knew that ten minutes before the curtain Vasili Vasilyevich would come once more to check my makeup, that Elizaveta Timofeyevna would tidy up my hairdo, and that Vera would fasten the last hook. And they knew that my whole performance often depended on how they looked at me during those last seconds before I walked on stage. Together, we would get nervous and break out in red spots; and with them, I could yell or go into hysterics. They, as masters of restraint, could only mentally send me to the devil – I hope they did. They probably didn't. They were fond of me, as I of them.

Now, in that empty dressing room, I ask them to forgive me. I ask them to stay at my side. I stand in front of the mirror and feel their solicitous hands on me. They fuss about and get me ready. In my ears all the melodies of my operas tumble over one another and I feel myself falling from one role to the next, as if I were on a film in fast forward. But now I am made up and perfectly coiffed, and the fit of my dress is impeccable. Vera picks up my long train. 'Well, let's go, Your Majesty!' And we head for the stage. We stand together in the wings, and I know her heart is beating as loudly as my own.

'Galina Pavlovna, your cue!'

One more step, and I am on stage. All the sounds die down . . . No one. Empty. Only the splendid hall, the vast stage, and an eerie silence. Easy now, easy . . . just a little farther across that space, whose every last centimeter is so familiar to me . . . I stand in the very center of the proscenium, relax the muscles of my tense body and check my breathing . . . I'm ready.

I'm leaving this stage. It is here, now, and alone – with no audience and with no artists – that I can fully realise the step I have taken. Yes, I'm leaving. Whether I come back in two years or five, I'll never return to the Bolshoi again.

I am in my prime, only forty-seven, and at the height of my

fame; in that season of maturity when the artist gathers the fruits he has lovingly cultivated all his life. As the peasant works the land, I, too, have sowed, cultivated, labored . . . But now, that harvest time has come, my crop – my standing field of grain – has been demolished, and I am left with naked ground. There is no longer time enough to cultivate again. I'm leaving twenty-two years of my life here, and there won't be another twenty-two. If I had my life to live again, I would do no differently.

I find myself standing in exactly the same spot, in the very center of the proscenium, where I always sang Tosca's aria, *'Vissi d'arte, vissi d'amore* . . .' I slowly cross the stage where all my heroines lived and died. Here, in my last role, the Polina of Prokofiev and Dostoyevsky cried out, broken, humiliated. That last desperate cry of mine . . . it seems to hang in the rich folds of the curtain, in the corners of the gilded loges, and above that stage where I have sung at least a thousand times.

Farewell, Bolshoi! How many great artists of Russia have given you their art, and I with them! I came to curse you, but find I have neither hatred nor spite enough. I feel only the injury, the pain . . .

I lie face down on your floor, pressing against you, holding you close. I love you deliriously. For me, you were everything: husband, son, lover, brother. To no one else on earth did I give so much love, so much passion, as I gave to you. I deprived my children and my husband to give you all: my youth, my beauty, my blood and strength. And you took it greedily.

No, no, I don't reproach you. In return for my reckless love you raised me up on a pedestal, you gave me everything: a gratifying career, honor, recognition, fame. I was absolute ruler here for many years, with no rivals. But why, in my hour of need, did you not defend me?

'Well, Galina Pavlovna, did you come to say good-bye?'

'Who's there?'

'It's me. Don't be alarmed.'

'I thought no one was here.' It's the old cleaning woman, clutching her buckets and rags in work-worn hands.

'I was mopping the floor, and saw someone over here walking, walking. What is it? Is something troubling you?'

'Something, yes.'
'Well, be patient, dear. He who is patient . . .'
'I'm patient . . . patient.'
'Well, good. Just stay here, then, I'll be by later. Good-bye!'
GOOD-BYE . . .

It finally came, the day before our departure – a day for taking leave of the living and the dead. Early in the morning I went to the Novodevichy Cemetery. I don't like that museum-cemetery, that apotheosis of bad taste and vulgarity, which so clearly reflects the spiritual essence of the Soviet elite. I once told Slava that it reminded me of a reception *à la fourchette* in St George's Hall of the Kremlin Palace: everyone strains to squeeze up closer to the high government officials, to soak up their aura and yet to behave with enough individuality to be noticed by them and among them.

The Novodevichy is the burial place of members of the government, marshals, ministers, and the most acclaimed of scientists, academicians, and writers. Here, for the most part, are only the victors.

I hurried along the familiar path to Melik-Pashayev's grave in the old part of the cemetery where the artists are buried, and where everything is more modest and simple. Prokofiev's grave. Slava had been here often. Before every important event he had come to his friend and teacher for support and help. And there is the grave of Alexander Shamilyevich . . . I wanted to sit here alone and pour out my grief to him, but tension gripped my soul like iron pincers. I adorned his grave with flowers, and tried to summon memories of that time long ago when, standing on stage, I saw his happy, smiling face before me. The only thing that rose to memory was a mournful mask.

'Look how many flowers she's brought. He must have died only recently.'

'No, read it. Ten years already.'

A crowd of curious people had gathered around me. Time to leave.

Good-bye, dear, unforgettable friend! I'll come back again some day.

Now only the last and most difficult thing remained: I had to go to the dacha, to Zhukovka, and take my leave of Shostakovich. Until the very last day I couldn't make up my mind whether or not to go and see him. Shostakovich was the dearest of all I was leaving behind and the only one who could make us reverse our decision. I was afraid that before him I would lose all self-control and succumb to his unquestionable authority. But he knew that was the case, and didn't press me. He understood very well what was in store for us, and that our only way out was to disappear for a few years.

We sat in his study as we always had, with Dmitri Dmitriyevich across from me in his armchair. I didn't hear a word of what he was saying. Or was he talking? Perhaps we were both silent. I tried to force myself to look at him without breaking into sobs. I knew that he was fatally ill, that I might be seeing him for the last time.

I remember standing with him a few years before near the open coffin of his dead secretary, Zinaida Merzhanova. When it came time, I kissed her on the forehead and hand, as is the Russian custom. I returned to my place beside Dmitri Dmitriyevich and I saw that he was deathly pale.

'What's the matter, Dmitri Dmitriyevich?'

'You kissed a dead woman just now. Weren't you frightened?'

'Why, no. What's there to be afraid of? Remember how it goes in your *Lady Macbeth*? "Don't fear the dead, fear the living."'

'I simply don't understand such a strange custom – kissing the dead.'

'But you and I are Orthodox, it's in our tradition. We give the dead person our last kiss.'

He squeezed my arm. 'And will you kiss me like that, too?'

'Of course.' He tried to smile wryly, but the result was a pathetic grimace. 'And it wouldn't disgust you?'

'No.'

Now I was looking at that face, each line of which was familiar to me, and my heart was rent in two. How would I avoid showing him my despair? Where would I find the strength to get up and leave?

'I'm going, Dmitri Dmitriyevich . . . Good-bye.'

We embraced, and suddenly I realised he was sobbing.

On the verge of crying out, feeling that I could bear that torture no longer, I frenziedly kissed him on the face, the neck, the shoulder. And with difficulty, I tore myself from him – from the living as though from the dead – knowing I would never see him again.

'Come back, Galya. We'll be waiting.'

I looked into his tear-filled eyes – into his pale, distorted face, bared to me for the first time – and, not seeing anything for my own tears, I stumbled down the stairs past the weeping women there below.

That is how I remember him.

I walked home along the road I had trod often, but it now seemed infinitely long, unfamiliar, and strange. I felt myself cast from that huge land – from my people – like a tiny, unnecessary grain of sand; a terrible loneliness gripped my heart. I was simply no longer here, nor was my house. So where was I going?

Not walking as far as our dacha, I turned back to the station and headed for Moscow.

A year later, on August 9, 1975, we were at the music festival at Tanglewood where Slava was to conduct Dmitri Dmitriyevich's Fifth Symphony, and I was to sing Tatyana. We were dressed and getting ready to leave for the concert when Slava's sister called from Moscow. Dmitri Dmitriyevich had just died . . .

To the very end, the Soviet authorities remained loyal to their harshness and inhumanity. I had made a tape recording, singing fragments of Shostakovich's Fourteenth Symphony (he was very fond of that recording and listened to it often). His children had wanted it to be played over his coffin at the civil funeral, but the authorities categorically refused. They scoffed at him one last time – they couldn't resist.

I never saw Dmitri Dmitriyevich dead, and wasn't fated to pay him my last respects – to give him, as I had promised, that last kiss. Perhaps that is why I always think of him as alive, as living somewhere. Perhaps in a few years we shall meet. Until that day, I will never forget those wide-open, tear-filled eyes, the weak, distant voice: 'Come back, Galya. We'll be waiting.'

That last night in Moscow, many people dropped in to say good-bye – all except the singers from the Bolshoi. And yet there was one: Anton Grigoryev, a tenor. He showed up late, after midnight, when only a few people – all admirers of mine – lingered on in the apartment. He came without warning, and with a general at his side.

'Why have you come without telephoning, in the middle of the night, and with a stranger to boot?'

'Well, see, I was just passing by with a friend, and I knew you wouldn't get any sleep tonight. I wanted to say good-bye. After all, we've sung together for twenty years.'

'Please forgive me, but I have to pack. Go on into the living room and help yourself to a drink.'

I saw the general walking through all the rooms as if it were his own home. Anton trooped after him, looking around and simply gasping. 'But look! Your furniture is all here. They told me you'd sold everything.'

'Sold it? Are you out of your mind? How will I live without furniture?'

'But you're leaving . . . Sell it to me.'

'So in two years I can come back to an empty home? Be serious.'

'Yes, of course, you're coming back. But where is your luggage? May I help you?'

'You don't have to, Anton. I have only four suitcases, plus two for each of the girls.'

In the bustle of packing I had no time for Anton or his general. The latter's appearance in my home didn't even strike me as strange at the time. We didn't exchange a word. He moved through the apartment looking at my things, watched Rimma cover the couches, beds and chandeliers with sheets, and mingled with my friends. I didn't notice when he left. Exhausted, I went through the apartment like a sleepwalker, tossing totally unnecessary things into suitcases. Only at dawn did I realise that one persistent thought had been with me all night – one I couldn't resolve; namely, that I had met that general somewhere, but I couldn't remember where or when.

'Listen, friends, didn't it strike you as strange that Anton

Grigoryev should visit me so late at night, and with a stranger?'

'But you're so naïve, Galina Pavlovna. That was a KGB man with him.'

'Why do you think so?'

After exchanging glances, my friends looked at me as if I were deranged. '*Why?* But the man didn't conceal the fact. He came in full uniform. Couldn't you tell what he was?'

'But I don't understand these things very well.'

And then I was rooted to the floor: Vasili Ivanovich! Twenty years later! Could it be? Or was it just that they all had the same faces, all were thickset, with short legs. But the more I thought about it, the more I was convinced. It was he, Vasili Ivanovich. So Anton Grigoryev, who had joined the Bolshoi only a year later than I, had been recruited by the case officer the KGB had assigned to me; not only that, but Anton had been their stool pigeon ever since. And he had made no bones about bringing his protector to my home. What difference did it make? By now that behavior had ceased to have any meaning for me.

It was time to go. We sat for a moment before leaving, as is the Russian custom.

Six in the morning, and not a soul in the courtyard. We got into the car and finally pulled away. But why are we heading for the Bolshoi? 'Where are you going? We're supposed to go in the opposite direction.'

The driver turned around, smiling. 'But your friends asked me to drive you past the theater. They said it would please you.'

'Thank you, but don't stop – go faster!'

July 26, 1974. How empty Moscow is at that early morning hour. Would they really let us go? What if at the last moment they stopped us and did an about-face? Why is it taking so long to get there? The sooner to Sheremetyevo Airport the better . . .

'Galyunya, I didn't want to tell you at first, but I've changed my mind and decided I will: Nikandr Khanayev is dead. He's being buried at noon today.'

How strange that I should get the news of that old friend's

death just at that moment. They were parting words – a reminder of the very beginnings of my career, my audition, when the famous artist, with such kindness and magnanimity, had encouraged and supported me, a giddy, stupid girl.

'But why didn't you tell me sooner?'

'I didn't want to upset you. You've been overwhelmed as it is . . .'

'Then promise me that you'll go straight from the airport to Moscow, buy flowers, and take them to Nikandr Sergeyevich. Can you manage that?'

'Yes.'

'And tell him they're from me. Promise?'

'I promise.'

We were at Sheremetyevo. Someone opened a bottle of champagne. 'Galina Pavlovna, one for the road! Come back as soon as you can. How will we do without you?' I see the distraught faces of my loyal admirers. For how many years they came to hear me and followed my career! I was going out of their lives. My friend began to wipe my face with a handkerchief. Time to go . . . Passport control. If only they don't stop me!

'Pass through.'

Thank God! Faster, faster!

We're in the plane. Oh Lord, why are we here so long without moving? Each time a new passenger comes on board I'm convinced they've come for us; that they'll order us off the plane immediately. What will happen then? Bound to the seat by the seat-belt and rigid with tension, I feel that a few more minutes of this and my heart will give out. I close my eyes and begin to count the seconds, the minutes . . . Finally the doors are closed firmly . . . No. It's too soon to rejoice: they could so easily open the doors and take us out . . .

But now the plane has begun to tremble, and we taxi onto the runway . . . How wildly my heart is beating . . . The plane picks up speed: faster, faster, faster . . . And finally it pulls free of the ground . . .

> 'Farewell forever, unwashed Russia,
> Land of masters and their slaves!

And you in pale blue uniforms,
And you, people beneath their sway!"

'Mama! Mama! What are you saying? Stop crying! Stop it!'

The tears are flowing from my eyes. Moments ago my children had such happy faces, and now their eyes show fear and alarm. I don't want them to see me like this. Trying to keep from sobbing, I press my face to the window. Below, I see my land receding rapidly beneath my feet like a wide, black ribbon. I am being carried higher and higher into the sky.

The farther I rise above it, the more marvelously it changes color and outline under the penetrating rays of the sun. Suddenly, as though washed by a spring shower, it is transformed into emerald-green meadow. A little girl in a white, polka-dot dress with a red ribbon in her hair seems to be running across it . . . And now she leaves the earth and flies through the air, thrusting out her hands, beseeching me with them, 'Come back! Come ba-a-ack!'

But that's me, Galka the Artistka!

Oh Lord, help me! Give me strength, save me, have mercy!

'Farewell!'

The childish figure becomes smaller and smaller, turns into a tiny dot, then disappears. The earth's outlines merge into a formless, colorless mass, and the white clouds close over it like a shroud.

* The first stanza of a poem by Mikhail Lermontov. The pale blue uniforms were worn by the political police of Tsar Nicholas I.

APPENDIX

February 9, 1984

Dear Galochka and Slava!

As the tenth anniversary of my exile approaches, scenes of the terrible, trying years preceding it come alive. Alya and I have been thinking back: without your protection and support, I simply would not have survived those years. I would have foundered – my strength was already coming to an end. I simply had nowhere to live; in Ryazan they would have smothered me, and I would have had no quiet, no air, no opportunity to work. And without work, life is utterly strangled. But at your place, I wrote more than half of 'August' as well as a great part of 'October.' And you tended my solitude with tact, you didn't even tell me of the growing constraints and harassment you were subjected to. You created an atmosphere I never dreamed possible in the Soviet Union. Without it, I most likely would have burst, and wouldn't have held out until 1974.

To recall all that with gratitude is to say little. You paid a cruel price for it, especially Galya, who lost her theater forever. No gratitude of mine can compensate for such losses. One can only derive strength from the knowledge that in our time we Russians are fated to a common doom, and one can only hope that the Lord will not punish us to the end.

Thank you, my dear friends. Alya and I embrace you. Regards to Olya and Lena. We are overjoyed that Vanechka is well. If you're in Galino in February, you must visit us.

Katya sends you heartfelt regards as well.

Yours always,
Alexander Solzhenitsyn

An Open Letter
From Mstislav Rostropovich
To the Editors in Chief of the Newspapers Pravda, Izvestia,
Literaturnaya Gazeta, *and* Soviet Culture

To the Editor:

It is no longer a secret that A. I. Solzhenitsyn lives a great part
of the time at my home near Moscow. I witnessed his expulsion
from the Writers Union at the very time he was working on his
novel, *August 1914*, and recently I have witnessed his receipt of
the Nobel Prize and the newspaper campaign that followed. It
is the last-named which has prompted me to write this letter to
you.

As I recall, this is the third time a Soviet writer has received
the Nobel Prize. In two cases out of the three, we regard the
awarding of the prize as a dirty political game, and in one (that of
Sholokhov) as the just recognition of the leading world significance of our literature. If at the time, Sholokhov had refused to
accept the prize from the hands of those who awarded it to
Pasternak 'for considerations having to do with the Cold War,' I
would have understood that henceforth we could not trust in the
objectivity and honesty of the members of the Swedish Academy.
But now it turns out that, in a selective way, we sometimes
accept the Nobel Prize for Literature with gratitude, and at other
times we quarrel with it. But what if next time the prize were to
be awarded to Comrade Kochetov? It would have to be accepted,
would it not? Why, one day after the awarding of the prize to
Solzhenitsyn, did our newspapers publish a strange account of a
talk between Correspondent X and a representative of the
Secretariat of the Writers Union to the effect that the *entire*
nation (including, obviously, *all scholars, all musicians*, etc.)
actively supported his expulsion from the Writers Union? Why
did *Literaturnaya Gazeta* tendentiously select, from among many
Western newspapers, only what was said in the American and
Swedish communist papers, bypassing such incomparably more
popular and significant communist papers as *Humanité, Les
Lettres Françaises*, and *Unità*, not to mention many non-
communist ones? If we trust a certain critic by the name of

Bonosky, what about the opinion of such outstanding writers as
Böll, Aragon, and François Mauriac?

I remember, and I would like to remind you of, our newspapers
of 1948. How much claptrap they published about S. S. Prokofiev
and D. D. Shostakovich, now recognised as giants of our music!
For example:

> Comrades D. Shostakovich, S. Prokofiev, V. Shebalin,
> N. Myaskovsky, et al! Your atonal, cacophonous music is
> ORGANICALLY ALIEN TO THE PEOPLE . . . Formalist
> tricks come into play when there is little talent but great
> pretensions to innovation . . . We find the music of Shostako-
> vich, Myaskovsky, and Prokofiev totally unacceptable. It has
> no harmony or order, no tunefulness or melody.

Today, when you look at the newspapers of those years, the
shame for many things becomes unbearable. For the fact that the
opera *Katerina Izmailova* was not heard for three decades. That
S. S. Prokofiev, when he was still alive, did not hear the last
version of his opera *War and Peace* or his Symphony-Concerto
for Cello and Orchestra. That there was an official list of the
banned compositions of Shostakovich, Prokofiev, Myaskovsky,
and Khachaturian.

Can it really be that the times we have lived through have not
taught us to take a more cautious attitude toward crushing
talented people? Not to speak in the name of the entire nation?
Not to force people to utter opinions about things they have
never read or heard? I remember with pride that I did not come to
the meeting of arts people at the Central House of Workers in the
Arts, where B. Pasternak was smeared and I was supposed to
speak, where my 'assignment' was to criticise *Doctor Zhivago*,
which at the time I had not read.

In 1948 there were lists of banned works. Today they prefer
verbal BANS, on the grounds that 'there is an opinion that this is
not to be recommended.' But it is impossible to ascertain where
that opinion is, or whose it is. Why, for example, was G.
Vishnevskaya not allowed to perform, at her concert in Moscow,
Boris Chaikovsky's brilliant song cycle based on a text by Joseph

Brodsky? Why, on several occasions, did they obstruct a performance of Shostakovich's cycle based on a text by Sasha Cherny, although that text had been published in this country? Why the strange difficulties attending the performance of Shostakovich's Thirteenth Symphony and Fourteenth Symphony? Again, obviously, 'there was an opinion . . .' Who conceived the 'opinion' that Solzhenitsyn had to be expelled from the Writers Union? I have not been able to determine that, although I am very interested in it. It is hardly likely that five Ryazan writer-musketeers would have dared to do that without a mysterious 'opinion.' Plainly, OPINION has prevented my compatriots from seeing Tarkovsky's film *Andrei Rublev* which we sold abroad, and which I was lucky enough to see along with the enraptured Parisians. Obviously, it was OPINION that stopped the publication of Solzhenitsyn's *Cancer Ward*, which had already been set in type at *Novy Mir*. But if it had been published in this country, it would have been openly and broadly discussed, to the advantage of both author and readers.

I shall not touch upon our country's economic or political problems, since there are people who understand those things better than I. But tell me, please. Why, in our literature and art, is the decisive word always spoken by people who are absolutely incompetent in those matters? Why are they given the right to discredit our art in the eyes of our people?

I am stirring up the past not to grumble but so that in the future – say, twenty years from now – we will not be compelled to hide today's newspapers in shame.

Every person must have the right to think and express views fearlessly and independently about things that are known to him, that he has personally thought out and lived through – and not simply to offer weak variations on an OPINION implanted in him. It is our duty to arrive at free discussion without prompting or rebuffs.

I know that my letter will certainly be followed by the appearance of an OPINION about me as well; but I am not afraid of it, and I am saying openly what I think. The talents which are the pride of our nation must not be subjected to assault in advance. I am familiar with many of Solzhenitsyn's works. I like them, and I feel that he has earned through suffering the right to set down on paper the truth as he sees it. Nor do I see any reason for concealing my attitude toward him when a campaign is launched against him.

Mstislav Rostropovich
October 31, 1970

The Red House, Aldeburgh, Suffolk

14th December, 1961

My dear Mr Stepanov,

Please forgive me troubling you about the proposed visit of Madame Galina Vishnevskaya to the Coventry Festival in May 1962, in order to sing the soprano solo in the first performance of my new War Requiem.

I have been very sad to hear of the letter from Mr Shashkin, the Director of Gosconcert, to the Director of the Coventry Festival, indicating that this visit will unfortunately be impossible. May I ask you to reconsider this decision? This Requiem is perhaps the most important work I have yet written, and the dominating soprano part has been planned from the start for Madame Vishnevskaya. When I heard her sing in England this last summer I realised that she had the voice, the musicianship and the temperament that I was looking for. Since then, writing the work, she has been in my mind planning every phrase of the music.

I am sure you will realise in this case how extremely difficult it would be to replace Madame Vishnevskaya, and why I am therefore writing to you personally, and ask you to reconsider this decision.

With best wishes,
Yours sincerely

Benjamin Britten

Mr. V. Stepanov
Ministry of Culture
Kuibishev Street 15
MOSCOW

Teatro La Scala
Office of the Artistic Director

Milan, 20 March 1965

Dear Galina:

I am availing myself of our mutual friend Oldani's visit to Moscow to bring you the heartiest expression of my ever affectionate regards.

I am very curious to know how your work on Donna Anna is proceeding, and whether you would consider singing that part at La Scala between March 15 and April 20, 1966 with Ghiaurov as Giovanni.

This time I would like to mix Italian and Slavic voices together in an effort to avoid the Austro-Germanic method of interpreting Mozart, which does not blend well with the Italian voice – so dear to Mozart (who, from the first performance of 'The Marriage of Figaro' as well as 'Don Giovanni,' wanted the whole of the company to be made up of Italian singers).

As for the other operas we have discussed ('Adriana Lecouvreur' and 'Manon') scheduled between April 16 and May 5, we are not yet able to give you a definite answer as we are waiting to see if we can form an adequate enough singing group to render performances of the highest level.

I would like to know if you have ever sung Gounod's 'Faust,' which has always been performed in Italy with voices like Tebaldi's and not with lyric sopranos as has been the case in almost every theater in the world.

I will welcome the opportunity to read any news of your work and I beg you to remember me most cordially to your husband.

With most affectionate cordiality,

(M. Dr Francesco Siciliani)

REPERTORY

OPERAS

Role	Opera	Composer	Debut
Tatyana	*Eugene Onegin*	Tchaikovsky	1953
Leonore	*Fidelio*	Beethoven	1954
Kupava	*The Snow Maiden*	Rimsky-Korsakov	1955
Katarina (Kate)	*Taming of the Shrew*	Shebalin	1957
Cherubino	*The Marriage of Figaro*	Mozart	1957
Butterfly	*Madama Butterfly*	Puccini	1957
Aïda	*Aïda*	Verdi	1958
Liza	*The Queen of Spades*	Tchaikovsky	1959
Natasha Rostova	*War and Peace*	Prokofiev	1959
Alice Ford	*Falstaff*	Verdi	1962
Marguerite	*Faust*	Gounod	1962
Zinka	*The Fate of a Man*	Derzhinsky	1962
Violetta	*La Traviata*	Verdi	1964
Liù	*Turandot*	Puccini	1964 (La Scala)
Marina	*October*	Muradeli	1964
——	*La Voix humaine*	Poulenc	1965
Katerina Izmailova	*Katerina Izmailova*	Shostakovich	1966 (film)
Desdemona	*Otello*	Verdi	1969
Sofia	*Semyon Kotko*	Prokofiev	1970
Marfa	*The Tsar's Bride*	Rimsky-Korsakov	1970
Tosca	*Tosca*	Puccini	1971
Francesca	*Francesca da Rimini*	Rachmaninov	1973
Polina	*The Gambler*	Prokofiev	1974
Lady Macbeth	*Macbeth*	Verdi	1976 (Edinburgh)

ORATORIOS, SYMPHONIES, AND SONG CYCLES

Work	Composer	Debut
Ninth Symphony	Beethoven	1957
Requiem	Verdi	1958
Five *Satires* to texts by Sasha Cherny	Shostakovich	1961
Missa Solemnis	Beethoven	1962 (Edinburgh)
Songs and Dances of Death, with orchestra	Mussorgsky-Shostakovich	1962
War Requiem	Britten	1963 (London)
Second Symphony	Mahler	1963 (Vienna)
The Poet's Echo, six poems of Pushkin	Britten	1965
Fourth Symphony	Mahler	1965
Seven Romances to texts by Alexander Blok	Shostakovich	1967
Fourteenth Symphony	Shostakovich	1967
Sunless, six songs with orchestra	Mussorgsky	1972
Un enfant appelle loin, très loin	Landowski	1979 (Washington, DC)
Te Deum	Penderecki	1981 (Washington, DC)
La Prison	Landowski	1983 (Aix-en-Provence)
Polish Requiem	Penderecki	1983 (Washington, DC)

DISCOGRAPHY

Arias by Bellini, Boito, Gounod, Puccini, Verdi, and Wagner
G. Vishnevskaya, B. Khaikin and A. Melik-Pashayev (conds.). Bolshoi Theater Orchestra.
Selections: Bellini's *Norma*, Boito's *Mefistofele*, Gounod's *Faust*, Puccini's *Manon Lescaut*, Verdi's *La Forza del Destino*, and Wagner's *Tannhäuser*.
USSR: Melodiya D 014019/20

BEETHOVEN: *Fidelio*
G. Vishnevskaya, G. Nelepp, N. Shchegolkov, A. Ivanov, A. Melik-Pashayev (cond.). Bolshoi Theater Chorus and Orchestra.
USSR: Melodiya D 04518-23

BEETHOVEN: *Symphony No. 9 in D Minor, 'Choral,'* Op. 125.
G. Vishnevskaya, N. Postavnicheva, V. Ivanovsky, I. Petrov, A. Gauk (cond.). USSR State Chorus and Radio Symphony.
USSR: Melodiya D 0391
        D 03652-4

BRITTEN: *War Requiem*
G. Vishnevskaya, P. Pears, D. Fischer-Dieskau, B. Britten (cond.). London Symphony Chorus and Orchestra, 1963.
US: 2-London 1255
UK and France: Decca SET 252/3

DARGOMYZHSKY: *The Stone Guest*
G. Vishnevskaya, I. Arkhipova, A. Maslennikov, G. Pankov, B. Khaikin (cond.). USSR Radio Chorus and Symphony.
USSR: Melodiya D 08975-8
        S 0299-302

GLINKA: Songs
TCHAIKOVSKY: Songs
RACHMANINOV: Songs
PROKOFIEV: *The Ugly Duckling*
SHOSTAKOVICH: Act I Aria from *Lady Macbeth of Mtsensk*
G. Vishnevskaya, A. Dedyukhin (piano).

Selections: Glinka: 'Barcarolle,' 'To her,' 'Do not excite me without cause'; Rachmaninov: 'Oh, cease thy singing, maiden fair,' 'I wait for thee'; Tchaikovsky: 'Complaint of the bride,' 'Lullaby,' 'Why?'
US: RCA Victor LSC 2497
France: RCA 640.738 (Rachmaninov and Shostakovich not included)

MAHLER: *Symphony No. 4 in G Major*
G. Vishnevskaya, D. Oistrakh (cond.). Moscow Philharmonic.
US: Melodiya/Angel S-4006
USSR: Melodiya D 021039/40
             S 01583/4

MASSENET: *Werther* (selections)
VERDI: *La Traviata* (selections)
G. Vishnevskaya, S. Lemeshev, B. Khaikin (cond.). USSR Radio Orchestra.
France: Le Chant du Monde
USSR: Melodiya D 012155/6
             S 0613/4

MUSSORGSKY: *Boris Godunov*
G. Vishnevskaya, N. Ghiaurov, L. Speiss, M. Talvela, H. von Karajan (cond.). Vienna Opera Chorus and Vienna Philharmonic.
US: 4-London OSA 1439
             OS 26300 (highlights)
France: Decca SET 514/7
UK: Decca SET 514/7

MUSSORGSKY: *Songs and Dances of Death* and Six Songs
G. Vishnevskaya, M. Rostropovich (piano), I. Markevitch (cond.). Russian State Symphony.
Six songs (orchestrated by I. Markevitch): 'Cradle song,' 'The Magpie,' 'Night,' 'Where art thou, little star?,' 'The Ragamuffin,' 'On the Dnieper.'
US: Philips 500082 (Mono)
             900082 (Stereo)
France: Philips 6511029
USSR: Melodiya D 011031/2 (Six songs only)
             S 0425/6 (Six songs only)

MUSSORGSKY: *Songs and Dances of Death*
RIMSKY-KORSAKOV: Arias
TCHAIKOVSKY: Arias
G. Vishnevskaya, M. Rostropovich (cond.). London Philharmonic.
Selections: *Songs and Dances of Death* (orchestrated by D. Shostakovich), Rimsky-Korsakov's *Sadko* and *The Tsar's Bride*, and Tchaikovsky's 'Lel's Song' from incidental music to Ostrovsky's *Snow Maiden*.

US: Angel S-37403
France: La Voix de son Maître C 069-02942
UK: EMI HMV ASD 3431

MUSSORGSKY: *Songs and Dances of Death*
TCHAIKOVSKY: Three Songs, Op. 6, Nos. 1, 2, 6
PROKOFIEV: *Five Poems by Anna Akhmatova*
    G. Vishnevskaya, M. Rostropovich (piano).
US: Philips World Series 9138
    Philips 500021 (Mono)
          900021 (Stereo)
France: Philips A 02250 L
UK: Philips 6527 222
USSR: Melodiya D 013739/40
           D 9895/6 (Mussorgsky only)

PROKOFIEV: *Russian Folk Songs*, Op. 104
RIMSKY-KORSAKOV: Songs
    G. Vishnevskaya, M. Rostropovich (piano).
France: La Voix de son Maître C 069-03504
UK: EMI (Conifer) IC 065 03504

PROKOFIEV: *War and Peace*
    G. Vishnevskaya, V. Klepatskaya, I. Arkhipova, E. Kibkalo, P. Lisitsian,
A. Melik-Pashayev (cond.). Bolshoi Theater Chorus and Orchestra.
US: 4-Columbia/Melodiya M4-33111
    Melodiya/Angel S-40053 (highlights)
France: Le Chant du Monde LDX-A-8306/9
UK: EMI HMV SLS 837 (four records)
USSR: Melodiya D 0893-400
           S 0259-66
           SM 0259-66
           D9109/10 (selections)
           D 08759/60 (selections, plus final scene from Tchaikovsky's
                   Eugene Onegin and two arias from Verdi's *Aïda*)
           S 0177/8 (selections, plus final scene from Tchaikovsky's
                   Eugene Onegin)
           SM 02961/2 (selections)
           D 030751/2 (selections)

PUCCINI: *Madama Butterfly* (Butterfly's death scene)
    G. Vishnevskaya, A. Melik-Pashayev (cond.). Bolshoi Theater Orchestra
(*Stars of the Bolshoi Theater*)
US: Angel/Melodiya SR 40050

PUCCINI: *Tosca*
    G. Vishnevskaya, F. Bonisolli, M. Manuguerra, M. Rostropovich (cond.).

National Chorus and Orchestra of Radio-France.
US: 2-Deutsche Grammophon 2707087
France: DGG 2740-161
UK: DG 2708 087 (two records)

RACHMANINOV: Songs
GLINKA: Songs
    G. Vishnevskaya, M. Rostropovich (piano).
    Selections: Rachmaninov: 'Night is mournful,' 'Oh, never sing to me again,' Music,' 'Spring waters,' 'Vocalise'; Glinka: 'Doubt,' 'I remember the wonderful moment,' 'How sweet it is to be with you,' 'To her,' 'No sooner did I know you,' 'Night in Venice,' 'The lark,' 'Barcarolle.'
US: Deutsche Grammophon 2530725
France: DGG 2530725
UK: DG 2530 725

RIMSKY-KORSAKOV: *The Snow Maiden*
    G. Vishnevskaya, V. Firsova, V. Borisenko, L. Avdeyeva, E. Svetlanov (cond.). Bolshoi Theater Chorus and Orchestra.
USSR: Melodiya D 03774-83
                   D 015091-8
                   D 7249/50 (selections)
                   D 0007867/8 (selections)

RIMSKY-KORSAKOV: *The Tsar's Bride*
    G. Vishnevskaya, I. Arkhipova, E. Nesterenko, V. Atlantov, F. Mansurov (cond.). Bolshoi Theater Chorus and Orchestra.
US: 3-Melodiya/Angel S-4122
France: Le Chant du Monde LDX 78641/3
USSR: Melodiya SM 03899-904

RIMSKY-KORSAKOV: *The Tsar's Bride* (Marfa's Act II aria)
    G. Vishnevskaya. Bolshoi Theater Orchestra (*Rimsky-Korsakov: Operatic Excerpts*).
US: Melodiya/Angel S-40052

Russian Opera Arias
    G. Vishnevskaya, B. Khaikin and A. Melik-Pashayev (conds.). Bolshoi Theater Orchestra.
    Selections: Rimsky-Korsakov's *The Tsar's Bride* and Tchaikovsky's *The Oprichnik, The Maid of Orléans, Mazeppa, The Enchantress, Pique Dame*, and *Iolanta.*
US: Melodiya/Angel S-40220
USSR: Melodiya D 012493/4
                S 0685/6
                D 00011363/4 (Rimsky-Korsakov only)

D 027345/6 (*Mazeppa* only)
SM 02537/8 (*The Enchantress* only)
D 00015409/10 (*Pique Dame* only)

SCOTT (Cyril Meir): Song
DEBUSSY: Song
  G. Vishnevskaya.
  Selections: Scott's 'Lullaby' and Debussy's 'Beau soir'
USSR: Melodiya D 00010447/8

SHEBALIN: *Taming of the Shrew*
  G. Vishnevskaya, G. Deomidova, A. Eisen, N. Timchenko, G. Pankov,
E. Kibkalo, Chalabala (cond.). Bolshoi Theater Chorus and Orchestra.
USSR: Melodiya D 04510-5
          D 7605/6 (selections)

SHOSTAKOVICH: *Lady Macbeth of Mtsensk*, Op. 29
  G. Vishnevskaya, B. Finnilä, N. Gedda, D. Petkov, A. Haugland, M.
Rostropovich (cond.). Ambrosian Opera Chorus and London Philharmonic.
US: 3-Angel SX-3866
UK: EMI HMV SLS 5157
France: La Voix de son Maître 2C 167-03374/6

SHOSTAKOVICH: *Symphony No. 14*, Op. 135, for Soprano, Bass, and
Chamber Orchestra
  G. Vishnevskaya, M. Reshetin, M. Rostropovich (cond.). Moscow
Philharmonic.
US: Columbia/Melodiya M-34507
France: Le Chant du Monde LDX 78554
UK: HMV ASD 3090
USSR: Melodiya SM 04009/10

TCHAIKOVSKY: *Eugene Onegin*
  G. Vishnevskaya, L. Avdeyeva, E. Belov, S. Lemeshev, I. Petrov, B.
Khaikin (cond.). Bolshoi Theater Chorus and Orchestra.
US: 3-Westminster WAL 1303
    Monitor S-2072 (highlights)
            S-4072 (highlights)
USSR: Melodiya D 02920-7
              D 011287-92
              D 06463/4 (selections)

TCHAIKOVSKY: *Eugene Onegin*
  G. Vishnevskaya, T. Sinyavskaya, V. Atlantov, Y. Mazurok, M. Rostropovich (cond.). Bolshoi Theater Chorus and Orchestra.

US: Melodiya/Angel S-4115
France: Le Chant du Monde 78485/7
UK: EMI HMV SLS 951
USSR: Melodiya SM 02039-44
          SM 02963/4 (selections)

TCHAIKOVSKY: *Pique Dame* (The Queen of Spades)
     G. Vishnevskaya, R. Resnik, P. Gougaloff, B. Weikl, M. Rostropovitch
(cond.). Tchaikovsky Chorus and National Orchestra of Radio-France.
US: 4-Deutsche Grammophon 2711019
UK and France: DGG 2740-176 (four records)

TCHAIKOVSKY: *Pique Dame* (The Queen of Spades) (Liza's aria)
     G. Vishnevskaya, A. Melik-Pashayev (cond.). Bolshoi Theater Orchestra
(*Great Voices of the Bolshoi*)
France: Le Chant du Monde LDX 78467

TCHAIKOVSKY: Songs
     G. Vishnevskaya, M. Rostropovich (piano)
     Selections: 'Was I not a little blade of grass,' 'Believe me not, my friend,'
'The fearful minute,' 'Sleep, my wistful friend,' 'In this moonlit night,' 'Cradle
song,' 'Why?' (Op. 6, No. 5), 'At the ball,' 'If I'd only known,' 'It was in the early
spring,' 'Again, as before, alone.'
US: Angel S-37166

TCHAIKOVSKY: Songs
BRITTEN: *The Poet's Echo*, Op. 76 (1965). Words: Pushkin
     G. Vishnevskaya, M. Rostropovich (piano).
     Selections: Tchaikovsky: 'Why?' (Op. 6, No. 5), 'Mid the noisy stir of the
ball,' 'Over the golden cornfields,' 'O child, beneath thy window' (Serenade),
'Night,' 'Why?' (Op. 28, No. 3); Britten: 'Echo,' 'My heart,' 'Angel,' 'The
nightingale and the rose,' 'Epigram,' 'Lines written during a sleepless
night.'
US: London 26141
UK: Decca SXL 6428
USSR: Melodiya

TCHAIKOVSKY: Songs
GLINKA: Songs
     G. Vishnevskaya.
     Selections: Tchaikovsky: 'Why?' (Op. 6, No. 5) 'Cradle song,' 'Reconcilia-
tion,' 'It was in the early spring'; Glinka: 'Do not tempt me,' 'The pigeons have
gone to rest,' 'Song of Marguerite.'
USSR: Melodiya D 4498/9
          D 012115/6 (Glinka only)
          D 08555/6 ('Why?,' 'It was in the early spring' only)

D 0009681/2 ('Why?,' 'Cradle song,' 'It was in the early spring' only)

TCHAIKOVSKY: Songs
MUSSORGSKY: *Sunless* and Other Songs
SHOSTAKOVICH: Seven Poems of Alexander Blok and *Satires*
    G. Vishnevskaya, M. Rostropovich (piano and cello), U. Hoelscher (violin), Vasso Devetzi (piano).
France: La Voix de son Maître 2C 167-02726/8

VERDI: *Aïda* (selections)
    G. Vishnevskaya, I. Arkhipova, Z. Andzhaparidze, I. Petrov, Dimitriady (cond.). Bolshoi Theater Chorus and Orchestra.
USSR: Melodiya D 019247/8

VERDI: *Falstaff*
    G. Vishnevskaya, I. Arkhipova, V. Levko, V. Nechipailo, A. Melik-Pashayev (cond.). Bolshoi Theater Chorus and Orchestra.
USSR: Melodiya D 014197-202
           D 14393/4 (selections)

VERDI: *Requiem*
    G. Vishnevskaya, N. Isakova, V. Ivanovsky, I. Petrov, I. Markevitch (cond.). USSR State Chorus and Moscow Philharmonic.
US: 2-Parliament S-154
    2-Turnabout 34210/1
France: Philips 6701.016
USSR: Melodiya D 07645-8

VERDI: *Requiem*
    G. Vishnevskaya, I. Arkhipova, V. Ivanovsky, I. Petrov, A. Melik-Pashayev (cond.). Leningrad Glinka Chorus and Leningrad Philharmonic.
USSR: Melodiya D 035389-92

VILLA-LOBOS: *Bachianas Brasileiras Nos. 1 and 5*
    G. Vishnevskaya, M. Rostropovich (cello).
France: Le Chant du Monde LDX 78644

Vishnevskaya: Arias and Scenes from Prokofiev, Puccini, Tchaikovsky, and Verdi
    G. Vishnevskaya, V. Klepatskaya, K. Leonova, G. Ots.
    Selections: Prokofiev's *War and Peace*, Tchaikovsky's *Eugene Onegin*, Verdi's *Aïda*, and Puccini's *Madama Butterfly*.
US: Westminster Gold/Melodiya 8267
USSR: Melodiya D 08759/60 (except Puccini)
           S 0177/8 (except Puccini and Verdi)

D 0007377/8 (Verdi only)
D 00015383/4 (Verdi only)

Galina Vishnevskaya Sings Arias and Songs of Beethoven, Bellini, Boito, Debussy, Fauré, Puccini, Verdi, and Villa-Lobos

G. Vishnevskaya, M. Rostropovich (cello), B. Khaikin and Melik-Pashayev (conds.). Bolshoi Theater Orchestra.

Selections: Beethoven's *Fidelio*, Bellini's *Norma*, Boito's *Mefistofele*, Debussy's 'Beau soir,' Fauré's 'Après un rêve,' Puccini's *Manon Lescaut*, Verdi's *La Forza del Destino*, Villa-Lobos's *Bachianas Brasileiras* No. 5.

US: Artia 157

USSR: Melodiya D 5382/3 (Bellini, Boito, Puccini, and Verdi only)

D 0006047/8 (Bellini and Boito only)
D 005418/9 (Villa-Lobos only)
SM 04399/400 (Villa-Lobos only)

INDEX

GEOFFREY MOORHOUSE

AGAINST ALL REASON

AGAINST ALL REASON is a unique and illuminating account of the monastic life, which met with critical acclaim when first published in 1969. Today, more than fifteen years later, it is as perceptive and relevant as ever.

'Mr Moorhouse combines radical criticism with much inner understanding . . . an enquiry which might have been superficial and rather sensational is neither'
Michael Ramsey, then Archbishop of Canterbury, in the *Spectator*

'I have learned more from this outsider than from a dozen books by professionals within'
Martin Jarrett-Kerr CR, in the *Guardian*

'I think it is a noble achievement . . . a splendid book'
Paul Jennings, in *The Times*

'I must say at once that I find this an appalling book, but that is partly because it is so good. If Mr Moorhouse were sentimental, or had less sympathy and were less thorough, if his judgement was not so obviously balanced, the picture of conventional life he brings before us would have less force and therefore less power to disturb'
Stevie Smith, in the *New Statesman*

sceptre